ANGUS L. MACDONALD:
A PROVINCIAL LIBERAL

Perhaps one of the most influential Canadian premiers of the twentieth century and one of the leading political intellectuals of his generation, Angus L. Macdonald dominated politics in Nova Scotia for more than twenty years, serving as premier from 1933 to 1940 and again from 1945 until his death in 1954. One rival referred to him as 'the pope' out of respect for his political infallibility. From 1940 to 1945 Macdonald guided Canada's war effort at sea as minister of national defence for naval services; under his watch, the Royal Canadian Navy expanded faster than any other navy in the world.

This new work by T. Stephen Henderson is the first academic biography of Macdonald, whose life provides a framework for the study of Canada's pre- and postwar transformation, and a rare opportunity to compare the political history of the two periods. Macdonald's political thinking reflected a progressive, interwar liberalism that found its clearest expression in the 1940 Rowell-Sirois report on federal–provincial relations. The report proposed a redistribution of responsibilities and resources that would allow poorer provinces greater autonomy and reduce overlapping jurisdictions in the federal system. Ottawa abandoned Rowell-Sirois in the postwar period, however, and Macdonald fell out of step with the national Liberal party that he had once seemed destined to lead. Within Nova Scotia, however, his ardent defence of provincial powers and his commitment to building a modern infrastructure enabled him to win election after election and transform the face and identity of his province.

T. STEPHEN HENDERSON is an assistant professor in the Department of History and Classics at Acadia University.

T. STEPHEN HENDERSON

Angus L. Macdonald

A Provincial Liberal

UNIVERSITY OF TORONTO PRESS
Toronto Buffalo London

© University of Toronto Press Incorporated 2007
Toronto Buffalo London
Printed in Canada

Reprinted 2007 (Sept)

ISBN 978-0-8020-9231-1 (cloth)
ISBN 978-0-8020-9459-9 (paper)

Printed on acid-free paper

Library and Archives Canada Cataloguing in Publication

Henderson, T. Stephen (Terence Stephen), 1968–
    Angus L. Macdonald : a provincial Liberal / T. Stephen Henderson.

    Includes bibliographical references and index.
    ISBN 978-0-8020-9231-1 (bound)
    ISBN 978-0-8020-9459-9 (pbk.)

    1. Macdonald, Angus L. (Angus Lewis), 1890–1954.   2. Nova Scotia –
    Politics and government – 1923–1956.   3. Canada. Royal Canadian Navy –
    History. · 4. Prime ministers – Nova Scotia – Biography.   5. Cabinet
    ministers – Canada – Biography.   6. Canada. Dept. of National Defence –
    Biography.   7. Nova Scotia Liberal Party – Biography.   I. Title.

    FC2325.1.M32H45 2007   971.6'03092   C2006-903709-4

University of Toronto Press acknowledges the financial assistance to its
publishing program of the Canada Council for the Arts and the Ontario Arts
Council.

University of Toronto Press acknowledges the financial support for its
publishing activities of the Government of Canada through the Book
Publishing Industry Development Program (BPIDP).

This book has been published with the help of a grant from the Canadian
Federation for the Humanities and Social Sciences, through the Aid to
Scholarly Publications Programme, using funds provided by the Social
Sciences and Humanities Research Council.

Contents

Acknowledgments

This project has taken years to complete and was possible only with the support and indulgence of dozens of people and a few institutions. It began as a dissertation at York University, and I must thank my committee – H.V. Nelles, Christopher Armstrong, and Craig Heron – for providing rapid and insightful feedback. Del Muise of Carleton University served as external reader and made helpful suggestions. I also wish to express my gratitude for funding provided by an Ontario Graduate Scholarship, York's Faculty of Graduate Studies Research Costs Fund, and the Ramsay Cook Fellowship in Canadian History.

The community of York inspired and entertained me for seven years. The faculty, and in particular John Saywell, Adrian Shubert, and Bettina Bradbury, encouraged and supported my research and teaching. My fellow students, including Dimitry Anastakis, Steve Penfold, Sheila McManus, Matthew Evenden, Janet Miron, Audrey Pyée, Jeet Heer, Joseph Tohill and Patrick Connor, truly engaged me in conversation and camaraderie. James Muir, my close friend and roommate in Toronto, distracted me when necessary with instructive readings and arguments.

I completed many of the revisions while holding a postdoctoral fellowship at the University of New Brunswick, funded by Margaret Conrad's Canada Research Chair. Marg set the bar high for me, but it was still far below the one she sets for herself. Sean and Lisa Kennedy made my time in Fredericton very pleasant. My friends and colleagues at Acadia University have been invaluable, especially Barry Moody, Gillian Poulter, and Pat MacNutt. Len Husband of the University of Toronto Press demystified much of the publication process for me, and editors Frances Mundy and John St James patiently cleaned up the manuscript.

Several scholars have offered kind assistance over the years, exemplifying the best in the academic tradition. Peter Waite and J. Murray Beck imparted to me some of their extensive knowledge of Nova Scotian and Canadian political history. Barry Ferguson and Penny Bryden helped me develop some of my ideas on federal-provincial relations. Todd McCallum, Shirley Tillotson, Philip Gerard, and Jerry Bannister at Dalhousie University gave freely of their time and good advice.

During the course of my research, several people who knew Angus Macdonald or his associates kindly shared some of their insights into his personality. Though I have quoted none of these conversations verbatim, they all added to my understanding of Macdonald. The Hon Richard Donahoe and his wife Eileen Boyd Donahoe gave me an afternoon of their time and some laughter. George Hawkins and Dalton Camp offered me their views on postwar politics. All four have since passed on. Macdonald's surviving children have been most gracious, removing all restrictions on their father's papers, offering some family photographs, and answering some questions. Sister Margaret MacDonnell of St Francis Xavier University assisted me on one or two points and kindly provided a copy of Father Stanley Macdonald's speech at the Canso Causeway opening.

The efficient and friendly service I received in various archives made the hours and days pass quickly. I would like to thank all the staff at Nova Scotia Archives and Records Management, the Provincial Archives of New Brunswick, Queen's University Archives, and Acadia University Archives in particular. Kathleen MacKenzie at the St FX Archives enthusiastically assisted me in locating photographs and information on Macdonald's time in Antigonish.

My extended family never once tried to dissuade me from this path, though they knew it involved sacrifices. Rather, they have been a constant source of support and encouragement. My wife, Tracey Williams, has also tolerated the extended separations and mounting student loans required by this project. She even accepted my habit of working Angus L. Macdonald into every conversation for several years running. I hope that this book will serve as a small measure of my gratitude.

ANGUS L. MACDONALD:
A PROVINCIAL LIBERAL

Introduction

Two bridges span the Halifax Harbour: the A. Murray MacKay and the Angus L. Macdonald. These bridges carry thousands of vehicles per day, and anyone who listens to traffic reports in the metropolitan area is familiar with their names. Most do not know that Murray MacKay was an executive with the telephone company, a prominent fund-raiser for local charities, and the first chair of the Halifax-Dartmouth Bridge Commission. Most are aware that Angus L. Macdonald was a long-serving premier of the province, and almost every Nova Scotian born before 1950 could tell you that he was a political legend who 'built' the first Halifax-Dartmouth bridge and the Canso Causeway and who died suddenly in office.

In the years that I have lived with this project, I have had to explain it briefly to countless friends, relatives, and strangers who have not made the study of Canadian history their life's work (and to a number who have). To Nova Scotians of a certain age, I can say simply that I am writing about 'Angus L.' For others, I explain that I am studying a premier of Nova Scotia, and very often the span that bears his name becomes the common point of reference. 'Oh, the bridge guy!' someone will exclaim in a flash of enlightenment.

Macdonald held office as premier of Nova Scotia from 1933 to 1940 and – after serving as minister of national defence for naval services in the Second World War – from 1945 until his death in 1954. These two decades were perhaps the most transformative in the history of the province and its government. Macdonald's administrations created a modern infrastructure, established social insurance programs that touched a majority of the population, articulated a new tourist-friendly vision of the province, and increased government revenues and spending sixfold. Certainly the growth of the state was not due to Macdonald alone. The pace may have varied, but the roads would have been paved, the bridges built, the old age pensions paid eventually, whoever was premier. The memories of Macdonald would have faded quickly were he merely a road-builder. Rather Macdonald's endurance and importance lies in his articulation of an alternative vision of Canada.

Many observers compared Macdonald to his Conservative successor Robert L. Stanfield, but a better likeness would be Pierre Elliott Trudeau. Both were charismatic legal scholars who attempted to instil a pragmatic idealism into pubic service. Macdonald would have objected to Trudeau's penchant for unilateral action and his centralized federalism, but he probably would have respected the latter's reasoning. In his lifetime, Macdonald believed that expediency and a lack of political leadership led Canada to miss the opportunity presented by the chaos of the Depression: the chance to remake the constitution and balance Canadian federalism.

Several historians have identified Macdonald as an ardent defender of provincial rights, yet his motives and ideas have not been closely examined. Often it is assumed that his defence of provincial autonomy emerged only in the post-war period and only out of bitterness that he felt toward Prime Minister W.L. Mackenzie King and the dominion bureaucracy. Other scholars have dismissed him as conservative or reactionary for opposing the brave new world of expanded dominion powers and tax rental agreements.[1] Macdonald's views on federalism were shaped by his pre-Keynesian liberalism, out of fashion after 1945 but perfectly in step with the Rowell-Sirois report, the most comprehensive study of Canadian federalism ever undertaken. To dismiss Macdonald's argument for an alternative federalism as the 'provincialism' of a reactionary is to risk assuming inevitability.

Historians of Canada have traditionally written through an omnipresent nationalism, consciously or unconsciously assenting to the concept that the purpose of Canadian history is to strengthen the nation.[2] Even those who criticize nation-building history tend to validate it by leaving it unchallenged or by seeking to fit their narratives to its framework.[3] Furthermore, there has been an unfortunate conflation in the literature of 'federalism' with the interests of 'the federal government,' so that the former is bounded by the aspirations of the latter. The provincial component of Canada's federation is neglected or, worse, feared and mistrusted. 'Canada' becomes an unquestioned virtue, and alternative 'historical conditions of possibility' are dismissed as dangerous or petty. Ian McKay writes that many scholars use 'a well-established trope ... that of the "dream undone," the Canadian "nation" founded in 1867 undone by the pettiness of the provinces and racked by regionalism.'[4]

The lack of provincial perspectives in political history has been also a matter of timing. Historians of 'limited identities' – women, ethnic communities, and the working class, for example – challenged the nation-building narrative only in the 1970s. The 'new historians' sought to redress the imbalance produced by decades of privileging political history. Allied with these rivals to hegemony were historians of regionalism, armed in the Atlantic provinces with the journal *Acadiensis* and powerful interpretive tools, most notably underdevelopment.[5] A sense of grievance drove much of this scholarship, though important case studies did correct assumptions of 'national trends' in the new history.[6] Yet while regional studies have a close connection to provincial perspectives, those links typically remain unspoken and unexplored. The logical political representatives of 'regional' interests are the provincial governments, though how provinces voice these interests and whether they could build a coherent regional vision have not been addressed. Indeed, provinces barely appear in some accounts of regionalism in Canada. For example David Bercuson, introducing a study of regionalism, contends that the Senate was the body 'intended [and] created [to be the] effective guardian of regional interests.'[7]

John English notes that historians have left the field of constitutional and political history largely to political scientists. 'In limiting identities,' English writes, 'historians normally avoided the political and focused upon cultural, social, and economic concerns.'[8] In the absence of rigorous historical scrutiny of the development of post-war federalism, statements about the sweetness and light of Ottawa's side of the federal balance are accepted at face value. Similarly, articulations of provincial concerns about the federal system are often dismissed as petty, self-interested, and short-sighted.[9] Such prejudgment obscures the positions of participants in the historical discussion of the evolving Canadian project and assumes, like Dr Pangloss, that the federation is as it must be, in this best of all possible worlds.

Political scientists have paid closer attention to the subtleties of federal–provincial relations, often praising elements of 'classical federalism' in the constitution. Most studies of provincial autonomy, however, focus on the late nineteenth century or the period after Quebec's 1980 referendum on sovereignty. The first eight decades of the last century are disregarded, and even the monumental Rowell-Sirois report is viewed as irrelevant to contemporary federal discussions.[10] Donald Smiley made a very good beginning, examining provincial autonomy before the rise of the 'new history.'[11] Paul Romney makes a valiant defence of the compact theory of Confederation and accurately links classical federalism to the liberal concept of responsible government, but misreads the Rowell-Sirois report and is silent on post-war federalism.[12]

For Macdonald and his political cohort, though, Rowell-Sirois represented the culmination of the 'new liberalism' that had developed between the wars. The report proposed a standard quality of social services for Canadians, provided by whatever level of government could deliver them most effectively, and a system of resource-redistribution to ensure that financial hardship did not compromise provincial autonomy. Macdonald believed that Rowell-Sirois signalled the last best chance for liberals and provinces.

Liberalism has dominated Canadian political and economic discourse at least since the mid-nineteenth century, yet it would be foolish to imagine 'the liberal order' as monolithic and unalterable.[13] Rather Canadian liberalism has been protean, mutating to absorb competing ideologies for the purpose of eliminating or enervating them.[14] The transformative nature of Canadian liberalism – and its entanglement with a dominant political party – has created 'semantic excess and poverty' simultaneously.[15] Crudely, a liberal society may be said to support the equal rights of self-governing individuals to possess property, with a state that exists only to safeguard property and liberty.

Facing numerous challenges in the late nineteenth century – from anti-Confederates in the Maritimes, the Catholic church in Quebec, the working classes of southern Ontario and the Metis and Indians of the West – Canada's liberal order gradually adapted to accommodate marginalized groups, thereby strengthening its position.[16] The 'new liberalism' that slowly emerged between the 1890s and the Second World War placed greater emphasis on equality, seeking to extend individual political and economic rights to more of society's members. This more inclusive liberalism also accepted a positive role for the state in safeguarding equality, along with property, and in providing an atmosphere to promote individual 'happiness' or self-realization.[17]

John Stuart Mill laid the intellectual foundations for the new liberalism, drawing on the utilitarianism espoused by his father's colleague Jeremy Bentham. Mill believed that the liberal political and economic systems could not withstand the challenges mounted by the growing opposition to laissez-faire capitalism. Liberalism must ensure the self-realization of as many – and potentially all – individuals as possible or be destroyed.[18] Alfred Marshall, John Hobson, and L.T. Hobhouse in Britain and Thorstein Veblen and F.W. Taussig in the United States followed Mill, arguing for rational limits on economic activity in order to spread the realization of happiness. Their students in Canada taught at various universities and especially in the Department of Political Economy at Queen's University.[19] By the beginning of the Great War, the social tensions created by the vicissitudes of economic cycles and the stubborn resistance of an entrenched elite made reform of the liberal order all the more necessary.

Angus Macdonald inherited a local, partisan liberalism, but he developed it into a carefully considered political philosophy. Born in 1890, Macdonald came to maturity in the era of Sir Wilfrid Laurier and knew none but a Liberal government in Nova Scotia until he was almost thirty-five. His family's support for the Liberals may have been rooted less in ideology and more in candidates' personalities and the patronage that family members received, but the differences between Liberal and Conservative were increasingly distinct by the twentieth century.[20] Debates such as the ones over reciprocity with the United States, a Canadian navy, and Workmen's Compensation probably helped to sharpen Macdonald's self-identity as a liberal.

Macdonald's Catholicism also shaped his liberalism. Pope Leo XIII issued his famous encyclical *Rerum Novarum* the year after Macdonald was born, urging Catholics to work to reform the morality of capitalism without resorting to the errors of socialism.[21] At St Francis Xavier University Macdonald met the indomitable Rev. J.J. Tompkins, whose 'bootstraps' schemes relied on education and cooperative organization to assist primary producers and the working class in improving their material, intellectual, and spiritual development. Tompkins's ideas were safely within the bounds of social Catholicism and had more than a touch of communalism, but they were not at odds with Mills's position on the need to offer self-realization to the greatest possible number.

Macdonald may have encountered British students of the new liberalism while studying and teaching at St FX. In the mid-1910s, the university hired two professors from Cambridge and one from Oxford, largely on the initiative of Father Tompkins.[22] Macdonald certainly embraced legal realism – a movement to adapt the common law to the exigencies of the industrial twentieth century – in his graduate legal studies at Columbia and Harvard Universities. His doctoral thesis on the liabilities of property owners documented the weaknesses of traditional legal theory, which placed property rights above social safety concerns. Individual rights, Macdonald argued, must be balanced against their negative effects in real-world situations.[23]

Macdonald did not develop his liberalism in isolation, and his working friendships with academics and politicians from across Canada profoundly influenced his thinking. Within the Liberal party, Macdonald gravitated towards the veterans J.L. Ralston and T.A. Crerar, but also to the innovative members of his own generation, J.L. Ilsley and Norman Rogers. Macdonald's career as an academic made him open to scholarly opinions, and he often solicited advice from professors R.A. MacKay, H.A. Innis, and J.A. Corry. This combination of influences pushed Macdonald to balance pragmatism and principles in his political philosophy.

The formative event of Macdonald's political career was the interwar economic downturn. The chaos of the 1920s and 1930s demonstrated the shortcomings of the British North America Act, as the inequitable distribution of resources pushed some provinces to bankruptcy, and the muddled division of powers prevented the Dominion from responding adequately to the national crisis of unemployment. Ottawa offered help with grants-in-aid programs, including Old Age Pensions and moneys for public works, but these cost-shared schemes were beyond the means of the poorer provinces and compounded problems by confusing jurisdictional boundaries.[24] Macdonald favoured a more 'watertight' division of responsibilities and resources between the Dominion and the provinces. Such clarity would strengthen responsible government, creating a more liberal federal system.[25]

In the report of the Royal Commission on Dominion-Provincial Relations, Macdonald found his ideas laid out in a vision of a renewed federalism, based on the liberal principle of responsible government. Provincial autonomy, secured by an appropriate division of constitutional powers and resources, was absolutely central to the 'Fathers of Reconsideration.'[26] The commission represented one of the most important and impressive cooperative scholarly projects ever undertaken in Canada and developed a liberal vision of constitutional renewal for the maturing industrial state. The commissioners embraced most of Nova Scotia's brief, which had called for a renovation of taxation systems that would more effectively distribute the nation's wealth among the provinces to allow for local control of key state functions: health, welfare, education, and infrastructure. Not surprisingly, Macdonald fought vigorously for the report, believing it to be the best hope for the Canadian federation. The relative prosperity of the 1940s removed the sense of urgency – and with it, the political will – for reforming Confederation and strengthening the federal system.

At the core of Macdonald's liberalism lay the individual's development or self-realization. The liberal state had a positive role to play in this process by providing the necessary intellectual and physical infrastructure for development; his governments spent more than $100 million on roads, bridges, electrical systems, and public education. Yet this most powerful of public actors had to avoid treading directly into private affairs. Self-realization included 'character building,' which paternalist policies could subvert, even if the intent were to improve individuals in spite of themselves. Thus, Macdonald preferred to offer thousands of unemployed men relief work on highway projects in the 1930s rather than to turn to direct relief, lest it impair the character of the recipients.[27]

Macdonald's government continued to pursue this indirect approach to economic development after the Second World War. Between 1945 and 1954 Nova Scotia's economy grew absolutely but continued its decline relative to the rest of Canada, losing about one fifth of its per capita share of GNP.[28] Macdonald's liberalism limited his government's ability to stimulate the province's economy, even as the province spent millions of dollars on infrastructure projects. Macdonald rejected calls for public ownership of key industries and shied away from the financial and political risks of large loans to private corporations. Rather, his government followed a consistent program of modernizing the province's physical and intellectual infrastructure, trusting that these projects would improve Nova Scotians and their economy. The bridge over the Halifax Harbour is, therefore, a fitting monument to Macdonald's liberalism and its limitations.

1 Dunvegan to Halifax

Angus Macdonald grew up in Dunvegan, Inverness County, in the Diocese of Antigonish on the eastern shores of the Northumberland Strait. The waters of the Strait linked Macdonald's extended family; the judicial institutions of Inverness County and the town of Port Hood gave his father work and an identity; the priests of the diocese educated young Angus and watched over his early spiritual and intellectual development; the Empire commanded his loyalty, and Canada equipped him to fight in its defence. The Province of Nova Scotia had meaning for only the small political and commercial elite and not the overwhelming majority of the 350,000 souls described as 'Nova Scotians' in the 1891 census. Only as a man in his thirties did Macdonald begin to recognize the development of a provincial polity as Nova Scotia became a practical fact in the lives of its citizens.

After he became premier of Nova Scotia, Macdonald portrayed himself as a Highland chieftain, but his ethnicity reflected the diversity of the Strait 'sub-region.'[1] Before roads and rails, the villages and towns ringing the Northumberland Strait were linked by water and developed commercial and social ties across colonial and provincial borders. Macdonald's ancestors hailed from Irish and Acadian communities in addition to Scottish, though all were Catholic. Each ethnic group had suffered under British imperialism, yet each existed with relative comfort in the Empire. In British North America, these communities managed to preserve much of their ethnic identities while making some accommodation with each other and with Britain.

The absence of a powerful, homogenizing state apparatus made this accommodation easier. Recognizing the limits of imperial control, colonial officials tolerated and even fostered local institutions of authority in British North America in exchange for loyalty and obedience to the Empire.[2] In Nova Scotia many of the commercial and political elite, such as Joseph Howe, favoured homogenization, but without a strong colonial or provincial state, local institutions and sub-regional communications persisted through the nineteenth century.

Macdonald's family traced its roots in the Maritimes to an Acadian community on the western shores of the Strait. His maternal grandfather Stanislaus François Perry descended from the Poirier family of Tignish, Prince Edward Island. Stanislaus anglicized his surname and married Margaret Carroll, an immigrant from Ireland and relative of the prominent nationalist Edmund Dwyer Gray. Perry enjoyed success as an Acadian Liberal in provincial and federal politics; between 1854 and 1898, he was elected to the local assembly ten times and to the federal parliament four.[3]

His father's family came to North America as part of the Scottish Highland diaspora of the early nineteenth century. The Highland emigrations were driven partly by England's pacification policies after the Battle of Culloden in 1746, but mainly by the destruction of the clan system of agriculture.[4] Between 1802 and 1840 about 20,000 Gaelic-speaking Highland Scots settled in Cape Breton. Among them were Alasdair Mhor Macdonald and his family from the Kinlochmoidart district of Inverness County, descendants of the clan chiefs of Moidart.[5] Angus Macdonald liked to boast that his great-great-great-grandfather Alasdair Og of Kinlochmoidart drew the first sword for the Jacobites in the cause of Bonnie Prince Charlie.[6]

After roaming the Strait for two decades, Alasdair Mhor, Angus's great-grandfather, settled with his family on the northwest coast of Inverness County at Broad Cove, where he received two land grants in 1832, totalling just under 1,000 acres.[7] The land on the Inverness shore was suitable only for mixed, subsistence farming. Alasdair's eldest son James established himself on the land but most of James's ten children could not survive by farming. The girls either married or took employment as domestics, while most of the boys left the farm in search of their own or other employment.[8] One son, Lewis, tried his luck westward down the Strait in Prince Edward Island. Near Tignish, he met and married nineteen-year-old Veronica Perry, a local schoolteacher, in January 1875. Lewis came from a proud family and attended school, but Veronica – who had attended Prince of Wales College in Charlottetown and had played hostess for her widowed father – stood above him socially.[9]

Lewis and Veronica remained in Tignish for the births of three children but returned to Broad Cove, probably in 1880. Lewis's share of the farm amounted to 100 acres at the edge of an arable plain, a barn, and a four-room farmhouse for a dozen people.[10] The Macdonalds presumably grew potatoes, turnips, and grains and kept a few milch cows.[11] It is also possible that Lewis worked for the Broad Cove Coal Company in the 1880s and 1890s.[12] He held the respect of his neighbours in Broad Cove – renamed 'Dunvegan' in 1885 – and was appointed a justice of the peace in the 1880s.[13]

Veronica gave birth to Angus Lewis Macdonald on 10 August 1890, the ninth of fourteen children, eleven of whom survived to adulthood. Oddly, Macdonald's parents made several repetitions of names among the boys. Angus shared his middle name with his brothers John and Donald or 'Dan,' and John Lewis shared his first name with his younger brother John Colin.[14] The nine boys and two girls were brought up speaking English in the small farmhouse, though many of their neighbours were raised in Gaelic. As Veronica was not a native Gaelic speaker, the family functioned in English. The children learned some French and Gaelic, but Angus did not consider himself bi- or trilingual, contrary to some popular accounts.[15] Music was common in the house, and the children learned to step dance in the Highland fashion.[16]

The Macdonald family valued education and pushed the children to excel in school. Eventually, six of them received post-secondary education at St Francis Xavier University, and five went on to further study after receiving undergraduate degrees. Stanley entered the seminary and became a priest; Mairi, Sister St Veronica, earned her MA in history from American University in Washington, DC, and became the first woman to teach at St FX in 1937; William, Angus, and Oswin attended law school; and Dan Lewis attended St FX and became a school teacher. Veronica appears to have been ambitious for her children to become professionals, though none rode education to great fortune. She made sure that Angus, in particular, studied diligently at home; he had potential, but learning did not come as easily to him as to some of his brothers.[17]

In the last decades of the nineteenth century, Lewis Macdonald supported the Liberals in Inverness County. His attachment to the party may have been motivated by his father-in-law's career, by a strong faith in responsible government and individual liberty, or simply by antipathy to Confederation. Religion did not direct him, as the bishop of Antigonish instructed his flock to vote for the Conservatives, and theories of a 'Catholic voting bloc' have been shown to be almost groundless.[18]

Nor is it likely that Lewis inherited his political leanings, since Nova Scotian political allegiances were almost wholly remade in the 1860s. The flux in partisan positions began with the Confederation debates of 1864 to 1867, but was exacerbated by Joseph Howe's defection to the Conservatives in 1869, when Ottawa granted 'better terms.'[19]

Lewis's brother Alexander Macdonald flirted unsuccessfully with politics. Alex practised law in Halifax in the 1880s but returned to Port Hood, where his Gaelic, English, and French might better serve his purse.[20] In the 1901 provincial election, he ran as an independent, finishing last with just 7 per cent of the vote.[21] He was appointed stipendiary magistrate for Port Hood in 1904, but died before the town incorporated in 1905.[22] Lewis inherited his brother's house, job, and social position. In 1905 he sold the farm at Dunvegan and moved the family forty kilometres to Port Hood, where he served as stipendiary magistrate for the next two decades. Stipendiary magistrates were appointed by the provincial government after 1900 and were expected to remain politically neutral.[23] Now past sixty, Lewis appeared as a distinguished gentleman, and most people greeted him as 'Judge Macdonald' as he strolled about town.[24]

Southern Inverness County rode a small coal boom at the turn of the century, with collieries at Port Hood, Dunvegan, and Inverness town. After several false starts, eighty kilometres of railway line were constructed from Point Tupper on the Strait of Canso to the Inverness colliery between 1899 and 1901.[25] Inverness and Port Hood incorporated in anticipation of rapid expansion, but the boom was small and short-lived.[26] The colliery at Dunvegan closed shortly after 1900, and Port Hood's had closed by 1920. Coal mining at Inverness became unprofitable in the 1920s but, with government assistance, continued for another thirty years. Port Hood settled into place as a small town with a stumbling economy and a steady stream of emigrants.

Education had become the best road to social mobility for rural Nova Scotians, and Angus performed well enough at Port Hood Academy to earn admission to St Francis Xavier University. Financing his post-secondary education would always be a concern. Even had his parents been able to afford his tuition, they could not have funded all his siblings. Angus followed a path familiar to many university students at the time, teaching school to earn money for tuition and accommodation at Antigonish. At sixteen, he obtained a Grade B teaching licence and taught for two years; by the time he enrolled at St FX in 1909, he had saved enough to pay for one and a half years' costs.[27] He gave the university a note for the last half of his second year and left to teach in 1911 to 1912 to pay his bill and earn more tuition money. By borrowing and interrupting his studies to work, Macdonald paid his way through his bachelor's degree, graduating in 1914 at the age of twenty-four. He considered this process perfectly normal, and it fit well with his ideal of individual development.

The bishop of Arichat had established St Francis Xavier College in Antigonish as a Catholic institution in 1853.[28] In the middle third of the nineteenth century immigration had altered the composition of the diocese, which included the mainland counties of Pictou, Antigonish, and Guysborough, as well as the four counties of Cape Breton Island. Scottish Catholics replaced Acadians as the most populous ethnic group by the 1870s. John Cameron, an early instructor at St FX, was appointed bishop in 1877 and formally moved the see to Antigonish in 1886, combining the site of the college with that of the diocese.

Cameron had come to maturity under Pius IX and sought to extend the ultramontane influence in the diocese. Between 1829 and 1922, thirty-five seminarians from Antigonish – including Cameron and several St FX faculty members – went to the Urban College of Propaganda at Rome. As coadjutor to the aging Bishop Colin F. MacKinnon from 1870 to 1877, Cameron strongly argued against participation in the 'Halifax University' project of 1876, the provincial government's plan to create a large, non-denominational school in the capital. Cameron opposed non-sectarian education and refused to cede any authority over his congregation to Protestants.[29]

In 1882 Bishop Cameron had his friend John Thompson – a convert to Catholicism who sat for Antigonish provincially from 1877 to 1882 and federally from 1885 to 1894 – shepherd an act of incorporation for St FX through the provincial assembly. The university's historian argues that the creation of a board of governors increased the independence of St FX from the church and introduced some lay influence.[30] The act stipulated, however, that all the governors must be Catholic and it preserved the bishop's veto power over decisions and appointments made by the board. Bishop Cameron and his successor, James Morrison, insisted on complete obedience to episcopal authority.

In addition to a university, the diocese had its own newspaper, the *Casket*, published in Antigonish. Though nominally independent until 1919 when the diocese purchased a controlling interest, the *Casket* generally obeyed the will of the bishop. The Reverend Neil MacNeil, rector of St FX, became editor of the newspaper in 1890. Bishop Cameron wished to use the *Casket* to further the campaign of Thompson, but MacNeil observed strict political neutrality in the 1891 federal election. Cameron suspected him of participating in a Liberal plot and banished him to a small parish in the diocese. MacNeil overcame exile and was later named bishop of St George's, archbishop of Vancouver in 1910, and finally archbishop of Toronto from 1912 to 1934.[31]

By the time Angus Macdonald arrived, St FX resembled a modern liberal-arts university. Intellectually and physically, it had outgrown its college roots. The driving force behind this growth was the Reverend James J. Tompkins, vice-president of the university from 1907 to 1922. Born in Inverness County, Tompkins had travelled to the Urban College for post-graduate work, but was conservative in neither philosophy nor method. During his time as vice-president, Tompkins relentlessly solicited donations for St FX, pushed for specialization and higher standards among the faculty, drove the students to meet their potentials, and tried to use the university as an agent for social change. Too unorthodox to be considered a liberal, Tompkins nonetheless shaped Macdonald's ideas about the university's place in a liberal society.[32]

At the turn of the century, a handful of faculty members taught a narrowly classical curriculum. Tompkins demanded specialization among the faculty and more relevant subjects for the students. He did not believe that one professor could teach adequately a range of subjects such as Latin, mathematics, chemistry, and English. Just over half of the faculty had done graduate work, and only a few had earned doctorates. On his return from the Congress of Empire Universities, held in London in 1912, Tompkins brought with him two PhDs from Cambridge and one from Oxford.[33] He was determined to make St FX a real university.

Student life on campus in the decade before Macdonald's arrival had changed as well. Though religious worship remained a dominant feature, athletic and social clubs had emerged on campus by 1900. In his years at St FX, Macdonald played rugby, joined the debating team, and edited the student newspaper, the *Xaverian*, in his senior year.[34] Even the board of governors acknowledged that a university should develop the character of its students, and Tompkins argued that this involved more than providing religious instruction and proscribing certain behaviours.[35]

Macdonald blossomed in this environment. He roomed with Neil MacNeil – later an editor at the *New York Times* – and quickly struck up a lifelong friendship. Macdonald overcame his natural shyness to become one of the most popular students on campus. He was elected president of his class in his sophomore, junior, and senior years and graduated valedictorian, claiming the gold medal in seven of eight courses.[36] He spent 1914 to 1915 teaching English and mathematics to high school students at St FX's academy to pay off his student debts. He also joined the university's Canadian Officers Training Corps (COTC) and soon began recruiting for what would become the 185th Brigade. Little wonder then that he made a deep impression on faculty and students at St FX.[37]

The Congress of Empire Universities in 1912 inspired Father Tompkins to pursue change throughout the whole diocese, using 'adult education' to address the needs of 'the masses.' In 1913 Tompkins began the Antigonish Forward Movement, a precursor to the Extension Movement that later brought international renown to the university. Aiding Tompkins in this endeavour were his cousin, the Rev. Dr Moses Coady, the Rev Michael Gillis, and the Rev 'Little Doc' Hugh MacPherson.[38] Tompkins drew from two main models for this program of education for farmers, fishers, and industrial workers: the Workers Educational Association of England and Bishop Edward O'Dwyer's discussion of a Catholic university for Ireland.[39]

The Forward Movement sought to stimulate local development by making primary producers more efficient and giving them confidence in their abilities. Tompkins believed that centralizing economic forces were draining the diocese and destroying communities; he hoped to reverse the trend of out-migration and rural depopulation in eastern Nova Scotia by improving the economic performance of the region. His plans were of a 'bootstrap' nature and never included significant government intervention as a means of redressing the uneven capitalist development of the region.[40] The experiment – largely confined to columns in the *Casket* and small study groups set up by Tompkins and associates – lasted until 1915, when the war effort deprived it of resources and participants.[41]

Many things grew from Tompkins's 'Bolshevism of a Better Sort,'[42] though progress was slow. Tompkins had gathered around him a cadre of 'reform priests' at St FX, but Bishop Morrison and Rector MacPherson were resistant to change. They favoured an idyllic rural past, overseen by parish priests; Tompkins and his supporters pushed for scientific management and aggressive organization, preserving local settlements but connecting them through agricultural and fishing cooperatives. Cooperatives and a decentralized adult education program – the Extension Movement – did not fully develop until the 1930s, after

Tompkins had left St. FX, yet Tompkins and his supporters had for years contemplated this 'third way.'

It is doubtful that Macdonald could have escaped the influence of Father Tompkins, even had he tried. Tompkins was quick to spot, inspire, and exploit talent among the students, and Macdonald's abilities to write and debate must have caught the priest's attention. The familiar manner in which Tompkins called upon Macdonald in 1922 suggests that the two had had a previous collaborative relationship.[43] Yet Macdonald did not accept his mentor's social Catholicism in its entirety. He respected the potential of organized cooperatives, but his individualist predilections favoured 'natural' limits on the size of these cooperatives, preferably the boundaries of a community. He also shared Tompkins's faith in education, though he emphasized the creation of a top-class university more than People's Schools.[44] Most significantly, Macdonald did not accept Tompkins's view of modern society as starkly divided between 'the people' and 'capitalists.' He believed, perhaps from reading *Rerum Novarum*, that all members of society had a common interest and that the state could help elicit their mutual potential.

When the Great Powers of Europe stumbled into war in the warm summer of 1914, Canadians, especially those of British descent, eagerly responded to the call to arms. In addition to catastrophic destruction and slaughter, the war brought 600,000 men into direct contact with the Canadian state. They may have been fighting for King and Empire, but they were organized, outfitted, trained, shipped, and eventually led by agents of the Canadian government as part of the Canadian Expeditionary Force. For the soldiers, the only sub-national entities were regionally organized regiments and battalions. After March 1917 these were arranged as 'Territorial Regiments' named for provinces but without any relation to provincial governments.[45] For Macdonald and his cohort in this most formative of experiences, the nation was much more real and relevant than any province.

Macdonald joined the COTC in April 1915 and was made a provisional lieutenant in May.[46] In February 1916 he enlisted in the 185th Battalion – the Cape Breton Highlanders – under the command of Lieutenant-Colonel Frank Parker Day, and in June 1916 became a captain, second in command of 'A' Company. Macdonald later wrote the official history of the short-lived 185th.[47] The battalion left for Britain in October 1916 to begin more intensive training in preparation for action on the Western Front. Macdonald spent the next year in pursuits as often intellectual as military; he taught a course in Latin to the enlisted men in the Khaki College and ruminated on poetry when writing to his sister. His letters focused on his spiritual state, and he wondered at the courage and nobility of those who marched to their deaths in battle.[48]

The High Command gradually dismantled the 185th and sent men from its ranks as reserves to units at the front. Macdonald often escorted men to France, which brought him tantalizingly close to the action, but he remained in Britain for most of 1917, nervously anticipating his chance to fight and agonizing over the dismemberment of his unit. His brother John Colin, a sergeant in the Cape Breton Highlanders, voluntarily reverted to the ranks and transferred to the Royal Canadian Regiment in late February 1918, just as Canadian military leaders officially disbanded the battalion.[49] Macdonald felt that the battalion's demise was a betrayal of the pledge he had made to recruits and their families in Cape Breton that he and the other officers would take personal responsibility for the men.[50] He himself voluntarily reverted to the rank of lieutenant and, on 28 May 1918, joined the 25th – Nova Scotia's oldest and most storied battalion – in France. Given the nature of 'war by attrition,' the majority of casualties occurred among enlisted personnel and junior officers; Macdonald had little chance of getting into combat as a captain.[51]

By the summer of 1918, Macdonald had seen considerable action.[52] Letters from Colin and Angus reveal complete confidence in the cause, but also an understandable fear.[53] While still in England, Angus wrote Sister St Veronica that he had 'an idea I shall be wounded but killed never ... I believe my fortune will stick to me.'[54] During the Allied offensive at Arras in August 1918, he went from leading a platoon to leading the entire company when all of the other officers in his unit became casualties. He credited his survival to 'the designs of Providence,' prayer, and the saints' medals given him by the family. His fear became adrenaline in the letter and he marvelled at the courage of his men. He tried to offer some comfort in closing: 'I have not heard from Collie yet but I imagine that if he were hit, they would let me know at once.'[55]

Colin, however, had been shot through the chest at 10 a.m. on 26 August. He could not be carried from the trenches, which were under heavy enemy fire, and died about eight hours later. When Angus learned the news, he wrote a lengthy, reflective letter to his sister, praising his brother as a martyr to a righteous cause. He passed along details of Colin's death but promised his sister that it was painless. He attempted to reassure her and himself that the cause was just and that fate would be kind:

There is no death so noble as that which he has died, with his honour stainless and his record clean, and victorious comrades passing on and beyond him, to the greatest triumph in the history of Canadian arms. Out here we see so many men go out, that the chief thing in our minds is how they died – and no one could desire a more glorious end than that of our brother. All our boys are filled with a zeal that is almost holy. They feel they are right and those who die are reverenced by those left behind. I grieve for him as the playmate of other days, the nearest to me of all the band of boys, but bitter as is the cup of my sorrow, it is not unmixed with solemn pride that one of my brothers has been tried in the furnace and proven true, and that he has laid down his life in a great and just cause.

The war was a world apart, where Macdonald and his comrades lived with death on a daily basis; the need to justify their collective sacrifice, and Colin's in particular, inevitably led Angus to the language of religion.[56]

After spending most of October in the rear, the 25th was ordered back to the front to play a role in the final push. On 7 November, the battalion's last day in the lines, Macdonald led his company into Belgium. On the outskirts of the village of Elouges, a German sniper spotted the group. Macdonald was hit; the bullet entered the right side of his neck and exited between his spine and his right shoulder blade, missing all the major blood vessels and nerves.[57] One of the men helped him into a house and dressed the wound. The sniper shot eight of the company's officers, but the enlisted men suffered relatively light casualties and reached the objective a few hours later.[58]

To his mother, Macdonald emphasized that he had done his duty with the dignity of an officer, lest she worry that his reputation had been sullied:

My arm fell limp by my side but I held on to my revolver which I was carrying in my right hand at the time. My first thought was one of anger that I should have been thus deprived of seeing the thing through ... I did not lose consciousness for an instant. I knew that I was useless as a fighter as my arm was absolutely limp and had to be put in a sling. I got out my maps and orders and sent them to the officer next in rank and ordered him to lead the company.

I was always in control of myself and walked 4 miles after being hit ... The victory is absolute and decisive, though the cost has been high. However, let us forget the sacrifices and remember what the fruits will be.[59]

Of course, the fruits would not be as sweet as imagined late in 1918.

Macdonald remained in hospital for two months and spent another six convalescing in England.[60] By the time he returned to Canada in the late 1919, his sister Margaret had died during the Spanish influenza epidemic. Sister St Veronica later described Angus as 'tense, restless and preoccupied when he came home.' The family agreed never to mention Colin; Angus spoke rarely of the war and never of his brother.[61] The war had made him more serious and less self-confident. He was deeply struck by the willingness of so many to march to horrible deaths in the name of an abstract principle. Perhaps he wondered if he were worthy of survival.

The generation of veterans returned, many prepared to reap public rewards for their sacrifices on the battlefields of France and Belgium, or at least to continue in the service of their communities. A favourite song of the 185th Battalion was an adaptation of 'Donald from Bras D'Or,' a folksong about a naive-but-remarkable young Highlander.[62] After defeating 'the Kaiser' in his unorthodox, simple Canadian way, Donald returns home to represent his riding 'down in Ottawa.' Like Donald from Bras D'Or, Angus Macdonald returned to Port Hood determined to make his mark on his community and country. His aspirations were not focused on any particular office, but his desire to enter politics was apparent.

The economic outlook for the region, and for much of the world, was bleak by the summer of 1919, but Macdonald had saved his officer's pay and had his discharge settlement; he required only a small loan to complete Dalhousie University's two-year program in law.[63] He received encouragement and probably financial support in his studies from Donald 'Little Danny' MacLennan. MacLennan, a young lawyer and Liberal Member of the Legislative Assembly, shared the magistrate duties of Port Hood with Lewis Macdonald.[64] Once he finished his studies in Halifax, Angus articled with 'Little Danny' in Port Hood.

At Dalhousie Macdonald studied with those who would become the legal, political and economic elite of the region. Graduating with Macdonald were H.P. MacKeen, a future corporate lawyer and lieutenant-governor of Nova Scotia; Josiah MacQuarrie, future attorney-general in Macdonald's government, and Norman Mackenzie, later president of the University of British Columbia. Vincent Macdonald, later a Supreme Court justice of Nova Scotia, edged out Angus for the gold medal in the class of 1921. In other classes were Sidney Smith, future president of the Universities of Manitoba and Toronto; George Nowlan, later of John

Diefenbaker's cabinet; Leonard Fraser, the provincial Conservative leader in the 1940s; J. Keiller MacKay, later justice and lieutenant-governor of Ontario, and future members of Macdonald's cabinets, including Ronald Fielding, Malcolm Patterson, and his roommate for a year, L.D. 'Lauchie' Currie.

Almost thirty and a veteran of the trenches, Macdonald commanded an instant respect from his classmates, whom he surely engaged with his warm personality, his wit and his play on the rugby pitch.[65] His academic ability impressed the faculty and especially Dean D.A. MacRae, who hired him as a part-time lecturer in the fall of 1922.[66] After his graduation, Macdonald also was hired for the newly created position of assistant deputy attorney-general on the recommendation of MacLennan and the faculty at Dalhousie. Attorney-General Walter J. O'Hearn wanted an assistant to serve as junior counsel when he prosecuted cases in person.[67] Macdonald thus began his formal public career.

Many people recognized the talents of the young lawyer and veteran, and he was very nearly drawn into a political career straight out of Dalhousie. The federal election of 1921 provided an opportunity that Macdonald might have pursued if his ambition had been keener than his judgment. In the first contest after the Union Government election of 1917, political positions appeared muddled, and many voters believed the old parties were doomed. In Nova Scotia, Farmer and Labour groups emerged, inspired partly by the examples of the United Farmers of Ontario and the Progressive Party forming in the West. In the provincial election of 1920 Farmer candidates won seven seats, and Labour took four; together they captured more than 32 per cent of the vote. George Murray's Liberals took twenty-nine seats, while the Conservatives were reduced to just three.[68] The end of the two-party system, if not the whole system, seemed at hand.

Dr A.W. Chisholm had held the federal riding of Inverness for the Liberals since 1908 and showed no inclination to retire; the party executive in the riding supported him. Disgruntled Liberals formed an independent association to contest the election and sought Macdonald as a candidate. Macdonald sent word that he would accept the nomination only if it were for the Liberal candidacy and implied that he would not force the incumbent out.[69] In the end, only Conservative I.D. Macdougall ran against Chisholm in Inverness. Fresh out of law school and not yet working for the province, Macdonald stumped for Chisholm, who won as part of a sixteen-seat Liberal sweep in Nova Scotia.[70] Macdonald might have entered a fight against Chisholm for the Liberal nomination but he wisely judged that he could win only a Pyrrhic victory, creating powerful enemies in the riding.

Work in the attorney-general's office for Macdonald was mainly administrative. He appeared in court on only a few occasions as the Crown tended to rely on local prosecutors, though he did assist O'Hearn in the 1923 prosecution of labour leader J.B. McLachlan.[71] He had enough spare time to lecture at the law school on a part-time basis from the fall of 1922 until the spring of 1924. He also served as the first editor for the *Gazette*, the official Catholic newspaper for the Archdiocese of Halifax founded by Monsignor William Foley, one of the most respected prelates of the city. Coincidentally, the monsignor's niece, Agnes Mary Foley, was the attorney-general's secretary and the love interest of the deputy assistant attorney-general.

Macdonald had met Agnes while at Dalhousie, but his appointment to the attorney-general's department allowed them to spend more time together. They were a good match: Agnes was clever and shared his love of poetry; Angus was a charming young professional, whose habits had been refined by six years of university and three years as an officer. He had long been surrounded by intelligent and assertive women – his mother, his sister Mairi, and his close friend from law school, Emelyn MacKenzie – and fell in love with another strong woman. They were married on 17 June 1924, honeymooned in Port Hood, and moved into a small house on Atlantic Street, in the South End of Halifax.[72]

Macdonald's first foray into public debate came in a nasty political and religious dispute in 1922, one that tested his loyalty to his former diocese even as it drew him closer to a provincial identity. At the request of his former mentor, Father Tompkins, Macdonald deployed his skills as a writer, debater, and academic to try to convince the Diocese of Antigonish that the proposed federation of the Maritime colleges was not a scheme of the Orange Lodges.

By 1921, the magnanimity of the great American philanthropists such as Andrew Carnegie and John D. Rockefeller was well known and slavishly coveted by universities in Canada. The Carnegie and Rockefeller Foundations had already contributed $1 million to put Dalhousie's Medical School on a solid footing.[73] After solicitations from Tompkins of St FX and A. Stanley Mackenzie of Dalhousie, the Carnegie Foundation expressed interest in assisting higher education in the region generally. Drs William S. Learned, of the Carnegie Foundation, and Kenneth C.M. Sills, president of Maine's Bowdoin College, toured the universities of the Maritime provinces in the fall of 1921 and released their findings in May 1922.[74] The report recommended that the smaller colleges pool their resources and federate into one regional university, preferably at Halifax. The new University of Nova Scotia would assume all degree-granting powers, save for theology. The denominational colleges would remain, provide the first two years of undergraduate study and all divinity programs, and hold authority over their respective students. To help the colleges with the move, the Carnegie Foundation offered to contribute $500,000 to each of the five colleges – St FX, Dalhousie, Mount Allison, Acadia, and Kings.[75] It was anticipated that the Rockefeller Foundation might also contribute to such a scheme, and at the very least, the proposal would free the province to grant moneys to the university. As matters stood, the government made no contribution to any general university operations, as a grant to one college would have to be matched to all the others.

Tompkins gleefully welcomed the Learned-Sills report, seeing in it an opportunity to establish a first-class university in Nova Scotia that might return prosperity to the region. Using an advance copy of the report, he openly praised federation in two columns in the *Casket* in late April 1922.[76] In Tompkins's vision, the smaller, denominational colleges would play a role in undergraduate and divinity education but would find their real niche as 'People's Schools,' following his St FX model. The University of Nova Scotia would be large and wealthy enough to afford the best faculty, exceptional research facilities, and real graduate programs. Tompkins began marshalling support for the federation scheme, securing unanimous support for a St FX faculty resolution in favour of university federation in January 1922.[77] His supporters at St. FX shared his optimism, and two faculty members from Britain wrote positively of the Catholic experience at Oxford and Cambridge. The Dean of St Michael's College, part of the University of Toronto, favoured federation, as did Toronto's archbishop, the former rector of St FX, Neil MacNeil.[78] Yet the opponents of the scheme were present and powerful, if silent in the first six months of 1922.

The president, H.P. MacPherson, opposed federation from the start. James Cameron locates MacPherson's hostility to the scheme in his optimism for the school. It had defeated earlier attempts at federation and had managed to raise almost $500,000 since 1910. Given what the university had survived, MacPherson reasoned, it would be criminal to let it be swallowed up now by a larger entity. MacPherson found an ally in Bishop James Morrison, whose suspicions of Protestant domination were piqued by the federation scheme. At the first inter-university conference held on 7 July 1922 to discuss the Learned-Sills Report, St FX displayed caution by sending a Halifax lawyer as a silent representative. A few weeks later, Morrison announced that public discussion of the question of federation was forbidden until the Maritime bishops had reached a decision.[79] Remarkably, Tompkins held his tongue though he must have been frustrated.

Meeting in late July, the council of bishops decided nothing. Archbishop Edward J. McCarthy of Halifax and Bishop Much of St John's favoured federation, while Morrison and New Brunswick Bishops Edward-Alfred LeBlanc and Patrick Chiasson were opposed. The council instructed Morrison to seek Rome's opinion, but he delayed. The bishops met again on 19 October and adopted a resolution opposing the federation proposal *as it stood*, but favouring greater 'efficiency ... with proper safeguards of conscience,' leaving the door open to some form of federated university. At a 20 October St FX board of governors' meeting, Morrison misleadingly reported that the Maritime bishops had rejected federation; the board duly passed a resolution preventing the university from participating in the scheme.[80] The *Casket* announced that St FX would not participate in federation and declared the matter closed and beyond debate as the decision was an episcopal edict.[81]

Tompkins was livid. In good faith, he had remained publicly silent since July, though he complained bitterly to supporters about some of the less-than-honourable tactics of the anti-federation side. For example, Rector MacPherson allegedly attempted to convince someone of the evils of federation 'by telling him how many Harvard students had syphillis.' Tompkins remained confident that the logic of federation and the influence of its supporters – including Monsignor Foley and Archbishop McCarthy – would carry the day.[82] Once Morrison's forces had pronounced against the scheme, Tompkins urged Macdonald into the fray. To oppose the bishop within the Diocese would be dangerous and nearly impossible, as he controlled the *Casket*. Macdonald could use his Halifax *Gazette* to express Catholic support for federation, though the paper was new and had a small circulation.[83]

Macdonald opened his campaign by challenging the *Casket*'s claim that Morrison's decision against federation had the unanimous support of the clergy of the diocese and the faculty of St FX. On 30 November 1922 Robert Phalen, editor of the *Casket*, picked up the gauntlet with a front-page editorial assailing the supporters of federation, who were trying to keep alive a question that had already been settled. Phalen concluded his lengthy attack by implying that he would return to the debate in future issues.[84]

Tompkins exhorted Macdonald to keep up the pressure, confident that federation represented the best interests of 'the people.' He was even willing to play martyr for the cause, being banished to the remote parish of Canso for his efforts to promote federation.[85] He urged Macdonald to gather around him a group of talented young men to assist him. 'We need a league of youth and a few Mussolini's. Can you start an organization through the colleges? This part of the country would go *en masse* if we had a few young, vigorous leaders.' In Tompkins's opinion, Macdonald would receive 'a great training' by participating in the debate, making allies who 'will vote for you when you run for premier.'[86]

In December, Macdonald attempted to speak directly to the Diocese of Antigonish. Dr D.J. MacDonald had written an anti-federation report that called non-denominational universities 'amoral and materialistic' and cited 'un-Catholic' statements by American professors. The report circulated among the board of governors of St FX, and when Bishop Morrison finally wrote to Rome for direction on the question of federation, he included a copy.[87] Angus Macdonald wrote a critique of the report and submitted it to the *Casket*. Phalen refused to publish it, even as he attacked Macdonald personally: 'We find the man interesting for just a moment; we put our finger on him just long enough to say: Here is the sort of Catholic that we may logically expect to find graduating from your merged colleges. We do not want any more of his sort; the few we have are too many.'[88]

Macdonald took his case to another major paper of eastern Nova Scotia, the non-denominational *Sydney Post*. As Phalen's weekly editorials continued on the theme of federation, the *Post* agreed to run a series of ten columns by Macdonald, and for the next three months, Phalen and Macdonald squared off.[89] Phalen wrote of scarlet temptations to which Catholic youth would be exposed in a federated university and cited authorities – including Thorstein Veblen[90] – to support his argument that small colleges produced more capable students than did large universities.

Macdonald, now teaching part-time at Dalhousie's law school, quickly conducted some research to counter Phalen's bleak picture of life for Catholics on American campuses. He circulated a questionnaire to Newman Clubs – named for Cardinal John Henry Newman, the English man of letters who converted to Catholicism – which tended to the needs of Catholic students at non-Catholic universities. Respondents were asked if they were aware of any anti-Catholic teaching by faculty or discrimination against Catholic students. Yale, Harvard, Illinois, Wisconsin, and other universities responded, all attesting to the positive experiences of Catholic students.[91] Macdonald also contacted Veblen directly to check Phalen's interpretation of his writings. Veblen denied that he was opposed to federated universities, noting the destructiveness of competition and the waste of duplicate courses.[92] Macdonald contrasted St FX's meagre resources with the large endowments of the smaller schools Phalen had cited as examples of excellence. He quoted several leading Catholic scholars to support the position that universities were places of inquiry, where explorations for truth might include a range of ideas, not all of them consistent with Catholic theology. Finally, Macdonald carefully spelled out the role of denominational colleges within a federated university, underlining the protection that a Catholic college would enjoy.[93]

The debate in the *Casket* and *Post* persisted after the issue was dead in Antigonish. Only Rome could have overruled Bishop Morrison, and he nullified this chance by submitting a leading question to the Vatican in November 1922. Morrison asked if it were permissible for Catholic colleges to submerge themselves inside non-denominational universities; no mention was made of constituent denominational colleges as envisioned under the Learned-Sills scheme. On 22 March 1923 the Congregation of Seminaries and Universities responded in the negative to Morrison's question, and Pope Pius XI supported the decision.[94] In February 1923, the Baptist board of governors of Acadia University had voted against federation, effectively killing the scheme.[95] All that came of the Carnegie Foundation's efforts was the merger of the small and nearly bankrupt King's College with Dalhousie in the summer of 1923.[96]

For Macdonald, the debate brought both notoriety and praise. The affair tarnished his image as a 'golden boy' in Antigonish and irreparably strained his relationship with Bishop Morrison.[97] He drew some favourable letters for his criticisms of Phalen and Morrison,[98] and increased his public profile as a reformer, but the line from the federation debate to the premier's office was not as straight as Father Tompkins believed. Tompkins had told Macdonald to 'Go for the premiership on a policy of a state university ... We shall make you Premier of N.S. ... Everybody in N.S. knows you now and that is something to start with.'[99]

Taking such a public and polemical stand forced Macdonald to think and speak politically. In future debates, outside election campaigns, he tended to be much more diplomatic than he had been with Phalen, but always he addressed his arguments to the reason and not the passions of his audience. Macdonald believed that excellence in education held the key to individual and communal self-realization. This principle took precedence even over his devout Catholicism. Religion belonged to the private sphere of the individual; civil society must be secular to ensure the greatest progress. 'Our people have not the same sense of public or patriotic duty that Protestants have,' he wrote Father Tompkins. 'Our priests have too long been either intimating or openly saying that so long as people went to Mass on Sunday, etc., the State could go to blazes.'[100] In Halifax, he was farther away from the Diocese of Antigonish than he ever had been in France.

Macdonald settled easily into a professional, intellectual life in Halifax. In 1924, he left the attorney-general's office for a full-time position teaching at Dalhousie, apparently because of limited prospects as a civil servant. He loved teaching and believed strongly in the three elements of Dalhousie's 'Weldon Tradition': adherence to the highest academic standards, the encouragement of 'unselfish public service,' and an open door policy for students seeking guidance from professors. One of the most popular faculty members on campus, Macdonald developed close and lasting friendships with students and other colleagues.[101]

His family blossomed as well with the birth of Aileen Veronica in April 1925, followed by Angus Lewis Jr thirteen months later. A young, middle-class couple, he and Agnes had a close circle of friends, some of whom Macdonald had known from Inverness County but more whom they had met in Halifax. They played bridge as a couple, and he took up curling and golf with a passion, revelling in the Scottish heritage of the sports. He also played a prominent role in several bourgeois social groups including the Knights of Columbus, honouring his Catholic faith, and the North British Society of Halifax, honouring his Celtic heritage.

Macdonald continued his intellectual development with a year of 'special studies' in law at Columbia University in 1925 to 1926; most of his work at Columbia seems to have been carried on by correspondence, though he spent the summer of 1926 in New York.[102] At the time, the legal realists were taking charge at Columbia, pursuing a more flexible jurisprudence, one informed by the modern social sciences and able to adapt the common law to the needs of industrial society.[103] Macdonald used his work at Columbia as a basis for later graduate studies at Harvard.

His new family and his academic life demanded almost all of Macdonald's time and seem to have precluded a political career in the mid-1920s. No evidence appears in his papers that he weighed the possibility of embarking on a political career in the elections of 1925 or 1926, though his office-mate Horace Read noted that by 1928 he clearly had the political itch.[104] He continued his loyal service to the Liberal party by speaking in the provincial and federal election campaigns of 1925 and 1926, but Nova Scotia's voters turned increasingly to the Conservatives.

A stubbornly persistent economic slump, out-migration, and violent labour unrest plagued the Liberals from 1921 to 1925. Premier George Murray retired early in 1923 after more than twenty-six years in office; Ernest Armstrong succeeded him but managed only to preside over the Liberal party's near demise in the 1925 election.[105] The Conservative party played on the resentments built up in the province by years of despair and hardship, developing a provincial and regional campaign of 'Maritime Rights.' The movement phrased dissent in terms of contractual obligations, founding agreements now reneged upon by Ottawa and Central Canada.[106] The Intercolonial Railway, Conservatives charged, had been an inducement to union, intended to move Maritime goods to Central Canadian markets cheaply; it was never intended that the ICR would turn a profit. Ottawa had broken faith when it placed the ICR under the Canadian National Railway and within the jurisdiction of the Board of Railway Commissioners, which pursued the equalization of rates. The sharp increases in rates between 1917 and 1920 provided the final nail in the coffin of many Maritime businesses, according to the Conservatives. In addition the federal government had deprived the Maritime provinces of their share of the nation's wealth when it alienated the Northwest Territories by giving them to the Western provinces, Ontario, and Quebec. Conservatives also maintained that tariffs were too high on manufactured goods and not high enough on coal, steel, salt fish, and other Maritime products.[107] The dismal economic prospects led the youngest and ablest to leave the province in a steady stream.[108] 'Maritime Rights' made for a powerful platform.

In Nova Scotia's provincial election of 25 June 1925, the Conservatives enjoyed other advantages as well. The Liberal government showed signs of entropy after forty-three years in power, and limited revenue streams precluded a provincial government response to the economic slump. Though no evidence of stupidity or outrageous corruption could be found, neither were there signs of acumen. For example, the province leased a half million acres of woodland in Cape Breton for just $6000 per year. On top of this, the government relied on rather antiquated accounting practices and rejected calls for an independent audit. George Murray had cultivated the image of being a 'man of the people,' eminently approachable and eager to hear the opinions of others; Armstrong, by contrast, seemed aloof to voters, though too friendly to the British Empire Steel Corporation (BESCO).[109] Finally, the government badly bungled the coal strike of 1925.

On 6 March 1925, District 26 of the United Mine Workers of America (UMW) went on strike against BESCO and its president, Roy 'the Wolf' Wolvin. Wolvin planned to starve the miners out: 'They can't stand the gaff,' he said. Between two seemingly intractable sides stood the provincial government, and Armstrong tried to remain uninvolved. When the Conservative opposition organized relief for miners' families, however, Armstrong reluctantly provided indirect assistance to the mining communities. A.S. MacMillan, minister of highways, went to investigate conditions in the mining communities. He reported that there was poverty, but foolishly added that some families were 'shiftless' and had not prepared for 'a rainy day.' On 3 April, the government voted $20,000 to the Red Cross to help the miners and their families. When BESCO police shot and killed a miner on 11 June, many Nova Scotians thought that the government shared at least some of the responsibility. Conservative lawyer Gordon Harrington, meanwhile, was legal adviser to District 26 and did much to secure the support of labour for the Tories in the election.[110]

In the provincial election of 1925 the Tories exploited the issue of Maritime rights, which the Liberals had used successfully in the 1921 campaign. Stumping for the government, Macdonald found himself in the awkward position of defending Nova Scotia's treatment within Confederation. 'I have no very clear idea of what this "Maritime Rights" means,' he said:

> I have never seen a clear definition of it ... I know among other things that the high freight rates our farmers, fishermen, lumbermen and mine operators have to pay tend to make business unprofitable. They have increased comparatively in recent years. But don't lose sight of the fact that the cost of operating railways has also increased.

Macdonald also called the Murray-Armstrong government 'a friend to the miners,' arguing that nowhere were there better regulations for the safety and protection of coal miners.[111] This may have satisfied the party faithful on the question of the government's inertia, but it provided no comfort to unemployed voters and could not forestall the Conservative victory.

On its side the Conservative party survived a sloppy change of leadership when leader William L. Hall became embroiled in a domestic scandal. On 21 May 1925, the party executive forced Hall to resign in favour of Edgar Nelson Rhodes, who had been sent by Prime Minister Arthur Meighen to assume the leadership of the provincial party. In spite of his cold demeanour, Rhodes was widely rated as one of the best orators of the day in English Canada. The Tories won the largest share of the popular vote in Nova Scotia in the twentieth century and took forty of the forty-three seats in the Assembly. Minister of Mines William Chisholm was the only Liberal cabinet minister to survive the carnage.[112]

The Liberal retreat continued in the October 1925 federal election, when Conservatives took eleven of fourteen seats in Nova Scotia. In the King-Byng election eleven months later, the Conservatives added another seat to the tally.[113] Macdonald had either been very astute or very lucky not to have entered politics in the mid-1920s. Dalhousie proved a comfortable place to wait for more propitious times, and Macdonald took advantage of the next few years to build up some political capital.

Macdonald's reputation as an able lawyer grew, and in 1927 a group of dissident employees of the Inverness Railway and Coal Company asked Macdonald to represent them on a conciliation board. The miners had left the UMW in a dispute over local control and mismanagement of funds, choosing instead to join the One Big Union (OBU). Though the OBU was a spent force in the Canadian West by the mid-1920s, it persisted in Nova Scotia; it muted its revolutionary rhetoric in Inverness County, stressing that its members were skilled workers and property owners, and built its campaign on appeals to local autonomy and lower union dues.[114] The OBU believed it had won the support of most of the miners.

In February 1927 Inverness Railway and Coal demanded that its workers accept a 10 per cent pay cut. In March UMW miners walked out, while those with the OBU kept working but began the process to initiate a strike under the Industrial Disputes Investigation Act (IDIA). In April the UMW agreed to a contract that included the wage cut but made the mine a closed UMW workplace. As the IDIA process ground on, the federal government established a Board of Conciliation, and the OBU miners chose Macdonald as their representative, possibly on the recommendation of Lauchie Currie. Inverness Railway and Coal chose Sydney barrister Robert S. MacLellan as its representative, and Rev. Dr John M. Shaw of Pine Hill Divinity College served as chair.[115]

The board sat at Inverness for two days in May, hearing evidence from OBU and UWM representatives. The company also sent representation but it was satisfied to let the UMW take the lead in the dispute. Local UMW vice-president P.M. Muise said that the UMW could supply all of the company's labour needs and argued that the OBU miners were really not unionized at all, though they were welcome to apply to rejoin the UMW. In the meantime, he said, 'We cannot permit non-union labour to work with us under the conditions of our contract.' He implied that 'the people of Winnipeg' or the '3rd International of Russia' led the OBU, which had no place in the Inverness mine. The board heard rumours that the provincial government had conspired with Inverness Railway and Coal to keep the OBU out of Nova Scotia, but found no evidence to substantiate the charge.[116]

The board shifted to Halifax, where further talks were held with company officials. Macdonald and Shaw then wrote the majority report, recommending that the OBU workers be allowed back into the mine and that a supervised referendum on union affiliation be held within three months. MacLellan's minority report recommended that the two factions be 'fused' within the UMW.[117] The company and the UMW simply ignored the board's report, leaving the OBU miners out in the cold. Macdonald sympathized with his clients, but advised them to rejoin the UMW rather than take direct action against the rival union and the company. His failure to secure victory for the OBU probably weakened Macdonald's reputation among Inverness's working class.

The Liberal party remained powerful in the province, the results of the 1925 elections notwithstanding, but it lacked a 'bureaucratic' organization. In the early 1930s Escott Reid studied local party organizations across the country, interviewing politicians and political workers.[118] From Reid's work we can see that each riding had an executive and patronage committee, but these existed primarily to distribute jobs and to 'get the vote out' at election time. The first task of the committee involved watching public servants during election campaigns, looking for anyone who worked for the opposition. When a patronage job became available – and there were only a handful that the federal government controlled in Halifax – the committee had to consider carefully the applicants and advise the local member whom to hire. A wise choice merely shored up existing votes, while a poor decision could anger party supporters and affect a future election.[119]

Getting out the vote included compiling accurate lists of potential voters, offering transportation to the polls, and, increasingly, purchasing votes. Three senior Liberals, Don Sinclair, William Chisholm, and Fred Pearson, were quite candid about the process of vote-buying. They maintained that the practice had grown more prevalent with the 1917 federal election, driving up the costs of running for office. Sinclair estimated that a pre-war election cost about $5000 per constituency – Pearson put the figure at $1000 – while elections in the 1920s cost more than $20,000 per riding. Party workers typically supplied liquor at campaign rallies and cash or bottles of liquor on election day. Chisholm, a Liberal MLA, noted that 'people who never touched liquor at any other time would always want it at election time.' Rum had been 'the traditional political drink,' but many women thought it cheap and insisted on being given gin instead. The organizers Reid interviewed did not care for these practices, but neither did they view them as especially corrupt. As Pearson put it, 'At present the effective bribes are not given to Tories to make them vote Liberal or vice versa but to Liberals to make them vote at all.'[120]

Macdonald had been active in party organization at least since 1925 and probably assisted in getting Liberals to the polls in the South End of Halifax. Towards the end of the decade he increasingly advised Colonel J.L. Ralston on matters of federal patronage.[121] Ralston began his political career at a young age and had a sterling war record.[122] When E.M. Macdonald retired from federal politics in 1926, Ralston was a popular choice to replace him as the Nova Scotian minister.[123] Angus Macdonald revered Ralston for his personal integrity and his wartime service. Ralston in turn offered political advice in 1930, attempting to steer Macdonald safely into the waters of federal politics.

The Nova Scotia Liberal Association (NSLA) served both the federal and provincial parties. This arrangement made it difficult for provincial candidates to distance themselves from unpopular federal measures, such as tariff and transportation policies. After the debacle of 1925, the Nova Scotia Liberals formed a small provincial opposition and had just a few seats in Ottawa. Rejuvenation of the party seemed imperative, and Macdonald and other young Liberals pushed for reforms to make the party more than just a distributor of patronage when it returned to power. They worried that it might go the way of the Liberal party in

Britain, with progressives abandoning it for Labour, or some such entity. Macdonald wrote Lauchie Currie that they should work to 'return to the principles of liberalism ... [to get] back to the fundamentals and [get] rid of a few men who have led [the Party] into the bog.'[124] For Macdonald, these principles centred on individual self-realization.

With most Liberals, Macdonald shared a faith in lower tariffs and expected that freer trade would stimulate economic activity everywhere. More important, high tariffs involved the government directly in the private sphere and infringed on an individual's liberty to trade. Macdonald also criticized favouritism shown to certain large companies by the province. The Murray-Armstrong government had catered to the demands of the coal companies and especially to BESCO. The new Rhodes government seemed to be at the beck and call of Royal Securities, its chief counsel J. McG. Stewart, and its subsidiary the Mersey Paper Company.[125] Such interference by the state greatly tilted the economic playing field and made citizens cynical about government.

Macdonald did not favour an idle state; rather, he supported government social-insurance programs to protect the weak and improve the general welfare. He spoke warmly of the provincial Workmen's Compensation Act, passed by the Murray government in 1908, and of the federal Old Age Pension Act, passed by the King government in 1927. Ensuring the well-being of society's deserving poor was a sound, liberal policy. So too was promoting progress and development through infrastructure and education. Thus, Macdonald advocated the improvement of harbours, railways, and bridges and backed greater public funding of education.

Parallel to the economic and intellectual development of the individual was a citizen's social development, achieved through participation in democratic government. Macdonald believed it essential for liberals to involve themselves directly in the state and society's decision-making processes. Responsible government carried the burden that voters, along with the press, were responsible for holding a government to account. He worried that the traditional parties had alienated voters and now functioned in the interests of the commercial and political elite.

Macdonald believed that the best vehicle for a rejuvenation of liberalism would be Young Liberal Clubs. J.L. Ilsley, a successful Liberal from the Annapolis Valley in the federal election of 1926, supported Macdonald's idea and suggested that the clubs obtain a weekly page in the Liberal's leading paper, the *Halifax Chronicle*.[126] Macdonald worked with Ilsley in the Valley, Currie in Sydney, Josiah MacQuarrie in Pictou, Ronald Fielding in Dartmouth, W.P. Potter on the South Shore, and Florence Clark in Antigonish to establish organizations of young Liberal men and women around the province. Macdonald knew MacQuarrie, Fielding, and Potter from law school, and Clark was a Liberal organizer who went to Ottawa as J.L. Ralston's secretary in the 1920s.

Potter suggested that with a properly devised constitution, the 'Young Liberals of Nova Scotia' could replace the existing NSLA as the heart of the party. He recommended that the organization be open to men and women, but that no one over forty-five or fifty be allowed to serve on the executive. Similarly, any candidate for federal or provincial office would be barred from serving as president, vice-president, secretary, or treasurer of the association. These restrictions 'would prevent the recurrence of conditions now obtaining.' The motto of the new group would be 'Liberalism from the ground up.'[127] Such an association was never formally established, but as Tompkins had suggested, Macdonald had developed a network of young political supporters throughout the province. Within the talented group almost any member could have emerged as leader, but Macdonald was among the oldest and had assumed a leadership role some time ago, in most eyes.[128] He had a personal bond with this group, based on close friendship and trust. Macdonald had ambitions for public office but, as he had shown in 1921, he was not prepared to have it at any cost.

Macdonald put his political career and his job at Dalhousie on hold for a year, while he took advantage of a post-graduate fellowship to Harvard Law School.[129] He had made all the arrangements with Dalhousie, rented out his house, and leased an apartment for his family in Boston when Premier Rhodes asked the lieutenant-governor to dissolve the Assembly on 5 September 1928. The snap election caught almost everyone by surprise and deprived Macdonald of even considering a run for office.

The Conservatives had made some progress in their first three years in power. A thorough audit revealed that Armstrong had left office with a $1.1 million deficit, making the Tories' deficit of just $227,000 all the more impressive. The government succeeded in abolishing the appointed Legislative Council, though it had required an appeal to the Judicial Committee of the Privy Council. In March 1928, the government announced construction of the Mersey pulp and paper mill on the province's South Shore, valued at $14 million. Finally, the Maritime Rights agitation – driven home by Conservative successes in the 1925 and 1926 elections – had forced the King government to appoint a Royal Commission on Maritime Claims under the auspices of Sir Andrew Duncan.[130]

Following four decades of Liberal rule, the Conservatives inevitably faced significant problems of political management. Their 1925 victory had been so overwhelming that it produced far more claimants for political favours than reasonably could be satisfied. Even a rigorous purging of government rolls could not eradicate all the Liberals who were publicly employed nor provide rewards to all the Conservative mendicants. The party also failed to create an efficient system of patronage distribution, and at least one MLA resigned over cabinet interference with patronage decisions in his riding.[131]

Rhodes excused the early election by arguing that the abolition of the Legislative Council left the Assembly in need of an 'enlarged mandate.'[132] Liberals, however, warned that deficits were increasing, in spite of the $875,000 windfall in federal grants resulting from the Duncan Report. Also, the government closed the door on the Old Age Pension (OAP) scheme passed by the King government in 1926 as too expensive for Nova Scotia, with its relatively high average age.[133] The Conservatives failed to hold onto support from the disillusioned Liberals who had backed them in 1925. On 1 October 1928, they squeaked past the resurgent Liberals, taking twenty-three of the forty-three seats in the Assembly.[134]

At Harvard, Macdonald worked with some of the leading legal theorists in the United States, including Roscoe Pound. A respected scholar of jurisprudence and a 'moderate' legal realist, Pound saw the law as a tool for 'engineering' social growth and development, to be used by the state to improve social conditions.[135] The faculty also included Francis H. Bohlen, an expert on tort law, and Felix Frankfurter, founder of the American Civil Liberties Union and future Supreme Court justice. The school had a reputation for realism, attempting to discern what the law *should be* as opposed to understanding what the law *was*.[136] The students were exceptional, and Macdonald encountered several bright young men, including Paul Martin, then studying for his LL.M. For most of his year at Harvard, however, Macdonald laboured to complete coursework and a doctoral thesis within ten months.

Bohlen supervised Macdonald's thesis, 'Liability of Possessors of Premises,' which offered a realist exploration of civil law. Surveying the case law relating to property liability, Macdonald expressed his unease with the semantic exercises of some judges who wished to serve the ends of justice while generally adhering to established legal categories that did not fit a modern 'sense of justice.' As an example, Macdonald pointed to decisions that called child trespassers 'virtual licensees,' people who had the possessor's permission to enter a property and therefore could sue the possessor for injury. The common law did not distinguish between child and adult trespassers, and Macdonald found it farcical to construe any trespasser as a licensee. Better, Macdonald argued, to drop the old categories and adopt 'a general standard ... to which the conduct of the possessors of premises, must attain.' In a clear break with classical liberalism, Macdonald sought to expand the social responsibility of property holders to more realistically meet the conditions of industrial society.[137]

In the spring of 1929, as Macdonald was finishing his thesis, word came from Dalhousie that Dean John Read was leaving the law school to act as solicitor for the Department of External Affairs in Ottawa. Read had recommended Macdonald and Sidney Smith as possible successors. Horace Read, Vincent Macdonald, and Smith all thought Angus Macdonald was the best person for the job. He was just thirty-eight, had been on the full-time faculty of the law school for four years, had some courtroom experience, and was in the process of earning a well-respected doctorate. According to Horace Read, several members of the university's board of governors favoured Macdonald as well. Macdonald, however, thought Smith better suited as he was trained in the case method of teaching and was only thirty-one. Smith worried the job might be offered to an older man – a mistake, in his opinion, as such a man would stay only because he was a 'failure' in other avenues. On the other hand, one of the university's governors felt there was no point in giving the deanship to a young scholar. 'In a few years he would get "a call" elsewhere and we could not hold him.'[138]

Macdonald faced a dilemma. He intended to return to Halifax and to take up private practice, but the possibility of serving as dean of the law school intrigued him. Smith told him that if he were going into private practice, he should do it in Montreal or Toronto, 'where law is not a profession, it is a business.' He also cautioned Macdonald on the fickleness of the political gods, though he acknowledged that Macdonald would not be happy until he had his 'fling at politics.' His former mentor D.A. MacRae also advised against Macdonald's committing to the deanship: 'The Angus L. of today has no authority to sign a long term contract that binds the Angus L. of three or five years' hence,' he told Smith.[139] The deanship could postpone a political career for some time.

In late March 1929, Dalhousie President Stanley Mackenzie saved Macdonald some agony when he travelled to Ontario to offer the position to Sidney Smith. Smith accepted on four conditions: he wanted salaries improved, the faculty increased from three to four full-time professors, a limit of eight hours' teaching per week – with the understanding that the faculty would spend more time on research and publishing – and he insisted on having Angus Macdonald back at the law school. After some cajoling from Smith and Horace Read, Macdonald agreed to return to Dalhousie for one year.[140]

Macdonald maintained a physical presence in Dalhousie's Forrest Building during 1929 and 1930, but his mind wandered increasingly towards politics. Though Macdonald enjoyed the reputation of being the best professor in the law school, Richard Donahoe, a student of his that year, found his lectures disappointing as Macdonald appeared distracted much of the time.[141] Classes had not begun before another opportunity presented itself for Macdonald finally to stand for election. On 2 September 1929, popular Conservative MLA John Mahoney died in a car accident, leaving vacant Macdonald's own riding of Halifax South. Mahoney's death left the Conservatives with the slimmest of majorities, making the 21 January 1930 by-election 'one of the most important ... in provincial history,' according to Murray Beck.[142]

The local Liberal association asked Macdonald if he would consider standing for the nomination. Macdonald went to Stanley Mackenzie and Board of Governors chair Fred Pearson for their opinions. Mackenzie thought Macdonald's offering would be in line with the Weldon tradition of public service, but Pearson, a key Liberal lawyer, thought his candidacy would interfere with his teaching duties, and advised him not to stand. Macdonald concluded that he could not leave the law school before the end of the academic year and declined to stand for the nomination. At the same time, he submitted his resignation to Mackenzie, effective May 1930, so that he could freely pursue a political career.[143]

Macdonald contented himself with succeeding Ronald Fielding as president of the Halifax County Liberal Association in November 1929. R.E. Finn, a Murray Liberal whose best days seemed behind him, won the Liberal nod for the traditionally Irish Catholic seat.[144] Macdonald arranged meetings and probably spoke as well, but the Liberals lacked some of the vigour of the Conservatives. While Conservative MPs joined Rhodes and his cabinet on platforms throughout the riding, Mackenzie King observed his rule of keeping the federal government out of provincial politics.[145] The Conservative candidate, Dr George Murphy, defeated Finn by more than 5000 votes, a tremendous expression of confidence in the government.[146] Once more Macdonald was fortunate to have been excluded from the race.

The result breathed life anew into the Rhodes government and stalled the Liberal advance of 1928. William Chisholm, the interim Liberal leader since 1925, decided that he should step aside. In poor health, he saw himself as merely a 'stop-gap' at a time when party conventions were widely viewed as the best way to choose a leader. Furthermore, he did not believe that he, as a Catholic, could lead the party to victory in Nova Scotia.[147] Chisholm agreed to lead the Opposition through one more session, but by May 1930 plans were well under way for a convention.[148] Before a date could be set, however, the prime minister called a federal election.

Macdonald got the news from Ralston on 6 May 1930 and began looking for two candidates for the dual Halifax riding. Long-standing tradition stipulated that each party run a Protestant and a Catholic – usually Irish – candidate in the federal election. In 1930 the Protestant Liberal candidate was Peter Jack. Macdonald quietly hoped that the past Catholic candidate, E.J. Cragg, would not re-offer, leaving the nomination open to him. 'A good many of my friends indicated that since I had resigned from the staff of the Law School and was now free, I should take a place on the ticket. I believed at the time, and I still believe,' Macdonald wrote in 1937, 'that had I so desired it, the nomination would have come to me.' While awaiting a nomination meeting in Halifax, Macdonald received an invitation to stand for Inverness County.[149]

Unsure where he should run, Macdonald sought advice. Fielding and Ralston asked him if he could win in Inverness, and he assured them he could. They told him to run in Inverness, as there were no guarantees a Liberal could win in Halifax. Macdonald should have been less sanguine about the prospects in Inverness. Though the nomination came to him easily, Liberal forces there were deeply divided around three perennial contenders: Dr A.W. Chisholm, Dr M.E. McGarry, and Donald MacLennan. Dr Chisholm had represented the riding in Ottawa from 1908 to 1925, when he lost to Ike Macdougall. Just sixty-one, he was still an important figure in Inverness politics. Dr McGarry sat in the provincial house for Inverness and had his own circle of supporters. Finally, 'Little Danny' MacLennan, who had supervised Macdonald's articles, had been the provincial member from 1911 until 1925. Had any of the three contested the nomination, Macdonald might have lost.[150]

During the campaign, the three Liberal factions did not openly fight, but neither did they fully cooperate. Drs Chisholm and McGarry were not on speaking terms, and relations between Chisholm and MacLennan were cool. MacLennan served as Macdonald's campaign manager, but his brother Allan MacLennan held some grudge against McGarry that led him to work for the Conservatives. Macdonald's own brother Stanley, a parish priest in Judique, embarrassed him with some poorly timed gripes against Mackenzie King. Macdonald later criticized the local organization for 'too much use of liquor and too little attention to business in certain quarters.' He noted that the Liberal headquarters in the town of Inverness became an informal tavern, where people came to drink and listen to music, not to discuss politics.[151] He was not yet fully acclimatized to the seamy realities of political campaigns.

In Ike Macdougall, Macdonald faced an abler opponent than he at first had assumed. A respected veteran and popular glad-hander, Macdougall enjoyed the position of incumbent while being able to attack the unpopular King government. The mine in Inverness operated only on the sufferance of the Eastern Trust Company with support from the provincial Conservative government, and Macdougall hinted that the mine would close if the voters of Inverness chose Macdonald. The local economy had been depressed for most of a decade, and Mackenzie King's Old Age Pension scheme was so much pie in the sky, as the provincial government could not afford to implement it. Bennett, Macdougall promised, would introduce a pension plan wholly funded by Ottawa within three months of winning the election.[152]

Nova Scotia had never fully recovered from the slump of 1920, and the sharp contraction of 1929 made matters worse. To Macdonald fell the task of defending the King government at the outset of the Depression. He pointed to decreased taxation and predicted that the government's 'broad and comprehensive plans for industrial and trade expansion' would surely lead to 'a lengthy period of unprecedented prosperity.'[153] He held aloft a cable from Labour Minister Peter Heenan promising an eight-hour day and fair wages on all government projects.[154] Yet Macdougall called into question Macdonald's record on labour, spreading word that Macdonald had betrayed the OBU miners in 1927. Macdonald obtained a telegram from Dr Shaw, chair of the board of conciliation, attesting that he had represented the miners honestly and to the best of his ability, but it is unlikely that this carried much weight in Inverness town.[155]

Macdonald's confidence waned as he sensed the strength of the Conservative trend. A friend pulled him aside with ten days left in the campaign and said that many good candidates had lost elections. Macdonald took his meaning and prepared himself for defeat.[156] His war record and his academic reputation could not match Macdougall the campaigner. Macdougall spoke well and could tell a colourful joke, while Macdonald shyly withdrew from large groups and eschewed vulgarity, even when the situation might have called for it.[157] On election day, several communities he had counted in his favour voted against him – including Port Hood, where his father had been a magistrate for two decades – and Macdougall prevailed by 189 votes overall.[158]

Macdonald returned immediately to Halifax and opened a law office to support his family. In August 1930, the Macdonalds were expecting their third child. His income as a professor had been relatively modest, and whatever savings he and Agnes had were surely eaten up by a year of graduate study in Boston and the campaign in Inverness. The economy of Nova Scotia had been depressed for a decade and now proceeded to get worse. Macdonald must have longed for the stability of a professorial income as he stepped into the uncertain world of private practice.

His retreat into law was made easier by the presence of political friends. He opened his own office in the Roy Building in Halifax, but shared a law library and secretarial services with Ronald Fielding, J.L. Ilsley, and M.B. Archibald.[159] Other lawyers often consulted him as an expert on tort cases, and his brother Oswin articled with him. He also mulled over his return to public life. The embarrassment of losing in Inverness probably made him more cautious in selecting his next political venture.

The party shuffled towards its leadership convention in the autumn of 1930. The by-election loss in January and the federal defeat in July left many disheartened. As well, four Liberal MLAs – D.A. Cameron, E.J. Cragg, E.C. Doyle, and J.J. Kinley – had resigned their seats to contest the federal election, leaving the Conservatives with a stronger majority in the Assembly. Rhodes felt safe enough to take a seat in Bennett's cabinet, handing the reins of power to Mines Minister Gordon Harrington.[160]

As the convention approached, Macdonald resumed his organizational role, working with D.A. Cameron, NSLA president Don Sinclair, and *Chronicle* editor George Farquhar to draft the party platform for presentation at the meeting.[161] The fifteen-point platform contained few explicit promises, other than an eight-hour day for workers and free schoolbooks for students through grade eight. Every other point criticized the Conservative government, especially the pledge to reclaim 'responsible government,' won almost a century before by another great Liberal, Joseph Howe. For Macdonald, the most important plank was the last: the pledge to conduct an inquiry into Nova Scotia's economy and its place within Confederation. Overall the platform articulated Macdonald's vision of an expertly guided liberal state, fostering broad economic and social development.[162]

The structure of the convention stirred little debate within the party, and most members seemed to approach it as a large riding convention. Members of the federal and provincial caucuses and the most recent failed candidates qualified as delegates. Each riding association could send ten delegates, though these appear to have been chosen by riding executives and not by local membership votes. The Nova Scotia Women's Liberal Association also received a handful of delegates.[163]

Liberals all over the province speculated as to who would run for the leadership, but when the convention opened on 1 October 1930, there were just two declared candidates: J.J. Kinley and William Duff. Every other potential contender either lacked confidence in himself or the party or hoped to capture the momentum of the convention. Observers saw Kinley as safe but uninspiring. He sat for Lunenburg under Murray and Armstrong without distinguishing himself.[164] Duff, an occasionally unscrupulous merchant who probably smuggled some rum on the side, had been an MP since 1917 and performed well in opposition.[165] Kinley relied on the support of the provincial caucus, and Duff apparently counted on a few well-placed local organizers to achieve victory.

A.S. MacMillan, minister of highways under Armstrong and another obvious contender, refused to run, later claiming to be bound by the caucus vote supporting Kinley.[166] Macdonald again pressed Ilsley to run in the interests of the Young Liberals, but Ilsley replied: 'Absolutely nothing doing.'[167] Chisholm, not satisfied with Kinley or Duff, asked George Farquhar to stand, but Farquhar pleaded poverty and argued that he would be more effective as an editor than as a leader.[168] The presence of only Kinley and Duff both frustrated and excited delegates; if voting on the floor of the convention decided the leadership, instead of negotiations in the backrooms, a young, dark horse might indeed win.

Macdonald shared the dissatisfaction of others on the eve of the convention. He rejected several suggestions that he enter his name, but he did not dismiss the idea entirely.[169] Days before the convention Mr Justice William F. Carroll, a former Liberal MP from Cape Breton, told him that their mutual friend Malcolm Patterson, a Sydney lawyer, had circulated his name as a contender. 'On the spur of the moment, I said that if the offer were made I should not decline it,' Macdonald recalled. 'So far as I know, that was the only definite statement that I made on the matter.'[170] When he went to the Nova Scotian Hotel for the convention, he had grudgingly decided to vote for Kinley.

The party executive met all morning on 1 October, discussing the agenda. When the delegates gathered at 2:00 p.m., they quickly voted to adopt the proposed platform. J.L. Ralston and Alice Hatfield, president of the Nova Scotia Women's Liberal Association, then paid glowing tribute to Will Chisholm. Sinclair, the convention chair, opened the floor for nominations at 3:30. Cumberland native John Smiley nominated Duff; Michael Dwyer, mayor of North Sydney, seconded. MacMillan rose to put forward Kinley's name, which was endorsed by Dr McGarry's wife.[171] MacMillan later wrote that he rushed to nominate Kinley to quash any movement to nominate him, as he was interested in maintaining party discipline. This explanation, coming years later, seems self-serving, as he added: 'If my name had gone before [the convention] undoubtedly I would have been selected.'[172]

Sinclair asked if there were any further nominations. Fielding, standing in a group around Macdonald, urged him once more to accept. Even as he refused, Truro's Prescott Blanchard stood and said he wanted to nominate 'a young man who had no political sins to answer for,' unlike the members of the Armstrong government.[173] Macdonald, standing on the other side of the room, strained to hear this man he did not know and 'wondered what name he had in mind. I thought of Ilsley, MacQuarrie, Patterson, but when he mentioned my name I was ... probably more surprised than anybody in the hall.'[174]

Amid 'pronounced' applause, Lauchie Currie made his way to the podium to second the nomination 'in a speech of considerable fire and vigour. Currie declared that no one who was associated with the Government of 1925 should be considered, and that what was needed was a new man.'[175] He said that workers in Cape Breton were looking for leadership from the Liberal party. 'The people expect to find that leadership I refer to in our young men.'[176] Currie drew the line clearly between the Young Liberals, cultivated over the last few years by Macdonald, Ilsley, himself, and others, and the party establishment, which hoped for an orderly transition of leadership.

Macdonald reflexively declined. 'I got to the stage and, as I remember it, stated that it was a great honour to be at a Liberal Convention of this kind, and an even greater honour to have one's name submitted to it for leadership of the Party, but that being a poor man and having just opened a law office, I could not possibly accept.' Perhaps he feared that another political embarrassment, coming on the heels of his defeat in Inverness, might severely damage his career. He could not gauge at first how Currie's speech had stirred the crowd and he did not appreciate that the circumstances obviated the need for a well-developed campaign. Only when he began to leave the stage and the excitement of the crowd persisted did he sense he could win. A clutch of friends, including Ilsley, Fielding and Currie, encircled him and urged him to change his mind. Senator H.J. Logan grabbed his arm and hissed: 'Don't be a fool. This is a thing that only comes along once in a lifetime.' Macdonald returned to the podium and accepted the nomination.[177]

Years later, the *Ottawa Journal* wrote that Macdonald won the leadership with a single speech,[178] but his second address was remarkable only for its context and not its content. He agreed the party had strayed from 'the real principles of Liberalism,' and said 'it was the duty of the Liberal Party to carry on the tradition of Howe and other great Liberal leaders.' He attacked the tariff, 'which had just recently been raised substantially at the short session of the Dominion Parliament.' He then urged the delegates to vote with reason and not to be swayed by any demonstration. In another setting he would have drawn polite partisan applause, but in the atmosphere of a reinvigorated convention where all bets were now off, the majority of delegates rose to their feet and cheered. Nominations closed – who dared to follow that drama? – and voting commenced. At 6:00 p.m. Sinclair announced that Macdonald had won almost two-thirds of the ballots.[179]

Dr G.M. Logan, a Halifax dentist who sat as a Liberal under Macdonald from 1933 to 1937, judged that Macdonald's victory came off too smoothly not to have been organized in advance, though Logan had not been in the Nova Scotian Hotel.[180] Fielding and Gordon Isnor, who were closer to Macdonald and present at the convention, both asserted that it was entirely unscripted.[181] Press coverage also points to a spontaneous campaign for Macdonald; if it was scripted, he and his associates acted brilliantly and with the utmost discretion before 1 October.

Macdonald's unexpected win resulted in part from his organizational work over several years and his unsuccessful-but-respectable showing in the recent federal election, but it was also a product of luck and the divisions between young and established Liberals. In their party's first leadership convention, potential candidates were overly cautious, afraid to campaign lest they appear egotistical or corrupt. Blanchard could have offered at least a handful of names to similar effect. Macdonald would prove to be wildly successful for the Liberal party, but no one could foresee that in 1930.

2 The Macdonald Decade

The 1930s belonged to Angus L. Macdonald. He began the decade as an unknown professor of law and ended it as perhaps the most respected provincial premier in the country. He overcame religious bigotry and inexperience and established himself as an electoral power, delivering Liberal majorities in provincial and federal contests. He shunned the novel and more radical political trends of Ontario and the West, remaining within the tent of Liberal orthodoxy while lobbying for significant constitutional reform. Nova Scotia endured its second decade of depression, but his yearly budgets glistened with black ink even as the province borrowed heavily to modernize its infrastructure and provide relief work to thousands of unemployed. Finally, he developed a national reputation as a gifted politician and, on the eve of the Second World War, seemed destined to succeed William Lyon Mackenzie King as prime minister.

Liberals in Nova Scotia awoke on Thursday, 2 October 1930, wondering if the previous day's events had really occurred. Had they chosen a little known, forty-year-old Catholic academic, whose only electoral outing had been a failure, to lead the party of Howe, Fielding, and Murray? Had they really turned their backs on such experienced politicians as John Kinley, William Duff, and Stirling MacMillan? The novelty of Angus Macdonald was briefly captivating, but for the long haul was the man worth the risk? Many observers recognized his potential, including his former mentors, prominent young Liberals in the province, and those with whom he dealt in Ottawa.[1] Macdonald's fast track to the leadership, however, struck many as unwarranted. Other men had earned the opportunity to lead the party by standing for office and fighting the Conservatives in the Legislative Assembly and in Parliament. Macdonald had assisted the party with campaign speeches, some organizational efforts, and one unsuccessful stand for federal office, but had sacrificed little more than his time.

Macdonald inevitably faced some animosity. His easy victory bruised the ego of every Liberal politician who, by virtue of service, talent, or age, believed himself worthier than the lucky young professor. Kinley accepted defeat with grace, but Duff nursed bitter feelings towards Macdonald for the rest of his career. A.S. MacMillan, who served as House leader of the Liberals for the next three years, remained convinced that he could have won the leadership if he had offered, and could never treat the younger man as a superior.[2] Macdonald's survival depended on the Young Liberals and his ability to fashion his own provincial organization.

Macdonald had time, personality, and vitality in his favour. He entered provincial politics at the shallow end of the pool and had three years to learn to swim. Since Gordon S. Harrington's Conservative government refused to hold by-elections to fill six vacant seats in the Assembly, Macdonald was spared a direct contest. The premier could not issue a writ for just one by-election and did not wish to risk the government's five-seat majority outside of a general election. In public Macdonald scored points by lamenting 'the loss of responsible government,' as so many Nova Scotians remained without an MLA and the Opposition without its leader. In private Macdonald delighted at Harrington's predicament, later telling one supporter, 'If the truth must be told, I was sometimes afraid that they would open up a seat and deprive me of this sort of ammunition.'[3] He watched the legislative sessions from the press gallery, relying on daily caucus meetings and scribbled notes to help direct the Liberal forces.[4]

Macdonald drew friends and supporters with his warm personality, exhibiting a genuine interest in the lives and stories of the people he met. He had a natural shyness in large gatherings – revealed in his tendency to look at the ceiling while he made a speech – but overcame it in small, conversational settings. Among friends Macdonald often shared a song or a tale.[5] His friendships usually lasted for life and were not bound by political stripes; among his closest friends were several important Tories, including lawyers John Walker, J. McGregor Stewart, and H.P. MacKeen. Macdonald's charm sometimes made up for his early political inexperience. In 1932, seventeen-year-old Henry Hicks accompanied his father and uncle to a Liberal meeting in Kentville, down a dusty road from their Bridgetown home. The Hicks brothers were dry Baptists who were suspicious of Catholics. Macdonald could hardly have made a worse first impression when he offered them a drink, yet by the end of the conversation he had won their firm support.[6]

Most important, Macdonald symbolized the revitalization of the Liberal party in Nova Scotia and, later, in Canada. He emerged from a group of young professionals who wanted to re-commit the party to liberal principles. Influenced by the economic devastation of the 1920s they were convinced that the state had a significant part to play in the economy. The dominance of 'machine' politicians and their corporate clients had bred a cynicism that could be removed only by sharply broadening political participation. This push for greater democracy in the province matched the rhetoric of equality common in Macdonald's circle: their opinions mattered as much as those of the older generation. Young people were drawn to the party by virtue of his leadership and his image as a reformer. J.L. Ilsley, who could just as easily have won the leadership, coolly assessed the results: 'Had I gone into it and carried the convention it would have been bad for the party in Kings and Hants [Counties] – and I cannot see why you are not in every way as strong as I would be and I have a suspicion that you are stronger ... and the best of it is that a whole lot of young men are feeling more like working for the party than ever before.'[7]

It is probable that Macdonald's views on 'reform' and 'liberalism' differed from those of some of his supporters. After more than a decade of economic decline, many simply wanted the state to do *something*, anything to improve conditions. When Macdonald spoke of reform, he meant government by political principle, rather than political expediency. He believed in studying problems and applying liberal principles to solve them. He did not propose to change the political or economic order, but he did want to make government less arbitrary and more responsible to the majority of Nova Scotians.[8]

Macdonald's liberalism in the early 1930s closely resembled Mackenzie King's. Neither gave a precise definition, but their speeches and writings focused on personal and political freedoms, freer trade, and the protection of the weakest members of society. Each saw a positive role for the state, guided by expert advice, in providing an automatic, means-tested safety net and indirectly promoting economic development. They believed in the 'opening of channels for the free flow of every form of legitimate activity,' but also in limiting private freedoms when they became 'public wrongs.'[9] Each spoke in favour of lower tariffs, but neither stood for complete free trade. Rather, they sought to balance the interests of primary producers and manufacturers, to adjust tariffs and freight rates 'so as to do the greatest good to the greatest number.'[10] They held that responsible government was a liberal concept and that the Liberal party was the party of democracy and equality.[11]

Macdonald later hailed King as the 'champion' of liberalism for staking out a middle ground between R.B. Bennett's Conservative government and J.S. Woodsworth's democratic socialism.[12] In response to a 1933 resolution by Woodsworth calling for state control of natural resources and the machinery of production for the 'interests of the people and not for the benefits of the few,' King first rejected the anti-communist hysteria of the Conservatives in response to the resolution and then calmly described the collectivist elements of the Liberal party. Public ownership and operation of utilities, for example, were appropriate only where 'the greatest good for the greatest number [was] likely to be brought about,' King argued. Though social legislation might be a good thing, 'a socialist state' was not. Moreover, he maintained, 'Most of the social legislation on the statute books of different countries throughout the world today is the result of great Liberal battles.' A Liberal government would balance freedom and security.[13]

From 1930 to 1933, Macdonald spoke constantly of the need to apply liberal principles to the problems of government. He presented himself as being above the sordid and undignified activities of partisan politics and his public speeches dealt mainly with liberalism and the party's platform that he had drafted for the 1930 convention. Macdonald spoke at length of free trade, more educational opportunities, and the need for government to secure expert advice. The job of chronicling the Conservative government's blunders and attacking its policies fell to members of the Liberal caucus, led ably and doggedly in the House by A.S. MacMillan. MacMillan may have been overly aggressive at times; after one particularly heated debate in the House in March 1931, MacMillan exchanged punches with Conservative MLA R.H. Butts.[14] The Liberal press referred to Macdonald as 'a professor' who would elevate the tenor of politics in the province and apply careful study to solve the province's problems.[15] At least one scholar has called Macdonald a 'populist,' but he always expressed complete faith in existing political institutions, save perhaps the Canadian Senate.[16]

In one of his first moves as Liberal leader Macdonald created a study group to examine the party's platform and philosophy. Not an especially creative thinker, Macdonald's method of scholarship had always involved thorough study, discussion, and careful consideration of alter-

natives and consequences.[17] His study group included Liberal politicians, party organizers, and academics, all drawn from outside the pool
of Murray-Armstrong Liberals. Wishart Robertson, MLA from Shelburne and future government leader in the Senate, joined Halifax MLA
Gordon Isnor on the committee. Party insiders included George Farquhar, editor of the *Chronicle*, M.B. Archibald, a legal colleague of Macdonald's, and party secretary J.W. Godfrey. Dalhousie professors R.A.
MacKay and W.R. Maxwell also joined. The group met every two
weeks, beginning in January 1931, though interest in the meetings may
have waned after a few months.[18]

The study group focused on economic problems rather than party
organization and favoured the liberal position of 'lower tariffs as a general principle.'[19] The first subject for discussion was the economic
inquiry promised in the party's platform. Though the nature of the
inquiry had not been spelled out in the platform, the group identified
tariffs and freight rates as the two central issues. At the group's second
meeting, Professor Maxwell delivered a report on tariffs and the province's economy. He noted that the existing tariff structure benefited
'domestic' as opposed to export industries, but noted that for the
domestic industries of Nova Scotia – especially coal – the tariffs were too
low to exclude foreign competition. Domestic and export industries
both languished in a semi-protectionist limbo. Macdonald reasoned
that if Nova Scotia 'could not get a lower tariff where we think it is
important, we should get some other compensating advantage, such as
lower freight rates.'[20]

As Macdonald toured the province building support for a renewed
Liberal party, he continued to call for careful investigation of problems.
In most of his speeches, he posed as a man above crass politics. 'As a
matter of fact we have too much politics in N.S.,' he told an audience in
Halifax. 'Too much of the cheap type of politics – too much of the ward-
healer, too little of the statesman – too much political so called oratory –
too little political thinking – we cannot have too much of that.'[21] This
aloofness had hurt his candidacy in Inverness in 1930, but as party
leader trying to rekindle idealism, it now lent him the aura of a statesman. He was not fighting an election but rebuilding the confidence of
Liberals.

Meanwhile, the Liberals in the Assembly kept up their attack on the
Harrington government and did not want for ammunition. The administration was not inept but it behaved timidly in the face of the depression, constrained by economic orthodoxy and limited resources. It had
counted on the federal government to bolster provincial revenues, but

Bennett found the nationwide pleas for help overwhelming. Liberal critics in Halifax focused on inadequate relief, the decline of the coal and fishing industries, and pieces of legislation that were poorly written and open to abuse by friends of the government.

The economic contraction that began nationally in 1929 was less pronounced in the Maritimes than in other regions of the country, but only because the 'incomplete recovery' from the post-war recession meant that the region's economy could not sink much lower.[22] The Conservative government had run yearly deficits since it was elected in 1925 and did not wish to expand the province's debt further by borrowing to participate in federal matching-grant programs. Annual revenues had grown from $4.8 million in 1925 to $9.3 million in 1931, yet the government anticipated its seventh consecutive deficit – $320,000 for the 1931–2 fiscal year – as it spent $850,000 on unemployment relief and $360,000 on mothers' allowances. Both programs were inadequate, and where relief work was provided Tories often were hired ahead of Liberals. The government finally predicted a tiny surplus in 1932, but when that failed to materialize the Conservatives became associated with endless red ink.[23]

Strained finances led the Conservatives down the politically dangerous path of government-controlled alcohol sales. As an issue, liquor could earn a government little support but much enmity. The government sponsored the 1929 plebiscite in which voters authorized the repeal of the province's Temperance Act and established the Nova Scotia Liquor Commission (NSLC) in May 1930. Liberals criticized the autocracy of the NSLC, but voted in favour of the Liquor Control Act rather than take a divisive stand on the issue. Liquor sales boosted provincial revenues, but not enough to overcome relief expenditures.[24]

The liquor trade offered both political parties a new and substantial source of funds. Brewers, distillers, and distributors of imported wines and spirits were asked to contribute to party coffers to ensure that their products were marketed on government-owned shelves. In addition, the profits generated by liquor sales were large and relatively nebulous; if some friends of the government received contracts with the NSLC, who could say whether they were overly generous? Tory organizer J. McG. Stewart purchased the Pentagon Building, in the heart of Halifax's commercial and legal district, a few days before the passage of the Liquor Control Act of 1930. The building then housed the NSLC and the Nova Scotia Conservative Association.[25] The NSLC also tended to rent space for its stores from good Tories at above-market rates.

In the provincial election of 1928, the Conservatives had been hurt by their failure to introduce Old Age Pensions (OAPs). Nova Scotia had limited revenues and an older population; the government said it simply could not afford the program as designed by King's Liberals. In the 1930 campaign, R.B. Bennett had promised that OAPs would be fully funded by the federal government within four months of the election; nothing was done until mid-1931 when Ottawa agreed to cover 75 per cent of the costs of the program.[26] The Conservative government of Nova Scotia – whose members had repeated Bennett's promise on the federal hustings and whose leader was now minister of finance in Ottawa – decided that it could not afford even this cheaper plan. Harrington became tied to Bennett's undelivered promise.

The national depression pushed the Dominion Steel and Coal Company (DOSCO) deeper into the red, and in 1931 it insisted its miners take a 12 per cent wage cut. The United Mine Workers of America (UMW) District 26 summarily rejected the demand, and Harrington appointed a commission of inquiry to forestall a strike. The commission's report, issued on the eve of the 1932 session of the Assembly, supported the wage cut and the closure of some collieries. The UMW rejected the report and continued to work without a contract, mollified by a deal for an increased coal subvention that Harrington had negotiated in Ottawa. According to the premier, the deal would create orders for an extra million tons of coal yearly. When the orders never materialized, the UMW grudgingly accepted the wage cut, but not before passing a motion of censure against Harrington, their former legal counsel.[27]

Two Conservative bills, in particular, exposed the government to charges of cronyism. Bill 151, passed in 1930 but never proclaimed, gave cabinet the power to ban exports of unprocessed pulpwood from woodlots of more than one thousand acres. Intended to promote forest conservation and the development of a pulp and paper industry in the province, the bill was attacked by Liberals as 'legalized public theft,' marking 'the death knell of Responsible Government.' Inflamed rhetoric aside, woodlot owners argued that even if it were not enforced, the bill depressed the value of their land.[28]

More damaging to the government's reputation was the Electoral Franchise Act of 1931. The franchise bill had been presented late in the 1931 session and passed with only muted debate.[29] Traditionally, municipalities updated voters' lists every year; as the majority of municipalities were under Liberal control, Conservatives argued that they had lost seats through rigged lists. The act provided that provincially appointed registrars would prepare new lists on the eve of the next general election, striking the names of deceased persons. Registrars were then to post the revised lists 'in conspicuous places.' The most controversial clause of the act stipulated that a revising officer had just three days in public hearings to make all corrections. The *Chronicle* warned that the act was open to abuse by the party in power and rhetorically asked if this were the intention.[30]

Liberals began taking a closer look at the Franchise Act the next year, in anticipation of an election. One county warden alerted Macdonald that 'the damnable Franchise Act of the present Government [is] designed with its many traps to put nothing but Tories on the list, and deprive others of their franchise.'[31] E.M. Macdonald, a veteran of many federal campaigns and Angus Macdonald's closest adviser among the older Liberals, urged him to have Liberal workers prepare voters' lists in each county. This would allow the party to mail out campaign literature and to check the official lists when they were posted. The older Macdonald also attacked the Redistribution Bill of 1932 – which reduced the number of seats in the Assembly from 38 to 30 in the interests of economy, a decline from the 43 seats contested in the 1928 election – as 'nothing but a bold attempt to steal the election.'[32] In the House, A.S. MacMillan introduced a resolution calling for changes to the Franchise Act, but the government brought the session to an end before the resolution could be discussed.[33] MacMillan pressed the government to make changes to the act by order-in-council, but the Conservatives ignored him, handing the Liberals a big stick with which to beat the Tories during the campaign to come.

Harrington's government had a difficult session in 1933, the last before an election had to be called. Shortly after the throne speech the Nova Scotia Steel and Coal Company went into receivership, threatening 3200 workers with unemployment. The provincial treasurer predicted yet another deficit, the eighth consecutive under Conservative rule. The government delayed almost two months after the House rose before calling the election for 22 August 1933, and the campaign slowly lurched into motion.[34]

Though the Liberals did not control provincial or federal patronage they were able to raise funds. Somewhat cryptic notes in Macdonald's diary indicate that MLA Wishart Robertson, whose seat had been eliminated by redistribution, and C.W. Ackhurst, a Liberal bagman, made a reasonably successful fund-raising trip around the breweries and distilleries of Central Canada in June.[35]

The Conservatives released their manifesto on 22 July, and the Liberals on 2 August 1933. The programs were similar, suggesting that platforms did not determine the result. Both parties promised to continue relief payments and mothers' allowances and to introduce the OAP, Harrington by 1 July 1934, and Macdonald immediately upon taking office. Both offered free schoolbooks, though Macdonald's plan was universal through grade eight, while Harrington's targeted only needy children. Both emphasized economy in government, better marketing of natural resources, and improvement of roads, and the Liberals sketched a tentative paving program. The Conservatives broke new ground by promising to bring electricity to every home in Nova Scotia; the Liberals pledged to conduct an inquiry into Nova Scotia's economy and the effects of national policies on it.[36]

In a study of Nova Scotian politics in the 1980s, Ian Stewart demonstrates that election campaigns tend to be driven by events rather than philosophy. Prime Minister Kim Campbell's famous 1993 observation that an election campaign was no time to debate policy was, perhaps, more accurate than her critics could admit. Activists are drawn to a particular party based on a presumably shared ideology, but during campaigns parties try to woo voters with 'pragmatic programs.'[37] The similarities in the 1933 manifestos should not distract us from the differences between Liberals and Conservatives. Macdonald and his supporters, for example, were far more inclined to embrace indirect intervention in the province's economy.

The Liberal manifesto also included a pledge to 'restore Responsible Government,' threatened by the 1931 Franchise Act. By leaving the compilation of voters' lists to government-appointed registrars and allowing only a few days for corrections, the Franchise Act was clearly open to abuse. Some Conservative workers gave into temptation and tried to keep the party in power by manipulating the lists. The ensuing scandal damaged the reputation of the Conservative party, and Macdonald managed to dredge up the affair in each of the next four elections he fought.[38]

The centre of the storm was Halifax, where the returning officers had appointed just one registrar for each city riding, North, Centre, and South. Early in the campaign, Macdonald cabled Harrington and Attorney-General John Doull, arguing that one registrar for the 11,000 voters of Halifax South was insufficient and pressing them to name more. If the government failed to act, he would have to seek redress in the courts. Harrington invited Macdonald to pursue that route, weakly arguing: 'it is not my function to instruct Returning Officers as to their duties.'[39] Foolishly allowing Macdonald to play the defender of democracy, the Conservatives compounded their blunder by opposing a writ of mandamus to secure more registrars in a late-night session of the Supreme Court. The court granted the application, more registrars were named, and the Liberal press hailed Macdonald as the greatest hero of Nova Scotia since Joseph Howe.[40]

When voters' lists were posted thousands of names – mostly Liberal ones – were absent. The skewed lists were produced in spite of continuous *Chronicle* editorials lambasting the Conservatives for the Act and predicting that such lists were in the works. An inquiry conducted by Justice Hugh Ross after the election showed that 45 to 65 per cent of eligible voters were left off preliminary lists in Halifax.[41] Liberals suspected that Tory organizers in the Pentagon Building had drawn up the lists. The *Chronicle* named Charles Stayner, an employee of the Highway Board and denizen of the Pentagon Building, as one author.[42] A *Herald* reporter told Macdonald that prominent Tory organizer Col. E. C. Phinney and Provincial Secretary Fred Fraser were behind the scheme.[43] Some registrars throughout the province abetted the fraud by attempting to hide the incomplete lists. One registrar, followed by Liberal workers trying to discover where he would post his lists, sought assistance from the Halifax police; the officers detained the Liberals while the registrar went about his business. A few lists were posted just before the midnight deadline on 23 July, high on utility poles and in other inaccessible places. In Shelburne, lists were posted at 5:00 p.m. in a store that closed at 6:00. In three districts in Kings County, the lists could not be found; the registrars claimed that they had posted the lists in 'conspicuous places' but refused to say where exactly.[44] Liberal workers, motivated by a sense of fighting injustice, used ladders, flashlights, and car headlights, working late into the night to read and copy the lists. Macdonald later boasted that his workers were able to add 4600 names in Halifax South in three days.[45]

And still the Conservative hijinks continued. Some registrars in Halifax refused to issue copies of voters' lists where the originals had been destroyed or stolen, forcing the Liberals to return to court to get copies. A few, when sitting for revisions, seemed determined to slow the process by asking senior citizens for proof they were twenty-one and women if they were Supreme Court justices. The *Chronicle* ran daily photographs of long lines of 'disenfranchised voters' waiting to register. Macdonald pressed Harrington to order the registrars in Halifax to sit beyond the deadline to ensure that all voters were registered; Harrington complied, but some registrars closed up shop in front of long lines nonetheless.[46]

Even Conservatives were offended by the blatant manipulation of the lists and the audacious behaviour of some registrars. Harrington attempted to dismiss concerns about the Franchise Act, arguing that it had worked 'excellently' outside Halifax. Liberal lists, he maintained, had been riddled with fraud:

> When we came in we found lists that were inactive and that carried a lot of dead people and didn't carry enough living people. That was notorious throughout the Province, and also the fact that our opponents had made personation a science ... Being Christians we might think that we will see the friend again in the Great Beyond, but we do not expect to have him turn up and vote against us ... I am told 30,000 voters have been registered from a total population of 59,000. Now we might not have the dead with us, but we might have too much of the living because there are not 30,000 voters in the City of Halifax.[47]

Harrington had a point about the old lists, but the franchise affair was a serious gaffe on the part of the Conservatives. More than any other issue, it allowed Macdonald to cast himself in the role of reformer, enhancing his image as a young, intellectual leader of integrity. Murray Beck writes: 'No newcomer to the provincial political scene has ever become so quickly, widely, and favourably known in such dramatic fashion.'[48] The actions of a few short-sighted Conservatives helped to transform Macdonald into the unbeatable 'Angus L,' the undisputed leader of the Liberal forces.

The campaign dragged on for almost a month after the climax of the franchise affair, but the Conservatives could not slow the Liberal juggernaut. Some local campaigns of religious bigotry appeared, mounted mostly by Orange lodges. Pamphlets warned of Macdonald's 'secret campaign' to introduce separate schools and predicted, 'Our Protestant children will be compelled to attend convent schools because no others will exist in the very near future.'[49] After the election, a bitter Harrington grumbled that a Roman Catholic conspiracy had been mounted against him, but the Liberals tiptoed around the religious question, hoping to let sleeping dogs lie.[50]

Macdonald ran in Halifax South, the Irish Conservative bastion in the capital, where Conservative George Murphy had won by 5000 votes in 1930; Macdonald carried a 400-vote majority less than three years later. The Liberals trounced the Conservatives throughout the province, sweeping the five Halifax ridings and taking twenty-two seats to the Conservatives' eight. Five cabinet ministers were defeated, and the new Opposition found itself confined almost exclusively to Colchester County and Cape Breton Island. The franchise incident spurred 86 per cent of eligible voters to cast ballots, giving the Macdonald government a strong mandate.[51]

The result reflected the sins of the Conservatives more than the virtues of the Liberals. Yet Liberals in Nova Scotia were excited about their future and especially about the new premier. He had shown himself to be articulate, passionate, and popular. By the end of the campaign, he had become known affectionately throughout the province as 'Angus L.'[52] Cartoonist Bob Chambers consistently sketched him as earnest and dignified, always ready to lead Nova Scotians out of danger, to offer them a lifeline, or to direct them to a promised land, usually labelled 'A New Deal,' reflecting the tremendous influence Franklin Roosevelt's new government had north of the border. Macdonald was not a populist, but the image the Liberals presented between 1930 and 1933 certainly had populist elements. Though his favourite topics in speeches were liberalism, tariffs, and freight rates, some saw him as a fighter for 'the little man.' Significantly, Chambers was in the process of developing a 'little man' as his central, stock character. This short, balding, bespectacled fellow looked as if he were perpetually sighing at the forces arrayed against him.[53]

Macdonald's campaign tirade against the Royal Canadian Mounted Police (RCMP) accentuated this image. The RCMP began operations in Nova Scotia in 1932, replacing the provincial police force as a cost-cutting measure. The Nova Scotia Provincial Police provided 110 officers and cost $325,000; the RCMP cost the province just $150,000 and provided 150 officers. Within a year, the RCMP had become associated with incompetence and dangerous recklessness following the shootings of several innocent people.[54] Early in the campaign, Macdonald addressed the issue of policing and, perhaps caught up in the excitement of a rally in Amherst, proclaimed that the Liberal party would drive the RCMP out of Nova Scotia all together. His colleagues were embarrassed and surprised at his foolish outburst; he avoided the subject for the rest of the campaign. After the election, Macdonald considered carrying through on his pledge, if only because he had made it. His caucus dissuaded him, emphasizing the added expense of the provincial force.[55]

Harrington was eager to hand over the reins of government, and Macdonald had to choose his cabinet quickly. Some appointments to the nine cabinet posts were obvious, beginning with A.S. MacMillan as minister of highways, John A. McDonald as minister of agriculture, and Michael Dwyer as minister of mines. MacMillan and McDonald were part of the old guard, and the new premier found it useful to cultivate an image of stability. An experienced contractor, MacMillan had served as chair of the Provincial Highways Board under Murray and Armstrong. MacMillan was not unopposed; J.D. McKenzie, a new MLA from the Annapolis Valley urged Macdonald not to include MacMillan in his cabinet, noting that he 'is not a "NEW DEAL."' McKenzie offered to resign his seat so that Macdonald might get J.L. Ilsley to come into the government as his right-hand man.[56] Had Macdonald passed over MacMillan, however, he would have created a nasty internal power struggle that he might have lost at that stage of his career.

McDonald was an Annapolis Valley farmer and former president of the Nova Scotia Fruit Growers' Association.[57] Dwyer, a former coal miner, had risen into management before becoming mayor of North Sydney; he came highly recommended by the mining communities.[58] Geography dictated other cabinet appointments. Macdonald passed over Dr M.E. McGarry from his home county of Inverness and named Dr Frank Davis from Lunenburg County on the province's South Shore as minister of health. C.W. Anderson, representing an Eastern Shore riding, was made minister without portfolio, and another minister without portfolio, J. Willie Comeau of Digby County, represented the Acadian community. Macdonald also had to consider the religious balance of the government. Counting himself, Dwyer, and Comeau, there were three Catholics in the cabinet, forcing him to hand the attorney-general's office to Josiah MacQuarrie, rather than his old friend Lauchie Currie. This was not a step down in quality by any means, but Currie did have a strong claim on Macdonald's loyalty. As premier, Macdonald held the posts of provincial secretary and provincial treasurer.

The new premier demanded some deference from his caucus. John Smiley, one of the MLAs from Cumberland County, mounted an aggressive and shameless campaign for the post of attorney-general. He had more than a dozen of his constituents write separate but identical letters to Macdonald on his behalf. Smiley then wrote the premier himself, saying that he expected to be made attorney-general and reminding Macdonald of 'the interests with which I am connected.'[59] Smiley never received a cabinet post, though Mackenzie King appointed him to the bench in 1938, presumably on Duff's recommendation.

The new administration was an able one, by all accounts. Murray Beck rates it as 'probably Nova Scotia's strongest.'[60] The ministers were fresh, motivated, and knowledgeable about their portfolios, with the sole exception of Macdonald as treasurer. Macdonald had no professional experience in finance, but neither had any other member of the Liberal caucus. He believed that by soliciting expert advice from his civil servants and outside auditors, and by following established rules of government finance, he could safely manage the province's treasury.

Macdonald did not relish the post-election wave of partisan hirings and firings. As he explained to his brother, 'I have never believed in being brutal in the matter of patronage.' He often intervened to spare Conservative government employees whose families were in need, though he could be vindictive in some cases, as with one public employee who had campaigned against him in Inverness in the 1930 election.[61]

For the most part, patronage appointments and dismissals were handled by a committee in each riding, which made suggestions to the Liberal MLA or the defeated candidate.[62] The committees compiled careful lists, scrutinized employees for inappropriate political activity and rated prospective candidates based on what they or their families had done for the Liberal party.[63] At least one committee used a set of questions for screening applicants that emphasized the importance of political orthodoxy:

(a) Is he a Liberal?
(b) Did he work at last election?
(c) Capabilities for position?
(d) Is he needy?
(e) Do you recommend him? How strongly?[64]

By the spring of 1934, the government had dealt with most of the patronage matters.

Nova Scotia's governments customarily had considered religion in distributing patronage, and Macdonald followed this practice. While his liberal preference may have been a merit-based system of appointments, he defended the 'just claims' of Catholics to every third hiring, reflecting their share of provincial population.[65] He was not wholly comfortable with the accommodation of communal interests that his Catholicism required of his liberalism. During his first term, Macdonald heard some criticism that he had not done enough for Catholics nor shown sufficient deference to Church leaders. 'I am not the Catholic Premier but the Premier of all the people and I have to do what I think is in the general interest,' he wrote to his brother.[66]

The patronage dismissals followed traditional practice, but were muted by an increasing trend to bureaucracy. Nova Scotia did not yet have a professional civil service, but most positions – especially those with greater specialization – had already become non-partisan. For example, Macdonald retained C.D. Dennis, the provincial auditor appointed by E.N. Rhodes, over the objections of a close adviser.[67] A study of the civil service by R. MacGregor Dawson revealed that just 289 of 1585 employees had been dismissed between 1 September 1933 and 1 September 1934. Dawson noted that few of the dismissals involved skilled positions.[68] Macdonald may not have initiated the transition from patronage to bureaucracy in government employment practices, but the trend accelerated under his administration.[69]

After being sworn into office on 5 September, the cabinet immediately set to work on three important tasks: finding economy in the government, providing relief in economically depressed areas, and preparing for an economic inquiry. The problems faced by the new government were daunting. In late 1933 and early 1934 tens of thousands in the province were impoverished and unemployed. A hurried report presented to the new government showed that 40,000 people were on direct or indirect relief in the summer of 1933; it was expected that 75,000 – one in every seven Nova Scotians – would become dependent on some form of relief that winter. Conditions were worst in urban areas, especially Halifax and industrial Cape Breton, where 25 to 40 per cent of the population were on the relief roles.[70]

Macdonald threw himself into his job in the first months, sacrificing his health in attempting to solve the problems of unemployment. He usually went to the office seven days a week and brought work home with him as well. The very fact that as premier of a small province he could know and influence almost all of the government's affairs led him to overtax his strength. He reportedly reviewed every dismissal and hiring in the civil service and sought to understand all aspects of relief and key industries in the province.[71] Macdonald's appearance in late November 1933 so worried Mackenzie King that he had his physician in Baltimore write Macdonald to urge him to relax and to invite him to come to Johns Hopkins for a thorough examination. Macdonald made the trip in 1934 and, for the rest of his life, went yearly to Baltimore for check-ups and treatment.[72]

As Macdonald came to learn the shortcuts of the premier's office, he managed to slow his pace, regaining some weight and colour. He was bothered by a persistent ulcer, however, and his health would remain rather delicate for the rest of his professional life.[73] During his term as naval minister (1940–5) – and probably at the approach of every legislative session, as estimates and legislation were being prepared – he suffered from insomnia. Certainly his habits did nothing to lessen the load; Macdonald's yellowed teeth were evidence of his feverish smoking, and he enjoyed a scotch whisky and soda. Several of his brothers and many of his political colleagues suffered from alcoholism, but Macdonald appears to have kept his drinking under control. If he did overindulge, his ulcer would have exacted a heavy price.

Macdonald's compassion for the poor did not overcome his concern for their moral integrity. Believing that self-realization began with the development of an individual's 'character,' Macdonald held that it was as necessary to care for 'pride and self-respect' as it was to feed, clothe, and shelter the poor. Direct relief might be cheaper than providing relief work, which required materiel and machinery, but it risked demoralizing its recipients.[74] He agreed with a government report on the relief situation:

> Direct Relief has been all spent for consumption goods leaving no asset except the maintenance of the population. Many economists, however, hold that the greatest asset of any country is a good class of people ... The Province could stand three more years without the matter being serious from a financial standpoint, if normal conditions returned by that time. The most serious matter is the impairment of the morale of our people, and especially the younger ones, if present conditions continue.[75]

The Macdonald government devoted most of its relief spending to public works projects but found it necessary to provide supplemental direct relief.

To get people through the winter of 1933–4, relief work projects were designed quickly for the areas of greatest need. Negotiations with the Conservative government at Ottawa did not proceed smoothly, however, as partisan suspicions and a dejected federal government delayed financial agreement. Macdonald had to pester W.A. Gordon, the federal minister of labour, to agree to pay the Dominion's share of $1,000,000 in relief projects for the province, about $350,000 by Macdonald's calculation. Gordon warned that municipalities would try to take advantage of the federal and provincial treasuries if they were allowed to propose relief projects on their own. Macdonald answered that the province had approved the projects and that 'all moneys will be spent with Scottish frugality and care.' Gordon then fretted over reports of political partisanship on relief work projects, but some were finally approved.[76]

Macdonald proudly reported in the government's first throne speech that many municipalities had not needed to issue direct relief through the winter.[77] Later in the session, he also announced that those overseeing direct relief would be put on the provincial payroll to foster greater efficiency.[78] The Canadian economy finally grew in 1934, and Nova Scotia shared in this modest recovery.[79] The acute stage of the depression passed, though relief work remained central to the survival of thousands of families in the province throughout the decade.

Macdonald also introduced Old Age Pensions, perhaps his most popular move. Both parties had promised pensions since the early 1930s, but Macdonald claimed credit for it. His mother informed him that one pensioner had sent part of her first cheque to have a mass said for him.[80] A friend wrote that some people in Cape Breton were naming their dogs 'Angus L.' – a true honour, formerly reserved for the likes of 'Borden and Tupper.'[81] Bringing in pensions did not strain the public purse as much as Harrington had feared; E.R. Forbes notes that many recipients were transferred to the new plan, where the province paid just a quarter of the costs, from direct relief rolls, where the province had paid as much as half.[82]

The most important project for Macdonald was the royal commission of economic inquiry, first promised in the party's 1930 platform. He anticipated that the commission could suggest productive economic policies to help the province deal with the depression and that its report would provide an intellectual foundation for future constitutional and fiscal negotiations with Ottawa. Macdonald planned to have a respected industrial or academic figure from Britain chair the commission, with a Nova Scotian and a Canadian from outside the region to round out the panel. In the 1930s, any respectable commission required a British chair, partly to provide a sense of impartiality but also an aura of dignity in the minds of Canadians still fond of colonial trappings. Macdonald particularly wanted a Briton for the sake of impartiality, given that this was an inquiry into relations between Nova Scotia and Ottawa.[83] To add to the legitimacy of the venture, Macdonald intended to have an independent academic prepare the brief of the government of Nova Scotia and to invite the federal government to participate in the hearings. Ottawa,

however, was not inclined to cooperate with a commission apt to criticize it.

Five weeks after taking office, Macdonald asked Norman Rogers to
'prepare Nova Scotia's case' and to present it at the inquiry.[84] Rogers
was well qualified to act as the province's representative. Hailing from
Charles Tupper's home of Amherst, Rogers had served overseas, won a
Rhodes scholarship, and trained as a lawyer and an academic, much
like Macdonald. He taught history at Acadia University from 1922 until
1927, when he became King's personal secretary and clerk of the Privy
Council. He returned to academia just before the fall of the King government, teaching political science at Queen's University from 1929 to
1935. From Queen's he remained a keen observer of the country's governmental and constitutional affairs.[85]

Macdonald then began a frustrating search across the Atlantic for an
available and respected British chair. He cabled invitations to Sir Walter
Layton, editor of the *Economist*, Sir Andrew MacFadyean, secretary for
the Commission on German Reparations, and Sir Hubert Llewellyn-
Smith, who had just conducted a four-year survey of London's working class; each rejected the offer.[86] None wanted to be part of a provincial ambush on the federal government in spite of Macdonald's claims
of impartiality. Finally, after six months' searching, Nova Scotia convinced J. Harry Jones, professor of economics at Leeds, to head the
commission.[87]

Former deputy minister of marine and fisheries Alexander Johnston
agreed to serve as the Nova Scotian commissioner. Johnston began his
career as a journalist in Sydney, before serving as a Liberal MLA
under George Murray from 1897 to 1900. He won a federal seat 1900
and held it until 1908, remaining in Ottawa thereafter. He then was
named a senior civil servant in Fisheries from 1919 to 1932. Johnston
came to know Macdonald well through the latter's trips to Ottawa
after he had become premier. Until his death in 1948, Johnston, the
'Old Sage,' remained one of Macdonald's most trusted advisers on
matters political.[88]

Macdonald pursued W.F.A. Turgeon, a justice on Saskatchewan's
Supreme Court, as the 'outside' Canadian commissioner. When the
Department of Justice refused to grant Turgeon leave to participate in
the inquiry, Macdonald believed that the Bennett government was
working behind the scenes to scuttle the exercise.[89] Rogers quickly suggested Harold Adams Innis, a professor of political economy at the University of Toronto, as the third commissioner. Innis was developing an

impressive reputation in Ontario's academic world, and three field trips to study primary industries in the region had made him very familiar with Nova Scotia's economy and geography.[90]

When the commissioners assembled in Halifax on 8 August 1934 to begin five and a half weeks of hearings, the government asked them to investigate the impact of Canada's fiscal and trade policies on the economy of Nova Scotia, as well as 'the adequacy of present financial arrangements' between the province and Ottawa, with special regard to constitutional responsibilities. The government also solicited suggestions for improving the economic welfare of Nova Scotia. Macdonald briefly welcomed Jones, Innis, and Johnston before ceding the floor to Rogers, who presented the province's brief. After two weeks of hearings in humid Halifax, the commission toured eighteen municipal centres throughout the province, taking evidence from more than two hundred witnesses.[91]

The Jones Commission proved to be a very influential forerunner of the Rowell-Sirois Commission. In addition to Roger's much sought-after brief for the province, the commission received reports from professors R.A. MacKay on fiscal relations between the province and Ottawa, from R. MacGregor Dawson on a permanent civil service, and from S.A. Saunders on municipal finance. Along with Innis's complementary statement, the Jones report comprised the leading scholarship on dominion–provincial relations to that point.[92]

The commission concluded that three main factors had contributed to Nova Scotia's relative economic decline: tariff policies, transportation costs, and centralized, protected industries. The commissioners avoided a conclusive statement on the tariff, recognizing that a sharp drop in tariffs would have unpredictable consequences in different regions of the country, but they did push for lower tariffs generally and for consultation with the provinces – as representatives of regional economies – in setting rates. They echoed the findings of the Duncan Commission that the Intercolonial Railway had been built to provide Maritime manufacturers with competitive access to Central and Western Canadian markets. The report also recommended a Federal Trade Commission with regional boards to police 'dumping' and unwarranted price spreads.[93]

In analysing federal–provincial fiscal relations, the report concluded that current subsidies were 'seriously inadequate.' 'The fundamental weakness of the original financial arrangements between the Dominion and the Provinces lay in [the Fathers of Confederation's] assumption that the expenditures of the provinces would be determined in the main by growth of population rather than by acceptance of new governmental responsibilities.'[94] The Jones Commission argued that it was Ottawa's task to 'establish equity' among the provinces because its economic policies differently affected the several regions of the country. It pushed the federal government to assume responsibility for some services currently provided by provincial governments and for 'other services, such as health and employment insurance, that may be established in the future.' The report also stated that Ottawa could also create 'a fund for allocation among the different Provinces in accordance with their needs ... [calculated by] impartial study.'[95] As a result of the Jones Commission, provincial subsidies based on 'fiscal need' became central to Macdonald's thinking on constitutional reform.

The commission offered a number of other suggestions to the provincial government. It strongly urged the immediate creation of a permanent civil service, under the direction of an independent commissioner. It pushed for a pension fund and a classification of positions for standardized promotions and pay rates. In his complementary report, Innis warned that unless Nova Scotia developed a strong civil service, it would be dominated by Ottawa's bureaucracy, leading to a centralization of administration.[96] The commission advised the provincial government to establish a Department of Municipal Affairs to work closely with the municipalities to standardize and coordinate their accounting procedures. It counselled the government to focus more attention on marketing Nova Scotia's products and to create an economic council to oversee industrial research. The commission encouraged the government to continue paving the province's highways and suggested that it mount a program of rural electrification, extending this modern convenience throughout the province to convince young Nova Scotians to remain on family farms.[97]

On the question of fisheries, the commission recommended that the province assume some control over the industry, going so far as to establish its own department. Johnston and Innis voiced strong objections to licensing steam trawlers for use off Nova Scotia's coasts, arguing that they would destroy the livelihood of inshore fishers. Jones did not address the subject, arguing that he was not familiar enough with the local industry, though the trawler question in Britain had been settled a generation earlier.[98] Opposition to trawlers remained very vocal in the province until the late 1940s. Macdonald viewed trawlers as progressive technology that could help expand the fishery; he favoured granting licenses if the fishing companies agreed to purchase the entire catch of inshore fishers, but he noted that he was alone in this stand within his government.[99]

Having invested a great deal of effort in the Jones Commission, Macdonald and his colleagues were understandably infuriated with a Canadian Press (CP) story that distorted the recommendations of the report. The province released a synopsis of the report to the press on 7 December 1934, and the full report the next day. CP reporter Andrew Merkel wrote that the commission had been appointed to determine whether Nova Scotia should secede from Confederation and whether Ottawa had engaged in 'deliberate tariff oppression.'He said the Jones report rejected both these ideas and was therefore a blow to the Macdonald government.[100] An enraged Macdonald suspected that the *Halifax Herald* had written the story and handed it to Merkel.[101] Macdonald blasted Merkel's interpretation at a press conference, forcing the CP to apologize for 'having given cause' to Macdonald to make his attack.[102] In Ottawa, the reception was better; both R.B. Bennett and Fisheries Minister R.B. Hanson congratulated Alex Johnston on the objectivity and 'restrained' tone of the Jones report.[103]

Macdonald grew increasingly hostile towards Conservative Senator W.H. Dennis's *Halifax Herald*. He may have been frustrated that it outsold the Liberal *Chronicle* by more than two to one and that much of the work he and his government accomplished went unreported in the *Herald*.[104] He certainly believed the newspaper crossed the lines of partisanship, deliberately distorting the public record of events and damaging Nova Scotia's tourist industry in particular. At a Liberal meeting in the summer of 1934, Macdonald called the *Herald* 'Public Enemy Number One,' charging that its depictions of dusty roads ignored the government's paving and extensive gravelling programs and kept tourists from visiting the province.[105] Macdonald's attack fit well within the partisan divisions of Nova Scotia's newspapers, but his tendency to 'have at' the fourth estate did not suit the broader political landscape he would face as naval minister.

Though Macdonald's performance as premier over the first eighteen months strengthened his hold on the party's leadership, Conservatives still charged that Stirling MacMillan really ran the government. Beck writes that Macdonald's maiden speech in the Legislature 'demonstrated that he would become one of the great orators of the Nova Scotia assembly, so effective that only a few years later the opposition would sometimes be reluctant to launch criticism for fear of devastating replies.'[106] His first budget showed red ink, but he managed to trim slightly the deficit inherited from the Conservative government.[107]

The government's most important measure of the 1934 session was the Gasoline Licensing Act. The volatility of the unregulated gasoline industry in Nova Scotia enhanced the power of the large oil companies. More than 4000 retailers – servicing fewer than 42,000 vehicles – were bound by exclusive contract to just a few wholesalers who retained control of the equipment they leased to the retailers. The glut of outlets and high equipment rentals forced retailers to keep gasoline prices high, on average 31 per cent higher in Halifax than in Toronto.[108] The government's bill sought to eliminate 'wasteful and uneconomic' practices and to restrict 'the excessive number of outlets'; it required retailers to secure licences from the Public Utilities Board by demonstrating that their outlets were necessary for 'public convenience.'

This remarkable foray into regulation worked quite well and illustrated the 'new liberalism' of the premier. The province reduced licensing fees for drivers and vehicles and raised gasoline taxes from six to eight cents per gallon. Macdonald could accept state intervention to prevent chaotic and ruinous competition in the marketplace; furthermore, he believed that the gasoline tax was a fairer distribution of the costs of infrastructure than licence fees, as it reflected drivers' use of the province's roads. Even with the extra taxes – the revenues of which were applied to the province's paving program – gasoline prices fell by 1½ cents per gallon under the new regulatory system.[109]

Macdonald also performed well in negotiations with the Bennett government, appearing as a moderate, articulate premier. At Dominion-Provincial Conferences on unemployment in January and July 1934, Macdonald joined with other premiers in calling for comprehensive discussion of the problem of unemployment. Bennett ignored this request and told the provinces that federal relief aid would be cut off on 15 June. Continued economic and political pressure forced Ottawa to extend the deadline to 15 July, and finally Bennett offered lump-sum payments to the provinces, saying his government was washing its hands of responsibility for relief.[110]

After the July conference, Macdonald and the premiers of New Brunswick and Prince Edward Island remained in Ottawa to lobby the federal government – with Macdonald as 'lead counsel' – for a re-examination of subsidies to the Maritime provinces, as recommended by the Duncan Commission. Bennett appointed former Finance Minister Sir Thomas White to chair a commission on the question. White's 1935 report recommended increased subsidies: an additional $425,000 for Nova Scotia to complement the $875,000 annual grant based on the recommendations of the Duncan report. Macdonald received this as a mixed blessing; his government got badly needed revenue, but the new money became part of a fixed subsidy, not tied to the province's relative economic position.[111]

The arrival of summer also revealed the success of the government's paving program. MacMillan, who had travelled throughout North America studying various techniques of hard-surfacing, selected a mixture of asphalt flexible enough to withstand Nova Scotia's winter frost and spring thaw. Upon taking office in 1933, the Macdonald government found just 45 kilometres of paved road; by the end of 1936, it had paved a total of 605 kilometres, and by 1939, it had paved almost 1300 kilometres of the province's 18,000 kilometres of highway. It funded this program of capital expenditures with the gasoline tax and the sale of debentures at very low interest rates. For example, in 1937 Nova Scotia raised $8 million by selling bonds at 2.5 and 3.5 per cent, $7 million of which went to the Department of Highways.[112] The highway program allowed the government to mount public works projects and avoid paying direct relief. These projects were labour-intensive and flexible in terms of cost and duration. Highway work could be organized on short notice to meet acute and localized unemployment crises, common in both coal mining and the fishery. The Rowell-Sirois Commission later praised the province's use of cheap money to modernize its infrastructure and minimize reliance on the dole. In 1937 Nova Scotia spent just 3 per cent of its budget on direct relief, against a national average of 11 per cent.[113]

Beyond the short-term benefits, the Macdonald government believed a modern highway system would lower transportation costs for local industry. The Maritime Freight Rate Act (MFRA) of 1927 had provided subsidies to the railways to reduce freight rates by 20 per cent on goods leaving the Maritimes. Nova Scotia complained that these reductions were offset by the railways' lowering of freight rates in Central Canada to meet the competition of that region's trucking industry.[114] Macdonald hoped that decent highways would lead to the development of a healthy trucking industry in Nova Scotia, forcing down shipping costs within the province.

Most important for Macdonald was the impact of paved roads upon the tourism industry. In addition to allocating most of the province's financial resources in the 1930s to highway construction, Macdonald spent much of his own time promoting the province as an idyllic tourist destination. While the government went to great lengths lobbying on behalf of the fishing, coal, steel, lumber, and apple industries, it undertook tireless efforts to boost the tourist industry. Under Macdonald, Nova Scotia's government mounted a consistent tourism advertising campaign. It worked to raise the minimum standards for tourist services by offering cooking classes to restaurant and hotel workers and granting small loans to hotel, motel, and cottage operations to improve their accommodations.[115]

For Macdonald, the tourism industry held great promise but needed leadership and direction. The dominant players in the field were the railway companies, which promoted only their own hotels and only certain sections of the province.[116] Most tourism entrepreneurs eked out sparse, seasonal incomes catering to wealthy summertime residents, hunters, and sport fishers. Macdonald constantly urged the quantitative and qualitative improvement of services for tourists – especially those travelling by automobile – believing that this industry had a brighter future than any other in the province.[117]

In addition to promoting better meals and accommodations for tourists, Macdonald preached the economic value of history and ethnicity. He sensed that North America's middle-class families were drawn to images of a simpler, nobler past, complete with romantic historical narratives. He frequently used 'positive ethnic stereotypes' to evoke these images. In a speech given to the St Patrick's Society of Montreal on 17 March 1934, for example, Macdonald paid tribute to four of Canada's dominant 'races.' The English, he said, had a 'passion for justice, for honesty, for fair dealing,' while the Scottish settlers possessed 'undying devotion; bringing to this country the stern and rugged character that they drew from their native hills.' He called the French 'the immortal race,' and praised the 'warmth and generosity of the Irish heart, the gaiety of the Irish spirit, the wit of the Irish tongue, the deep feeling of the Irish soul.'[118] Nova Scotia could offer beautiful coastlines, mountains, valleys, lakes, and rivers, but it was also packed with 'history', if properly presented. Communities of Acadians, Germans, Mi'kmaq, and especially Scots could be found throughout the province, with flashes of 'typical' dress and languages. Though Macdonald would not have used the terms, he believed Nova Scotia's greatest asset was its antimodern folk. In brochures, books, magazine advertisements, short films, and speeches, the government of Nova Scotia presented the province as a place where urban, middle-class families could go to 'step back in time.'[119]

While the government led this effort, various 'independent cultural producers' gladly cooperated. McKay focuses on folklorist Helen Creighton and Mary Black, a handicraft specialist, but mentions others as well. For example, Macdonald's former comrade-in-arms Will R. Bird produced a number of brochures and books on Nova Scotia as a haven of the folk; some of these were commissioned by the government, as Bird's day job was in the province's civil service. Other friends who turned their pens to the aid of Nova Scotia tourism, directly or indirectly, included George Matthew Adams, Thomas Raddall, *New York Times* journalist and editor Neil MacNeil, and novelist Frank Parker Day.[120]

For Macdonald, the romanticized culture of the Highland Scots took pride of place. His most beloved tourism project was the creation and development of the Cape Breton Highlands National Park in the 1930s and 1940s. In 1934, Dalhousie geology professor Donald S. MacIntosh bequeathed one hundred acres on Cape Breton's northern shore to the province, along with instructions to construct a 'lone shieling' on the property. A verse from 'The Canadian Boat Song' inspired MacIntosh's unusual request for a shieling, a crude, thatched hut:

> From the lone shieling of the misty island –
> Mountains divide us, and the waste of seas –
> Yet still the blood is strong, the heart is Highland,
> And we in dreams behold the Hebrides.

Macdonald worked to set aside more than a quarter of a million acres for an adjacent park, completing a deal with the federal government early in 1936.[121] The province constructed a resort hotel in the park, and Ottawa paid for the development of a stunning Stanley Thompson golf course. Macdonald believed he had created a piece of Scotland for tourists in the New World.

The tourist program attracted more visitors and some cash to the province but had its greatest impact on the provincial identity. McKay argues that before 1933, 'no single vocabulary of "Nova Scotianness" was in use.'[122] In his drive to lure tourists, Macdonald expanded the shared reality of Nova Scotians. They witnessed the provincial state constructing an elaborate network of modern roads; they read books and brochures extolling the beauty of the province, and they heard their premier waxing romantically about the pure, simple nobility of their ancestors. The communal identity being developed by these means was certainly conservative, but most seem to have received it warmly. Macdonald's efforts at promoting Nova Scotia and the tourism program were mutually rewarding: more tourists came and his image as the representative of the province grew.

Like Mackenzie King, Macdonald believed that government should play only an indirect role in the economy.[123] He did not oppose public ownership of certain industries in the interests of regulation or sheer necessity; for example, Macdonald supported strict regulation of the sale of alcohol through the NSLC. He also backed public ownership of utilities where service was necessary though perhaps not profitable enough to attract private capital, as with the Nova Scotia Power Commission. Mostly, however, he favoured investing public moneys in infrastructure. Just as he believed governments should adjust the tariff schedule to provide the greatest good for the greatest number, he held that the state must provide an environment conducive to economic and individual development. This led his government to pursue capital investments in highways, rural electrification, and schools. Macdonald also believed that the state should promote and conduct research for industry. In 1934 his government sent representatives to Britain to help sell the province's fruit and lumber; it created a marketing board to encourage higher standards of production of fish and agricultural products, and it established an Economic Advisory Council and later a Research Foundation to assist provincial industries with information but not funding.[124]

Macdonald's role in the 1935 federal election reflected his developing stature in Canada. The National Liberal Federation decided to use Canada's more popular Liberal premiers to stump around the country, sending Saskatchewan's James Gardiner and Ontario's Mitchell Hepburn east, while Macdonald toured Southern Ontario. He spoke to good reviews at St Thomas, Woodstock, and Kingston, where he appeared on behalf of Norman Rogers, who was making his first venture into electoral politics.[125] He also performed his rigorous campaign duties in Nova Scotia, including playing host to Mackenzie King at a large rally in Halifax. The latter wrote in his diary: 'McDonald made a splendid speech, was quite eloquent in his style and use of language, he looks much better, and is a really first class man.'[126]

King's overwhelming victory was highlighted by the Liberals' sweep of Nova Scotia's twelve seats. The swing to the Grits had begun provincially in Nova Scotia in 1933, and over the next twenty-six months, five more provinces elected Liberal governments.[127] J.L. Ralston had retired to private practice in Montreal, and Macdonald became a leading candidate to be Nova Scotia's representative in the federal cabinet. With Ernest Lapointe, King discussed his choices for cabinet:

> I told him that I had spoken to Macdonald, the Premier, and I had asked him if he would care to consider Ottawa, but he said he thought he ought to stay in Nova Scotia. I then asked Macdonald whom he would suggest, and he said Ilsley was the only person. We both agreed that Duff would make a lot of trouble and would be nasty. I said I certainly would not take him in the Cabinet.[128]

Macdonald declined King's invitation, arguing that he had a lot of unfinished work in Nova Scotia.[130] Old Age Pensions and a paving program had been established, but budget deficits continued and he looked forward to serious discussions on constitutional reform.

Disappointed at being denied a cabinet post, William Duff immediately lobbied for a Senate seat. Many believed that former Liberal leader William Chisholm had first claim to the seat from eastern Nova Scotia, but Duff whispered that Chisholm was too ill to be considered. Ilsley supported Duff's appointment, arguing that he had been passed over for many things and that something had to be done for him. Macdonald warned Ilsley: 'I am probably biased on the subject of Duff, but I do not think that his political ambitions are at all dead. I think that he will make whatever trouble he can for you, and that being the case I think you would be better off with him as an open enemy than as a treacherous friend.'[130] Macdonald was wary of ambitious men.

Ilsley and Macdonald discussed a number of post-election appointments, though each respected the other's prerogative in the federal and provincial fields. Beyond their common reference in the advice of Alex Johnston, Ilsley and Macdonald each had developed his own cortège of trusted workers. Macdonald gave Ilsley his opinion of candidates for federal posts, but clearly left the decisions to the new minister of national revenue. Likewise, when Macdonald passed over Ilsley's friend, Colonel James Regan, for the position of Ottawa bagman for the Nova Scotia Liberals, Ilsley accepted the verdict. For his part, Macdonald trusted Ilsley's judment enough to hire Regan as the province's tariff consultant.[131]

After the heavy-handed unilateralism of the Bennett government in federal–provincial relations, most observers anticipated a more agreeable atmosphere under the King administration. Within weeks of his victory, King invited the provinces to a conference slated for 9 to 13

December 1935, promising cooperation and consultation. The conference focused on three issues: provincial finances, an amending formula for the British North America (BNA) Act, and unemployment and relief. The presence of seven Liberal premiers and the good humour of two more promised more harmony than Bennett ever had known. Trouble loomed, however. The only substantive plans the dominion put forward involved a Loan Council that could veto risky proposals and further restrict provincial borrowing privileges.[132]

Ontario's Hepburn objected to the Loan Council and expressed disappointment with Ottawa for its unwillingness to refinance national and provincial debts. He proposed 'converting' the debt, most of which was paying 5 per cent, into new bonds at the rate of 3 per cent. Federal officials explained that much of the debt was held abroad and an announcement of compulsory refunding would damage Canada's credit rating. It is possible that Hepburn felt King had snubbed him while forming his cabinet. Amid rumours that he might be invited into King's cabinet, Hepburn had suggested that his friend Arthur Slaght be made a minister. King rejected Slaght, and when presenting his cabinet to the public, announced that he had consulted no premier on the matter, a direct embarrassment to Hepburn.[133] Hepburn and King would agree on little in the future.

The question of an amending formula made some progress. Premier L.A. Taschereau of Quebec reversed his position from 1927 and agreed that the power to amend the constitution should lie in Canada.[134] Ontario presented a plan for a flexible amending formula – written by Attorney-General Arthur Roebuck and Toronto law professor W.P.M. Kennedy – that was to dominate constitutional talks for the next fifteen years. It divided the BNA Act into four categories of clauses, each with its own amending formula. Clauses that involved the federal government alone could be amended by a simple act of Parliament; those that involved Ottawa and certain provinces were amendable by the respective legislative bodies. Fundamental rights, such as language, required unanimity of Parliament and the provincial legislatures. All other clauses could be amended by Parliament and two-thirds of the provincial legislatures, provided they represented more than 55 per cent of the population.[135]

Most premiers welcomed this as a basis for future discussions, but New Brunswick's attorney-general, J.B. McNair, objected to even the mild resolution, stating that Canada should take control of its constitution when an acceptable amending formula had been agreed upon.[136]

At a meeting of dominion and provincial officials in January and February 1936, the compartmental amending formula was presented as a possible constitutional amendment; New Brunswick objected, fearing that the other provinces could gang up on the Maritimes. Another meeting in March heard a proposal to allow provinces to opt out of particular amendments, but this idea did not receive broad support. The amending formula talks then adjourned.[137]

At this critical juncture in constitutional discussions, New Brunswick's constitutional policy was shaped largely by A.P. Paterson, minister without portfolio. Paterson was a veteran of the Maritime Rights movement of the 1920s, recruited by Alison Dysart's Liberals in the 1935 campaign. He had little formal education but claimed to be a self-taught expert on the BNA Act. He held to a confused version of the compact theory and argued, in the face of New Brunswick's crushing poverty, that no constitutional changes were necessary; if only Ottawa would honour the terms of the Confederation contract, New Brunswick would become a land of plenty. It is not clear that McNair and Dysart agreed with Paterson, but they had offered him the role of constitutional adviser to secure his candidacy as a Liberal. To keep him in the government, they now opposed even discussing an amending formula, lest one of the amendments prove to be bad for the province.[138]

The December 1935 conference had not ended in confrontation, largely because the dominion's proposals on unemployment and relief funding satisfied the premiers. To labour minister Rogers's delight, the conference agreed to the appointment of a National Employment Commission to investigate the problem of unemployment. The premiers welcomed Ottawa's offer to increase relief grants by as much as 75 per cent. Macdonald judged the conference to have been a good 'preliminary' effort, with 'the real work remain[ing] to be done.'[139]

Grattan O'Leary, editor of the Conservative *Ottawa Citizen*, was fast becoming a friend of Macdonald and praised his performance at the conference.[140] He was the third-longest-sitting premier present, but still felt very much a novice with just two years' legislative experience. Interestingly, Macdonald resented the impression given in a December story in the *Financial Post* that Mitchell Hepburn had been the driving force of the conference.

> To begin with, all this talk of Hepburn formulating a plan and working it on other delegates is purest bunk. Hepburn was never seen by any other delegates, save the Ontario delegates, except at the conference meetings.

He took no part in the social side of the conference, nor did he after hours discuss things with any other delegates. No single Province at any time said 'amen' to his conversion scheme ... In a personal way I have nothing at all against Hepburn; on the contrary, I am quite friendly with him, but the stories coming out of Toronto that Ontario took their tremendous brain-trusters and smart politicians and dominated the whole conference nauseates me ... This, however, is not in the true spirit of Christmas, rather with Tiny Tim should I say – 'God bless us everyone – even the people of Ontario.'[141]

Though not averse to ensuring positive coverage of his government's activities, Macdonald wondered at Hepburn's shameless self-promotion. After his 1935 speaking tour of Ontario, he wrote to his brother: 'Unfortunately, I was not able to do as Hepburn did, take along a special correspondent of my own, and consequently some of the reports were not what they otherwise might have been.'[142] Macdonald enjoyed friendly relations with many journalists, but did not focus on courting the press.

Nova Scotia's paving program and deficit reduction continued apace, and 1936 saw some improvement in the economy. Relief payments in the province had dropped from $1.9 million in 1933 to just under $1 million in 1936. A by-election on 2 March 1936 brought the government candidate, former *Chronicle* journalist Harold Connolly, into the Assembly with a large majority.[143] Even misfortune played into the government's hands. On 13 April 1936, three men from Ontario – investors Dr D.R. Robertson and lawyer Herman Magill and the mine's timekeeper, Alfred Scadding – were trapped by a cave-in forty-three metres below the surface in the Moose River gold mine. For the next ten days, the rescue effort played out on newspaper front pages and on the radio; much of the Western world watched as rescue miners raced against the clock and unstable mine shafts to pull the men out alive. A pipeline for communication reached the men by 19 April, a few hours before one died of pneumonia. A telephone line was established, and the trapped men were interviewed on the radio over the final three days of their dramatic ordeal.[144]

Macdonald spent many hours at the site, and Minister of Mines Michael Dwyer, a former miner, took an active part in the rescue effort. At a dinner in Stellarton to honour the rescuers, Macdonald made his memorable 'Sons of Martha' speech, broadcast on a national radio hook-up. He drew the title from a Rudyard Kipling poem, referring to the biblical sisters Mary and Martha of Bethany, honouring 'those who work and serve.' The well-crafted speech was later published in booklet form.[145] The opposition, jealous of the attention paid to Macdonald and his government, could do nothing except call for an inquiry to see if the mine had been properly inspected.[146]

The Macdonald family kept the young premier going but brought with it pressures, financial and otherwise. After their home was struck by lightning in a summer storm in 1935, Angus and Agnes sought a new house to match the stature of the premier of the province. They settled on a large, handsome house in the Marlborough Woods overlooking the beautiful Northwest Arm.[147] Macdonald considered a Gaelic name for the house to match his self-image as a Scottish chieftain. Father Stanley suggested several names that could refer to the view of the Northwest Arm – 'Inverard,' 'Camberard,' or 'Kinlochard,' for example – but Angus decided to limit his invention of tradition and retained the name 'Winwick.'[148] The new home stretched the family's budget but it admirably filled the role of executive residence. Two days before his forty-sixth birthday, Angus welcomed his third daughter, Oonagh.[149] The family usually had one servant, a dog or two, and a couple of cats, so the house was teeming with activity, though Macdonald's work schedule kept him outside the circle for the most part. Even when in Halifax, Angus worked at the office for ten or twelve hours, almost every day. His career kept him somewhat distant from his children.[150]

His siblings were not immune from the effects of the depression and partisan politics, and Macdonald was often drawn into their battles. When his brother Joseph returned from Detroit looking for work, Angus got him a position at the Inverness mine as safety inspector.[151] Oswin, or 'Sweeney,' was now practicing law in Antigonish, and Angus hoped that he would develop into a politician under the tutelage of William Chisholm. Sweeney tended to drink and neglected his debts, however, remaining in perpetual dire straits. Chisholm wrote of his lack of direction, something Sweeney shared with many veterans: 'Altho he has the ability for some reason or other difficult to understand, he has not grown as was expected, and has not the prestige in this County he ought to have.'[152] Angus also tried but failed to get his brother W.A. elevated from the District Court to the Supreme Court of Alberta. Federal justice minister Ernest Lapointe had a rule not to elevate judges from district courts, lest they attempt to curry political favour, and W.A. had to wait for promotion until Louis St Laurent took over Justice during the war.[153]

Angus intervened on Father Stanley's behalf in a dispute with Bishop James Morrison of the Antigonish diocese, though his participation probably hurt the priest more than it helped. Angus and the bishop nurtured an animosity from the university federation debate; the premier saw the bishop as a Tory, and the bishop saw the premier as disobedient. Matters did not improve with Macdonald's elevation to the highest political office in the province. Macdonald and Morrison squabbled over who would get a licence to distribute mass wine in the diocese, the bishop's choice being unacceptable to the Liberal government. Macdonald also offended the prelate by neglecting protocol shortly after his election: 'In my own case, Bishop Morrison, I understand, grumbled because I did not call to see him on my first visit to Antigonish. I was there only a short time, only a few hours as a matter of fact, and I was very busy while I was there.' On his second visit, he called on Morrison and was treated coldly, even rudely. 'It would be long before I call upon him again.'[154]

Morrison continued the petty squabble by denying Macdonald a tribute from his alma mater. The faculty of St FX voted to grant Macdonald an honorary doctorate in 1937, but the bishop exercised his veto as chair of the board of governors. The faculty then voted unanimously to honour no one before Macdonald, and so from 1937 until the bishop relented in 1946, the university gave out no honorary degrees.[155]

Father Stanley had been transferred from his parish at Judique in 1930 for intemperance and neglect of his parish duties. In 1933 Morrison removed him from a curacy in New Waterford for arguing with his priest there, leaving him without any means of support until early 1937, when he was appointed curate to the small parish of Pomquet. Father Stanley thought the post beneath him and appealed to Rome. Through an intermediary Angus asked the opinion of the Secretary of the Apostolic Delegate in Ottawa, but received an unfavourable reply.[156] Father Stanley's appeal to the Vatican was rejected, and he remained a curate for a number of years before securing appointment to the parish of Big Pond, on Cape Breton Island.[157]

In the six-week session of the Assembly in 1937, the Macdonald government presented an ambitious pre-election package of legislation, including a program of rural electrification, an 'independence of Parliament' bill, and amendments to the Workmen's Compensation Act that improved benefits.[158] The 'independence of Parliament' bill prohibited business transactions – other than of a 'casual' nature – between MLAs and the government. The Opposition objected to the vagueness of

'casual,' hinting that MacMillan and other government members prof-
ited from public contacts.[159] Macdonald revealed the government's
trump card when he proudly reported to the Legislature that the 1935–
6 fiscal year had brought not the predicted $360,000 deficit, but a sur-
plus of more than $150,000 and that the estimates for 1936–7 showed
another surplus of just over $100,000 with some minor tax reductions.
Conservatives sat in stunned silence as Macdonald detailed the province's first surplus in fourteen years.[160]

Macdonald skilfully handled a potentially damaging scandal involving a lesser light from his cabinet when he forced the resignation of
minister without portfolio C.W. Anderson. When Macdonald learned
of Anderson's business improprieties he decided to air them publicly.
The province's chief forester testified before the Public Accounts Committee of the Assembly that Anderson's Scotia Lumber Company illegally had cut almost 29,000 cords of wood from Crown lands; the
government fined Anderson $42,513 the next day. By ousting Anderson
and presenting all the relevant information to the Legislature, Macdonald took the sting out of the opposition's attack and preserved his
image as an honest reformer.[161]

The most important piece of legislation the government passed in
1937 was its Trade Union Act. Liberals and Conservatives attempted to
outshine each other as the party of the worker because of organized
labour's renewed strength. In 1935 the Communist International
shifted its strategy from one of divisiveness to that of a 'popular front,'
lending their remarkable organizing strength to the non-Communist
labour movement. Workers in North America saw the rapid growth in
industrial unions, led in the United States by John L. Lewis and his
Committee for Industrial Organization (CIO). Once despised for his
business-friendly policies and autocratic methods, Lewis was now
'rehabilitated' in the eyes of radical miners committed to building a
united front. Lewis appointed UMW executive Silby Barrett to shepherd Sydney's steelworkers into a union under the auspices of the
CIO.[162]

Providing a backdrop to the resurgence of labour in industrial Cape
Breton was the remarkable confrontation in Oshawa, where Mitchell
Hepburn showed a determination to resist the expansion of the CIO
into Ontario. The Ontario premier backed management in a two-week
strike in April over union recognition at the General Motors plant.[163]
Hepburn wanted to keep the CIO out of Northern Ontario's mines, but
the presence of a militant union in Nova Scotia's mines was an irrevers-

ible fact in 1937. Macdonald and his government calculated that if industrial unionism were coming, it would be wise to institutionalize collective bargaining and curry labour's favour, rather than resist and earn its enmity.[164]

Macdonald approached the UMW leadership through Father Stanley, whose labour sympathies had been sharpened with three years of work in the mining town of New Waterford. Father Stanley arranged a meeting in late January 1937 between Macdonald and officials of the. nascent steelworkers' union at the Isle Royal Hotel in Sydney. At this meeting – over a bottle of bootleg rum brought by the premier – Canada's first piece of modern labour legislation was created.[165] The union leaders provided a draft based on the American Wagner Act, which compelled employers to recognize the union chosen by their workers. Macdonald took this back to Halifax, intending to introduce it to the Assembly.

Conservative leader Gordon Harrington tried to steal Macdonald's thunder by introducing a compulsory collective bargaining bill early in the session. The Liberal benches erupted in howls, accusing Harrington of introducing government legislation. Macdonald quickly rose to move an amendment to Harrington's bill, demonstrating his pro-union credentials. The final bill was a mixture of proposals by the UMW, Harrington, and the government. It compelled employers to recognize and bargain with the union chosen by a majority of their employees; it prohibited 'yellow dog' contracts and dismissal of employees for organizing a union, and provided for a check-off deduction of union dues where check-offs for any other purpose existed.[166]

The bill faced opposition in public hearings, where representatives of the Canadian Manufacturers' Association denounced it as giving too much power and money to 'foreign agents and agitators.' Nevertheless, government and opposition MLAs worked well past midnight on the penultimate day of the session to pass the Trade Union Act unanimously. Within a week, steelworkers at DOSCO had voted to be represented by the CIO-affiliated Steelworkers' Organizing Committee (SWOC).[167]

Once the lieutenant-governor prorogued the Assembly, Angus and Agnes were off to Britain for the coronation of King George VI. They had an enjoyable crossing on the *Empress of Australia* with Mackenzie King, Ernest Lapointe, Charles Dunning, T.A. Crerar, Ian Mackenzie, and Napier Moore, editor of *Maclean's*. Before the coronation ceremonies, the Macdonalds went sightseeing to Oxford University, Paris, and

Versailles and dined with all the proper people, including Vincent Massey, David Lloyd George, and the king.[168] Immediately upon returning to Halifax, Macdonald assembled his cabinet and within two hours announced a general election for 29 June 1937.[169]

Perhaps the most remarkable feature of the campaign was the prominent role played by Bob Chambers's cartoons in the newspapers of both parties. The *Herald*, which had hired Chambers away from the *Chronicle* on the eve of the election call, ran his cartoons on the front page of the paper almost every day for five weeks.[170] The *Chronicle* hired Ted Sellen as its cartoonist for the campaign, but found his work less effective than that of Chambers.' Although Sellen's cartoons were more polished than Chambers', they lacked any humour. He drew his characters with over-sized heads, and often featured a dimple-chinned Macdonald being thanked by an attractive woman for fulfilling a promise from the Liberals' 1933 platform. To supplement Sellen's work, the *Chronicle* ran many of Chambers' cartoons from the 1933 campaign, often on the front page.[171] Chambers's new work for the *Herald* proved entertaining, but hardly damaging to the government. Every cartoon featured a woodpecker gradually wearing away a vacant cabinet chair, a reference to Anderson. The government countered this by charging a former Conservative cabinet minister with illegally cutting wood on Crown lands.[172]

Macdonald ran on his government's record, offering no promises to voters. Throughout the province, he proclaimed that the government had fulfilled all of its platform promises from 1933; he asked his audiences, did they wish to return to the deficits of the Rhodes-Harrington years? Could they trust the men who had perpetrated the iniquitous 'Franchise Scandal'?[173] There was no need to make reckless promises when he had every confidence in his government's victory.

Harrington campaigned on promises of social legislation and rural electrification, but devoted most of his energy to attacking the Liberals. The government, he charged, had balanced the budget on the backs of the taxpayers and had driven the provincial debt to dangerous heights, borrowing for public works projects. Liberals attacked his social program as too expensive without federal assistance and noted that Bennett had ignored Harrington's earlier requests to call for a constitutional amendment making Ottawa responsible for social security. Macdonald, meanwhile, could point to King's recent announcement of a royal commission on dominion–provincial relations. The government walked to victory, taking twenty-five of thirty seats, including Harrington's. Voter turnout was again high, and the Liberals slightly increased their share of the popular vote from 1933.[174] The Conservatives won the double ridings of Cumberland and Colchester counties, and secured a seat in Queen's County on the South Shore. The new Trade Union Act helped the Liberals capture the labour ridings of industrial Cape Breton and Pictou County. With consecutive majority governments under his belt, Angus Macdonald had earned the reputation of being a political winner.

Friends and political observers had been anticipating Macdonald's move to federal politics for some time. Macdonald had declined King's earlier invitation of a cabinet post in 1935, saying that he had more work to do in Nova Scotia. He wrote one friend that provincial tasks, such as balancing the budget, modernizing the highways, and negotiating a constitutional settlement, would keep him in the province until 1938 or 1939.[175] Most of these tasks were now complete or well in hand, and speculation of a move resumed. Macdonald's relative youth, his speaking ability, and his impressive demeanour at dominion-provincial conferences marked him as a man of talent who could build a national following. His frequent trips to Ottawa and his journey to London with the prime minister for the coronation in 1937 sparked rumours that he would join King's cabinet immediately after the provincial election.[176]

Macdonald, however, awaited the opportunity to put forward his case for a more rational, balanced federalism before the Royal Commission on Dominion-Provincial Relations, better known as the Rowell-Sirois Commission. The economic relapse of 1937 left most provinces either tremendously upset with the King government or willing to embrace unorthodox theories to deal with crushing poverty. King faced simultaneously the looming bankruptcy of Manitoba and Saskatchewan, rumblings of revolt in British Columbia, Alberta, and Ontario, and a National Employment Commission proposal for a federal program of unemployment insurance. He breathed a sigh of relief when the cabinet agreed to a commission to investigate matters between Ottawa and the provinces.[177]

By 1938 Macdonald fully accepted Norman Rogers's argument that 'constitutional changes are essential to the maintenance of national standards.'[178] Macdonald was willing to sacrifice some provincial prerogatives to achieve a better distribution of powers and resources, with an eye to strengthening the Canadian federation. He himself wrote most of Nova Scotia's brief for the Rowell-Sirois Commission, though he fretted that his other duties made him feel rushed and left the brief 'imperfect.'[179]

The Rowell-Sirois Commission sat in Province House in Halifax hearing evidence from 3 to 8 February 1938. Macdonald adroitly presented the province's brief to the commission, proposing that constitutional powers and responsibilities be adjusted to meet the needs of an industrialized nation, that taxation systems be rationalized to give each level of government exclusive fields and necessary revenues and that national wealth be redistributed among governments to provide a 'national minimum standard' of services. It is not surprising that most of Macdonald's suggestions anticipated the final report of the commission; Nova Scotia had been studying the subject for some years. Macdonald's familiarity with his subject struck one observer: 'He is the first witness to testify with utter self-confidence, no fumbling for words or ideas, and something like a prose style.'[180] As well, Macdonald had personal and professional relationships with many of the leading academics who helped to shape the report, including R.A. MacKay, counsel J. McG. Stewart, economic adviser S.A. Saunders, and, of course, Norman Rogers, the strongest supporter of the commission within cabinet.

Macdonald began by proposing an amendment to the BNA Act that would allow Ottawa and the provinces to alter the constitution without appealing to Westminster. He did not suggest a specific amending formula but said it should be 'determined by agreement between the Dominion and the Provinces.' He nevertheless expressed support for the compartmental idea – different amending processes for different sections of the BNA Act. Macdonald further suggested that a delegation mechanism be put into the constitution, allowing the federal government to transfer legislative authority to a province and vice versa. In terms of specific powers, he argued that Ottawa ought to accept responsibility for matters of labour and social welfare that should be national in scope. Nova Scotia offered to cede control over maximum hours, minimum wages, marketing, and labour in general, and asked that Ottawa assume responsibility for OAPs, an unemployment insurance scheme, and mothers' allowances.[181] National standards were needed to protect provincial economies, because differences in provincial minimum wages, for example, would compel provinces to sink to the lowest level to attract and retain industry.

On matters of taxation, Macdonald argued strongly for progression and rationalization. He conceded that if Ottawa accepted responsibility for OAPs, unemployment insurance, and mothers' allowances, it would require more money; he signalled his willingness to hand over income tax and succession duties to Ottawa, implying that they should form the core of revenues. Nova Scotia recognized that the federal government 'is able to administer such duties and tax more effectively, economically, and uniformly throughout Canada than can be administered by nine separate provincial authorities or, in the case of income tax, their municipal delegates.' To guard provincial autonomy, Macdonald insisted that provinces be given the right to collect indirect taxes, such as a sales tax, and that they have exclusive control over minor tax fields, such as gasoline and electricity taxes. The revenues these taxes could offer were of secondary importance to the discretionary power that exclusive tax fields would ensure.

Macdonald spent some time addressing the harmful impact of federal tariff policy on Nova Scotia over the years and pointed out that the province ranked last in per capita wealth. He then made his familiar appeal for provincial subsidies based on the principle of fiscal need, rather than population. Macdonald argued that fiscal need had always been the main element in calculating federal subsidies: Nova Scotia's original eighty cents per capita subsidy had been considered sufficient to cover the needs of the province in 1867. The subsidy system's rigidity, however, made it outdated. 'Whether the original coat was well tailored is not to the point,' the premier went on.'The boy has outgrown it.'[182]

Macdonald suggested the creation of a Federal Grants Commission to calculate fiscal need and oversee subsidy payments to the provinces. It would also have the power to make emergency grants when conditions warranted. Thus, provinces could 'maintain the standard of government services normal throughout Canada upon the basis of a rate of taxation normal throughout Canada.' Where people in a province suffered as a result of national policies such that their standard of living was below the national average, they 'should be compensated by appropriate special consideration.' Macdonald drew his idea of a grants commission from the Australian model and had closely studied Australia's *Report of the Royal Commission on the Constitution*.[183] He did not offer a specific formula for determining 'fiscal need,' but suggested that subsidies could be adjusted with every decennial census, taking into account factors such as, but not limited to, population change, relative economic performance, and the taxable capacity of a province.

Macdonald again referred to Australian practice and recommended fixed, annual conferences of federal and provincial officials.[184] Regular meetings would create 'the opportunity for discussion and for creating a spirit and an attitude of cooperation among the Provinces and the

Dominion, and a willingness based upon sympathy and understanding, on the part of one section of the Dominion to assist in so far as possible in correcting the difficulties of another section.' This was clearly a reference to the attitude, if not the rhetoric, of Hepburn, whose jeremiads about Ontario's playing milch cow to the poorer provinces were well known.[185] Macdonald believed that greater attention to federal relations would draw provincial and federal leaders out of their narrow self-interests and strengthen national unity.

Macdonald had wrestled with the question of fisheries in preparing his brief. Indigence pervaded fishing communities, and the decline of the salt fishery only worsened conditions. The number of workers in the industry had increased by almost twenty percent since the start of the Depression, yet the value of fish landed dropped by more than 12 per cent between 1930 and 1937.[186] Macdonald wrote of his dilemma to Alex Johnston:

> I am somewhat concerned about the matter of fisheries. I have a feeling that we could do the job better than it is being done now, apart from international complications. Just in what ways we could do it better I find it difficult to say specifically, and I cannot find anyone here who can give me definite arguments to support me ... Certainly the present handling of the fisheries problem is not satisfactory to us, and our people look to this government rather than to Ottawa for help.

Johnston, a retired deputy minister of marine and fisheries, was distressed by the general poverty of fishers, but could provide no direct arguments for provincial control of fisheries.[187] Macdonald told the commissioners that successful management of the fishery required too many dominion powers – over transportation, marketing, and international treaties – and therefore Nova Scotia would not request oversight of the fishery.[188]

'The Fathers of Reconsideration,' as reporter J.B. McGeachy called the commissioners, seem to have been impressed with the Nova Scotian brief, though Rowell's biographer dismisses it as 'the deeply rooted provincialism of the Maritimes.'[189] The idea of a Federal Grants Commission did not appeal to the chief justice, and he asked Macdonald if such a commission might not award a lower subsidy or none at all. The premier agreed and pointed out that he was not calling for a raid on the federal treasury. 'Instead, Ottawa could serve as the distributing agent for the wealth of [richer] provinces ... It was only reasonable that some of that wealth [built up from certain national policies] "should be distributed on what we think is a more equitable basis."'[190] The other four commissioners found much to suit their tastes in the brief, and after Rowell retired from the commission, they adopted most of Nova Scotia's proposals.

The King government tabled the *Report of the Royal Commission on Dominion-Provincial Relations* on 16 May 1940. The main recommendations were presented in two plans. Plan I, the one favoured by the commissioners, involved significant changes to Canada's constitution and to government finance. Plan II merely advocated the transfer of responsibility for 'unemployed employables' to the federal government. Plan I was quite similar to Nova Scotia's brief, differing only slightly in some areas. It called on Ottawa to assume responsibility for unemployed employables and OAPs, though it chose to leave mothers' allowances to the provinces. It also supported Macdonald's ideas on federal control of marketing and a constitutional amendment allowing delegation of powers. The report lauded the idea of fixed, annual dominion-provincial conferences and quoted King as favouring them. In addition, the report called for exclusive dominion control of progressive or 'justly distributed' taxes, including income and corporate taxes and succession duties, making the bulk of the taxation system more efficient and rational.[191]

On the key issue of provincial subsidies, the commissioners adopted Macdonald's proposals almost to the letter, though they chose the name 'National Adjustment Grants' (NAGs), to be administered by a Finance Commission. Emergency grants would be given 'whenever a provincial government established that it could not supply Canadian average standards of service and balance its budgets without taxation (provincial and municipal) appreciably exceeding the national average in relation to income.' The commissioners spelled out the centrality of NAGs to the philosophy of the report:

[They] are a complete break from the traditional subsidy system and the principles ostensibly underlying it. They make provision for the Commission's recommendations (other than those for the relief of unemployed employables) on the major subjects of public welfare, education, and provincial development and conservation expenditures. They illustrate the Commission's conviction that provincial autonomy in these fields must be respected and strengthened, and that the only true independence is financial security ... They are the concrete expression of the Commission's conception of a federal system which will both preserve a healthy local autonomy and build a stronger and more united nation.[192]

Macdonald could not have asked for a stronger endorsement of his vision of federalism.

After seeing the commissioners on their way, Macdonald faced the 1938 session of the Legislature able to project the province's third consecutive surplus.[193] The Conservatives brought the *Herald*'s six-month campaign against the steam trawler into the Assembly and demanded that Macdonald take a public stand. He refused, saying that it was a federal matter, but then charged that the *Herald* distorted the case with false statistics. It led its readers to believe that trawlers landed 90 per cent of the total catch when really, the premier said, they accounted for just 10 per cent. Furthermore, the paper appeared determined to destroy the reputation of the capital according to Macdonald:

> Statements such as those constantly appearing in the *Herald* to the effect that grass will shortly grow on the docks of Halifax, that the City Home is nothing but a hovel, that the members of the City Council are stupid and corrupt, that 'public authority' generally is derelict in the discharge of its duties, and the like – all these must create a decidedly unfavourable impression abroad.[194]

An irritated Macdonald wrote to Grattan O'Leary: 'It seems to me that today the large section of the press is placing too much emphasis on freedom and not enough on responsibility.'[195] Macdonald continued to be overly sensitive to criticism in the press.

Though Nova Scotia's economy largely escaped the slump of 1937, it suffered serious setbacks during 1938, and the *Herald* incessantly pressed the provincial and federal governments to take action. Coalfields in Inverness and Pictou Counties were unprofitable and at risk of closing. Prices in the fishery declined a further 12 per cent during 1938, and the salt-fish industry all but collapsed in spite of a government bonus program. Macdonald suggested granting trawler licences to companies that agreed to purchase the fish caught by inshore fishers. He also tried to negotiate a deal with General Seafoods whereby the company would build a cold-storage plant in Canso in exchange for a trawler licence or two. Ilsley noted that Ottawa planned to renew the licence for Maritime National's two trawlers, but feared the political costs of granting one to General Seafoods, given the hostility against trawlers raised by the *Herald*'s campaign.[196]

In August 1938 the *Herald* began writing about the poverty of some Nova Scotia communities. Evelyn Tufts, its parliamentary gallery reporter, took the *Globe and Mail*'s Harold Dingman on a tour of some fishing villages, leading to a series of articles describing cruel poverty and exploitation. Dingman described fishing families living in 'grim squalor' on $25 per year, getting paid just twenty-five cents for 300 herring. Ottawa-based Norman MacLeod wrote of three fishers working four months to earn $10 to split among themselves. Tufts reported that fishers were paid 1½ cents per pound for haddock, which was sold in Halifax for twelve cents.[197]

Macdonald in Halifax and Ilsley in Ottawa railed against the stories for their inaccuracies and sensationalism.[198] Macdonald met with Dingman for three hours to confront him on his facts. Dingman admitted that he had visited only about two dozen families in the poorest communities. From this, he estimated that fishers' average gross income was about $75 per year. Macdonald told him he had been used by the *Herald* and showed the reporter statistics indicating average gross earnings of more than $330. Dingman replied 'that he had not met anyone who had earned $300.00, and that as between government reports and the statements of individual fishermen, he would take the statements of the individual fishermen.' By the middle of September the *Herald* had stopped its campaign without conceding anything to the federal or provincial governments. Macdonald believed that the reactions of the *Herald*'s readers had forced a halt. 'There is not much doubt that many Conservatives have cancelled their subscriptions, and generally, I think, the pride of Nova Scotians was deeply hurt by the efforts of these outsiders to picture the worst side of conditions here.'[199]

Beyond his defensiveness in the area of Liberal policies, Macdonald's passions were inflamed by the external criticisms of his province. Poverty undoubtedly existed in many areas and touched Macdonald's compassion, but he would not stand to have these realities pointed out by 'outsiders.' He asked former temperance inspector Rev. C.W. Rose to conduct a personal investigation of some fishing communities. Rose reported that after a bad season, some families were living on about $100 per year, but pointed out that most owned their own homes and kept gardens as well. There was no evidence of 'immorality and illegitimacy' – key concerns for Rose – and some relief work on the roads would tide families over until spring.[200]

Problems continued to plague the fisheries into the winter, leading to harsh words between Liberals in Ottawa and Halifax. Storms destroyed thousands of lobster pots in the Maritimes, and the federal government considered a compensation package for fishers. Macdonald opposed 'handing out money and material gratis,' as he believed this would set a bad precedent. Lobster pots were lost every year, and paying fishers for equipment destroyed by 'acts of God' invited other industries to seek compensation in similar circumstances. 'It may be that the time is coming when the governments of one sort or another must pursue this fairy godmother policy, but it seems to me that we should endeavour to postpone that time.' He favoured relief work for the fishing communities and told the minister of fisheries, J.E. Michaud, that if Ottawa intended to provide direct relief, it could do so alone. He noted angrily that Ottawa was quick to announce unilaterally relief plans that required provincial cooperation and participation.[201]

Macdonald's resistance to the compensation prompted a sharp attack from Halifax Liberal MP R.E. Finn, who praised Michaud and the governments of New Brunswick and Prince Edward Island for moving swiftly to pay fishers. He urged Ottawa to pressure Macdonald to sign on to the plan.[202] Macdonald responded in the press, arguing that the overwhelming majority of Canadians preferred work to handouts and saying that his government had a road works project ready to assist fishers in need. MacMillan supported this stance, telling Ilsley that 'Nova Scotia would have no part in distributing doles,' and asking Ottawa to put up $75,000 for relief work projects.[203] This was perhaps the first instance of Macdonald's criticizing a Liberal government in Ottawa for failure to consult the province on a matter of mutual interest.

After winning two majority governments, balancing the provincial budget three years running, and presenting the province's case to the Rowell-Sirois Commission, Macdonald began preparing his path to federal politics. One MP from Peterborough, Ontario, wrote that he had 'an idea that King is going to ask you to join his Government when he goes to the country. You have made a very fine impression throughout Ontario and apparently your own Province, and the Quebec members think just as highly of you as the rest of us.'[204] A friend from Alberta wrote: 'It is rumoured that King will retire either before or immediately after the next election. Is it your modesty that prevents you from making any statements or predictions?'[205]

Alex Johnston and T.A. Crerar advised Macdonald to take a tour of the Canadian West to raise his image as a national figure. Crerar planned to escort him in the autumn of 1938 through Manitoba and Saskatchewan to Yellowknife, Vancouver, and Edmonton, introducing him to Liberal organizations along the way. The Munich Crisis kept Crerar in Ottawa, and Macdonald had to remain in Nova Scotia after the death of the Speaker necessitated a by-election; the trip was postponed for a year.[206]

King George VI and Queen Elizabeth disembarked at Quebec City on

17 May 1939, the first reigning monarchs to visit Canada. The trip had a number of unspoken purposes – Mackenzie King anticipated that the royal tour would boost the Liberal cause in the coming election – but its most important goal was to strengthen the ties of the Commonwealth in anticipation of a European war. After making their way across Canada and part of the United States, the king and queen arrived in Halifax on a lovely June day. Macdonald played host with all the requisite dignity and polish, and his young daughter Coline remained composed and graceful as she presented the queen with a bouquet on the steps of Province House.[207] He received compliments on his performance, even from the queen – passed on through the Crerars – who 'voiced tremendous admiration' for Macdonald and said that Halifax had been the highlight of the trip.[208]

Angus Macdonald, not yet fifty, now prepared for a more direct introduction to Canadian voters. He made a quick trip to Baltimore for a physical inspection before setting out on a tour of Western Canada. It began in Toronto on 8 August 1939, as the Liberal party fêted Mackenzie King on the twentieth anniversary of his selection as leader. Macdonald, quoting from H.H. Asquith, said of King:

> He has brought to the work of leadership the most priceless of all assets – the asset of Character. Believe me, however deceptive appearances may be, however low (in the language of the Stock Exchange) character is quoted in the market for the moment, it is, and thank Heaven it will always be, the one sure passport to the respect and homage of the British people.[209]

Though the occasion called for hyperbole, Macdonald delivered his speech with sincerity. He and the prime minister shared a mutual admiration in addition to their liberalism, and many observers expected them soon to share a council table.

After seeing Agnes on her way back to Halifax, Macdonald boarded a plane with C.D. Howe, the minister of transport, who was travelling west on an inspection tour of 'his' Trans-Canada Airlines.[210] Howe and Macdonald made stops in Winnipeg, Regina, Lethbridge, Calgary, Vancouver, Victoria, Jasper, and Edmonton, before returning to Ottawa via Winnipeg. The trip began with good press coverage, but Macdonald and Howe soon found their speeches buried in the back pages, as the situation in Europe turned from bad to worse.[211] By the time he spoke to the Edmonton Chamber of Commerce on 21 August, a Nazi-Soviet agreement had been announced, and a major European war seemed imminent. Back in Ottawa late on the 22nd, Macdonald considered meeting with King to urge him to make a 'reassuring statement' on Canada's position, presumably regarding its loyalty to Britain. Howe and Alex Johnston favoured the idea, but Macdonald reasoned 'that King would be busy and perhaps in any event it was not my place to give advice.'[212] He returned to Nova Scotia to await developments in Europe.

The Second World War violently disrupted the anticipated progression of Macdonald's career from provincial to federal politics and possibly to the leadership of the national Liberal party. The war changed the dynamics of politics in Canada completely. Mackenzie King came to be seen as perhaps the only leader who could keep Canada united, and most Liberals recommitted themselves to his leadership for the foreseeable future. The war effort eventually demanded undreamed of levels of state involvement in the economy – something that even ten years of depression had not produced – and Macdonald's liberalism suddenly seemed out-of-step with the times. Macdonald did move to Ottawa, but not on his own terms or with his own power base. These factors contributed to his ineffectiveness and unhappiness on the national scene.

3 Macdonald versus King

Angus L. Macdonald had made the transition from peace to war in the late summer of 1939 much as other Canadians did. He knew well the horrors of war and was not blinded by loyalty to the Empire. He believed simply that Nazi Germany had to be defeated and was prepared to accept vastly expanded state powers to bring about this defeat. Macdonald noted that Canadians did not greet war with the enthusiasm and momentum of 1914, but he judged them to be more determined, 'spurred on' by Hitler's audacity. He argued that the Allies had to win a 'decisive victory,' even if the war were to last years.[1] Macdonald left the premiership of Nova Scotia to perform war work in Ottawa and, while he may have dreamed of earning a significant peacetime role there, he put the war effort before his political ambitions.

The Ontario Legislature, rather than Germany, made Canada's war effort the subject of national attention in January 1940. Conservative leader George Drew criticized Mackenzie King's leadership, and Liberal premier Mitchell Hepburn presented a resolution damning Ottawa's prosecution of the war to that point.[2] Macdonald understood the criticisms offered in the Ontario Legislature, but firmly backed King:

> I suppose that in a democracy where the feeling toward defence was not altogether unanimous a year ago, it might have been difficult to make adequate preparation and spend money against possibilities which might never be realized. On the whole, however, in times like these it seems to me unwise to make too open criticism, unless the matter admits no other remedy.[3]

After a brief hesitation, King decided to use Hepburn and Drew's criticisms as an election issue. Parliament met on 25 January; Governor

General Lord Tweedsmuir announced the dissolution in the throne speech, shocking members of Parliament and Canadians as a whole.[4]

To news that King had called an election the day Parliament met, Macdonald replied that, like a prize fighter, he was 'groggy but game.' He believed the Liberals would be returned, if only for a lack of a real alternative. He thought most Nova Scotians viewed '[J.S.] Woodsworth and his crowd [the Co-operative Commonwealth Federation] as a pacifist, near-Communist group' and showed no enthusiasm for Conservative leader Robert Manion's call for a National Government coalition. Macdonald stumped for the federal Liberals all around Nova Scotia, but declined invitations to speak in Ontario, citing his preparations for the spring sitting of the Nova Scotia Legislature.[5]

On 26 March 1940, Canadian voters chose to put the war effort into the hands of the Liberal party. Mackenzie King's government won the largest majority in Canadian history to that date – 181 of 245 seats – based on an as-yet-modest war effort and a commitment not to impose conscription for overseas service.[6] The Canadian electorate, it appeared, agreed with King and not Hepburn on the appropriate size of Canada's war effort early in 1940.

The German blitzkrieg of April, May, and June banished all thought of a limited war. Pressure intensified on King to form a coalition by taking the 'best brains' in the country into his cabinet, regardless of their political stripe. Recalling the Union Government of 1917, Manion's Conservative party had changed its name to the 'National Government Party' for the March election; the move drew little support then, but after the fall of France calls increased to shelve party politics for the duration. The Conservatives even suggested in the House that King step aside for someone better able to manage a 'full war effort,' much as Chamberlain had resigned in favour of Winston Churchill. The leading candidate to replace King seems to have been J.L. Ralston, minister of finance since September 1939.[7] Ralston refused to listen to such talk, saying he had faith in 'King's ability to hold the country together – Quebec-wise' and citing King as 'the hinge between Churchill and Roosevelt.' Senator Norman Lambert believed that 'Ralston would be impossible and could not hold Quebec. Ralston is impossible because he is unable to delegate work and has already become the bottleneck of the government where he is.'[8]

King argued that his unprecedented majority made his government 'national.' Nevertheless, King rarely could resist public pressure, and even members of his cabinet pushed for the inclusion in the government of strong figures to boost confidence, to help with the war effort, and especially to answer the government's critics. King approached Tom Moore, president of the Trades and Labour Congress, to serve as minister of labour and invited J.W. McConnell, publisher of the *Montreal Star*, to take over the portfolio of national security. Both declined, and King furiously wrote that they did not want to 'run the risk of spoiling their own reputations by taking responsibilities, yet those of us who have assumed this job and are carrying it out are being criticized for not taking these "best brains" and "best minds" into the Cabinet.' The search for new ministers intensified with the death of Defence Minister Norman Rogers on 10 June 1940. Rogers, one of King's ablest ministers and few friends, died in a plane crash en route to Toronto. This tragedy had a silver lining for King in that he could shuffle the cabinet without admitting that his government had not been up to the task.[9]

Shortly after Rogers's death, King asked Ralston to take over Defence. Ralston agreed on condition that he get an assistant minister and that J.L. Ilsley replace him as minister of finance. On 27 June, King suggested C.G. 'Chubby' Power as minister of national defence for air and Angus Macdonald as minister of national defence for naval services.[10] Ralston and Power 'strongly favoured this,' and King called Macdonald the next day. The two men had talked about such a move in discussions early in June, and King reminded Macdonald 'of his promise to help in any way he could' and said that he expected that Ralston, Power, and Macdonald would work well together. Macdonald asked for time to consult his colleagues, but made it pretty clear that he would come to Ottawa.[11] A few days later, the *Toronto Evening Telegram* guessed that King would bring Macdonald into his cabinet:

> A dual purpose move which not only will permit him to proclaim that he has strengthened his cabinet for the prosecution of the war but will also bring into the federal limelight a new figure to assume the mantle of leadership when he lays it down, is now believed to be contemplated by the Prime Minister ... If and when the necessity arises for Mr. King to lay down the leadership of his party, Mr. Macdonald would be 'a natural' ... Mr. Macdonald has a reputation for considerable initiative and ability. Mr. King might very well use him as material to proclaim that he is 'strengthening' his cabinet – without going outside the Liberal field.[12]

From Halifax, Macdonald had admired Mackenzie King as the principled successor to Sir Wilfrid Laurier. Four and a half years spent working with him in Ottawa, however, led Macdonald to despise King and his equivocations. For his part, King came to view Macdonald as a viper, ready to strike out of sheer jealousy. That division emerged within a government prosecuting a war was inevitable, but Macdonald and King's mutual animosity and mistrust threatened the ability of the government to function. King spurned Macdonald's good-faith gestures and watched always for evidence of his hidden agenda. For his part, Macdonald instinctively dismissed King's careful consideration of all aspects of a problem and believed the prime minister had abandoned liberal principles for self-preservation.

The first snag in the relationship involved the question of which riding Macdonald would represent. King favoured Kingston, Ontario; it had been Sir John A. Macdonald's riding and usually went Conservative until Norman Rogers won it in 1935. King believed the Liberals could keep it without a fight if Macdonald agreed to run there. Macdonald asked for time to think about the matter, and clearly favoured a seat in Nova Scotia. At least one MP from Nova Scotia offered his seat, though he undoubtedly expected to be repaid with a Senate appointment.[13] Macdonald knew the political and religious conditions of Nova Scotia and feared stirring up anti-Catholic prejudices in Kingston. The familiarity of his home province would allow him to spend less time on constituency matters and more on his ministerial role. Moreover, if he chose to stay in federal politics he would not have to change seats. Nothing had been decided when Macdonald's train pulled into Ottawa late in the evening of 12 July 1940.[14]

King, J.L. Ralston, J.L. Ilsley, C.G. Power, Cabinet Secretary Arnold Heeney, and Chief of the Naval Staff (CNS) Vice-Admiral Percy Nelles greeted Macdonald at the station and took him to Government House, where he was promptly sworn into the cabinet by the governor general. After the ceremony, King and Macdonald went out to Kingsmere and chatted until past two in the morning. King pushed the idea of the Kingston seat. Macdonald later wrote: 'I told Mr. King that I did not know Kingston at all, nor its problems, nor its people, that there might be resentment in Ontario – particularly among Cabinet aspirants – Nova Scotia was a surer way and [Antigonish-Guysborough MP Ralph] Kirk and others were willing to resign.'[15] Eventually, he relented and said he would sit for Kingston if he could be guaranteed an acclamation, but that he would want to return to Nova Scotia in the next general election. Macdonald hoped that Kingston Conservatives would offer a challenge, allowing him to stand for a seat in Nova Scotia without directly defying the prime minister.[16]

Negotiations began with the Conservatives in Kingston to arrange a 'saw-off.' They agreed not to run a candidate against Macdonald for Parliament, and the Liberals agreed not to oppose Conservative candidate Colonel T.A. Kidd for the provincial legislature. Division soon arose among the local Tories, however; some wanted to challenge Macdonald on the basis that he was a Liberal, not a National Government, candidate. Key Conservatives – including Colonel Kidd, who declined the nomination of a splinter group – supported Macdonald's acclamatión, however, and he won Kingston without a fight on 12 August 1940.[17] The result pleased King, but he found Macdonald's reluctance to fight rather short-sighted and self-interested. Macdonald's friends and colleagues in Ottawa cautioned him that King was acting entirely within character. Ilsley told him that 'the P.M. he thinks will be entirely selfish, will do whatever he thinks best for himself and will pay no attention to my interests.'[18]

The obstacle of a seat behind them, King found Macdonald a valuable addition to the government. King liked his broad view on subjects and compared him favourably to the minister of finance: 'Ilsley has a very narrow mind; has no vision with regard to international problems. Is of the old colonial mind. Might be a better resident of Newfoundland than of N.S. Angus Macdonald, quite a different person. He will forge way ahead of Ilsley.'[19] Coming to Ottawa as a wartime minister with the probability of a secure post to return to at the conclusion of hostilities, Macdonald could afford to be above much of the petty politics and patronage that necessarily occupied the other ministers. Though he tended to some constituency business in Kingston, Macdonald really acted as an MP-at-large and did not attend either Ontario or Nova Scotia caucus meetings. Combined with his avid interest in world affairs, Macdonald's 'independence' allowed him a longer view of Canada's part in the war.

In 1940 Macdonald and King agreed on the direction Canada's war effort should take. Each believed that this would be a war of materiel, not men; they favoured concentrating Canada's resources in production and on the air force and navy to help defend and supply Britain, rather than on a large army to fight the Great War over again. Macdonald also sided with King in resisting British requests and imperial impulses to send more men and money overseas. King wrote, 'The younger and newer men in the Cabinet, with the exception of Macdonald, are of very little help. Indeed it would be much easier to conduct proceedings without the presence of most of them as is the case in the War Committee.'[20]

King had appointed Macdonald minister of national defence for naval services because, 'living at Halifax, he would be familiar with the Atlantic Coast and would be an invaluable addition to the Cabinet in wartime.'[21] Macdonald knew nothing about organizing a navy, but neither did anyone else on the Canadian political horizon. He dutifully took up the joint tasks of overseeing a significant naval contribution to the war and firmly establishing a permanent Canadian navy.

The Royal Canadian Navy (RCN) grew from a skeletal fleet to become a crucial defender of Allied supply lines. In September 1939 the RCN had just thirteen ships and about 1800 personnel. When Macdonald arrived in July 1940, it had grown to 100 ships and more than 7000 personnel, though few of its ships and sailors were ready for service at sea. Macdonald's appointment and the organization of Naval Affairs as a separate department provided a boost to the RCN, which mushroomed over the course of the war to include about 400 fighting ships, almost 500 auxiliary craft, 90,000 male and 6500 female personnel. Canada's navy expanded by fifty times its original strength during the war, whereas Britain's Royal Navy (RN) and the United States Navy (USN) grew eight and twenty times as large, respectively. During the war, the RCN performed roughly 40 per cent of the Allied transatlantic escort duty. Though lacking glamorous headlines, the 'silent service' played a role at least as important in securing final victory over the Axis powers as the other branches of Canada's armed forces.[22]

By 1944 King believed his naval minister had imperialist intentions of making the RCN a fleet arm of the RN. In reality, Macdonald saw the war as an opportunity to realize Sir Wilfrid Laurier's dream of an independent Canadian navy. Marc Milner argues that 'the war fought by the RCN between 1939 and 1945 was as much to anchor the navy permanently as to beat the Germans.'[23] For Macdonald that meant 'Canadianizing' the RCN: eliminating unnecessary mimicry of the RN and allowing the service to establish its own traditions. Given that all the RCN's senior officers had trained with the RN, and that many – including CNS Vice Admiral Nelles – were well-known anglophiles, it is not surprising that Macdonald's program for a national navy met resistance.[24]

Macdonald's administration of Naval Affairs did not rise to brilliance, and he does not get high marks from naval historians.[25] Yet the problem may have lain more with the senior naval staff than with Macdonald. Horace Read, recruited in 1943 to revise the Naval Regulations, rated Macdonald's administrative abilities highly, provided that he trusted his underlings.[26] Lacking any naval training, Macdonald relied entirely on the officers at Naval Services Headquarters (NSHQ) for advice on the service's requirements. Though he had broad goals for the RCN, his inability to separate the wheat from the chaff of technical information often limited his ministerial control over the department. Ralston described his role as a defence minister to Grant Dexter: 'He was minister but must act upon the advice of his staff of professional soldiers. Being a civilian, he could not set aside his advisers simply because he disagreed with what they said. They knew: he did not know.'[27] Macdonald generally saw himself as the advocate of the Naval Staff in the War Committee of the cabinet; he acted as a liaison with other departments and faithfully represented the Naval Staff's views, intervening only when an issue threatened to cause political damage.

Although Macdonald thoroughly enjoyed his association with the navy, the post may not have challenged him fully. In late 1942, Chubby Power proposed a reorganization of the War Committee, making it smaller and more focused on the war effort. To this end, Power suggested limiting the committee to King, Ralston, Minister of Justice Louis St Laurent, and Macdonald. St Laurent had a 'light' portfolio, and Ralston and Macdonald could be relieved of mundane departmental duties. Power wrote: 'Macdonald, having had a long and successful experience in general administration could give valuable counsel on all questions of general interest; besides, he could be looked upon as representing Munitions and Finance. Furthermore, the job he has at present is not commensurate in importance with his ability and capacity.'[28]

Macdonald agreed with Power that administrative meetings took up entirely too much of his time – six to eight hours a day – and that meetings of the Naval Council, War Committee, and Cabinet dealt with too many frivolous matters, but he blamed the problems on too many levels of bureaucracy and the close scrutiny of the Treasury Board.

As it is today, so far as the Department of Naval Services is concerned, outside of the actual operation of ships, the Department is completely bereft of any real power. It cannot buy as much as five cents worth of any material without the approval of either the Department of Munitions and Supply, or the Department of Finance, or of both. The tendency to centralization and to reach out for more and more power is evident in the attitude of certain controllers and others appointed here since the outbreak of war, and it is causing, I believe, a great deal of resentment in the country, and among the Members of the House of Commons.[29]

He begrudged the bureaucratic curtailment of his discretion as a minister of the Crown.

The bureaucracy at Naval Service Headquarters grew and changed shape as Macdonald settled into his office. He quickly established a Naval Council in August 1940 to advise him on the RCN's program of expansion. The minister found the council's meetings too time-consuming and detailed, however, and early in 1942 it was replaced by the Naval Board, on which Macdonald did not sit. The deputy minister – a civilian, beginning in 1942 – took over as liaison with Munitions and Supply.[30] For his personal staff, Macdonald called on some familiar faces, people whose ability he knew first-hand. He brought Doris Bentley, a secretary from his office in Nova Scotia, with him to Ottawa as his assistant private secretary. He made Walter Gilhooly, a classmate from St Francis Xavier, controller of naval information. He appointed Benoit Comeau, son of Nova Scotia cabinet minister Willie J. Comeau, a close assistant, and he seconded Sydney P. Wheelock from Ilsley to serve as his private secretary.

To secure competent, civilian advice, Macdonald found it necessary to recruit someone on whom he could rely completely. By early 1942, he had chosen John J. Connolly. An Ottawa lawyer and erstwhile academic, Connolly had taught philosophy at Notre Dame before moving to the law firm of Senator Charles Murphy. On the advice of Alex Johnston and others, Macdonald sought Connolly out in late 1941 and appointed him his personal secretary. Macdonald soon developed tremendous faith in Connolly's judgment, and the two established a close, lifelong friendship.[31]

The RCN's very development from 1910 and its tradition of officer training made it a 'junior' RN service. The RCN cherished and cultivated its British roots perhaps even more than the RN. In 1944 Macdonald described his frustration with anglophile officers to Admiral Nelles, whom he presumably included: 'From a Canadian point of view, it would seem that it will never be possible to create a navy in this country if it is merely an appendage of some larger Navy. Unfortunately, there seem to be some Canadian officers who are content to accept this decision.'[32] The RCN clung to certain traditions of discipline even after the RN had done away with them; Macdonald abolished 'pack drill' – marching at double-speed with a pack full of bricks – when he discovered its use in 1942. This won him favour with RCN ratings, if not senior officers.[33] After the war, the Canadian navy resisted the use of French – though not from a concern for operational efficiency

– and many officers resisted 'spoiling' their uniforms with 'Canada' shoulder flashes.[34]

Macdonald found the RCN using the RN's King's Regulations and Admiralty Instructions, sections of which dated to the reign of Charles II. He commissioned his former Dalhousie colleague Horace Read from the University of Minnesota 'to write the Declaration of Independence' for the RCN. From September 1943 until December 1945, Read supervised the work of forty-five consultants on the project, producing a comprehensive set of Canadian rules and regulations to govern the organization and operation of the RCN.[35]

The policy of Canadianizing the RCN extended to its operational role. Shortly after Macdonald arrived in Ottawa, the Naval Council prepared an appreciation which said that the RCN should look to the defence of Canadian shores and harbours and achieve a maximum complement of 4500 personnel by 1943; any recruits in excess of this figure should be sent directly to the RN.[36] As the U-boat campaign spread into the North Atlantic, Canada's anti-submarine (A/S) role expanded in a haphazard way. Initially, the RCN shared convoy escort duty with the U.S. Navy as far as Iceland. After the Japanese attack on Pearl Harbor, the U.S. Navy focused its resources on the Pacific, leaving the Northwest Atlantic almost wholly to the RCN. Not until 28 May 1942 did the Naval Board reluctantly confirm that the RCN's primary role would be anti-submarine escort; it delayed authorizing A/S modifications to some of its destroyers until October 1942, still hoping that they might be used in fleet battles.[37]

By 1942 some journalists were expressing disappointment in Macdonald's performance in Ottawa. Several members of the press gallery wondered aloud at the basis of his glowing pre-war reputation, and Macdonald did little to court journalists. After one of his first press conferences, a reporter printed something that had been told in strict confidence, souring the naval minister on the whole process. The *Globe and Mail* reported that Macdonald had not achieved any 'growth in political stature' in fifteen months in Ottawa. In late 1942 the press gallery considered Ralston or Ilsley – not Macdonald – as the top candidate to replace King.[38]

Macdonald developed a particularly antagonistic relationship with journalist Austin F. Cross. In 'Career Sketches,' a collection of brief biographies of King's ministers that appeared in *Canadian Business*, Cross sharply criticized Macdonald. While praising most of the other members of King's government, Cross wrote that Macdonald had fallen short of the 'wonderful reputation' that had preceded him to Ottawa and that he had not made the necessary adjustments: 'Bluntly, Macdonald seems a fish out of water.' Cross implied that the naval minister squabbled openly with reporters: 'Macdonald has handicapped himself by failing to understand the press. Refusing to give press conferences, touchy about this and that, Angus L. tends to spurn the hand that would help him.'[39]

Kenneth McArdle, managing editor of *Canadian Business*, forwarded the article to Macdonald together with a form letter, which read: 'We have published an item about your good self. I sincerely trust our comments please you.' Macdonald replied, 'I doubt if many people, after reading the article, would conclude that there was very much good about me.' McArdle invited Macdonald to write a rebuttal, but Macdonald declined: 'I do not think that anybody who knows the man would pay much attention to anything written by Mr. Austin Cross. He may be able to write rather interestingly for children, about little tiny railroads, and that sort of thing, but when he comes to anything requiring brains or judgment, he can be written off as a complete loss.'[40]

Cross's opinion may have been that of a journalist who had been snubbed. Macdonald had close relationships with several leading reporters and editors in Ottawa, including Grattan O'Leary, the Conservative editor of the *Ottawa Journal*, Bruce Hutchison of the *Vancouver Sun*, and especially Grant Dexter of the *Winnipeg Free Press*. Dexter, for example, wrote a very flattering piece on Macdonald for *Maclean's*, portraying him as a modest but hard-working minister: 'He thinks of his service in Ottawa as war service. His record as Minister of the Navy is one of unclouded success but, strangely, in achieving this success, he has made no deep impression on the Liberal Party or on the nation-at-large. And he has not desired to do either.'[41] Nevertheless, Macdonald's failure to achieve full journalistic acclaim did not strengthen his position in Ottawa and may have contributed to his longing for Nova Scotia.[42]

Canada's war effort steadily grew, involving unprecedented levels of state control of the nation's economy and human resources. Germany's near-supremacy in Europe pushed Canada into closer economic and military integration with the United States, as outlined in the Ogdensburg and Hyde Park Agreements. To avoid rampant inflation, Ottawa gradually introduced wage and price controls, made more effective and less liberal as the war progressed.[43] Orders-in-council – easier and faster than the parliamentary legislative process – were issued dealing with appointments, labour relations, military bases, and other varied subjects. Macdonald worried that some ministers and civil servants had developed a taste for shortcuts.

One key expansion of federal power came in the area of taxation. Shortly after Ilsley took over the Ministry of Finance, he sought larger and more secure sources of revenue for the war effort. The Rowell-Sirois report offered an attractive plan for a rationalization of the taxation systems. The report recommended that Ottawa assume exclusive control of income and corporate taxes and succession duties, giving the provinces 'adjustment grants' based on fiscal need to ensure that all provinces could provide a level of social welfare programs equivalent to the national average without having to impose taxes in excess of the national average. The report had some support from the poorer provinces, but those that held the lion's share of the national wealth did not warm to it at all. The prime minister wanted to set it aside for the duration of the war and did not relish the idea of a public discussion of its recommendations. Ilsley and his staff, however, pressed for a conference on the report for the sake of the war effort if not for constitutional renewal.[44] After some debate, the cabinet agreed to hold a Dominion-Provincial Conference.

The conference opened on 14 January 1941 and collapsed the next day in failure. King's opening address took a conciliatory tone, but Hepburn responded by lambasting the 'five hundred thousand dollar report – the product of the minds of three professors and a Winnipeg newspaper man' and compared its proponents to 'the enemies of civilization' currently afoot in Europe.[45] Alberta's William Aberhart and British Columbia's Dufferin Pattullo joined Hepburn in refusing to consider the report.

Macdonald abstained from the discussion, lest he be seen as a second representative of Nova Scotia. From the Dominion's side of the table, however, he quietly tried to salvage something from the conference. He passed a note to King, urging a signal of flexibility: 'Mr. Aberhart is willing to consider the Sirois report, along with other matters. Hepburn is willing to talk about the war. If we accepted the idea of discussing *something*, could we by degrees get to a consideration of the Report?' No one yielded, however, and the conference broke up after Ilsley warned that Ottawa would have to take over tax fields anyway, for the war effort.[46]

It is possible that Ottawa not only expected but also hoped that the conference would collapse swiftly. J.L. Granatstein notes that Hepburn,

Aberhart, and Pattullo were roundly criticized as opponents of rational change, while Ilsley was able to make a case for drastic changes to the taxation system.[47] Christopher Armstrong argues that a 'skilfully orchestrated meeting which broke up in disagreement could provide an excuse for the prime minister to act unilaterally to deal with pressing national problems.'[48] Ottawa did press ahead with the expansion of federal power; in his 29 April budget speech, Ilsley announced that his department would impose heavy taxation on personal and corporate incomes, along with other lesser fields, as a 'temporary wartime expedient.' Any province that wished to voluntarily concede its prerogatives in these fields could 'rent' them to the federal government for the duration of the war.[49] Premiers who refused to vacate the tax fields in question almost surely would be vilified for impeding the war effort and imposing 'double taxation' on their constituents.

Though Macdonald certainly regretted the failure of the conference, he did not despair over the fate of the Rowell-Sirois report. Along with J.W. Dafoe and T.A. Crerar, he assumed that the logic of the report would make it indispensable to Canada in the reconstruction period. The economic disaster of the 1930s and the inherent problems of the British North America Act surely demonstrated that the recommendations of Rowell-Sirois were essential to the nation's health.[50]

The expanding military and industrial war also raised the spectre of a debate over conscription, King's greatest fear. Even as the government attempted to balance the national war effort, it faced incessant pressure from vocal segments of society to extend that effort to full capacity; eventually, the limits of voluntary human resources at its disposal would be reached. King became consumed by the struggle to limit Canada's war effort, if politically possible, to avoid conscripting soldiers for combat overseas.

Allied losses in Europe in 1940 had made plain the threat to Canada, and on 18 June the government presented the National Resources Mobilization Act (NRMA) to the House. It gave the government 'special emergency powers to mobilize all our human and material resources for the defence of Canada,' but clearly spelled out that these powers 'will relate solely and exclusively to the defence of Canada on our own soil and in our own territorial waters.' To calm Quebec's fears, King assured the House that 'no measure for the conscription of men for overseas service will be introduced by the present administration.'[51] Quebec MPs in Ottawa fidgeted nervously, and a handful spoke against the bill, but it passed into law on 21 June.

King's opposition to conscription rested entirely on political grounds. In his diary he wrote: 'Conscription is sound in principle but has to be related to all factors which are important in their political bearing.'[52] He also told *Free Press* editors Ferguson and Dafoe that he did not oppose conscription on principle and that it might indeed become necessary, but that he would probably have to resign rather than bringing it in. King may have thought of putting the question to a national referendum or general election.[53]

Macdonald recognized the political problems conscription could cause in Canada, but in a December 1941 cabinet discussion he supported it on principle:

> I said the logic of the case was all for Conscription. Nearly all Continental countries had it – U.S. would have it soon. State demanded taxes, obedience to law and in cases of capital crimes, a man's life. There was no distinction between service in Nfld, Iceland etc. and in England or the Continent ... The question of whether this was the time or not was another matter.[54]

Macdonald believed conscription to be the best way to fairly and rationally distribute the burdens of war. The structures of liberalism were supported by and embodied in the Canadian state. A threat to that state constituted a common emergency, temporarily overriding citizens' liberties to choose their own responses.

Pressure to bring in conscription for overseas service began to emerge in the spring of 1941. Members of the Conservative party and certain senior army officers led the push, but without a tangible threat or broad-based public call for conscription, the government could ignore the issue for the time being.[55] Only the navy and the Royal Canadian Air Force (RCAF) had seen significant action, and throughout 1941 those services faced no shortage of volunteers. In fact, the navy and air force turned away thousands of applicants even as they rapidly expanded. Neither did the Canadian Army lack recruits to fulfil its authorized program.[56]

King continued to fret over the size and direction of the war effort; he may even have considered resigning, rather than facing the tremendous pressure of governing. After one War Committee meeting, King expressed despair at Canada's burdens. He spoke to Macdonald and Ralston alone, saying that

> he felt he could no longer go on as Prime Minister, and that it was quite evident there were developing in Cabinet two groups, one more aggres-

sive than the other, wanting this country to undertake practically everything that was suggested to it. He felt he was out of sympathy with that
group, and that it would be better if somebody out of the more vigorous
party were selected as leader, and he said that one or the other of us should
take on the task. He continued by saying to Ralston, 'I do not think you
want the job. You have only come in for the war, and would be glad to be
relieved at the end of the war.' Ralston immediately said he would be very
happy to serve under me. I then told the Prime Minister that I thought he
was tired and worried, and that he did not really mean what he said, and
that he should think the matter over.[57]

Macdonald interpreted the prime minister's words as an honest invitation to succeed him. In reality, King hoped to force his ministers back in
line by his familiar trick of threatening to resign and he assumed he had
been understood: 'I could see that they both realized just where the
Government was likely to be if either of them were left to take responsibility of leadership, and Macdonald said I was quite right in not having Canada take on things she could not do.'[58]

In the autumn of 1941, Ernest Lapointe's health failed, leading King
and T.A. Crerar to discuss their own political futures.[59] Neither wished
to consider running in another general election. Crerar informed King
that he had consulted Dafoe on the question of a successor to the prime
minister, but they had reached no conclusion. Crerar 'then went on to
say that none of them could see anyone else in sight from any party. We
both felt that Angus Macdonald had many of the qualities required but
had certain obvious limitations.'[60] Unfortunately, these limitations
were so obvious to King that he did not record them in his diary, leaving us to speculate. The obstacles to Macdonald's assumption of the
Liberal leadership probably involved his health, his small base of support, his religion, and his frank support for conscription.

The naval minister suffered from a duodenal ulcer and insomnia.[61]
Although there was little Macdonald could do about this, King was not
sympathetic to ministers who let their health slip for the sake of work.
Clearly a weakened minister was not fit to assume even heavier responsibilities. Macdonald also lacked a national profile. Coming from the
Maritimes and with only a loud and perhaps superficial popularity in
Ontario, Macdonald could not 'bring' much of the country with him in
an election, nor had he cultivated a strong image in the press. Religion,
of course, remained a political issue in the 1940s, and Macdonald's
Catholicism would not be much of an asset outside Quebec. In that
province, the bastion of Liberal power since 1896, he cast little or no

shadow, and his willingness to countenance the use of conscription for overseas service might have crippled the party.

The debate over conscription for overseas service developed in earnest in November and December 1941. The Conservative party, trying to recover from its woeful showing in the 1940 election, recalled Arthur Meighen from the Senate in mid-November. Meighen returned to the leadership reluctantly, but with a determination to see Canada fight the war with all the tools at its disposal, including a national (coalition) government and unrestricted conscription.[62]

Just before Japan entered the war, the defence ministry presented to cabinet its plans for a 'Big Army' program for 1942–3 – an army of two corps, made up of five divisions, three infantry and two armoured. The government established a Labour Supply Investigation Committee to see if the country could support five divisions. It reported that there were only 609,000 men left in Canada who might be eligible to serve, provided 500,000 women joined the labour force. From that 600,000, many would be needed in key industries, and the navy and air force required 175,000. Ralston estimated that the army would need a steady supply of 6000 recruits per month until March 1943. Asked if he could achieve these figures without resorting to conscription, 'Ralston said he was not prepared to say there should never be conscription.' King said he would support the program if it were the army's last demand and if the army would give assurances that it could be done without conscription. They summoned General Kenneth Stuart, chief of the General Staff, who assured them that the army's plans had been drawn up with the concerns of the government in mind. The War Committee decided to place the question before the entire cabinet on 9 December 1941.[63]

The Japanese offensive of December 1941 fundamentally changed the situation facing the cabinet. Although cabinet could not gauge the significance of the Japanese moves in the North Pacific, they did seem to underline the importance of home defence, perhaps eliminating the case for conscription for overseas service. Before 7 December 1941, Macdonald had grown frustrated with the chronic indecision of King and the cabinet. Grant Dexter spoke with Alex Johnston and Macdonald on 6 December:

> [Johnston] said that Ralston, Angus and Ilsley were agreed on the need to settle the conscription issue forthwith. Angus was present and discussed conscription in a general way. He seemed very fed-up with Ottawa and keen to get back to Nova Scotia ... Angus said that it might well be too soon

to face the conscription issue but he was sick and tired of listening to the Quebeckers saying that it couldn't happen. He was in favor of settling the matter as soon as possible, regardless of the military situation.[64]

Macdonald believed the Quebec ministers were isolated and out of touch on international matters. At a cabinet meeting in early 1942, Macdonald squared off with P.J.A. Cardin, who believed that Canada had been drawn into another imperial war. Dexter paraphrased Cardin: 'It would be a good thing for Canada if Britain is licked: then our Imperialists would disappear. Cardin definitely likes Pétain and Vichy: likes this kind of government setup. He certainly is no democrat.'[65]

The discussion of conscription before the entire cabinet took two days, and saw the introduction of the new Quebec minister and successor to Lapointe, Louis St. Laurent. Each minister laid out his views on conscription, and King and Macdonald recorded the opinions in their diaries.[66] Nine opposed conscription. C.D. Howe, Minister of National Revenue Colin Gibson, Minister of Labour Norman McLarty, and Postmaster-General William Mulock all agreed that conscription was not necessary at the moment, but that the government should keep its options open. Only the three Nova Scotians unreservedly supported conscription, but none of them felt it was time to impose it. They argued merely that the government ought to be prepared to implement it if necessary.

Howe had said that Ralston, Ilsley, and Macdonald formed a subcabinet in themselves. King would have agreed and attributed their support for conscription to an imperialist sentiments common to Nova Scotians. 'As I think matters over, I begin to see that in Ralston, Ilsley and Macdonald, we have three men from the Maritimes. They still have the kind of attitude toward Britain that Fielding and others of the Maritimes have had.'[67] Macdonald, for his part, thought King and the Quebec ministers had failed to provide leadership and education on the issue. He accused them of focusing on 'political considerations' and said, 'They are *not* thinking of the war but of Quebec.'[68] Macdonald and King each believed the other was short-sighted: King thought Macdonald too focused on the Empire rather than Canadian unity, while Macdonald found King concerned primarily with maintaining Liberal support in Quebec as opposed to defeating Hitler.

Pressure for conscription mounted both inside and outside the government. Inside, Ralston seemed determined to secure approval for the Big Army program over the protests of King, Howe, and Crerar. King opposed the program for fear that sustaining the program might necessitate conscription down the road; Howe and Crerar opposed it because they believed that production of essential goods and mechanized war materiel was far more important than an extra division or two of Canadian troops. Outside the government stood Meighen and the Tories, determined to press for conscription for several reasons. First, they believed – and estimated that most voters believed – that conscription was the only way Canada could properly conduct a total war. Second, they saw this as the best way to oust Mackenzie King, something that did not escape his notice.[69]

King answered the pressure for conscription by employing part of a formula first proposed by Sir Wilfrid Laurier. Facing a Union Government intent on conscripting 'slackers' to fight in the trenches of Europe, Laurier had called for a national referendum on the idea. All Canadians would have to submit to conscription if it were the clearly expressed will of the majority, Laurier argued, but the people had to be consulted.[70] King favoured a national vote to settle some of the questions surrounding conscription, though not a direct vote on conscription for overseas service. On 18 December, he proposed asking Canadians for *the power* to send troops outside Canada, thus cancelling the pledge of 1939 and 1940. To maintain its legitimacy with the Canadian public, the government could not appear to be constrained in anyway in its war effort.[71]

Before the timing of the plebiscite could be worked out, Franklin Roosevelt called King and his defence ministers to Washington to meet with Churchill, the latter having just flown in. The Canadians arrived on Boxing Day without any clear agenda, and the gathering turned out to be simply a meet-and-greet. Churchill returned to Ottawa on the train with the Canadians, affording the opportunity for a lengthy chat about the war. Churchill told King that Britain could use all the manpower Canada could send, and that an armoured division, though expensive, was worth three infantry divisions, adding credibility to Ralston's Big Army program.[72]

Early in 1942 cabinet was still debating the army's proposals, and Ralston implied that either he would have his two corps or King would have his resignation. King worried that if Ralston resigned, Macdonald would follow, and the prime minister feared the government could not survive that.[73] Macdonald later speculated to Dexter that King might replace Ralston with General Andrew McNaughton, General Officer Commanding, First Canadian Corps, in which case Macdonald would resign. 'He points out that the winning of McNaughton would be, politically, a master-stroke which would far outbalance the loss of Ralston and himself.'[74]

Cabinet struck a deal by approving the Big Army and opting for a plebiscite to free the government's hand. Ralston and Macdonald agreed to oppose conscription for overseas duty publicly on the grounds that it was unnecessary at present, divisive to the country and detrimental to the war effort, provided that the government have the power to impose conscription if it became necessary.[75] Macdonald had not been a member of the government in 1939 and 1940 when it pledged not to impose conscription for overseas service. Thus, he did not feel bound by the pledge but welcomed the plebiscite as a method of removing the moral dilemma for other members of the government. In addition, he believed that the exercise of the plebiscite might help to educate, if not shift, public opinion in Quebec.

It took cabinet three days of wrangling to set the wording of the plebiscite question. The throne speech would announce that 'the magnitude and balanced nature of the war effort are being obscured and impaired by unnecessary controversy' involving the NRMA. Ottawa, therefore, would ask Canadians: 'Are you in favour of releasing the Government from any obligation arising out of any past commitments restricting the methods of raising men for military service?' The wording, of course, had been a compromise; as two historians have noted, 'Mackenzie King carried the art of oblique references to its very pinnacle.'[76]

On 26 January, Quebec Premier Adélard Godbout argued in a speech in Montreal that to impose conscription now 'would be a crime' and said that King agreed with him.[77] Macdonald and Ralston went to see King to clarify their respective positions. King denied saying anything to Godbout and gave Macdonald permission to say publicly that he would support conscription 'when the necessity for it arose,' as long as he also said that it was not now, nor might ever be, necessary. Macdonald was growing uneasy:

There is some doubt in my mind as to what will happen if the plebiscite carries and the time comes when many of us will feel that conscription should be in force. I fear that the P.M., by use of the phrase 'considering everything,' will say, 'Conscription might give you a few more men here and there, but it would create a terrible situation in the country and consequently will not be worthwhile.'[78]

Macdonald wisely doubted King's understanding of the word 'necessary'; it proved the key to the second conscription crisis.

Even before the vote the plebiscite proved beneficial to the King government. It temporarily stifled unrest in the cabinet, as all but Cardin agreed with the move. More important, the announcement of the plebiscite took the wind from the sails of the Conservative party and probably helped to defeat Meighen in a by-election by 5000 votes. Combined with the victories of Liberal candidates St Laurent and Humphrey Mitchell, the King government appeared to have 'a striking endorsement' of its policies.[79] The results of the plebiscite, held on 27 April 1942, seemed clear enough: 64 per cent of Canadian voters opted to release the government from its pledge not to impose conscription for overseas service. A closer look at the figures, however, opened the door to myriad interpretations. In Quebec, where the original pledge had been made, 72 per cent of voters opposed releasing the government from its commitments.[80] The government's hand had been freed, but to do what?

The question of what to do with this qualified release followed on the heels of the plebiscite. In cabinet on 28 April, Ralston and Ilsley argued that the government must move decisively towards enforcing conscription for all theatres. King proposed repealing section 3 of the NRMA, which barred the government from sending conscripts beyond Canada's borders, but only 'as far as Nfld. and other American Continental outposts are concerned.' Macdonald warned 'that it would be a mistake to take two bites at the cherry.' St Laurent and J.E. Michaud, minister of fisheries, opposed removing section 3, as they worried that conscription for overseas service would be applied at once. Macdonald disagreed, though he did not go so far as Ralston and Ilsley: 'I said that the repeal of Sec. 3 would mean that we should have the legal right to impose conscription. The moral right had been given by the people yesterday. When we should exercise the right was another matter.'[81] Macdonald's view carried, though another stumbling block remained: determining what to do when conscription became necessary.

From this point on, the question became one of parliamentary procedure. Section 3 would be repealed after a debate in Parliament, leaving the government free to bring in conscription if necessary. King did not wish to bear the responsibility alone; he favoured returning to Parliament for a full debate before authorizing conscription for overseas service. Macdonald and Ralston fought against this plan, fearing that a second debate would cause a dangerous delay at a time of military crisis and raise the entire controversy afresh in the future. Crerar suggested returning to Parliament after imposing conscription only for a vote of confidence. St Laurent, now the de facto Quebec lieutenant, hinted that he might accept this idea, as long as the government returned to Parliament.[82]

As the debate in cabinet wore on, tensions grew. King wrote: 'Macdonald has become very aggressive and more or less unpleasant in his attitude ... I fear there has not been a real effort on Ralston's part to seek to meet the rest of the Cabinet, and as for Macdonald, I have lost faith in his political judgment.'[83] King told cabinet that he was bound by his past speeches and that his words in Hansard were terribly important; he had an 'obligation to redeem every letter and semi-colon.' Macdonald told him that Canadians 'didn't give a damn about fine-spun argument over words. The country had voted for conscription and wanted conscription when it was necessary – not words.' Macdonald shared his frustrations with Grant Dexter: 'Angus had kept notes of King's speech to caucus [on 12 May] and went over them to show that King never once made a direct statement. Weasel words popped out of every sentence.' The government's direction on this central issue troubled Macdonald, and he considered resigning. He, Ilsley, and Ralston could not accept a second debate. At the same time, he recognized that King might resign and take the bulk of his ministers with him, leaving one of the conscriptionist ministers to form a government. After a talk with Macdonald, Dexter wrote, 'If anyone accepted a commission to form a government, and he quite sincerely rated himself as the least worthy among the three, a dissolution would be inevitable and in the long run it would mean crucifixion in the national field.'[84]

Through Dexter, Macdonald solicited the advice of Winnipeg's Liberal oracle, J.W. Dafoe. Dafoe cabled that the idea of a second debate was senseless, unless it could prevent disunity now and assure united action later. He backed Macdonald's position but advised against resignation: 'There should be no precipitate action by anybody while the situation is being thoroughly explored. Disruption would be complete negation of any claim to statesmanship or patriotic concern for country by parties responsible.' Macdonald welcomed the advice and said he would follow it.[85]

King learned through Crerar of Macdonald's appeal to Dafoe and vented his hostility in his diary:

> Why Macdonald should be communicating with Dafoe as to his resigning, I cannot understand, unless it is that he feels he would like to become the possible head of a conscriptionist government; or whether he feels he has an exceptional sense of his own importance. He takes himself a little too

seriously and wishes to put himself in the position where he can say that he has consulted with some of the leading men in the country, etc., possibly building up a case for himself as to why he has not left the government at a particular time. Macdonald is a very vain man and has an exceptional opinion of himself. Undoubtedly, he came here expecting to possibly lead the Liberal party later on but has found that he will not be able to command the following that he expected and that, lacking leadership, and having been Premier of his own province, he would prefer to get back there and take that position again as something more secure, at any rate from the time of the next general election on.[86]

King's habitual hatred of any rival combined with his fear of conscription to poison his mind against Macdonald in most future encounters.

The government introduced Bill 80 to repeal section 3 of the NRMA on 11 May 1942, and over the next two months, as much debate went on around the council table as on the floor of the House. On 8 May, King told cabinet that he would 'make no commitment either for or against going to Parliament first or later, and would decide it in light of circumstances at the time.'[87] At the end of a 27 May caucus meeting, however, King said that 'if conscription is necessary, Parliament must decide the matter. He will not take that responsibility.'[88] Macdonald rushed off a letter to King objecting 'that the statement does not accord with what was decided at Council.'[89] King met with Macdonald later and said that 'he had no idea of having two debates. There would be only one debate.' Macdonald concluded that King had moved closer to the position taken by him and Ralston.[90]

Indeed, King had moved significantly. 'Having fully decided to avoid any second debate,' he wrote in his diary, 'I still want to leave myself free to have Parliament know that I intend, if at all possible, to have expression of confidence in the government before any action in the way of applying conscription for overseas.'[91] The prime minister delivered a long and tortuously worded address to Parliament on 10 June, made famous by his description of the government's policy: 'not necessarily conscription, but conscription if necessary.'[92] Few understood what he actually said; Grant Dexter initially thought he promised *not* to return to Parliament after imposing conscription by order-in-council, but King's assistant J.W. Pickersgill later corrected him.[93] The struggle to find an acceptable process continued.

In cabinet on 12 June, King proposed returning to Parliament for a short debate and vote before imposing conscription. Macdonald objected, pointing out that there was a significant difference between going to the House before imposing conscription and going afterward asking for a vote of confidence. He reasoned that if Quebec MPs were presented with conscription as a fait accompli and asked for a vote of confidence, they would stand with the government rather than risk giving power to the Conservatives. If, on the other hand, the door were left open to defeating conscription by making a vote of confidence a prerequisite to imposing it, they would feel beholden to vote against the government. For his part, Ralston worried that a delay of even a day or two at a crisis point could endanger the lives of soldiers at the front.[94]

When cabinet adjourned, Ralston told King privately that he would have to resign. King dismissed the idea and said that if Ralston quit, he would as well. Ralston held off, and several mediators intervened. T.A. Crerar worked to soften Macdonald's position and keep him in the cabinet; Macdonald, in turn, undertook the same mission with Ralston. Meanwhile, Dafoe met with King on 16 June and seemed to convince him to choose a procedure more palatable to all sides. If conscription became necessary, the government would pass an order-in-council imposing it, but would return to Parliament for a vote of confidence and a debate not longer than forty-eight hours before signing the order.[95] The cabinet crisis dragged on for four more weeks, but little new was added.

Macdonald played a delicate role. He disagreed with Ralston on the size of the Army and the proper balance between military strength and war production, yet he appears to be the only cabinet minister, save perhaps Ilsley, to whom Ralston would listen.[96] He also recognized that he and Ralston were threatening to resign over a relatively minor matter of procedure. In cabinet on 7 July, King again went over his proposal. This time, Ilsley and Howe joined Macdonald and Ralston in their opposition; Howe agreed with Macdonald that it would be wiser to ask for a vote of confidence *after* signing the order-in-council. That evening, Ralston gave King his resignation; King urged him not to go, arguing that the distance between them was not so great.[97]

Macdonald agreed with King and firmly decided against resigning. 'If going back to Parliament means a delay of only one week, the ground of difference seems to be too narrow.'[98] He then began counselling Ralston to stay on. Ralston pondered his position all week, and on 11 July King gave him a letter promising him freedom of movement on the question in the future; Ralston would not be bound to support the government in a future conscription crisis if he believed an independent course of action was 'necessary and in the national interest.' Ralston agreed to stay on, and the crisis passed along with Bill 80.[99]

Compromise and equivocation had not settled the matter of conscription, and there was no shortage of ill will within the cabinet. Most of the ministers were upset with Ralston and Macdonald for their rigidity, and several – including Howe, Crerar, and St Laurent – thought it would be best if Ralston did resign. The crisis caused a rift even in the solid friendship between Macdonald and Crerar, who did not discuss politics for much of July. Most importantly, however, the dispute forever altered the relationship between Macdonald and King. From that point on, Macdonald assumed that King would never make a direct statement, let alone a grave decision. King came to view Macdonald as a Meighen in his midst, believing that the Nova Scotian lay in wait to destroy his government for the sake of the British Empire.[100] Furthermore, the fundamental issues remained unsolved: how would the government determine that conscription had become 'necessary'? What did 'necessary' mean? Did it mean 'necessary to win the war' or 'necessary to support the troops at the front'? Fear of splitting the government prevented the working out of a clear answer, but this point almost caused the government's collapse in 1944.

For the Royal Canadian Navy, 1942 marked the beginning of its most serious growing pains. Now in charge of the Northwest Atlantic, the RCN assigned almost every ship that could float to convoy escort duty. Corvettes, Bangor-class minesweepers, motor launches, armed yachts, and a few destroyers carried the burden of convoy protection. Understandably, the main tactic of the RCN at this time was avoidance of the enemy. To limit contact with German submarines, the navy relied on air support to keep submarines 'down' as much as possible, and convoys zigzagged and changed routes to bypass suspected U-boat locations. In cases where U-boats made contact with convoys, escorts were often satisfied with chasing the enemy off to a safe distance. Until 1943 these techniques proved remarkably successful in the North Atlantic. Along the RCN's main convoy route from New York to the Grand Banks, only one ship was lost to U-boats in 1942.[101]

Avoidance tactics were of little use, however, in the Gulf of St Lawrence and in the river itself. In such tight spaces, convoys could not avoid established routes. Moreover, an idiosyncratic combination of underwater geography, currents, sediment, and temperature gradients in the area – subjects of the infant sciences of hydrography and bathythermography during the war – allowed U-boats to hide with relative ease. The main tools for locating U-boats were radar for surfaced vessels and asdic, an early form of sonar, for underwater searches. Even had it possessed the latest equipment and skilled technicians to use it, the RCN would have found the task of locating enemy submarines almost impossible. The USN and the RN attributed the success of the U-boats in Canadian waters to the RCN's lack of modern equipment and skilled operators. While these charges had merit, the obstacles to using asdic in the area were just as significant.[102] German submarines managed to sink twenty Allied vessels in the St Lawrence River and Gulf in 1942.

On 9 September 1942, the Naval Board elected to close the St Lawrence River and Gulf to international shipping because of its vulnerability to U-boat attack and the disproportionate amount of RCN resources that would have been required to reduce this threat. Until this point, Ottawa had not developed the ports of Halifax and Saint John and the eastern rail lines for larger wartime roles, meaning that the St Lawrence handled half of Canada's east coast shipping in 1941. The area remained closed until late in the 1944 shipping season, putting tremendous strain on Canada's transportation infrastructure.[103]

This 'tactical defeat' in the St Lawrence embarrassed the RCN and the government.[104] J.S. Roy, MP from the Gaspé, raised a question in Parliament about the sinking of ships in the St Lawrence, and the press reported it, a serious breach of standard naval secrecy. After praising the Gaspésians for helping to rescue sailors, Macdonald delivered a stern lecture about the need for strict secrecy. He argued that revealing such information would give comfort to the enemy, keep the Germans up-to-date on the activities of their U-boats and relieve the U-boats of the necessity of using their radios, something that placed them in danger of discovery and attack. Macdonald then criticized Roy, and apparently French Canadians in general, for being so self-centred:

> I would say further that there are other people in this country, other citizens of Canada, who are in greater danger, or are much nearer the battle line, much nearer the danger zone, than his constituents; and not once have I heard from that easternmost part of Canada any break of this kind. Not once have I heard an hon. member from the easternmost provinces of Canada rise in his place and ask questions of this kind.[105]

At the height of the 1942 conscription debate, Macdonald's normal diplomacy deserted him. In October he again reacted badly to criticisms coming from Quebec ministers about the St Lawrence situation.[106] This situation hurt the government, but unlike the coming crisis over training and equipment, little could be done to relieve matters.

The winter of 1942-3 had revealed the consequences of the RCN's rapid expansion and over-reliance on the RN. Britain requested that Canada's navy be removed from Mid-Ocean Escort Forces until the ships could be modernized and the crews properly trained. This came at the height of the Battle of the Atlantic as Germany's U-boats mounted a tremendous offensive, later met by an even more successful Allied counter-offensive. The RCN continued with some convoy duty, but was largely sidelined in terms of sub-hunting for the rest of the war.[107]

The RCN's equipment and training problems were partly unavoidable, partly the fault of the British and partly self-created. The sheer magnitude of its expansion meant that the RCN would encounter difficulties; Canada had very little experience in constructing warships in 1939 and depended almost entirely on Britain for technical guidance and specialized equipment. The British Admiralty, of course, looked to its own needs first, leaving the Canadians waiting for technical drawings and materiel. In addition to ships, Canada undertook the construction of radar sets and other technical equipment. Here, too, delays and inefficiency hampered Canadian efforts. When the radar sets were completed and installed on RCN ships, they were badly out-of-date and proved to be almost useless for spotting U-boats on the surface even in calm seas.[108]

From the start of the war, Canadian ships and crews lagged behind their British and American counterparts in efficiency, and they fell back steadily. Corvettes, designed for inshore service, were being widely used for ocean-going convoy escort by 1941 and needed to be refitted almost constantly, first to handle mid-ocean service and second to accommodate developing anti-submarine equipment. The shortage of ships and trained sailors, combined with lengthy maintenance schedules – a consequence of service on the cold and heavy seas of the North Atlantic – precluded the speedy modernization of the fleet, even if up-to-date gear had been available. As matters stood, the latest equipment usually had not been ordered by NSHQ, was rarely available in Canadian shipyards, and took months rather than weeks to instal if it could be found. When the U-boat offensive began in late 1942, RCN ships proved dangerously inefficient.

The same could be said about Canadian sailors. RCN crews operating in the North Atlantic in 1942 had little advanced training in A/S tactics. For the most part, they had learned their jobs at sea, as limited resources did not allow crews to be pulled off the ocean for months at a time to complete courses. The rushed training and second-rate equipment of the Canadian escort groups was exposed by a mounting U-boat campaign: of eighty ships sunk on the mid-ocean route in the last six months of 1942, sixty were escorted by the RCN or the USN.[109]

The Canadian government and its navy could no longer ignore the situation, especially as Britain took the trouble to point it out to them officially. On 17 December 1942, Clement Attlee, secretary of state for dominion affairs, cabled King formally requesting that some RCN groups be removed from mid-ocean escort until they were up to snuff:

> A careful analysis of attacks on our trans-Atlantic convoys has clearly shown that in those cases where heavy losses have occurred lack of training of the escorts both individually and as a team has been largely responsible for these disasters ... [T]he expansion of the RCN has created a training problem which must take time to solve.[110]

The Admiralty told Churchill the RCN had bad leadership, bad training, and a 'bungled expansion.' It recommended putting the RCN groups on the Britain-to-Gibraltar convoy route for several months. The Gibraltar route offered continuous air cover, better weather, and excellent training and repair facilities in British ports, all of which, it was hoped, would allow the Canadians opportunities to improve their efficiency.[111]

In Ottawa, Macdonald seemed not to know the reasons for the British request. CNS Nelles and several of his staff cited delays in getting modern equipment and a persistent shortage of destroyers for the poor Canadian showing.[112] The CNS told Macdonald in a memo that there simply were not enough escorts; he also hinted that Gibraltar was a tougher and therefore more prestigious route, given the threat of German air power there. Ironically, NSHQ had finally taken the matter of destroyers to the political level and got Ottawa to formally request fourteen destroyers from the RN on 5 December 1942. The War Committee allowed Macdonald to bargain with Britain, offering the Tribal destroyers under construction in Canada for escort destroyers now.[113] On 21 January 1943 Britain offered the RCN six destroyers.

Of the CNS's response to Attlee's message, David Zimmerman writes: 'If Nelles were not guilty of deceit then he was incompetent and ill-informed on the serious state of affairs within the navy: either way the results were the same.'[114] Marc Milner concedes that Nelles was 'less than honest' and agrees that he ought to have been fired. Yet Milner also sees the incident as evidence of Macdonald's incompetence: 'He, too, perhaps even more than Nelles, had power well beyond his ability to wield it.'[115] Macdonald had authorized the navy's long-term construction program while at the same time accepting a burdensome level of escort duty. He did not recognize how badly behind their British counterparts Canadian escort groups were and, lacking independent, informed advice, Macdonald accepted the vice admiral's excuses without further questions.[116]

The Naval Board endorsed the Admiralty's recommendation to the War Committee, with the proviso that the groups be returned to the MOEF no later than May 1943. The groups were rotated to the Gibraltar route, and the RN saw that they received new equipment in Londonderry and intense training in Scotland. In the meantime, the Battle of the Atlantic moved into the endgame. By March 1943, Germany had sixty U-boats operating in the mid-Atlantic air gap; it had deciphered Admiralty codes and knew with great accuracy when and where convoys were crossing, and it had re-encrypted its own codes, leaving the Allies 'deaf' for the first three weeks of March. During this period wolf packs intercepted every transatlantic convoy and sunk a fifth of all ships in the convoys. The green light for the return of the RCN groups to the North Atlantic came in late February, and the groups began returning by the end of March.[117]

In the last week of March, the Admiralty cracked the German codes and dispatched an impressive concentration of naval and air power against the wolf packs. The RN operated five 'support groups,' designed not for convoy escort but for hunting and destroying submarines. The Allies also introduced forty-one very long range (VLR) aircraft. In the first five months of 1943, Allied forces destroyed fifty-two U-boats in the MOEF zone, and on 24 May the Germans withdrew their U-boats from the major shipping lanes. The climax of the Battle of the Atlantic had passed without significant participation from a key player: the RCN.[118]

Canadians did not know the dimensions of the Battle of the Atlantic and certainly were unaware of the absence of RCN escort groups during the crucial months of February, March, and April. Milner, however, argues that they restlessly awaited some evidence of their forces in combat, somewhere in the world. The most obvious and tangible evidence the RCN could hope to offer was, of course, U-boat kills. After a respectable showing in the last six months of 1942 – claiming four of nine U-boats destroyed in the North Atlantic – the RCN could boast only a share of a kill when Churchill announced victory in the Battle of the Atlantic in June.[119] The prime minister sensed that Canada's efforts were not being rewarded with headlines, though he blamed Churchill and Roosevelt for this, rather than the Canadian forces.[120]

Unable to point to evidence of the lethal capabilities of the RCN escort groups, Macdonald again had to defend its performance in home waters. In March 1943, Members of Quebec's National Assembly charged that Ottawa was neglecting the defence of their province.[121] J.S. Roy echoed these charges in the Commons, saying that thirty-seven ships had been sunk in the St Lawrence by U-boats in 1942; J.-F. Pouliot supported Roy, and called the minister of naval affairs 'incompetent.' Macdonald responded in carefully measured tones. He noted that only twenty ships had gone down in the St Lawrence River and Gulf; he argued that it would be impossible to prevent all attacks in the area, and he pointed out that at the farthest point up-river where U-boats had attacked, the St Lawrence was thirty miles wide, giving the enemy ample water in which to hide.[122] Just before the shipping season was due to open in 1943, the Naval Board chose to keep the river closed to all ocean-going traffic, focusing its resources on the Atlantic.[123]

The RCN's efficiency began improving significantly by the middle of 1943. On 30 April, Britain and the United States officially recognized the Northwest Atlantic as an area of Canadian command.[124] Exceptional intelligence, extended air cover, and the presence of support groups lightened the burden on the convoy escorts greatly. Furthermore, the RCN had a new, clear focus on its anti-submarine role and had formed its own support group in June.[125] All of this, however, came after the peak of the Battle of the Atlantic, and concerns lingered about the state of Canadian warships.

A series of observers with a range of expertise voiced concerns about the RCN's maintenance and equipment predicaments. In May 1943, the Allied Anti-Submarine Survey Board reviewed the RCN and its facilities and strongly urged that convoy escorts be given priority in shipyards. Later that month the captain in charge of destroyers for Newfoundland, J.M. Rowland (RN), and the flag officer for Newfoundland, Commodore H.E. Reid (RCN), submitted a report showing that Canadian corvettes were far behind those of the RN and petitioned NSHQ to give first priority to escort ships to be fitted with modern asdic and radar. In June the commanding officer of HMCS *Restigouche*, Lieutenant Commander D.W. Piers, informed his superiors that morale in the RCN groups of the MOEF was low. These observations were made within proper channels of command and were dealt with, ponderously, by the Naval Staff. RCN officers and ratings at sea could detect little action to rectify the problems and morale declined steadily. Only when official channels were circumvented did the minister of naval affairs take direct action.[126]

The assistant director of naval intelligence, Captain W.I. Strange, crossed the Atlantic in July 1943 aboard the HMS *Duncan* and learned from British officers of the woeful state of Canadian warships. Hearing similar opinions among RN and RCN officers in Londonderry convinced Strange that proper channels were ineffective. He decided to submit a report directly to the minister; on his return trip aboard HMCS *Assiniboine*, he spoke with Captain K.F. Adams, who concurred with the RN's criticisms and helped Strange prepare his memo. Adams also wrote one of his own and submitted it through channels on 9 August 1943.[127]

By the time Macdonald received Strange's memo from John Connolly on 20 August, Liberal political fortunes had ebbed.[128] Milner argues that the RCN's poor showing in the Atlantic contributed to the government's unpopularity, but most contemporaries pointed to the wage ceilings and the apparent lack of post-war planning.[129] Macdonald shot off a quick letter to Nelles, asking for an appreciation of the RCN's equipment vis-à-vis the RN's and instructing Nelles to spare no effort in his investigation. Macdonald cited Adams's report, but kept Strange's memo secret from his chief of staff.[130] Nelles replied with a discussion of RN and RCN equipment policies, but made no attempt to address Macdonald's explicit request. He later admitted that NSHQ did not have information about the equipment possessed by each RCN ship. Milner writes:

> [This was] not only an indictment of the Naval Staff but also an inadequate excuse in light of the minister's specific instructions that no effort be spared to obtain detailed information from operational authorities. Macdonald suspected a cover-up and was thereafter suspicious of anything Nelles said on the matter.[131]

Macdonald felt he needed reliable, independent information and sent his executive assistant overseas in search of answers.

Connolly flew to Newfoundland on 6 October 1943 and proceeded across the Atlantic on the corvette HMS *Nasturtium* for an eleven-day visit. He visited Londonderry before moving on to London, where those who had gripes about the Naval Staff in Ottawa welcomed him warmly. He heard ample testimony from RN and RCN officers that Canadian ships were not getting U-boat kills because they lacked modern equipment for anti-submarine warfare. He also heard that a combination of inexperience and red tape meant that refits which could be done in three weeks in Londonderry took six months in Halifax. Many officers pleaded for the RCN to cease its construction programs and to concentrate on modernizing its operational ships.[132]

On 15 November Connolly told the Naval Board that he heard similar arguments and evidence from all he talked to, adding weight to the points of Strange's memo. He noted that while all of the RN's Flower-class corvettes had been modernized, only 15 to 20 per cent of the RCN's had. Connolly recommended expansion of the technical liaison, both with the Admiralty in London and the shipyards in Londonderry. He also relayed requests for better communication between NSHQ and the Senior Canadian Naval Officer, London, and for more rapid handling of signals at NSHQ. Finally, he recommended that NSHQ secure a high priority from the Admiralty for RCN ships to receive the latest equipment. The chief of naval engineering and construction, Rear Admiral G.L. Stephens, pointed out that many of these changes were in hand, but the report did spark some action, especially in the liaison area.[133]

Connolly's investigation strained relationships within the Department of Naval Affairs.[134] Macdonald pressed Nelles for clearer answers. By this time, Connolly had turned up some of the memos from the spring that had been critical of NSHQ and left unanswered for most of the year. Macdonald accused the Naval Staff of lacking 'energy and capacity' and said that Nelles's 1 September memo was off-topic. If NSHQ had made him aware of the equipment problem earlier, he could have brought political pressure to bear in an attempt to solve it. As it stood, Macdonald wrote, the RCN had a great quantity of ships, but none of great quality. 'The price of this was the fact that of the last one hundred and fifty subs destroyed not one has definitely been destroyed by a Canadian ship of War.' If he had been unable to secure political action, Macdonald said that he would have been prepared to withdraw RCN ships from the North Atlantic.[135]

Nelles responded by sending Macdonald two memos and Naval Staff reports demonstrating what had been done since June 1943 to solve equipment problems. Nelles wrote that the minister's lack of awareness 'baffled' him, that the shortage of up-to-date equipment had been 'the state of affairs practically from the time you took office.' He claimed that he had been careful to keep Macdonald informed about equipment and especially about the uncooperativeness of the RN. Nelles denied that the RCN's construction program had any impact on modernization efforts and went on to say that Macdonald oversimplified the situation, as the tally of 150 U-boats included all theatres; the RCN's zone claimed just eighteen kills. Finally, Nelles scoffed that Macdonald's political pressure could have helped with procurement, though he noted that Connolly's visit to Londonderry had accelerated Canadian refits there.[136]

In reply, Macdonald dissected Nelles's case as if it were an opponent's legal brief. He acknowledged that he had been aware of expansion problems. 'I was prepared to accept from time to time conditions which would find us, as to some of our ships and equipment, slightly below the British standard.' He did not know the extent or persistence of this lag in modernization, and the Naval Staff did not spell it out for him. Nelles's job was to give him the best advice. 'This ought to be particularly true when the matters are technical and therefore of a nature with which a Minister is not ordinarily familiar.' He then got to the heart of the matter:

> The great questions are 'were our ships putting to sea inadequately equipped as compared to British ships, and were they doing so over an unduly long period of time?'
>
> The answer to both questions, in my considered judgment, must be a definite and unequivocal 'Yes.' Your memoranda and the supporting documents do not disprove these facts. Therefore, I must ask you to indicate who is to blame for these conditions.

Macdonald insisted that political approaches could have succeeded, if he had been advised to try them and he pointed to the results of Connolly's trip as evidence.[137] In January 1944 Macdonald named Vice-Admiral G.C. Jones Chief of the Naval Staff and sent Nelles to London as Senior Canadian Flag Officer, Overseas.[138]

Historians differ in their analysis of Macdonald's handling of the equipment crisis. C.P. Stacey, who dealt with Nelles's ouster as if it were a routine personnel change rather than a demotion, implies that the naval minister reacted appropriately. David Zimmerman presents Macdonald's actions as decisive and effective in the face of obfuscation from Nelles. Others find less to admire in Macdonald's actions. Tony

Macdonald Family, ca. 1909. In the back row are John Colin, killed in France in 1918, and Joseph, who found work in Detroit before the Depression. In the second to back row are Veronica, daughter of Stanislaus Perry, the leading Acadian politician from Prince Edward Island in the late nineteenth century, and Lewis Macdonald, then stipendiary magistrate of Port Hood. In the next row are John Lewis, William, who became a Supreme Court Justice in Alberta, and Angus Lewis. In the front row are Oswin 'Sweeney,' who had an undistinguished career in law, Mairi, who became Sister St Veronica and earned an MA in history, Donald 'Dan Lewis,' who ran for the Conservatives in the 1949 federal election, and Margaret, who died in the 1919 influenza pandemic. Absent is Stanley, then studying to become a priest. (Courtesy Macdonald Family)

St Francis Xavier University's graduating class of 1914. Macdonald, in the cen-tre, excelled at university socially and academically and was elected class pres-ident. He returned to Antigonish in the fall of 1914 to teach at the St FX Academy and pay off his debts to the university. He remained there running the university's officer training program until the spring of 1916 when he went overseas with the 185th Battalion, the Cape Breton Highlanders. (Courtesy St Francis Xavier Archives)

James Lorimer Ilsley (1894–1967). Macdonald shared a close friendship with Ilsley dating back at least to the latter's election to Parliament in 1926. They were never rivals, as each had his own sphere of activity at least until the Second World War. By 1942 Ilsley's star shone brighter, but Macdonald appears no longer to have aspired to a federal career. Their friendship survived the strain of the postwar tax rental negotiations, and they saw each other frequently after Ilsley became a Supreme Court Justice of Nova Scotia in 1949. (Library and Archives Canada C-029366)

Do you remember the iniquitous Franchise Scandal? Not many forget it.

On the eve of the 1937 provincial election, the Conservative *Halifax Herald* lured cartoonist Robert Chambers away from its Liberal rival, the *Chronicle*. The *Chronicle* hired Ted Sellen to replace Chambers, but found it useful to re-run his cartoons from the 1933 election, usually on the front page. This one, attacking Tory registrars for participating in the franchise affair, originally ran

Sellen was more of a caricaturist than Chambers, often using oversized heads and careful renditions of Macdonald paired with attractive women, as in this suggestive cartoon that appeared in the *Halifax Chronicle* on 29 May 1937. After the Liberals' victory, the struggling *Chronicle* had to let Sellen go. (*Halifax Chronicle*)

The first meeting of the Royal Commission on Dominion-Provincial Relations, Ottawa, 18 September 1937. Left to right: University of British Columbia's Dr H.F. Angus; Supreme Court of Canada Justice the Hon. Thibaudeau Rinfret, who soon resigned for health reasons, to be replaced by Laval University law professor Joseph Sirois; Ontario Supreme Court Justice the Hon. Newton W. Rowell, who also resigned for health reasons upon the completion of public hearings; *Winnipeg Free Press* editor John W. Dafoe, who directed much of the writing of the final report, and Dalhousie University's Dr R.A. MacKay. (Library and Archives Canada C-010403)

Agnes Macdonald, Angus Macdonald, Queen Elizabeth, and W.L. Mackenzie King in Halifax, 15 June 1939. Mackenzie King hoped that playing escort during the royal visit would boost his political fortunes in the anticipated federal election. Macdonald managed to impress the queen with his gracious hosting and no doubt benefited from the national media exposure. (Library and Archives Canada PA-800468)

Nazi victories in Western Europe forced King to bolster his cabinet in mid-1940. Macdonald, far right, agreed to become Minister of National Defence for Naval Affairs and abruptly left Halifax to perform 'war work' in Ottawa, arriving 12 July 1940. He was greeted at the train station by, left to right, Cabinet Secretary A.D.P. Heeney; Deputy Naval Minister Col. K.S. Maclachlan; Rear-Admiral Percy W. Nelles, Chief of the Naval Staff; Air Minister C.G. Power; and Minister of National Defence Col. J.L. Ralston. (Library and Archives Canada PA-134339)

In this wartime publicity photo, Agnes Macdonald plays the dutiful wife sending her husband off to his important job. Away from the camera, she was a published poet and intellectual. Angus appears uncomfortable, and indeed his failure to court Ottawa's press gallery contributed to the disappointment of his federal career. (Courtesy St Francis Xavier Archives)

Macdonald meeting with Sir Winston Churchill in London. To his left are Vice-Admiral Percy W. Nelles, Chief of the Naval Staff, and Captain F.L. Houghton, Senior Canadian Flag Officer Overseas. Macdonald never absorbed the technical aspects of the Royal Canadian Navy's dramatic expansion but when, in late 1943, he learned that severe equipment shortages placed Canadian sailors at greater risk and weakened their morale, he dismissed Nelles from his post. (Library and Archives Canada PA-134341)

The War Committee of Cabinet, 1943. Back row, left to right: Louis St Laurent, C.D. Howe, J.E. Michaud, and Angus L. Macdonald. Front row: J.L. Ilsley, J.L. Ralston, W.L. Mackenzie King, T.A. Crerar, and C.G. Power. King's government had barely survived the 1942 debate as to how to proceed should conscription for overseas service become necessary. Ralston had submitted his resignation, and several observers expected fellow Nova Scotians Macdonald and Ilsley to follow him out. Ralston relented, and cabinet trudged on until the next conscription crisis in 1944. Macdonald, Ilsley, Crerar, and Howe forced the government to impose conscription, but not before Ralston was summarily dismissed. (Library and Archives Canada C-026922)

Col. J.L. Ralston, Minister of National Defence, addresses members of the Princess Patricia's Canadian Light Infantry, Italy, 3 October 1944, on the eve of the conscription crisis. Ralston, a battalion commander in the First World War, put aside political caution when a shortage of trained infantry developed late in the war. He insisted that conscripted troops be sent overseas as reinforcements, sparking the cabinet crisis that led to his dismissal. (Library and Archives Canada PA-163657)

"Out Of The Frying-Pan Into The Fire"?

Robert Chambers captured the unease of many with Ottawa's postwar 'Green Book' proposals in this cartoon that appeared in the *Herald* on 18 October 1945. Certainly Angus Macdonald, recently re-elected as premier, believed that the new plan diverged sharply and dangerously from the Rowell-Sirois proposals. (Robert Chambers Collection, Acadia University Archives)

Candidates for the 1948 Liberal Leadership in Ottawa, 5–7 August 1948. Left to right: Jimmy Gardiner, C.G. Power, and Louis St Laurent. Macdonald considered entering the race but judged from the start of the convention that St Laurent could not be defeated. New Brunswick Premier J.B. McNair wanted Macdonald to stand as a protest candidate, drawing attention to the grievances of the Maritime Provinces. Macdonald refused, partly to maintain party harmony and partly to preserve his chances in the next leadership race. (Library and Archives Canada C-023549)

Princess Elizabeth chats with Angus Macdonald in 'Winwick,' his home in Halifax. Elizabeth and her new husband Philip were completing the Royal Visit of 1951, and Winwick was the only private home they visited on their trip to Canada. (Courtesy St Francis Xavier Archives)

The Macdonald family gathered for a publicity photo on the eve of the 1953 election. Back row, left to right: Coline Foley, Angus Lewis, Jr, and Aileen Veronica. Front row, Angus, Oonagh, and Agnes. Macdonald's political career demanded long hours and limited his time with family. Agnes believed that his exhausting schedule convinced his children to stay out of politics. (Courtesy Macdonald Family)

German writes that a 'devious' Macdonald cared only about controlling political damage. Richard Mayne calls Nelles's demotion a 'political execution.' Marc Milner characterizes Macdonald's charges as 'preposterous' and 'absurd,' and of his dismissal of Nelles, Milner says: 'There was nothing grand in Macdonald's subsequent action. Clearly the failure of the RCN to help deliver the government from crisis put him under pressure in cabinet and he had to find a scapegoat.'[139]

Milner is correct to focus on Macdonald the politician, as he certainly lacked naval expertise. Yet politics guided Macdonald's actions in the crisis only so far. As a former junior officer and advocate for veterans' rights, Macdonald cared very much about the well-being of those in the services. The disparities in equipment bothered him for two reasons: RCN sailors were not as safe as their RN counterparts if their ships were substandard, and their morale clearly suffered from their added risk and their backseat role in hunting U-boats. Furthermore, Milner, Mayne, and German overstate the 'political crisis' caused by the small number of U-boat kills attributable to the RCN. While the government may have wished for a higher tally about which to boast, there is no evidence that the press or public asked why Canadians were not sinking more U-boats. On the contrary, the government appeared delighted that the U-boat threat had largely been dealt with by the summer of 1943. For his part, the prime minister seemed quite unaware of the reasons for Nelles's transfer and assumed the navy was increasing its representation in Britain simply to match that of the army and air force in anticipation of the invasion of Europe.[140] Meanwhile, the press attributed the absence of reported RCN kills to the standard secrecy of 'the silent service.'

Macdonald could have been more involved in the routine discussions of the Naval Board, but in this he deferred to his expert advisers. In cabinet debates on the post-war navy, Macdonald fought doggedly for the interests of the navy, increasing his isolation from the prime minister. There is every reason to believe that he would have fought very hard to secure essential equipment had he understood the situation. Nelles's gravest error was his failure to make the equipment situation perfectly clear to Macdonald and to advise his political master to pressure the British government. In any event, Nelles did not fall very far; upon his retirement in January 1945, he was promoted to the rank of full admiral.

In August 1943, four separate by-elections were held in formerly Liberal ridings; in each, voters rejected the government candidate.

Throughout the country, the CCF seemed to be riding a wave of working-class discontent to popularity, if not to power. In the Ontario election of early August, the CCF became the Official Opposition to George Drew's Conservatives; an opinion poll in September placed the CCF narrowly ahead of the two old parties in public support.[141] Popular sentiment was to prove stronger than the Great Depression: it forced the Mackenzie King government to develop a social welfare system.

Unlike some members of cabinet Macdonald did not see the mid-war popularity of the left as cause for panic, though he did favour 'more social legislation – health insurance and things of this kind.' Again he solicited J.W. Dafoe's opinions on the subject; Dafoe cautiously advocated reform. 'I am hoping that the govt. will not try to compete with the C.C.F. in promising utopias – they haven't a chance along that line. This is not to say that there is not plenty of room for radical action in the field of social betterment. Family allowances would make a good start.' Dafoe wanted the Liberals to prepare a platform of social legislation 'which will make the socialist program appear the shoddy impractical thing it is.'[142] These two liberals anticipated the adoption of at least some of the Rowell-Sirois recommendations after the war.

On the subject of social welfare, Mackenzie King drifted with the winds of public opinion, only to convince himself later that his course had been as straight and narrow as the path to heaven. He had opposed opening Ottawa's purse strings in the name of social justice during the Depression and maintained his tight fist for much of the war. He addressed the Liberal caucus in March 1943: 'Speaking of social security, I said I would never allow an appeal to the people on social security measures at a time of war with a view to bribing them to support the govt. because of what it would pay out of the public treasury.'[143] After the omens of the late summer, however, King changed his tune. J.W. Pickersgill told Dexter:

He is nearing 70 and with him it is make or break now – in the next election. He is not going to officiate at the internment of liberalism ... If the reactionaries don't like it, they can get out and join the Brackenites. We are going to the left and with a vengeance. By the way King talks he cannot abide any substantial political party more radical than himself. He is the grandson of the little rebel and so on.[144]

Having decided on a shift to the left – albeit a conservative shift – King now had to lead his cabinet there.

Few of King's ministers seem to have been ideologically committed to creating a social welfare system, though many saw political potential in doing so. Ian Mackenzie strongly advocated such a system; it had been his Committee on Reconstruction and Rehabilitation that produced the Marsh report of March 1943, which proposed a comprehensive system of social welfare based on full employment, a minimum income, and children's allowances.[145] Grant Dexter interpreted Mackenzie's zeal for social justice as a means of atonement for his 1939 failure as minister of defence. 'The government as a whole isn't too enthusiastic on social security and certainly there ain't going to be any this session. Ian, however, has always been smarting over his demotion in favour of Norman Rogers and he has wanted to make a really big splash in his new portfolio.'[146]

The rest of cabinet reacted coolly to the Marsh report, though Mitchell, minister of labour, appeared to favour it for fear of being beaten by the CCF. Ilsley objected to the potential costs – estimated at $900 million per year – and Howe and Crerar expressed disdain. In June 1943, the prime minister dismissed the idea that people would be won over by social legislation; in the post-war period, he argued, the federal government would have to focus on the veterans, not old age pensioners. As late as a caucus meeting in September, King said that social security measures would have to wait until peace arrived.[147] In November Dexter judged the cabinet to be exhausted with war work and unable to focus on new ideas.[148] By the end of 1943, however, King had been convinced of the necessity of social welfare.[149]

The government now began to discuss post-war social policy in earnest. A Ministry of Reconstruction under C.D. Howe was suggested, even though Howe gave only qualified support to the government's proposals. In early December King gave a radio address in which he went 'a long way in stating govt. policy without further consultation with the Cabinet.' He spoke in favour of a floor for farm prices, a national minimum standard of living, a basic wage increase for labour, and compulsory collective bargaining. 'I think I have cut out the ground in large part from under the C.C.F. and the Tories alike and certainly have given the Liberal party a place of new beginning.' On 11 January 1944, the cabinet voted to create the Departments of Reconstruction, Health and Welfare, and Veterans Affairs; it then turned to writing the Throne Speech for the next session of Parliament.[150]

At this point, Macdonald raised some practical questions about the government's plans. In a memo he agreed that the Department of

Reconstruction would 'catch the popular fancy,' but saw several problems with it. He argued the government already had the organization in place to deal with post-war problems, save perhaps the housing shortage, and he cautioned that the proposed department would necessarily interfere in the work of other ministries. Finally, he warned that the department would contribute to a centralization of power, both within the federation and within the federal government. As an alternative, Macdonald suggested creating a National Development Commission and appointing a minister without portfolio to coordinate federal and provincial reconstruction programs. This minister could focus on research and planning and leave the implementation and supervision of projects to the appropriate departments. He identified the three 'great problems' of reconstruction as being health, housing, and education.[151]

A few days later, Macdonald wrote personally to King expressing his concerns that the social welfare scheme had not been fully thought out. Clifford Clark, deputy minister of finance, had told cabinet that family allowances would cost Ottawa between $175 and $200 million and that the post-war budget would be in the area of $1.75 billion. Macdonald supported the idea of family allowances, but urged that cabinet consider 'the whole social program' before moving ahead. He warned that Canada would probably have to maintain a much larger post-war defence establishment that it had in 1939 and he expected a drop in government revenue from the 1943 level. Ottawa might not be able to manage a budget that included these factors while spending $150 million on health insurance, $200 million on family allowances, $400 million on debt payments, plus expenditures for housing, veteran's pensions, and so on.[152]

In his diary, meanwhile, King had managed to square social welfare with his liberal philosophy:

> Where the State, through organization of industry, etc. being what it is, gives great opportunities to a few, and robs the many of many opportunities, it should become the duty of the State to work out some scheme of social justice which will see that opportunities are widened for the many and that at least for all there should be a minimum standard of life.[153]

Macdonald would have agreed with King on the importance of equality of opportunity, but he feared that Ottawa could neither afford the proposed social welfare system nor administer it without significant and dangerous expansion of the federal government's powers and its bureaucracy.

Macdonald was speaking in Winnipeg when cabinet debated the Throne Speech on 24 January, but Ilsley, Howe, Crerar, and Gardiner criticized the 'leftist' nature of the address, as written by King and his staff. They urged that some encouragement to business be added for balance. King agreed to drop a direct promise of health insurance. Nevertheless the speech pointed to a new social welfare state in Canada. The government promised to implement family allowances and to hold discussions with the provinces to secure health insurance and a more generous contributory pension scheme.[154]

By this point, Mackenzie King had convinced himself that the proposals for social welfare legislation came directly from the pages of his 1919 book, *Industry and Humanity*, and represented the logical culmination of his career as a humanist and friend of labour. King had considerable powers of self-persuasion, but those who knew him best recognized political opportunism when they saw it. C.G. Power, after reviewing Bruce Hutchison's manuscript for *Incredible Canadian*, dismissed the notion of a straight line from *Industry and Humanity* to family allowances:

> With regard to the planning of a sort of foreordained career apart from the fact that it was recognized that Mr. King always had the ambition to be Prime Minister and a determination to maintain himself in that high position, few of us ever dreamt that he had set his mind on achieving the social reforms which were brought about in his day. They appeared, I think, to be more a product of opportunity and political expediency than the fulfillment of any fixed ideal.[155]

King's faith in his 'mission' made him especially sensitive to criticism on the subject of social welfare. Those who opposed it, he came to believe, were conspirators who would stop at nothing to oust him and defeat his dream of social justice.

The House saw the bill for family allowances in June 1944. Cabinet debated some of the finer points of the bill, which King interpreted as an attack on his program. He wrote in his diary that Ilsley, Howe, and Macdonald now were opposing legislation to which cabinet had already agreed. In fact, Ilsley and Macdonald objected to paying a 'double allowance' to children of service personnel 'war pensioners,' who already received a dependents' allowance. St Laurent sided with them on this point. Nevertheless, King felt personally attacked and openly complained that he was the only radical in a cabinet of reactionaries.[156]

On 15 June 1944 T.C. Douglas led the CCF to its first win in a general election in Canada by taking forty-seven of fifty-two seats in the Saskatchewan election. Significantly, the CCF won more than two-thirds of the overseas soldiers' vote. Jimmy Gardiner, former premier of Saskatchewan and witness to the election, attributed the CCF's victory to a skilful campaign of sabotage against the Liberals and general public unrest with wage and price controls and the rationing of goods. Yet some of the cabinet, including the prime minister, panicked and suggested announcing new tax cuts in the budget speech. Ilsley said that if the cabinet voted to do this, he would resign; Ralston, St Laurent, and Macdonald supported him. No decision was made, but Macdonald saw this as a bad omen:

> It looks to me as if this Government would be badly defeated when it appeals to the country. It has been weak at all points where pressure has been exerted – on conscription, on labour matters, on financial concessions to this or that group ... This Government seems to have lost any appeal it ever had. The P.M. is responsible for this, more than any other member of it. He is naturally a compromiser.

Macdonald believed King personified the antithesis of leadership, and yet 'some members refer to him as our greatest asset.'[157] He worried that Canada would come to socialism in a haphazard, piecemeal fashion, led by a party pandering to voters' feelings of entitlement.

Though he never said so explicitly, King probably considered Macdonald one of the 'reactionaries' in cabinet by mid-1944. On labour questions – always near to the prime minister's heart – King's judgment of Macdonald fluctuated wildly for a time. In some of the Prime Minister's diary entries, Macdonald and King were completely in concert, especially when it came to supporting collective bargaining. King even went so far as to ask Macdonald to become minister of labour in September 1943.[158] A few months later, however, King portrayed Macdonald as anti-labour.[159]

The prime minister also feared that Macdonald's plans for a post-war navy would threaten spending on social programs. From the beginning of the RCN's expansion, the Naval Staff planned for a balanced post-war Canadian navy that could operate independently or, more likely, as a fleet arm of the Royal Navy. Such a navy would require larger ships at its core than the corvettes so essential to escort work. Macdonald favoured an independent Canadian naval service and brought his plans for a 'big ship' navy to cabinet. Mackenzie King's nephew, Captain Horatio Nelson Lay, aided the cause. In the spring of 1943 Lay broached the subject of aircraft carriers for convoy duty; he suggested to King that one or two carriers would provide invaluable air support for RCN convoys in the North Atlantic. A few weeks later, when Macdonald raised the subject of carriers in the War Committee, King endorsed the idea.[160] Though King's position did not rest solely on his nephew's advice, the prime minister undoubtedly found that advice more acceptable coming from a family member than from an admiral or naval minister.

At the first Quebec Conference the Naval Staff and the Admiralty arranged that Churchill and Admiral Sir Dudley Pound would ask the Canadian War Committee to operate some large ships for the RN. Pound said that Britain would appreciate Canada's manning one or two cruisers and two fleet destroyers, along with some auxiliary craft. Macdonald immediately said that the RCN could take on the cruisers and destroyers. A week later, the committee approved the scheme. The naval minister was elated: 'This step is very significant. The R.C.N. is stepping out of the small ship class – the Laurier plan is being realized after more than 30 years.'[161] Macdonald saw a direct link between his wartime work and Sir Wilfrid Laurier's scheme of an independent Canadian navy.

King soon began to smell an imperial rat in the RCN's expansion, however. Earl Alexander of Hillsborough, First Lord of the Admiralty, sent a message to Vincent Massey, Canada's High Commissioner to Britain, expressing His Majesty's Government's delight at seeing Canada uphold the Commonwealth naval tradition by getting into a 'big ship' navy. King flew into a rage when he read this, calling it 'old imperial stuff – a unified navy.' Macdonald interjected that he believed that 'Britain had not tried to direct us but was willing to let us run our own naval show. Alexander's words were intended to be complimentary.'[162] At that moment Macdonald was shifting Nelles to London, leading King to conclude that the RCN planned to transform itself into a fleet arm of the RN. As the German threat appeared to wane, King's habitual isolationism began to return.[163]

Canadian nationalism influenced both Macdonald and King on naval matters, but in very different ways. Macdonald believed that Canada should play a role commensurate with its post-colonial status as a wealthy, industrialized nation. In his mind, that meant a significant contribution against all Axis powers and a fleet strong enough to defend Canada in the post-war period. King, by contrast, feared any post-war commitments, especially ones that could be interpreted as maintaining imperial ties. A small or non-existent navy could not bind Canada to any actions in the future.

By the time of the Second Quebec Conference in the late summer of 1944, most politicians and military leaders were expecting a swift end to the European war and now focused on the war in the Pacific. King wanted to limit the Canadian contribution to the war against Japan as much as was politically possible. Major-General Maurice Pope, his personal military adviser, reported that the Americans did not ask for and did not seem to want Canadian participation at all. King grasped this intelligence as a reason to limit the Canadian role: 'I feel we must seek now to save both life and money.'[164]

On 6 September 1944, cabinet discussed Canada's contribution to the Pacific war. Every minister favoured Canadian participation. Macdonald argued that Canada had declared war on Japan independently in 1941 and now had to finish the job. As for the size of Canada's contribution, ministers had a variety of opinions, some advocating a large land force, while others felt that only the RCAF and RCN should go. Macdonald said the Naval Staff had prepared three or four plans: the smallest force would be 19,000 men; the next 25,000, and so on. Whether this force made its way towards the theatre of war through the Aleutian Islands or through the Indian Ocean had not been decided.

King said dispatches from England that spoke of 'Imperial armies and Imperial forces' disturbed him. Canada must not lose its identity in its war effort. 'He felt that our forces should not fight below the Equator. The climate in those areas was very unsuitable for our men ... We were a North American power.' He demanded that Canada 'have a national force and not be swallowed up in an Imperial Army. Otherwise we would lose the support of Quebec and the West.' Later he said, 'Our contribution in the Pacific should be as small as we could decently make it.' Macdonald found it 'fantastic' to imagine that a line of latitude should limit naval and air operations in wartime and he argued that Canadians would have to fight under either the Americans or the British. A smaller Canadian force would more apt to be 'swallowed up.' He proposed a naval force of 20,000 for the Pacific, though he added that 3000 of those would be in minesweeping and could possibly be dropped. 'Mr. King, with some heat, said that the figures were too high, and that he resented figures being presented which violated the understanding' reached earlier in cabinet.[165]

As the dispute dragged on, King grew absolutely livid that Macdonald would not accept what he believed had been an agreement of cabinet. Macdonald stubbornly, almost petulantly, held his ground. He refused to let political considerations determine strategy in the Pacific. The War Committee settled the matter on 11 October, voting to stay out of Southeast Asia and to commit a force of about 13,500 to the Northern Pacific.[166] John Connolly wrote in his diary that this represented 'a high water mark for ALM. He kept the navy on the map.'[167] That Macdonald's executive assistant hailed the decision as a great victory suggests that the minister had requested considerably higher numbers than he really hoped to secure. Yet the debate was just one more in a growing list of confrontations between Macdonald and King.

The conscription crisis that very nearly toppled the Mackenzie King government and divided the country in the autumn months of 1944 has been well documented and is one of the more familiar episodes in the story of the Canadian involvement in the Second World War.[168] From mid-October to early December, the government of Canada seemed to be in a constant state of crisis, threatening self-immolation at any moment. In the end, King's government endured, lost only two ministers, imposed a limited form of conscription, survived a parliamentary vote of confidence, and – after the end of hostilities in Europe – won the next federal election.

Many observers at the time, both inside and outside the cabinet, felt that the survival of the government could turn on Macdonald's decision whether or not to resign in support of his colleague and friend J.L. Ralston. While Macdonald is typically painted as an ardent supporter of conscription who was outmanoeuvred by King, his decision to remain in the government and his efforts to achieve a viable solution to the conscription crisis contributed substantially to the survival of the government and the preservation of unity in Canada, badly strained though it might be. For a brief period, Macdonald held the power to bring down King and his government; King knew it and resented him all the more.

The essence of the conscription crisis in 1944 concerned the shortage of infantry reinforcements for the five Canadian divisions and two armoured brigades fighting in Europe. Though Lieutenant-General Kenneth Stuart, Chief of Staff at Canadian Military Headquarters (CMHQ), London, assured the War Committee of cabinet on 3 August 1944 that there were 'plenty of reserves,' a shortage of infantry reinforcements was already developing.[169] British analysts had predicted that infantry would account for 48 per cent of the total casualties in the campaign to liberate France; in fact, they accounted for 75 per cent. Stacey points out that a deficiency in reinforcements had been perceived early in 1944, and that the General Staff had made some attempt to remuster troops from other arms to infantry service, a process that took some months' retraining.[170] There the matter lay until August and the height of the Canadian campaign in north-west Europe.

The day after Stuart assured the War Committee that there were enough reinforcements for the duration of the war, the commander of the First Canadian Army, General H.D.G. Crerar, cabled him with contradictory information. Crerar's telegram of 4 August read, in part:

> Am concerned about the infantry general duty deficiencies which approximate 1900. Our ability to continue severe fighting or to exploit a break out would be seriously restricted through lack of replacement personnel ... I consider this the most serious problem of Cdn Army at the moment and to require most energetic handling.

Crerar sent another cable on 8 August urging that 'vigorous remustering and strenuous conversion training' be initiated to solve the developing reinforcement problem.[171] In August 1944, however, Germany seemed on the verge of collapse, and it appeared that the war in Europe would end before the new year. Stuart, therefore, saw no reason to alarm the government.

Rumours that there was a crisis in reinforcements became public on 19 September 1944. The *Montreal Gazette* printed Major Conn Smythe's charges that men who were poorly trained and, in some instances, only partly recovered from wounds were being sent into battle, endangering the lives of all Canadian troops at the front. George Drew, now premier of Ontario, took up Smythe's accusations and again raised the clarion call for conscription.[172] Ralston left at once for Europe to assess the situation first-hand.

The minister of national defence returned on 18 October and went immediately to see the prime minister. Ralston told King that Allied command now expected the war in Europe to last into 1945, possibly into the spring, and that casualties among the infantry were far higher than had been anticipated. The pool of troops used to replenish frontline units was dangerously low and would be exhausted by the end of the year. To meet this shortage, the army required 16,000 trained infantry. Ralston felt that only by extending the terms of service of the NRMA troops to include duty overseas could the reinforcement situation be met. He presented his report on the reinforcement situation to the War Committee the next day. The debate began slowly, and members of the committee asked probing questions about Ralston's report. No one, save the prime minister, rushed to take a position for or against conscription at this point. Each may have sensed some truth in King's hyperbole that this was 'the most serious [question] that had come before the Cabinet since Confederation.'[173]

Over the next few days, King presented a lengthy and at times ludicrous list of arguments against imposing conscription for overseas service. He said that Parliament would have to be recalled for what would be a drawn-out and bitter debate, followed 'almost certainly' by an election. He would have to consult Churchill and Roosevelt. Civil war might break out in Canada. To use compulsion at this point would sap any Canadian will for participating in an international organization after the war; if Canada stayed out, so would all the smaller nations of the world. Thus, conscription in Canada would threaten the newly formed United Nations and world peace.

King grasped frantically at possible solutions that might stave off conscription. He suggested reducing the size of Canadian units and limiting the amount of fighting done by Canadian troops. Military advisers warned that reducing the size of Canadian units – probably by limiting the number of infantry companies per battalion – would increase the risks to soldiers in battle. To shorten the Canadian front line would have required approval and coordination from Canada's allies at the highest military, if not political, levels. King suggested giving NRMA soldiers 'gratuity privileges' from the moment they 'went active,' a financial incentive for them to volunteer for duty overseas. 'He would go himself to these men and urge them to volunteer.' He continually pointed to evidence that Germany would soon collapse and said that the war might be over before the matter could be settled in Canada.[174]

The crisis threatened the very existence of the government. King worried 'that Ralston himself may again take it into his mind to tender his resignation because of what he feels the reinforcement situation demands, and that Angus Macdonald may decide to leave the Government to go to Nova Scotia, Ilsley taking the view that he must stand by Ralston and Macdonald.'[175] All were from Nova Scotia, and King recognized that if two Nova Scotians left the cabinet, it might be politically impossible for Ilsley to remain. The loss of three key ministers could lead to the downfall of a government. Indeed, many members of the cabinet, including King, believed that Macdonald's resignation would precipitate Ilsley's and possibly others as well. Thus, J.E. Rea notes in his analysis of the situation, 'in the end, it seems Angus L. was the critical factor.'[176]

Macdonald sought a satisfactory solution, but he also stood ready to defend Ralston. Realizing that Ralston would grow only more entrenched in his position in the face of opposition as he had in 1942, Chubby Power urged King to get Macdonald and Ilsley to meet with Ralston to convince him not to resign. King wrote:

> I told him I would be prepared to talk to Ralston, Ilsley and Macdonald in the morning, but I felt both Ilsley and Macdonald had a dislike for me; that I had opposed increases to the Navy and use of our navy in the southern seas and Macdonald resented that. To this Power said, Macdonald may have felt a little hurt about that, but he was a politician and a Liberal. He would not wish to see the party destroyed.

King and Macdonald met the next day to discuss the crisis, and King testified to Macdonald's conciliatory attitude in his diary: 'Angus said he saw the difficulties. Was very much concerned about everything himself, but Ralston was hard to deal with.' Macdonald agreed that everything should be done to avoid conscription, but added that if it were the only means of providing reinforcements, it would have to be used. King recognized that Macdonald wanted to help. 'He impressed me as realizing more than heretofore the seriousness of the situation. I think he still holds to the desirability of attempting conscription.' Although Macdonald would not surrender his principles, he made every effort to avoid the very crisis King feared.[177]

Cabinet assigned Macdonald and Power to meet with Ralston and his advisers to go over the army's figures to see if the reinforcements could not be found without resorting to the NRMA. Power questioned the strict physical and mental standards required of infantry soldiers in this war. He found it incredible that while there were 120,000 general service – that is, volunteer – personnel in Canada and another 90,000 in Britain, a seemingly insignificant 16,000 soldiers fit for infantry service could not be found without resorting to conscripts. 'I began to suspect that in the minds of these generals the infantry man of today must almost be an honours college graduate.'[178] As well, the minimum age for infantry was set at nineteen years, although Power and others in the War Committee recommended lowering it to eighteen-and-a-half. Nonetheless, neither he nor Macdonald contradicted the General Staff's essential version of the situation. Their verification of the army's numbers convinced Crerar of Ralston's case for conscription.[179]

From this point on, the crisis played out in front of the full cabinet, where King thought the position of the conscriptionist ministers was not so strong. King calculated that in the War Committee he could count on only St Laurent, J.E. Michaud, now minister of transport, and possibly Howe. Ralston, Macdonald, and Ilsley would have the support of Crerar. He suspected that Power would vote with his fellow defence ministers, though in fact Power had decided to support King and to oppose conscription, even if it meant losing Ralston and Macdonald. Power was hospitalized with appendicitis at the end of October, and remained in Quebec City until mid-November. King believed the vote against conscription in cabinet would be about thirteen to eight.[180]

The change of venue from war cabinet to the full cabinet table failed to bring about a solution, but the two sides did come closer to a compromise after some tense moments. Ralston said he thought he would have to resign, and Macdonald and Ilsley said they would have to consider their positions. King asked them if they wished to try to form a government; all declined. Macdonald then indicated that he could accept King's proposal of one last appeal to the NRMA men to go active and have the appeal on King's terms. This meant that no decision would be made about conscription until the end of the appeal. Ralston, however, insisted on a commitment to conscription should the appeal fail.[181]

On 1 November, Ralston and Macdonald spoke by telephone with Major-General G.R. Pearkes, General Officer Commanding, Pacific Command. Pearkes oversaw most of the camps with NRMA personnel, and the two defence ministers hoped to get a clear picture of the potential success of another appeal to these troops. Pearkes advised Macdonald that it would take a few weeks to make the appeal, and then another week or two for the soldiers to make up their minds. He said that it would be possible to gauge the success or failure of the appeal by 30 November and advised against saying that conscription would be applied if the appeal failed, as most of the NRMA personnel would simply wait for the government to order them overseas.[182] Before the two ministers went in to that afternoon's cabinet meeting, Macdonald apparently had convinced Ralston to accept King's proposal of an appeal without a guarantee that conscription would be imposed should it fail.[183] In spite of Ralston's new willingness to compromise, however, this would be his last cabinet meeting.

King had been anticipating Ralston's resignation since the defence minister's return from Europe and considering a suitable replacement. He settled on Lieutenant-General Andrew McNaughton, who had been removed from the command of the First Canadian Army in 1943 at the urging of the Imperial General Staff, which felt he was not fit to command in the field. Despite McNaughton's and Ralston's bitter confrontation over the incident, McNaughton had returned to Canada without the public becoming aware of the reasons for his dismissal. Thus, his reputation as Canada's leading soldier was still intact when King approached him on 31 October to see if he would agree to replace Ralston and make an effort to secure the necessary reinforcements through the voluntary system. McNaughton said that he would come into the government and he expressed great faith in the voluntary system, believing that his personal reputation would go a long way to convincing NRMA soldiers to go active.[184]

King later claimed that he had thought of getting McNaughton to replace Ralston only on the morning of 1 November, the day Ralston was dismissed. In fact, he had been considering the general as defence minister since March 1942 and almost constantly during the latest crisis.[185] On 20 October King let St Laurent know of his plan and implied that the threat of McNaughton would compel Ralston and Stuart to be more compliant. Howe and Ian MacKenzie also had suggested that King inquire of McNaughton if he would be willing to replace Ralston.[186] If King did intend to use McNaughton to keep Ralston and his senior military advisers in line, it would make sense that the prime minister let slip his intentions so that Ralston would know of the threat. At least two observers outside the government either heard of or guessed King's plans. On the evening of 31 October, journalists Grant Dexter and Bruce Hutchison told Macdonald that they thought that King would bring in McNaughton to replace Ralston, but would introduce conscription before he allowed Ilsley, Macdonald, and possibly other ministers to leave the government. Thus, Macdonald knew of the possibility that McNaughton would replace Ralston, and this may have helped him to convince Ralston to be more conciliatory at the cabinet meeting on 1 November.[187]

Macdonald's efforts and Ralston's readiness to accept King's compromise were not enough, however, to prevent the prime minister from dismissing his minister of national defence. King now believed there was a conspiracy among the ministers urging conscription to oust him.[188] He saw conscription as a red herring; the conscriptionist ministers really wanted to get rid of him to scuttle his social security program. There is, however, no evidence to support the notion of a conspiracy beyond King's own assertions that the reinforcement crisis had been concocted to destroy him. King's suspicions prevented him from appreciating the efforts of Macdonald and others to build a consensus within cabinet.

In cabinet on 1 November, King observed that Macdonald made efforts to reach a compromise, noting that he 'was as conciliatory as possible and put forward, while Ralston was out of the room, what he thought Ralston was prepared to consider in further ways.' Macdonald said that cabinet must now decide whether to choose a path before or after the appeal to the NRMA men. He favoured waiting, as the question would be academic should the appeal succeed.This seemed an entirely reasonable position and could have kept the government together. King, however, looked for his opening and patiently waited for Ralston to say, as he had said before, that he would have to resign if his recommendation were not accepted; he waited for him to argue that the government must commit itself to conscription before launching an appeal to the NRMA troops. Ralston did neither, and King grew more suspicious. He feared that Ralston's amenable attitude was part of 'a scheme to make the situation still more difficult for me.' In fact, Ralston appeared to be following Macdonald's advice and trying to resolve the crisis.[189]

King could not wait for Ralston to resign. He informed cabinet that he felt an appeal to the NRMA soldiers to volunteer for overseas service could succeed only if organized by someone who believed it would succeed. Ralston had said that such an appeal would fail, and this would impinge on its effectiveness, King explained. He then announced that he had to accept Ralston's resignation, which had been submitted two years previously during the debate over Bill 80. General McNaughton would take over; King knew he would have the confidence of all Canadians and that by his reputation alone he would help to make the appeal successful. King summarily dismissed Ralston in front of his colleagues, and McNaughton became defence minister the next day. Macdonald told Grant Dexter that he thought of walking out with Ralston, but that Ernest Bertrand, minister of fisheries, restrained him. 'Angus said that if he had risen, he would have struck King. So he sat still, tearing his note paper into small pieces and dropping them on the floor.'[190]

Most observers have found it necessary to explain why, when King 'accepted' Ralston's resignation, no other member of the cabinet resigned in support of the defence minister. This question is especially intriguing when asked of Angus L. Macdonald. Macdonald would seem to be the cabinet minister with the least to lose. An 'outsider,' he had been appointed for service during the war and had already made up his mind to leave Ottawa.[191] Furthermore, Macdonald could be reasonably sure of regaining the premiership of Nova Scotia and therefore did not depend on Mackenzie King for his political future, unlike almost every other member of the cabinet. Macdonald had identified himself with conscription as early as December 1941, and King fully expected him to resign in favour of this policy. Other observers at the time saw Macdonald as one of the leading conscriptionists in the government, though he had always qualified his pro-conscription statements by saying 'when necessary conscription should be applied.'[192] Yet he did not resign either to force the issue or to support Ralston's position. Why did he remain in a government moving in a direction of which he did not approve?

The most common answer has been that Macdonald and the rest of the cabinet were stunned into passivity by King's swift move to fire Ralston. R. MacGregor Dawson, for example, argues that King's action was the best way out of a very perilous situation for the government. 'The move, as it was actually carried out, caught everyone by surprise and made instantaneous concerted action almost impossible, and once that dangerous corner had been turned the situation became relatively safe.'[193] In one of his early treatments of the event, J.L. Granatstein writes that Ralston's 'fellow conscriptionists were stunned into silence as King announced that McNaughton would put his enormous prestige into an all-out effort to persuade NRMA soldiers to volunteer for overseas duty. It appeared that King had carried the trick.'[194] C.P. Stacey, the official historian of the Canadian army, also takes this position: 'The Prime Minister's tactical plan had been a complete success. The conscriptionists, totally taken by surprise, were in no position to act together.'[195]

This assessment certainly has some merit; Crerar's, Ilsley's, and Macdonald's accounts of the 1 November cabinet meeting all describe their being surprised at King's move.[196] Surprise, however, wears off. Moreover, most of the cabinet members must have been expecting Ralston to resign at some point in the crisis and would have considered their positions accordingly. Though they may not have anticipated King's abrupt dismissal of Ralston, his actual departure could be foreseen. What kept the conscriptionist ministers from taking action shortly after the cabinet meeting, or even mentioning in cabinet that they might have to reconsider carefully their positions in the government, as Macdonald had said only the previous day? Macdonald and Ilsley later speculated why King had chosen to dismiss Ralston in front of the cabinet. While they agreed that it might have been intended to scare other ministers into line, Macdonald suspected that it also offered the convenience of keeping the issue covered by the code of cabinet secrecy.[197]

It is possible that the ministers felt obliged to give McNaughton a chance to meet the situation without resorting to conscription. Macdonald himself noted in a letter to A.S. MacMillan that he felt McNaughton ought to be allowed an opportunity to make the volunteer system work: if successful, he should be supported; if unsuccessful, the cabinet would then have to make up its mind as to the best course of action.[198] Still, McNaughton was not sworn in until the afternoon of 2 November, allowing Macdonald a small window of time to resign without appearing as if he had not given the general a chance. Furthermore, by acknowledging that McNaughton deserved an opportunity, Macdonald implicitly repudiated Ralston's position on the reinforcement situation.

In an interesting and persuasive shift away from traditional accounts of the conscription crisis, Rea argues that Ralston's colleagues who supported conscription did not walk out with him because they questioned his earlier judgment and possibly his assessment of the situation. In particular, some felt that Ralston had been badly advised by his army officers, who needed to be reined in. T.A. Crerar, for one, did not trust Ralston's department and had opposed almost every expansion in army numbers requested by the General Staff. He later told Macdonald that he thought Ralston's dismissal would be a good lesson for the General Staff. Certainly King attributed the situation directly to mismanagement on the army's part, and there is much evidence to support this view.[199]

The General Staff had perceived a shortage of infantry as early as January 1944, and yet it failed to implement an aggressive remustering program, even as other branches of the armed forces were discharging excess personnel. Had a more farsighted campaign of retraining soldiers for infantry been pursued throughout the summer of 1944, it surely would have eased the reinforcement crisis that arose in the autumn, though it may not have circumvented it completely.[200]

More significantly, army headquarters in Ottawa did not pass on to Ralston the August telegrams sent by General Crerar warning of an impending shortage of trained infantry reinforcements. Later, Stuart himself cabled Ottawa from London warning, in much less alarmist language, about a shortage of properly trained infantry replacements. Ralston ignored Stuart's message and he did not see Crerar's telegrams until 24 October.[201] Though the delivery of these telegrams might not have prevented the resulting crisis, Stuart's poor judgment seemed evident. In a War Committee meeting early in the crisis, King laid the blame squarely at Stuart's feet:

> I asked Stuart about his statement, his assurance two months ago as to there being plenty of reinforcements, and also about the additional brigade in Italy not making any additional drain on manpower. He gave some sort of an explanation about the latter that it simply meant changing over certain units; did not touch on the question of extra men involved. As to the former, he said he had made a mistake. Later I said to him that having given us the wrong information and having made a mistake, I hoped he would, as I knew he would, do all he could to help the govt. out of the present situation.[202]

Observers outside the government also criticized the General Staff. Victor Sifton, master-general of the ordnance from 1940 to 1942 and publisher of the *Winnipeg Free Press*, wrote Ralston on 1 March 1944 that

> a good many of your difficulties have arisen because a small group of G[eneral] S[taff] officers were determined to keep things in their own hands and in consequence recommended appointments of men who either were sympathetic to them or who they felt sure they could dominate. This has now produced the inevitable result, a lack of capacity in key positions.[203]

In a conversation inviting McNaughton to become minister of national defence, King asked if he would have any problem working with anyone in Defence; McNaughton said he 'disagrees cordially with Ralston on some of the things he has done and he says he does not trust Stuart's judgment at all.' When he moved into the department, McNaughton immediately got rid of Stuart.[204] Macdonald, too, had expressed his mistrust of the General Staff the previous year. He told Dexter that he thought the generals manipulated Ralston to secure more troops. 'Angus not nearly as keen on conscription as a year ago,' Dexter wrote to his editor in September 1943. 'Is now inclined to think that, on balance, King may have been right.'[205]

The behaviour of certain army commanders later in the crisis must have added to the scepticism about who was running the department. On 20 November, for example, General Pearkes allowed some of his officers to express their views freely about the NRMA situation to reporters. This was strictly against the King's regulations, and the prime minister interpreted it as an effort to embarrass his government into making a decision.[206] At all turns, King found the army less than cooperative.

King's military adviser, Lieutenant-General Pope, recommended easing the reinforcement problem by taking certain steps within the army itself. Specifically, he suggested trimming infantry battalions from four rifle companies to three, an organization that British and German forces used throughout the war. This would have reduced the reinforcements required, perhaps delaying the impending shortage by as much as a month. Pope also suggested lowering the physical and mental standards for infantry service. Each of these suggestions was rejected by army commanders, as being 'objectionable ... from a military point of view.'[207] King believed that the Army wanted to find a way to get the NRMA troops into action, as it resented the fact that these men would not volunteer.

One should hesitate to blame the General Staff for the entire conscription crisis. As Stuart pointed out in his 19 October report, in early August most of the Allied commanders felt that the war would be over by December 1944. German success at denying the Channel ports to the Allies, however, meant that the war would probably last well into 1945. Also, the Canadian army had been calculating its reinforcement requirements based on the British figures, which underestimated the rate of infantry casualties by almost half.[208] It is unreasonable to suggest that the Canadian commanders ought to have been any more prescient than their Allied counterparts.

Ralston stood by his advisers and had been intractable during the first few days of the crisis. King found his insistence on achieving his goals almost intolerable and noted on 21 October, 'I feel more and more, as McNaughton does, about Ralston; that there is something inhumanly determined about getting his own way, regardless of what the effects may be on all others.'[209] Both Howe and Crerar were 'impatient' with Ralston's demand for a large Canadian army and had been since 1941. A 'Big Army' competed with industry for male workers, and Howe had felt that his war production program was at least as important a contribution to the Allied war effort as Canada could make on the battlefield; Crerar also took this view.[210] In the crisis of late 1944, however, Crerar and Howe became convinced that the reinforcement situation demanded the introduction of conscription for overseas service.[211]

Throughout the crisis, Macdonald tried to achieve a resolution without abandoning his position that the troops had to be supported. When King first mentioned another appeal to the NRMA men, Macdonald voiced support. On the day of Ralston's dismissal Macdonald worked to prevent a major break, and while King seemed to notice this, his animosity prevented him from trusting his minister of naval affairs. The night of Ralston's dismissal, King wrote: 'Angus Macdonald has given the impression of trying to go very far to help all he can and has done well but I realize that behind it there has always been the laying of the ground for his leaving the govt. on the score of conscription along with Ralston and embarrassing the govt. as a consequence – not in desire but in effect.'[212]

After King fired Ralston, Macdonald sought advice as to what path he should follow. He spoke with the 'Old Sage,' Alex Johnston, and Ilsley. Johnston said this move was typical of King, who had no personal loyalty. Ilsley said he would not resign at present, and later he and Macdonald helped Ralston write a new letter of resignation. Macdonald put the matter clearly: 'Have we departed from the policy which we laid down in 1942 during the plebiscite campaign and the debate on Bill 80?' Macdonald sensed that they had, but as the cabinet had not come to a final decision, the issue was murky.[213]

The next day John Connolly laid out Macdonald's options. The reasons against his resigning included (1) if only Macdonald and Ralston left, their resignations would have no effect; (2) King's appointment of McNaughton was shrewd, as no one could say that this was a step down in capability; (3) the Liberal party would be hurt by further resignations; (4) the government's and McNaughton's prestige would be compromised and this might damage the war effort and especially the appeal for NRMA volunteers, which still might succeed; (5) party loyalists would accuse Macdonald of making Ralston's mistake, that is, accepting the army's appraisal of the situation; (6) Quebec would say that Macdonald wanted to 'foment racial disunity'; and (7) no one outside the inner circle would know the motives for Macdonald's actions, as King would use the tool of cabinet secrecy to conceal what had happened. Connolly, however, noted that '[t]he issue is important enough for you to [resign],' though the best time for that would have been before McNaughton's appointment, as a move at this point would hurt McNaughton's prestige. 'You cannot delay going out on this issue, if you are to go.' He also argued that if Macdonald were staying, he ought to make a statement that he thought the use of the NRMA men had become necessary but found McNaughton's views reassuring enough to warrant his remaining in cabinet. Connolly recognized that Macdonald held perhaps the most objective view of the entire situation. 'I sometimes think that if Colonel Ralston had been a bit more amenable to your way of thinking, the crisis would not have happened.'[214]

Macdonald contacted Kingston Senator Rupert Davies and Professor J.A. Corry of Queen's University, as well as Premier MacMillan and Frank Davis, Nova Scotia's minister of public health, to canvass their views. Senator Davies had often advised against conscription and, after McNaughton lost a February 1945 federal by-election, Davies wrote to Macdonald: 'Of course, if Ralston had come back with some kind of reasonable proposition, we would not have been in this kind of mess.'[215] During the crisis, Corry responded to Macdonald's request for advice and warned against taking the General Staff's position too closely: 'I find it hard to believe that the national honour is seriously involved by a possible reduction of one infantry division in the front line.'[216]

Macdonald wrote MacMillan of Ralston's dismissal and his thoughts afterward. 'I then had to consider what I should do. Should I go out or stay in? On this point let me say that from the time of the plebiscite in 1942 onwards, I had always understood that the Government, if the need for conscription arose, would apply conscription, would then go to Parliament and announce its decision, and ask for a vote of confidence.' He said that when McNaughton came in, he felt he should be given a chance to try the voluntary system, and if successful, he should be supported. MacMillan responded: 'If it is possible for you to remain for the present, it would be in your own interests to do so.'[217]

Macdonald wrote Frank Davis that he might soon be returning to Nova Scotian politics: 'For a time last week I felt my return might be hastened. In fact, that it might be almost immediately.' Did the Nova Scotia Liberal Association want him to have his old job back? Davis warned that further resignations could bring down the government, leaving the people who resigned to take the blame. In addition, Davis did not know if MacMillan would retire just yet. He advised Macdonald to stay put, if possible.[218]

Most of the advice Macdonald received in the period following Ralston's dismissal urged him to stay on. Fully disillusioned with Mackenzie King, Macdonald decided to remain only if the government would demonstrate aggressive action on the reinforcement situation. On 3 November, McNaughton told cabinet of his plan for the appeal to NRMA men, and the ministers struck a committee to oversee activity. Macdonald asked McNaughton his opinion of the reinforcement situation, and McNaughton said it was much the same as Ralston had reported. Macdonald asked if conscription had been ruled out, and McNaughton said that it had not been.[219]

Macdonald tried to fly to Nova Scotia after this meeting, but made it only as far as Montreal. There he spoke with veteran Liberal organizer Kirk Cameron, the promising MP from Westmount, Douglas Abbott, and even King's former minister of finance, Charles Dunning. Cameron and Abbott warned that if Macdonald and Ilsley resigned, King would have to call an election. Macdonald did not think so, but took their advice to heart. He felt at liberty to disclose to Dunning, a Privy Councillor, the week's events in cabinet. Dunning commiserated with him about the arduous task of working with King. Macdonald, who rarely recorded his own opinions in his diary, let Dunning speak for him:

> In his experience as Minister, he said that in the end King would usually agree with Dunning's views, but Dunning would have to make such a long and bitter fight to have his views prevail, that he would be worn out. He does not think King has a single friend in the world ... referred to the P.M. as a dirty little rat.[220]

Macdonald continued subtly to prod the cabinet on the matter of policy; he wrote King on 13 November, pressing for a definition of the word 'necessary.' Macdonald said he hoped to determine if the government had changed the policy it had adopted during the 1942 debate on Bill 80. King obfuscated in his reply, referring Macdonald to *Hansard* for his 10 June 1942 speech and adding that he did not wish to discuss the matter further while it was before cabinet.[221]

The government continued to dawdle on the appeal to the NRMA to go active. McNaughton gave a poorly received speech at Arnprior, Ontario, on 5 November, and King spoke over the radio on 8 November. King noted this in his diary: 'But what I fear is that now that both McN[aughton] and I have spoken, little else will be done. I don't know what further progress there has been in carrying out what the Committee recommended as to individual appeals. No one person seems to have that in hand. General McNaughton cannot be expected to follow it up.'[222] The prime minister did not divulge who, exactly, ought to be working to ensure the success of the appeal to the NRMA soldiers.

McNaughton's and King's efforts had little or no effect. A mid-November opinion poll showed no change in public attitudes on conscription since 1943 – 57 per cent of Canadians polled were in favour of conscription for overseas service, 36 per cent were opposed, and 7 per cent were undecided – and the number of NRMA soldiers volunteering to 'go active' did not increase appreciably.[223] Macdonald concluded that the appeal would fail and he lashed out at the French Canadian cabinet ministers for their lack of leadership and at King for his mendacity. 'A year after coming up here,' Macdonald told John Connolly, 'I realized, I could not stay. It is impossible to work under this man ... he is just not honest. I think I should have gone last week, but perhaps there will be a better opportunity later.'[224]

The naval minister considered his options, among them the forming of an independent Liberal party. Macdonald and Crerar discussed organizing the conscriptionist members of the government and some Liberal backbenchers into an effective group. On 10 November Macdonald wrote: 'Suppose some of us had to go out, can we stop there – merely get out of politics. C. doesn't think we can. Talks of a[n] independent Liberal party. Ralston leader. Dafoe told him a year ago that I should be next leader. C. thinks such a party would hold balance of power. C. seems to think perhaps of a Coalition with *Tories*.'[225] It appears that Ilsley did not play a large role in these discussions; although he supported conscription, he did not relish the thought of leaving the government.

On 18 November, Macdonald spelled out his and Crerar's plans to Ralston:

> Crerar thinks, however, that it is vital that by Wednesday [22 November] those who are going to break should do so, and provide a rallying ground for Liberal Members who will be dissatisfied with Government policy, assuming that that policy will be
> (a) one of no conscription; or
> (b) one of further delay.
> I agree that the sheep must have a shepherd ... There is no doubt in our minds that you would be the man whom the public would look to to head the group.[226]

While Ralston may have been too rigid within the cabinet to earn the support of his fellow ministers earlier in the crisis, his popularity among Canadians in favour of conscription had been strengthened. As the first minister to leave during this crisis, he would provide a natural rallying point for a conscriptionist government.

The conscriptionist wing in cabinet got a boost when McNaughton brought in his reinforcement figures on 20 November 1944. McNaughton predicted that there would be a reinforcement surplus of approximately 700 at the end of December, but that a deficit would soon develop. He expected this shortage to reach more than 2000 by the end of January and 9500 by the end of May. Except for Ralston's prediction of a deficit by the end of the year, the two defence ministers' numbers were very similar, especially for the four- and five-month projected shortages. Macdonald noted that these figures made much more of an impact on the ministers than did Ralston's, however, because they had been expecting better news. At this point, Crerar, Ilsley, and Macdonald again spoke of resigning if conscription were not imposed. They even mentioned a deadline for the appeal to the NRMA personnel: 1 December 1944. Howe argued that the government had to decide which path it would choose before it faced Parliament in a few days.[227]

On 21 November, King told cabinet that if the appeal failed, he would step down and let someone else lead the government when it imposed conscription; he would not. Macdonald argued that most of the cabinet and much of caucus would go with King, making the position of those who remained impossible. Though he had been considering an independent Liberal party to administer conscription for overseas service, Macdonald thought it would be difficult to draw MPs to the vestiges of the King government; better to allow King's failure to deal with the reinforcement situation to be aired in front of Parliament, which was to meet the next day. This would make it easier for the conscriptionists to pull together dissatisfied MPs and form a government. As an alternative to King's proposal, Macdonald suggested that he, Crerar, Ilsley, and the other pro-conscription ministers resign, leaving cabinet united in support of the voluntary system. Macdonald argued that King would be able to replace the departed ministers and carry on governing.[228] He wanted King to shoulder his share of the blame for any defeat the government might suffer.

Little happened at the meeting of caucus the next day, and both sides anticipated a break at that evening's cabinet meeting. In between caucus and cabinet, Macdonald gathered with the other conscriptionist ministers – Crerar, Ilsley, William Mulock, Colin Gibson, and, for the first time, Howe – in Crerar's office. They were all prepared to resign but they had heard that King intended to set a time limit on the appeal, and some of the group wanted to establish the date. Crerar suggested 30 November, and Ilsley, 2 December. Macdonald felt that the appeal had already failed and that a future deadline would be pointless, though he conceded that a deadline would help the Quebec ministers if conscription had to be implemented. Nevertheless, Macdonald implied in his diary that at 8:00 p.m. the six ministers went to cabinet intending to resign as a bloc.[229]

King did not know of the conscriptionist ministers' intentions but announced that, on McNaughton's advice, he proposed sending NRMA soldiers overseas. Each of the District Officers Commanding had signed a memo for McNaughton to the effect that the voluntary system had failed, and McNaughton warned King that they might resign, leaving the domestic army in a state of chaos. More likely, this move merely would have embarrassed the government. To convince St Laurent of the need to accept conscription, however, King privately hinted to him that a 'revolt of the generals' was imminent. King's message to St Laurent was kept secret for some years. When Power heard of it, he wrote to Macdonald: 'It would have been great fun, had your loyal and intrepid Navy turned its guns on Laurier House from its armoured rowboats in Dow's Lake.'[230]

Cabinet quickly agreed to McNaughton's recommendation for conscription. Power announced that he would have to resign, and for a time it appeared that Gardiner and Alphonse Fournier, minister of public works, might go as well, but they eventually stayed with the government. Needless to say, Macdonald and the other conscriptionists chose to remain. An order-in-council was signed on 27 November sending not more than 16,000 NRMA troops overseas. On 7 December the King government safely won a vote of confidence in the House of Commons.[231]

The image of Macdonald as one of the most ardent conscriptionists in King's cabinet during the Second World War obscures much of his role during the crisis in 1944. If one sees him only as a strong conscriptionist, his behaviour on 1 November and shortly thereafter appears timid and vacillating; if one views him as one of cabinet's leading mediators, however, his behaviour is more easily explained and appears more effective. Macdonald believed in conscription, but did not resign with Ralston because he recognized that his leaving would not solve the reinforcement crisis and might very well bring down the government. He disagreed with Ralston about the best path to follow to achieve a solution, urging him not to push for a commitment to conscription too early, but he also realized his own place in the scheme of things. King, St Laurent, Power, and cabinet secretary Arnold Heeney all recognized that Macdonald could be the linchpin holding cabinet together if Ralston left.

They all believed that if Macdonald joined Ralston, Ilsley would have to resign as well, possibly taking other ministers and causing the government's collapse.[232] It is not unreasonable to suggest that Macdonald had thought of this scenario. Thus, his conscious decision to remain in the cabinet when many of his principles seemed to demand his resignation can be seen as the defining factor in the successful resolution of the crisis.

The evidence of Macdonald's efforts to avoid a governmental collapse is apparent in several places. King's diary bears many references to Macdonald's helpfulness, at least until Ralston's dismissal; all references to Macdonald after this seemed tainted by King's suspicion that Macdonald was about to strike him down at any time.[233] Macdonald attempted to persuade Ralston to accept King's compromise – one final appeal to the NRMA men, after which a decision would be made concerning conscription – in the days before Ralston was dismissed. He wrote to his close friends and advisers that even after King's shoddy treatment of Ralston, he would give McNaughton a few weeks to prove his effectiveness.[234] Finally, when Macdonald felt that he must resign late in November, he attempted to establish a viable alternative party that could carry on running the country while imposing conscription to meet the reinforcement crisis.

Macdonald did not stay in the government after 1 November 1944 because he agreed with King that Ralston had to go; he believed simply that he must remain, for the sake of the infantry and the country, but also for the party and the government. To walk out would have created an irreparable split in the party – if Ilsley and others followed him – or allowed King to delay resolving the crisis, possibly to the point where soldiers' lives increasingly were jeopardized. Macdonald believed that the welfare of Canada's infantry could best be assured by sending NRMA troops overseas as reinforcements.

It seems that Macdonald also wanted to force King to make a decision, any decision. The prime minister's evasiveness and his determination never to be 'wrong' infuriated him. Power later wrote to Bruce Hutchison of King's fear of making an errant commitment. After a frustrating meeting of the War Committee, spent discussing the wording of a single telegram, Macdonald and Power used humour to soothe their aggravation:

Angus Macdonald who was with me said 'What's the use of getting mad, the urgent needs of my navy and your air will be looked after next week, but meanwhile we have been writing "the history of our times" and whatever may befall we will find that in this cable there are sufficient reservations for Mr. King's biographers to find that he was right.' We grew to look upon this writing of history with such ribald levity that I do not think I am much impressed with the idea of always appearing to have been right.[235]

King boasted of this very tendency in his diary: 'I think I have had some influence in persuading the group and my colleagues in Cabinet as well, to leave sufficient leeway to enable us to proceed by steps and degrees and to leave sufficient doorways open for necessary revisions as to save the situation.'[236]

Macdonald's last five months in Mackenzie King's government were a clear denouement, if not uneventful. The war in Europe entered its final stages, and the government concerned itself with routine administration, awaiting the end of the war so that it could safely hold an election on its post-war social program. Macdonald was something of a 'lame duck,' as the public knew of his looming retirement before the conscription crisis; yet as the only defence minister in the House of Commons he served a vital role for the final wartime session of Parliament.

Following the emergency session of November and December, Macdonald returned to Nova Scotia, where he scouted the political landscape and found it almost ready for his return. Stirling MacMillan was preparing to retire, though Macdonald's old college friend and cabinet colleague Lauchie Currie had some ambition to be premier.[237] In late January, Macdonald took his senior staff on a final tour of the United Kingdom, inspecting Canadian ships and establishments, bidding farewell to colleagues in the Royal Navy and exchanging jeremiads about King with Vincent Massey, Canada's High Commissioner in London.[238]

For his part, King consoled himself with thoughts of the political ruin of his new enemies and assertions that conscription had been unnecessary, the result of a vast conspiracy to ruin him. By early January 1945, he had convinced himself that there had been no crisis of reinforcements and that 'the whole business had been a mare's nest stirred up deliberately from political and personal motives.'[239] King had an interview with Grant Dexter and gave flight to his fancy that Macdonald was 'through.' King wrote that Dexter told him that Macdonald was being cut adrift by Nova Scotia's Liberals, but Dexter's account of the interview had King pronouncing the end of Macdonald's career. It seems probable that King's hatred of Macdonald and his awareness of a future audience for his diary led him to put his thoughts and desires into the mouths of Macdonald's friends.[240] He could forgive those ministers whose ambition made them dependent on his good will – Ilsley and Gardiner, for example – but those who sought nothing from him could not be controlled and were, therefore, beyond the pale. After some hesitation King honoured his long-standing promise to appoint Crerar to the Senate after the war.[241] Crerar remained vibrant in the upper house for almost three decades. Power remained on the periphery of the Liberal party, though he could rely on his personal popularity to get elected; he did not go to the Senate until 1954, on St Laurent's nod.

Ralston's replacement, General Andrew McNaughton, repeatedly demonstrated his political naivety. While Macdonald was in Britain, McNaughton told the press that the North Atlantic was still 'alive with U-boats' and that the Allies lost ships everyday. This overstated the threat and embarrassed both the Canadian and British navies. The First Lord of the Admiralty asked Macdonald why McNaughton would make such a statement when it was not his place to do so.[242] Macdonald felt obliged to contradict McNaughton in a press conference back in Canada on 13 February, much to the latter's chagrin. The general's political career suffered a mortal blow when he lost a by-election in Grey North on 5 February 1945, as voters expressed displeasure at King and his defence minister. After his defeat, McNaughton told cabinet that the campaign had turned ugly, with Orangemen taking shots at his wife's Catholicism. 'McNaughton said that no one had ever received such a tirade of abuse as he had,' Macdonald wrote. 'This was received with laughter by the others present who had experience in elections.'[243]

In April, King proclaimed dissolution and announced a general election for 11 June 1945. Although Macdonald had indicated that he very much wanted to be 'in at the end,' he accepted that he could not serve beyond the life of the current government and submitted his resignation, effective 18 April 1945.[244] King took a parting shot at Macdonald in his diary:

> I must say that I have been deeply disappointed with Macdonald. First of all, as a Liberal, because he has proved anything but such in his views, and secondly, to use an expression St. Laurent used this afternoon, of his intolerance. I thought he had a sunnier and more wholesome nature but I can see he is very vain, very selfish ... I will feel a great relief in having him out of the govt. altogether.[245]

Macdonald left the federal government 'unrewarded politically.'[246] He could be proud of his role in shepherding the RCN through a remarkable growth and making it a permanent navy capable of independent operation. He struggled against the weight of the Naval Staff to Canadianize the navy by commissioning an original, efficient set of guidelines and by fostering Canadian traditions within the service. Politically, however, his career in Ottawa had been disappointing: he did not become prime minister or even a likely successor to King. Yet Macdonald, as much as anyone, achieved his goals in the conscription crises, ensuring that a Liberal government survived and supported infantry soldiers in Europe. And while his running battles with King had drained and disillusioned him, he returned to Nova Scotia as something of a hero, all but unbeatable in provincial elections.

4 The Provinces' Champion

Angus Macdonald returned to his chair in the premier's office of Nova Scotia in the autumn of 1945, just after the abrupt end to the Pacific War. Macdonald's homecoming perhaps brought a sense of closure to the war effort for many Nova Scotians; they could pick up their lives where they had left off in 1939 now that 'Angus L.' had come back. Macdonald, too, took up a familiar task: working for a more equitable federation.

Canada felt the deserved pride of a victor, having mounted a significant and well-organized war effort. Many perceived an almost limitless potential at home and on the world stage. Yet this confidence masked fear of another depression, unemployment, and perhaps another war. VE day illustrated the complex range of Canadian emotions after the war; while most cities erupted in festive celebration on 8 May 1945, Halifax witnessed an ugly urban riot as some sailors, soldiers, and local citizenry needed little provocation to turn from parading to pillaging.[1] Few wanted to return to the way things had been before the war; most expected something better and looked to the state to guarantee a reward after fifteen years of hardship.

In the years after the war Angus Macdonald emerged as the leading figure in the area of provincial rights. Though he came from a poor, small province, he cast a national shadow thanks to the length of his career as premier, his federal war service, and his acknowledged understanding of constitutional issues. Garnering fewer headlines perhaps than Ontario's George Drew and Quebec's Maurice Duplessis – whose provinces' size and wealth ensured their status – Macdonald fell naturally into the role of representative of 'the lesser provinces.' He used this position to articulate an idea of a more clearly defined and balanced federalism shaped by the Rowell-Sirois proposals. Ironically, he briefly considered using the cachet of his 'provincial' persona to mount a campaign for the leadership of the federal Liberal party, before deciding that the timing and political forces were not right.

Macdonald resigned from Mackenzie King's government on 18 April 1945 and gradually wound up his life in Ottawa before taking a much-needed vacation. Almost immediately, some of Dalhousie's alumni recommended him for the university's presidency, made vacant by the board of governors' messy dismissal of Carleton Stanley.[2] Religion remained a dominant factor, however, and one board member privately wrote: 'Angus L. would undoubtedly make a good President for Dalhousie, but it is felt it would not do to have a Roman Catholic as President.'[3] Instead, the board safely hired Dr A.E. Kerr, principal of the United Church of Canada's Pine Hill Divinity College.

Many of Macdonald's friends thought he would go to the bench or the Senate, but King spitefully refused to consider any reward for his former cabinet colleague. King assumed for a time that Macdonald wanted a judge's robes after the war, but the latter made no request.[4] When John A. Macdonald, a Cape Breton senator, died on election night 1945, journalist Grant Dexter wondered, 'Will King now do the decent thing by Angus L.?'[5] Macdonald's preference, at least since October 1944, had been to return to his home province and his old job, and much groundwork for this had been done quietly in the interim. Yet King refused even to help clear the way for Macdonald's return to Nova Scotia; J.L. Ilsley recommended that A.S. MacMillan be appointed a senator, but King argued that MacMillan was too old.[6]

From the beautiful shores of the Bras d'Or Lakes, Macdonald spent much of the summer of 1945 awaiting the retirement of Stirling MacMillan. Between 1930 and 1933 MacMillan had served as House Leader for the Liberals in opposition; for the next seven years, he ruled the highways department as his own personal fiefdom, his pride occasionally hurt when praise was heaped on Macdonald. During the war, MacMillan finally could match his imperiousness to the title of premier. As the war ended, it seemed that so too would MacMillan's political career. He was seventy-three, not the ablest administrator, and surely tired after so many years of political battles.[7] But he was not yet properly honoured.

In February Macdonald suggested that MacMillan might retire at any time he wished; surely another minister could succeed him temporarily. MacMillan did not need to consider Macdonald's plans at all. MacMillan replied that he had not yet reached a decision on retiring, though he was planning on calling a convention to choose a leader. He added that, 'generally speaking,' the cabinet did not want him to go. Furthermore, the province and the party needed him: 'I am quite satisfied (although I may appear egotistical to you) that there is none of my colleagues who can carry on successfully.' Finally, in late June, Macdonald openly said that he would accept the premiership if MacMillan wished to retire and if the party would have him. Macdonald wanted the cabinet, the caucus, and the Nova Scotia Liberal Association (NSLA) to invite him to return, avoiding a convention; he said this would show that he was not taking his return for granted, but it also would be a wise move to assure unity behind his leadership. Macdonald wrote MacMillan that he would offer his name at a leadership convention only if unopposed.

> I would rather see somebody else selected ... than beg for support at a convention. I say this, not because I think myself so much better than anybody else, or because I think the world has to come to me with its gifts and favours, I say it simply because I was Leader of the Party for ten years and Premier of the Province for seven, and my work was, therefore, known to the Party.[8]

Macmillan remained mum about his plans for a few more weeks.

In early August King summoned the premiers to hear Ottawa's proposals for post-war reconstruction and federal–provincial relations. The 1945 gathering was more pleasant than the 1941 fiasco, partly because some of the more 'difficult' personalities were gone – Ontario's Mitchell Hepburn had been replaced by George Drew; Alberta's William Aberhart had been succeeded by Ernest Manning, and British Columbia's T. Dufferin Pattullo had given way to John Hart – and partly because the premiers met only to hear Ottawa's proposals, not to come to any decision.

In response to the failed dominion-provincial conference on Rowell-Sirois, Ilsley had announced in his April 1941 budget speech that Ottawa would raise income and corporate taxes sharply, effectively forcing the provinces from these fields. The federal government then negotiated 'tax rental' agreements with most of the provinces, whereby they surrendered the tax fields in question in exchange for payments that replaced the lost revenues. For its part, Ottawa was able to rationalize the taxation system and maximize its revenues. The tax rental scheme preserved the inequalities between provinces, however, as those who had large tax bases to give up got the most in rents. Nova

Scotia, which had no income tax and low corporate tax rates in 1939, got little from the federal treasury in its rental agreement. MacMillan was not pleased with the deal he signed in 1941, but felt obliged to support the war effort.[9]

In the summer of 1945, with Germany defeated and Japan collapsing, the federal government presented its plan for reconstruction to the provinces. Essentially, Ottawa proposed to centralize taxation and assume responsibility for some social welfare programs, but to leave constitutional questions aside. Keynesian monetary theories clearly influenced the federal plan, contained in 'The Green Book'; it promised to develop a depression-resistant economy through a centralized fiscal policy. Ottawa also proposed a substantial social welfare package, including universal Old Age Pensions and Health Insurance to go with the existing programs of Unemployment Insurance and Family Allowances. To entice the provinces to accept centralized economic planning, Ottawa offered relatively generous subsidies – Nova Scotia's subsidy would be $12 per person, adjusted with growth in the Gross National Product and provincial population – based on population and previous taxation capacity.[10] This scheme differed sharply from the Rowell-Sirois proposals:

> In the heady days of economic growth immediately following the war, the federal government chose to ignore, largely because of the opposition of the richer provinces, the recommendations of the Rowell-Sirois Commission for unconditional grants targeted to the poorer regions of the country. Instead, emphasis was placed on promoting aggregate economic growth and stability, and on creating the outlines of the modern welfare state.[11]

Most federal officials accepted the formula that growth of the national economy, combined with a social welfare net, would raise the standard of living in all provinces.

Ottawa's shift from Rowell-Sirois to the Green Book lay almost entirely with its senior civil servants and seems to have resulted from both fear and mental exhaustion. Queen's professor J.A. Corry conducted research for Rowell-Sirois and worked on the final draft of the commission's report; he returned to Ottawa in 1943–4 to advise on the shift to peace. Corry later wrote that those in Ottawa feared a post-war economic collapse without aggressive action:

> Almost all the attention during the discussions was focused on finding ways to extend the federal government's reach ... In the circumstances we

were then facing, the federal government, the one with the longest reach, was, of course, best equipped to take the lead in moving us from a war to a peace-time footing. But in later less critical circumstances, even strong nationalists are learning now that centralization of power and activity isn't automatically the best arrangement.[12]

Grant Dexter found a level of weariness in the planners at the end of the war. He spoke with most of the key figures in Ottawa in February 1945 as the Dominion's proposals were being prepared, including J.L. Ilsley, Alex 'Sandy' Skelton, and W.A. Mackintosh. Ilsley despaired of getting any agreement from the provinces, while Skelton trusted in the pragmatic needs and basic instincts of the premiers. 'The Dominion should buy out any or all provinces,' he told Dexter, 'and leave the offer lie. The weaker provinces would take it and the stronger would soon weary of their course.' Mackintosh warned against further centralization and believed that the Dominion's offer should emphasize 'not centralization but rationalization of taxation. Moreover rationalization would place the provinces in a sounder position.' Mackintosh, who was just leaving the Department of Finance to return to Queen's, told Dexter that he had been playing 'an intellectual form of volleyball – bouncing ideas off Mr. [C.D.] Howe's battleship steel headpiece. Some of 'em bounce pretty far ... He finds that Howe agrees but does not know what he is agreeing with.'[13]

Prime Minister King opened the conference on 6 August by echoing the conclusions of the Royal Commission on Dominion-Provincial Relations: '[W]e believe that the sure road of Dominion-Provincial cooperation lies in the achievement in their own spheres of genuine autonomy for the provinces. By genuine autonomy, I mean effective financial independence, not only for the wealthier provinces, but also for those less favourably situated.' Premiers Drew and Duplessis predictably responded with expressions of distaste for further centralization of revenues and responsibilities. Speaking for Nova Scotia, MacMillan criticized what he saw as Central Canadian hypocrisy; he said he welcomed the opposition of Drew and Duplessis to centralization and hoped that they would help in reversing the centralization of industry to Ontario and Quebec. This marked the limit of MacMillan's contribution to the talks. He explained with folksy humour that he did not have the time, and perhaps ability, to read and understand the Dominion's proposals.[14]

Once the conference had ended and the 'Captains and Kings' had departed, MacMillan sought out the oracle of Clemow Street, Alex

Johnston. MacMillan confided that he would resign, though he had told his cabinet nothing. He would call for a leadership convention and told Johnston that he expected no opposition to Macdonald. He also expressed the opinion that a general election should be held before the end of October. In the meantime, he had pressed Ilsley to get J. Willie Comeau appointed to the Senate, thereby quelling concerns that there could be four Catholics in the cabinet when Macdonald returned. Johnston then spoke with Lauchie Currie, Macdonald's former Dalhousie classmate, cabinet colleague, and long-time friend. Currie had once thought of challenging for the premier's chair, but his ambition waned by 1945 as he considered his future. Now, he told Johnston, he wanted only security if that were possible. A government sinecure for Currie would also improve the Catholic-Protestant ratio in the cabinet. Everything seemed prepared for Macdonald's return.[15]

MacMillan resigned on 22 August, and the NSLA announced a convention to select his replacement, slated for 31 August 1945. The Association arranged for Macdonald's coronation to resemble his initial victory in 1930: the convention returned to the Nova Scotia Hotel ballroom, and another Truro native, Major Hugh Dickson, nominated Macdonald. Senator William Duff, an ignominious loser of 1930, even got into the act by trying to stir up some opposition to Macdonald's acclamation, but to no avail. The crowd in 1945 was larger than in 1930, Macdonald noted in his diary, 'and the enthusiasm was all that could be desired. The occasion lacked the dramatic elements of 1930, of course.'[16]

Macdonald immediately began preparing an agenda for the coming provincial election. The evening of the convention, he called a caucus in the hotel, though at least two Liberal members had gone drinking and missed the meeting. The platform focused on the construction of highways, rural high schools, and technical schools, and included a significant improvement in teachers' salaries.[17] In line with Macdonald's pre-Keynesian liberalism, these programs involved government spending in the public sector to improve the province's physical and intellectual infrastructure, rather than making direct payments to its citizens.

Macdonald also spelled out his intention to be the champion of the province's interests soon after his return. The *Halifax Chronicle*, the province's leading Liberal newspaper, hailed him as the man who would 'hammer into the federal mind that we are against further centralization ... that we want nothing to do with any proposal to exchange what remains of our birthright for a slightly increased mess of federal potage.'[18] Conservative leader Leonard Fraser played into Macdonald's hand by raising the subject of relations with Ottawa during the campaign. Fraser argued that Macdonald would not be able to win a good deal for Nova Scotia in negotiations with the federal government.[19] He badly miscalculated in attacking Macdonald's strongest point. The Liberal leader had more experience in dealing with Ottawa than any other provincial politician of significance; he had been an articulate and thoughtful contributor to the Rowell-Sirois hearings in 1938, his knowledge of constitutional matters was widely respected, and most Nova Scotians recognized – and generally praised – his having been a thorn in the side of the King government during the last seven months of the war. Few believed that the inexperienced Fraser could do better than Macdonald, who assured his audiences, '[W]e will go to Ottawa fully equipped to guard the rights and interests of the people of this Province.'[20]

With the simple slogan 'Angus L.'s Back,' the Liberal Party of Nova Scotia rode their leader's coattails to a landslide victory on 23 October 1945, taking twenty-eight of thirty seats in the Legislative Assembly. Fraser's Conservatives were shut out, and the Co-operative Commonwealth Federation took seats in Sydney and Glace Bay, becoming the Official Opposition. Not all Nova Scotians were satisfied with Macdonald's government – the Liberals failed to hold the industrial Cape Breton ridings they had won in 1937 – but he had reached the peak of his political career, virtually unbeatable in his native province. Dalton Camp likened Macdonald to the pope: infallible in matters of politics.[21]

Solidly ensconced in Halifax, Macdonald prepared a response to Ottawa's offer of a tax rental agreement. When the conference of August reconvened in November, Macdonald presented a well-argued critique of the entire process, which included a call to revisit the Rowell-Sirois report. Paraphrasing the prime minister, Macdonald argued that 'the road to genuine provincial autonomy' was not necessarily 'the road of financial independence.' A balanced federal system also demanded a clear division of responsibilities and resources. Any discussion of fiscal issues was premature:

> To be strictly logical, it seems to me that we should make constitutional changes first and taxation arrangements afterward. This is indeed more than a matter of logic. It is the essence, for it is basic to a Federal system that the Constitution shall divide the responsibilities of a government first, and arm the responsible units with the legal power and sources of revenue appropriate to that division ...

When the Sirois Commission sat, the Nova Scotia Government of that day intimated its willingness to have the British North America Act amended so that the Provinces could delegate powers to the Dominion, and the Dominion could delegate powers to the Provinces. The Government of Nova Scotia still adheres to that view, and we are prepared to enter into discussions with the Dominion along that line.

Macdonald pointed out that the commission's report had been acceptable to Ottawa in 1941, even if the conference of that year had failed. The tax rental proposals were something new. 'I should like to know why the principles and conclusions of the Sirois Report, framed after such careful study, framed by a Commission appointed by the Dominion Government, approved by the Dominion Government, should now be disregarded and abandoned by that Government.'

Macdonald then put thirteen questions to the federal government, asking if it were planning on further invasions of provincial tax fields or if it would offer guarantees against this trend. He specifically asked if the federal government would vacate the fields of gasoline, electricity, and amusement/pari-mutuel taxes – fields that Ottawa had tapped during the war – and recognize them as belonging exclusively to the provinces.[22]

Ottawa responded the next week, refusing to commit itself to anything: 'The Dominion is not willing to give general commitments which might hamper, in unexpected ways, future budgetary policy.' While opening the door to abandoning the minor tax fields, it said it would do so only if compensated by the provinces for lost revenues.[23] Needless to say, this approach to reshaping the federation, which seemed to be both unilateral and centralizing, did not sit well with Nova Scotia's premier.

Some historians have viewed the Rowell-Sirois report as a call for greater centralization, a plan to allow Ottawa to securely dominate the provinces in the name of economic stability.[24] Much of the confusion certainly lies in the language scholars have used. Many casually contrast 'centralization' with 'provincialism,' failing to define either term. We can perceive that 'centralization,' for these authors, means 'overcoming regional prejudices' or 'working towards greater national unity.' 'Provincialism,' meanwhile, implies all that is negative about that word: 'narrow-minded' and 'working against national unity,' assuming that a united, uniform nation is a self-evident good. Thus, some have argued that a province's wealth determined its premier's 'provincialism.'[25]

Macdonald, in contrast, emphasized the provincial half of the federal equation. Centralization of powers and resources threatened the autonomy of the weaker provinces and, by extension, the Canadian federal system. He saw Rowell-Sirois as Nova Scotia's best chance for a viable future within Confederation. He was prepared to cede the major tax fields to the federal government, provided that the provinces receive exclusive control of the minor fields and that Ottawa redistribute national wealth – on the basis of fiscal need – to ensure that the provinces could meet their obligations. Resistance to these conditions, Macdonald felt, indicated 'a trend towards more and more centralization at Ottawa – a trend which, frankly, we do not like.'[26]

As Macdonald prepared his second response to the federal government, he consulted two of the leading academic experts in the country, Corry of Queen's and H.A. Innis of the University of Toronto.[27] Macdonald wanted to know if the logic of Ottawa's case was sound. 'Will centralization of taxing authority in these federal fields tend to promote employment and prosperity throughout Canada?' Corry was now away from the pressures of wartime Ottawa and had time for reflection, though he told Macdonald that he had been considering this question for several years and was still not sure of the answer. The economists he most respected were Keynesians, but he did not accept the applicability of the theories to Canada's federal, as opposed to unitary, system of government. Macdonald should be cautious in ceding fiscal powers to Ottawa. Provincial autonomy, Corry warned, 'is illusory unless it has a secure economic base.' He doubted as well that federal officials had the political will to follow the dictates of Keynesianism at all times and suspected that they would repeatedly opt for politically expedient solutions. Finally, he cautioned Macdonald that the size and ability of Ottawa's civil service corps put it in an advantageous position vis-à-vis the provinces; erudite Dominion bureaucrats could 'out-talk provincial civil servants and confuse them with massive statistics and recondite theoretical arguments.'[28]

Harold Innis responded by eschewing Keynesianism and calling Ottawa's faith in fiscal manipulation misplaced. This approach, he maintained, would do nothing to achieve parity between the Maritimes and the St Lawrence region because

uniform monetary measures will not operate to the equal advantage of all regions ... When the Dominion government has shown its ability to give intensive consideration to specific problems of a definitely regional character and its willingness to recognize to the full its necessity of overcoming the handicaps of the tariff and other measures then the government of Nova Scotia or of other regions similarly placed can perhaps afford to consider suggestions of an over-all character ... It seems to me that the federal principle disappears unless you continue to insist on your position in Nova Scotia.

Economic management necessarily would be centralized and could not be readily adapted to the regional patterns of Canada's economy. The problems of the Maritime provinces, he wrote, 'can only be met by piecemeal *ad hoc* considerations and not by overall blank cheques.'[29]

Macdonald continued to take the lead in developing his government's position on the tax rental agreements and held his ground when laying out Nova Scotia's case in January 1946. Though he preferred that constitutional discussions precede any financial arrangements, Macdonald insisted on a few key principles if financial talks were to continue. Provinces must have guaranteed and exclusive sources of revenue. Thus, Ottawa would have to vacate the minor tax fields – gasoline, electricity, and amusement/pari-mutuel taxes – and pledge not to expand further into other provincial fields. In exchange, Nova Scotia would be willing to recognize exclusive federal jurisdiction in the fields of income and corporate taxes and succession duties. Fiscal need, determined by what revenues a province required to meet a minimum national standard of services, must be the basis of determining provincial subsidies, rather than a rigid per capita formula. Finally, Macdonald insisted on fixed, annual federal-provincial conferences to discuss problems of shared jurisdiction and to keep constitutional talks moving forward.[30]

After delivering Nova Scotia's submission to Ottawa, Macdonald spoke rather candidly to the Halifax Board of Trade, criticizing the British North America Act. He argued that the failure to give direct taxes exclusively to the provinces was 'a great defect' in the act and opined that Nova Scotia's Fathers of Confederation had been too complacent in relying on subsidies. In 1867 subsidies had provided 70 per cent of the provinces' revenues; in 1946 they accounted for just 10 per cent. Macdonald generally opposed this system altogether: 'I think that one of the worst features of the subsidy system is that it helps to destroy the instinct for self help and the spirit of self reliance.'[31] Presumably, Macdonald preferred alterations to tariff and transportation policies, the assumption of certain responsibilities by the federal government or greatly expanded provincial powers of taxation to the subsidy system. As matters stood, however, Nova Scotia and most other provinces could not have survived without subsidies in 1947.

Responding to Nova Scotia's submission, the federal government either dismissed Macdonald's points or set them aside for future discussion. It repeated that it would not vacate the minor tax fields without compensation, but it was willing to discuss that compensation. Ottawa offered to cooperate on an amendment to section 92 of the BNA Act allowing provinces to collect a sales tax, but made no further mention of constitutional discussions. The federal government argued that per capita subsidies fulfilled virtually the same role that fiscal need subsidies would, and it rejected annual conferences as too rigid for Canada's parliamentary system.[32] Ottawa also set aside the question of a national health insurance scheme at the January gathering, arguing that it was too complicated and likely to lead to greater division.

The conference reconvened in late April 1946. Macdonald returned to his theme that fiscal negotiations were premature until constitutional responsibilities had been properly apportioned and he recommended discussions aimed at revising the BNA Act within three years, the proposed life of the tax rental agreements. He also repeated his demand that the minor fields be provincially managed, as these taxes had been first levied and administered by the provinces. Furthermore, these revenues were used for provincial purposes: gasoline taxes went towards road construction, electricity taxes supported rural electrification programs, and amusement taxes paid for provincial censor boards.

The lack of clearly defined responsibilities and resources, Macdonald argued, threatened federalism in Canada. As matters stood, the federal government could continue to enter into provincial fields of taxation or spending, gradually weakening the provinces' position. Provinces would be squeezed out of tax fields if Ottawa increased its taxation rates. Their resources would be drained by shared funding programs that Ottawa had announced unilaterally, or provinces would have to surrender further resources to the Dominion so that it could fund these programs alone. The results, Macdonald predicted with some hyperbole, would be catastrophic. 'Provincial autonomy will be gone. Provincial independence will vanish. Provincial dignity will disappear. Provincial governments will become mere annuitants of Ottawa. Provincial public life ... will be debased and degraded.'[33]

Macdonald's arguments swayed Mackenzie King, though the prime minister seemed to be a mere observer of events, without any power to influence the government's position:

Still, the Cabinet having reached agreement I have held with them ever since but I think the really sound position is along lines that would reserve definite fields of taxation to the Dominion and provincial governments respectively, avoiding double taxation and causing the government which has to do with the spending of public money to be obliged for the raising of the necessary revenues.[34]

J.L. Ilsley, however, rejected his friend's assessment. Fixed subsidies, he argued, were more dignified than fiscal need subsidies, which required a province to prove its penury.[35]

As a conciliatory gesture, Macdonald said that Nova Scotia was willing to compensate the federal government if it would vacate the minor fields; later he pledged that if Ottawa abandoned certain minor fields, his government would not increase taxes in those fields for several years, demonstrating that for Nova Scotia this was a matter of principle, not finances.[36] He suggested that the conference be adjourned for a time to allow all parties to consider the proposals and their positions. He noted that the talks that led to Confederation had taken more than two years and said that there was no need for haste now.[37]

The conference did adjourn, but the adjournment became permanent. King's government appeared once again to use a conference's failure to take unilateral action. In his June budget, Ilsley announced Ottawa's intention to obtain agreements on its tax rental proposals on a province-by-province basis, rather than at a general conference. Ilsley also indicated that the agreements negotiated would last for five years, not three.[38] Macdonald criticized the separate negotiations as 'undignified' and apt to promote jealousy, as each province would have to seek better terms than those who signed before them.[39] King's government, however, recognized that the provinces were much weaker and more tractable in individual negotiations, as compared to conferences.

Macdonald's opposition to the federal tactics and his continued refusal to sign a tax rental agreement over the next fourteen months made him rather notorious in political circles outside Nova Scotia. The national press frequently linked him with Drew and Duplessis, hardly a comfortable spot for a Liberal premier. Macdonald did meet with Drew and Duplessis in the Windsor Hotel in Montreal in November 1946 to discuss the tax rental negotiations, but he was seeking common ground in pursuit of a deal, rather than conspiring against Ottawa. Macdonald knew that if he could get Ontario and Quebec to approve a deal with which the other provinces could live, the federal government would pay a high price to ignore it.

Earlier in the negotiations, Macdonald had praised Drew's sincerity in attempting to find a solution though he found Ontario's proposals – which included the provinces' retaining the major tax fields but paying into an 'equalization fund' – were unrealistic, as they assumed the provinces had equal tax bases. Compared to Drew, Macdonald wrote his brother, 'Duplessis is more unpredictable and it is difficult to say just what his motives are.'[40] Macdonald appears never to have made a concerted effort to understand Quebec's position on constitutional matters, or indeed most political issues. Like most politicians outside Quebec, he got his information and analysis from anglophone 'insiders.' For example, Macdonald consulted with Quebec MP C.G. 'Chubby' Power, Montreal businessman and Liberal organizer Kirk Cameron, journalist Leslie Roberts, and McGill University's Colonel Wilfrid Bovey.

At the meeting in the Windsor Hotel Macdonald found that, away from reporters and political entourages, the sides were not as far apart as Ottawa thought. Duplessis indicated that he was willing to give up income and most corporate taxes but not succession duties. Drew said Ontario would surrender income and corporate taxes and succession duties, but not the minor fields. The three premiers discussed the possibility of Macdonald's hosting a conference of the provinces in Halifax. This would be a risky move: while a united front among the provinces would certainly compel Ottawa to be more flexible, failure at such a conference would just as surely strengthen the federal government's hand. The idea was eventually dropped.[41]

In January 1947 Macdonald chatted civilly with Mackenzie King in Ottawa for half an hour. King agreed with Macdonald that 'the Finance Dept. had in its original programme gone too far in what appeared to be taking from the provinces certain fiscal rights and leading to centralization in expenditure.' The prime minister, however, refused to reconvene the conference, more out of indignation than strategy:

> I told him there were times and seasons for all things – he could hardly expect, recalling the way Duplessis had behaved at the last conference and the way he talked, and of Drew speaking about the government being incompetent, etc., that men like St. Laurent, Ilsley, Abbott and myself could be expected to want to have annual conferences with them.[42]

At this stage of his career, King provided little if any leadership within the government. Even if he believed that the tax rental agreements were dangerous for the provinces, he would not rouse himself to change the direction of cabinet and the civil service.

Ilsley, Skelton, and others in the Department of Finance negotiated with individual provinces, determining what price was necessary to secure signatures on tax rental agreements. An exhausted Ilsley worked diligently with Macdonald to find an acceptable middle ground, even suggesting bargaining points that the premier could officially present to Ottawa. They could reach no agreement, however, and their twenty-year relationship must have been strained by this fundamental impasse on the future of the federation.[43]

By the end of 1946, New Brunswick, Prince Edward Island, Manitoba, Saskatchewan, and British Columbia had accepted tentative agreements after Ottawa increased the fixed per capita subsidy offer. Alberta signed a deal early in 1947, leaving just Nova Scotia, Ontario, and Quebec outside the tax rental scheme. As Macdonald predicted, the separate negotiations led to jealousy among the provinces. British Columbia signed in mid-December, receiving a subsidy of approximately $21 per capita; New Brunswick's premier J.B. McNair wired King in a huff, saying that British Columbia's deal 'violate[d] the basis of understanding' between Ottawa and Fredericton. 'We will therefore treat our negotiations as suspended.'[44] McNair, though, soon accepted the $15 per capita he had earlier agreed to.

Liberals across Canada grew displeased with Macdonald for his stand-off with Ottawa. Were some subtle constitutional points worth damaging the harmony of the party? After meeting with Senator Rupert Davies, owner/editor of the *Kingston Whig-Standard*, John Connolly wrote Macdonald of the criticism being expressed towards him: 'The great secrecy surrounding your position on Dominion-Provincial relations has always caused considerable speculations here. Rupert Davies was complaining about the damage being done to the Party in Ontario because of the fact that the Globe and Mail speaks of Drew and Duplessis and yourself in the same sense.'[45] Macdonald, for his part, grew frustrated with those who could not or would not understand his position:

I thought that Drew was a Christian and believed in God. Was it therefore to be expected that I should renounce my belief in a Deity? I cannot help it if on this point of Dominion-Provincial relations Drew's stand in several respects agrees with mine. I feel definitely sure that I am right – that is, it is impossible to talk of a federal state, unless Provinces have some tax fields of their own.[46]

Macdonald had supporters beyond Nova Scotia, but they tended to be 'on the outs' with the King government. Writing from the Senate, T.A. Crerar advised Macdonald that he was on 'solid ground' in his stand on federal-provincial relations.[47] Macdonald replied that he thought the Rowell-Sirois report was 'pretty profound.' He also said that the federal officials were too sanguine about their grand plan.[48] Chubby Power, another wanderer from King's cabinet, thought Macdonald's principles on this point were correct, though he chided Macdonald for his increasing infamy in Ottawa: 'I note with some interest that the practice of black-mail which legend hath said originated in the Highlands of Scotland is now being practiced with great success by one Rob Roy McDonald with a poor unfortunate Southron Abbot as the victim and as usual the peasantry and commonalty suffer.'[49]

Nova Scotia finally negotiated a deal with Ottawa in late April 1947. In exchange for vacating the fields of income and corporate taxes and succession duties the province received almost $11 million in annual subsidies, a significant figure in a time of $20 million budgets. Nova Scotia also received 30 per cent of the pre-war Duncan and White subsidies, totalling about $390,000. The federal government agreed to withdraw from gasoline taxes but not from electricity; as for the other minor fields, Finance Minister Abbott acknowledged the principle for which Macdonald had fought:

> The Dominion recognizes the desire of the Provinces to have taxation fields of their own. We are prepared, therefore, to say that in view of the nature of amusement and pari-mutuel fields, and of the special interest of the Provinces in respect thereto, it will be our policy to vacate these fields as soon as circumstances permit.

Finally, Ottawa agreed to hold a federal-provincial conference *at least* one year before the expiry of the tax rental agreement.[50]

Macdonald won a few small victories in the agreement, including getting Ottawa out of the field of gasoline taxes and, especially, securing its recognition that having exclusive sources of revenue for provinces was a desirable goal.[51] He did not, however, win other vital points. The federal government did not accept the idea of regular conferences, its statement about exclusive tax fields was ambiguous and unlikely to amount to very much, and the subsidies, though generous, did not establish fiscal need as the basis for redistribution of national wealth.

James Bickerton has argued that Macdonald signed the tax rental agreement because Liberal Party discipline finally brought him to heel.[52] It is true that Macdonald received only limited and insubstantial support from Liberals outside his province, and indeed some Liberals from Nova Scotia, who held or aspired to federal offices, seemed ready to speak against Macdonald publicly. Yet this analysis ignores Macdonald's extremely strong position in Nova Scotia. He could win elections seemingly at will, and his resistance to further centralization played very well in a province less than a generation removed from the rhetoric of the Maritime Rights movement. The political pressure Macdonald faced was negligible. Rather, he signed because of money and his belief that he had succeeded in shifting the course of federalism in Canada.

Nova Scotia's budgetary surpluses were dwindling as demands on the public treasury re-emerged after six years of war. Signing the tax rental agreement turned Nova Scotia's modest 1947–8 surplus of $122,000 into a whopping $9,500,000. The Macdonald government divided the windfall into three parts: $4 million was devoted to retiring maturing bonds, $4.5 million was earmarked for municipal loans, and $1 million was used for loans to industries for expansion in the province.[53] Without signing, the government would have struggled to balance its books; the agreement allowed Nova Scotia to begin important infrastructure programs, including highways and bridges, rural high schools, and municipal sewerage systems.

More important, Macdonald believed he had won the debate on the issue of mutual exclusiveness of tax fields. Though the federal government merely 'recognized the desirability' of this idea, Macdonald hoped that this would help shift momentum back towards securing provincial autonomy. He continued to refer to the Rowell-Sirois report, hoping that its guiding principles would not be lost. In announcing the understanding reached with Ottawa on tax rental, Macdonald hammered at this point once more:

> Even though there is inequality in the wealth of the various provinces, one is not justified in concluding from that fact that the provinces are not to have taxation fields of their own. Let them have their fields; let them do their utmost to raise the necessary revenues from these fields. Having done that, if they are still unable to maintain an average standard of services for their people, let them then have resort to some such scheme as that outlined by the Sirois Commission.[54]

Macdonald reiterated this to a delegate on his way to a Young Liberal convention:

> While the Dominion proposals give us much more money than we could get by ourselves, the same result could have been obtained in other ways without infringing so much upon provincial autonomy ... If the Sirois plan had been adopted, we would be getting more money, and while the Sirois Report recommended that we should give up income taxes, corporation tax and succession duties, it stated very definitely that if the Dominion got these fields of taxation they should be very careful to respect the provinces' rights in the remaining fields.
>
> In this instance, the Dominion started out by trying to take a great deal more than the Sirois Commission suggested and it was only after a very long struggle that we were able to beat them down to the present position.[55]

Macdonald's references to Rowell-Sirois became less frequent, but he still brought it up and drew important lessons from it.[56]

In the first half of 1947, the Macdonald government also reconsidered Nova Scotia's labour laws, once the most advanced in the country. The period from 1946 to early 1947 saw labour law shifted back to full provincial jurisdiction from the murky federal-provincial shared jurisdiction of the Second World War. Organized labour tried to retain and expand upon the gains it had made in the last years of the war, when King's government had introduced compulsory collective bargaining in many Canadian industries. Order-in-Council P.C. 1003, passed in March 1944, resembled Nova Scotia's Trade Union Act in that it required employers to recognize and to bargain with trade unions chosen by their employees. Unions welcomed the move, and most volunteered to forego collective action for the duration of the war. In 1943, more than one million working days had been lost to strikes in Canadian industry, but in 1944, fewer than half that number were lost.[57]

Once the war ended, organized labour attempted to use compulsory collective bargaining to entrench itself and improve the standard of living for workers. Frozen wages, government coercion, and employer discrimination against union organizers provided workers with causes enough to launch a wave of strikes that initially had some success in winning concessions. In 1945, the number of working days lost to strikes jumped to almost 1.5 million, exploding to 4.5 million in 1946, the peak until the 1960s. In the post-war period, many labour organizations attempted to negotiate industry-wide contracts, thereby strengthening their position considerably. A strike by steel workers in Nova Scotia and Ontario lasted from July to October 1946 and saw moderate union gains in a settlement reached under the aegis of federal concilia-tion.[58] Federal jurisdiction, however, would soon expire.

Federal and provincial labour ministers met in October 1946 to dis-cuss jurisdiction. Though trade unions were pushing for a national labour code, the ministers did not even attempt to develop a common model for labour legislation. In 1941 Nova Scotia's minister of labour, Lauchie Currie, had argued

> that industrial relations in connection with all our basic industries should be entirely directed and controlled from Ottawa. Neither the Provinces of Canada nor the States of the American Union are sufficiently able to enforce punitive measures [against employers] in the basic industries, and there is not much advantage in having Provincial Laws that cannot be enforced.[59]

Currie, however, raised no objection to the return of labour matters to provincial jurisdiction in 1946.

Two major strikes in Nova Scotia that followed the steel strike dem-onstrated that Macdonald's government was prepared to concede to labour gains that it could defend, but it would not offer new conces-sions, even when those concessions were consistent with its own labour law. The relatively successful strike by the well-established United Mine Workers of America (UMW) District 26 contrasts sharply with the crushing defeat suffered by the fledgling Canadian Fishermen and Fish Handlers' Union (CFFU). Macdonald's government worked closely with Ottawa to try to meet the demands of the coal miners, while it stood quietly by as the employers starved the fishers out.

The miners of District 26 went on strike in February 1947, protesting the appalling conditions in mining communities and demanding sig-nificant increases in compensation to improve the standard of living in those communities. Ottawa appointed Justice William Carroll to inves-tigate the dispute. Carroll recommended a wage increase of $1.40 per day, and federal labour minister Humphrey Mitchell thought that forty cents of that could be covered by a federal subsidy on coal, the rest by increased productivity. Carroll also recommended that a pension plan be established, funded by the companies, the miners, and the prov-ince.[60] Nova Scotia announced that it would contribute 20 per cent of its coal royalties to such a fund. It then worked with Ottawa and the

UMW's American headquarters to convince District 26 and the coal companies to accept the deal by June.[61]

In Nova Scotia's fishery, the CFFU also sought an industry-wide agreement, but had the ground cut out from under it by a court ruling, some red-baiting, and an uncooperative provincial government. In 1946 a handful of companies controlled the fishery in Nova Scotia, led by Ralph Bell's National Sea Products.[62] National Sea and its allied companies owned some trawlers but concentrated on buying, storing, and processing fish. Fishers in Nova Scotia were paid by the 'Lunenburg 64' system, which defined them as 'co-adventurers' rather than employees. Crews were paid according to a '60/40 lay,' whereby owners received 60 per cent of the value of the catch and the crews 40 per cent, after deductions had been made. As the major companies largely controlled fish prices, fishers were in a particularly vulnerable position.[63]

The Canadian Fishermen's Union (CFU) formed in 1939, but failed to win recognition from boat owners or fish companies. In 1945 it applied for certification to the Nova Scotia Wartime Labour Relations Board. The board, however, refused to define fishers as employees, invoking the nineteenth-century idea of 'co-adventurer.' An appeal to the National War Labour Relations Board (NWLRB) under P.C. 1003 in February 1946 succeeded, and the CFU received certification as the bargaining agent for the fishers of three vessels. The CFU merged with the Canadian Fish Handlers' Union in October 1946 to form the CFFU and began to negotiate with the fish companies. Negotiations failed, and on 28 December 1946 the CFFU voted to go on strike. The peacetime shift in jurisdiction, however, had opened the door for provincial courts to assume a new and significant role in labour matters. In mid-January, the Supreme Court of Nova Scotia ruled on an appeal of the NWLRB verdict, reversing the classification of fishers as 'employees' and finding that they had no right to unionize.[64]

From a weakened position the CFFU continued the strike – now for basic recognition – and lobbied the Macdonald government to alter its labour law. The well-capitalized National Sea could easily outlast the union and turned its efforts to a massive advertising campaign to prevent the CFFU from winning public sympathy. National Sea and its subsidiaries bought advertising space in the *Halifax Chronicle* and *Herald*, the *Bridgewater Bulletin*, and the *Saint John Evening Times-Globe*, in addition to publishing at least one pamphlet, *Christianity or Communism?*[65] Union leaders were accused of being communists; the traditions of individualism and masculinity in the fishery were extolled, and 'generous' fishers' incomes were revealed. Ralph Bell told Macdonald that fishers earned between $2200 and $4500 in addition to getting food and quarters while at sea.[66]

The charge of communism in the union leadership particularly hurt the CFFU, as there was some truth to it. The CFFU was affiliated with the Canadian Seaman's Union (CSU), headed by J.A. 'Pat' Sullivan, a known communist. Moreover, CFFU secretary H.C. Meade and his wife were members of the Communist Party of Canada, something discussed even in the pages of *Time* magazine.[67] This may have been the reason that in this dispute, unlike previous ones, the boat captains sided with the owners. Nevertheless, all but two municipal councils in the province – Lunenburg and Mahone Bay, where National Sea was strongest – presented resolutions to the province endorsing the union's position.[68]

In early February, Currie hinted that the government might expand the definition of 'employee' to include fishers when it revised its labour statute in the coming session of the legislature. The boat owners and captains hastily arranged a meeting with the government, and Currie retreated from his earlier promise. O.F. MacKenzie, Halifax's leading fish merchant, wrote Macdonald that the owners were 'exceedingly satisfied' with the meeting and added, 'Time and again recently I have had to declare that Lauchie Currie could be depended upon not to favour communism.'[69] Macdonald announced that in light of the Supreme Court ruling, his government could not compel recognition of the union; the two sides would have to work things out. He neglected to mention that it lay within the government's power to rewrite the labour law.[70]

The strike collapsed a month later, and the death blow came from another union leader. On 14 March 1947, Pat Sullivan resigned as president of the CSU, calling it a front for communists and renouncing his earlier political leanings. He specifically mentioned Meade, saying that he took his orders directly from Moscow. On the 19th, four hundred CFFU members passed two motions, one expressing confidence in its executive, and the other pledging to return to work. President Ben MacKenzie said the union and fishers could not afford to continue the strike. National Sea granted a 60/40 lay favouring the fishers, but it also unilaterally lowered the price of cod and haddock by 1½ cents per pound. In addition, fishers were required to sign 'articles of agreement' – non-union contracts – before every voyage.[71]

With the strike safely over, Currie met with a delegation of the defeated fishers on 21 March. They were seeking an expanded definition of 'employee' in the revised Trade Union Act, and Currie promised to help fishers bargain collectively. The government did not expand the act to include fishers, but it did pass the Fishermen's Federation Act in early May 1947. This paternalistic legislation allowed the organization of at least forty fishers on a county-by-county basis for the purposes of collective bargaining. Non-residents and non-fishers were expressly prohibited from acting as representatives.[72]

Jean Nisbet categorizes Macdonald as 'a fierce anti-communist,' using his role in the fisheries strike to support her view.[73] This rather oversimplifies Macdonald's position on communism. In the denouement of the fisheries strike, Macdonald did take direct aim at the 'Communist threat,' though in this case, it was the threat that communist agitators posed to 'industrial legality' and the collective bargaining process.[74] His speech to the House on 26 March emphasized the sanctity of collective agreements, implying that illegal strikes had to be proscribed. He then warned workers that communists might lead them to violate their collective agreements, as they cared more for 'the cause' than for the concerns of labour. He quoted Pat Sullivan and Communist Party leader Tim Buck on the political value of strikes to illustrate this point. Macdonald argued that, as it stood, communism was not a political party in Canada: it was a revolutionary party. 'I do not think there should be any place in this country for people whose fundamental purpose and aim is to destroy the democratic system.' Communism might be reformed in the future, Macdonald conceded, but 'in its present form and with its present objects it should have no place in this country.'[75]

Yet Macdonald, like his friend Tom Crerar, did not support the use of the state's power to eradicate a political ideology or to harass its adherents. They worried that St Laurent had been too willing to allow 'Gestapo tactics' by the RCMP in its hunt for spies following the Gouzenko affair.[76] Communism did not feature prominently in Macdonald's writings or speeches, indicating that he did not consider it a significant threat. More ominous to him, always, was the trend towards greater centralized, bureaucratic power in Canada, which limited the institution of responsible government.

Macdonald soon squared off in another contest with Ottawa. On 30 March 1948, the Board of Transport Commissioners (BTC) – the appointed regulatory body for railways in Canada – issued a decision allowing the members of the Railway Association of Canada (RAC) a 21 per cent across-the-board increase in freight rates.[77] This decision not only imperilled economies outside Central Canada, it was also badly flawed. The BTC had used Canadian Pacific (CP) as its model when studying the question of rates; this avoided the confusion of the details of all the smaller lines, and the RAC and provincial representatives had accepted this model. In calculating the liabilities of CP, the BTC included the debts and operating expenditures of its non-railway holdings, claiming that it could not distinguish between railway and non-railway liabilities. In determining how much revenue CP required to provide its shareholders with a 'reasonable profit,' however, the BTC refused to consider revenues from its non-railway activities. Thus, the rail operations of CP had to generate enough revenue to cover all of CP's operating expenses and debts and provide a net profit of 11 per cent.[78]

The governments of Ontario and Quebec paid little attention to freight rate battles given their advantageous location and the competition provided by an infrastructure of highways and water. Railway companies typically provided 'special rates' to Central Canada industries to better compete with trucking and shipping, so increases in freight rates often were not passed along.[79] Regional economies outside Central Canada were threatened by the rate increase, however, and outraged provincial governments quickly organized. A flurry of telegrams and telephone calls, directed mostly by Macdonald and Manitoba's Stuart Garson, led to a meeting on 28 April 1948 between the federal cabinet and the premiers of the seven provinces opposed to the BTC decision. With Macdonald acting as spokesperson, the premiers called for the suspension of the rate increases and a royal commission to investigate the whole question of transportation in Canada.[80] Clearly, Macdonald and the rest were hoping for another Rowell-Sirois Commission to give voice to regional concerns and to suggest practical solutions.

The minister of transportation, Lionel Chevrier, pointed out that he had ordered the BTC to investigate the general question of freight rates – even as he upheld the controversial ruling[81] – and argued that a royal commission would be redundant. Macdonald maintained that the board could not investigate itself and that it would be bound by past decisions. Moreover it was, by its own admission, not competent to deal with policies of economic development or questions of regional disparity. Furthermore, the premiers were so incensed by the latest ruling that they claimed to have lost all faith in the board. The 'Seven Premiers' acknowledged that the railway companies' costs had increased sharply, but pointed out that their profits had as well. Macdonald asked that the freight rate increases be suspended until an inquiry could be held. In the meantime, if the companies did lose money, they should be compensated either by direct subsidies from Ottawa or by the removal of the federal tax on passenger fares. Macdonald noted that this presentation did not constitute a formal appeal, a right the premiers chose to reserve at that time.

Two months after the Seven Premiers met with King and his cabinet, the prime minister replied. He opened by listing some moves taken to 'soften' the rate increases. These concessions included reducing the minimum rates on eggs from seventy-five cents to fifty, reducing the increase on rates for Nova Scotian coal from twenty-five cents per ton to twenty, and appointing as chief commissioner of the board Nova Scotia Justice M.B. Archibald, a former legal colleague of Macdonald. King then argued that a royal commission could not do better than to duplicate the board's investigation, especially as 'the amount of technical help is not unlimited and will be absorbed by the Board's requirements.' Ottawa refused to 'substitute its judgment ... for the judgment of the Board' and so would not suspend the rate increases, though it did invite the provinces to formally appeal if they were still unhappy with the ruling.[82]

The Seven Premiers kept a mostly united front – all but British Columbia refused to participate in the board's inquiry – and pressed for a royal commission. On 20 July they officially appealed the BTC decision to the Governor-in-Council, but made it very clear that they preferred a royal commission.[83] On the 27th the RAC showed its audacity by applying for a further 20 per cent increase in freight rates, leaving the provinces just thirty days to respond before the BTC.[84] With more telephone calls and telegrams over the next few weeks, Macdonald kept the premiers united in their refusal to deal with the BTC.[85] They gambled that it would be better to resist the BTC entirely than to quibble with each application put forward by the railways.

Macdonald threw himself into the campaign to prevent freight rate increases that would, he feared, prevent industries on the periphery from competing in central markets. His scepticism about Keynesian 'management' techniques did not signal that he rejected any economic presence for the state. He consistently argued that a liberal state should foster economic development through physical and intellectual infrastructure. After considerable and diverse political pressure, Lionel Chevrier hinted in a speech in Winnipeg on 10 August 1948 that Ottawa would give in to one of the demands of the Seven Premiers. Finally, on 29 December, Ottawa officially announced a royal commission to study the question of transportation.[86]

Early in 1948 another crucial issue arose: the selection of Mackenzie King's successor. King's retirement had long been anticipated, though cynics such as Macdonald and Alex Johnston believed rumours of his going were circulated merely to test loyalty. When King did announce his retirement at the National Liberal Federation dinner on 20 January 1948, Macdonald was in attendance and found enough qualifications in the prime minister's speech to conclude that 'it did not amount to a definite retirement.' A Nova Scotia delegate assumed that King did not unequivocally retire for fear that he would become a 'lame duck' in parliament. Macdonald reasoned that he had left open the door to being drafted at the convention.[87]

Discussion among Macdonald's circle of friends soon turned to leadership candidates.[88] All agreed that Louis St Laurent had the early edge if he chose to run. He was King's anointed and had a whiff of Laurier about him. Furthermore, he was sixty-six and would not be able to hold the office for three decades as King had done. J.L. Ilsley had earned a great deal of support through his integrity and Herculean efforts during the war but he was, physically and mentally, a shadow of his former self and was openly considering retirement. C.D. Howe was well known and popular in his way, but he lacked the necessary tact and patience for the office and he knew it. Then came the 'lean and hungry' men of cabinet whose ambitions were always barely cloaked: Jimmy Gardiner, Paul Martin, Douglas Abbott, and Brooke Claxton. Of these, Gardiner had seniority and at least the remnants of a personal political machine in the West. The others could temper their hopes with the knowledge that they were the generation of the next leadership convention.

Outside King's cabinet and nominally outside his control, the candidates were fewer. New Brunswick's J.B. McNair had earned his political spurs, but his wife's illness and his lack of a national reputation made his candidacy unlikely. Manitoba's Stuart Garson appeared young, energetic, able, intelligent, and bound for federal politics, but most saw him as belonging to the next generation as well.[89] That left Angus L. Macdonald as possibly the only 'outside' candidate.

Macdonald initially thought he had little chance. His determined fight in the negotiations over the tax rental agreement won him support in his home province and perhaps some admiration from constitutional observers elsewhere, but it did little to make him popular within the Liberal party. And although he was one of the most recognizable premiers, he was known as a wartime conscriptionist, something that would count against him in the minds of Quebecers and those who placed a great deal of value in keeping Quebecers mollified. Finally, he would be strongly opposed by King, and the departing prime minister had more allies than enemies within the party. Yet the course of events provided Macdonald with some tantalizing evidence that his leadership candidacy might succeed. St Laurent opened a dangerous door in a Winnipeg speech in which he said he would not run if his race or religion became an issue.[90] He hoped to keep the contest civil and the country united, but many suspected that Gardiner or his machine might raise one of the said issues to force St Laurent from the race. Macdonald's circle of friends considered that Gardiner would be a disaster as leader, as his political tactics were embarrassingly out of fashion at the national level in 1948.

Tom Crerar, Chubby Power, and Leslie Roberts worried that the convention would be but a tearful farewell to King and speech after speech of self-satisfaction by cabinet ministers. Power urgently wanted a restatement or clarification of Liberal principles, which might guide the party forward, but saw no signs of hope from Ottawa. 'With the leadership question out of the way and policy neglected, I fear that the much prayed for convention, instead of marking the beginning of a Liberal resurgence, will be the last nail in the coffin of both traditional Liberalism and new liberalism.' He summarized the work of the prime minister's colleagues by citing Sir Richard Acland: 'Of course, in any party there may be at any time too many people who are uncritically working to put or keep their party in power; and too few who are constructively working at the task of so serving their party as to make sure that it deserves political power.'[91]

Macdonald agreed that fundamentals must be restated at the convention, but he stressed the importance of the leadership race after 'a good many years of experience with compromise, expediency and appeasement as the guiding factors in politics.' Principles not implemented were useless.

> It must be remembered that no matter what policies may be laid down at a convention, these will be largely shaped and moulded by the leader of the party. Therefore, I cannot go all the way with Power, who in his [*Maclean's*] article last year seemed to think that the whole question was rather one of drawing up a truly Liberal platform without too much worry about who would be the leader.[92]

He feared that the next leader would learn too well from the Master.

Macdonald thought the prospects of the federal Liberal party none too bright and traced the problems back to King. A series of gaffes seemed to indicate either incompetence or arrogance on the government benches. In November 1947 Abbott announced a new tax – passed by order-in-council – on the radio, bypassing the authority of Parliament. In the 1948 session a resolution proposed by Abbott was defeated in committee, and he admitted to the press that he did not realize what was going on. Howe introduced a motion, changed his mind, and asked the House to vote down his own motion. Macdonald saw these moves as

> the motions of a tired organism – tired and I am afraid, just a bit contemp-tuous of public opinion. More than eight years of virtually unrestricted power, the excessive use of the Order in Council, the undue influence of men behind the scenes who are often anonymous and who are never accountable to the people in the sense that members of parliament are accountable have left their mark. When you add to this the next fact, namely, that the head of it all has his mind on other things, you have a combination of factors that, short of a miracle, is sure to produce the results that we see today. The ironic part of it all is that his apologists will say (assuming he goes out and that the deterioration continues until it results in defeat) that so long as he was leading the party, success generally smiled upon its fortunes ...
>
> The serious condition of international affairs will no doubt be used as an argument for continuing things as they are. Really, that condition should be the chief reason for a change. It is not a time for shilly shallyers, and for those who, in the last war did not contribute, so far as I know, one single constructive idea to our war effort, but on the contrary were always discovering dangers and difficulties where none existed, and raising pif-fling objections to well thought out plans.[93]

Macdonald's circle of supporters in Ottawa took his chances seri-ously. The chief architect of his non-campaign was John Connolly, his former executive assistant in naval affairs and chair of the Resolutions Committee at the convention. Connolly wanted to get things moving quickly, and attempted to launch several 'kites' in the press to stimulate a consideration of Macdonald as federal leadership material.[94] Con-nolly worked with Grant Dexter, now editor of the *Free Press*, and Sen-ator Davies, though little came of the work with Davies. Macdonald allowed these efforts to continue for a time, but steadfastly refused to work on his own behalf.

By mid-April, Macdonald had all but closed the door to offering his name as a candidate at the leadership convention, and the dispute over freight rates strengthened his resolve not to run. He gave Connolly a list of reasons why St Laurent would win on the first ballot of the convention: he would have the support of almost all of the cabinet and caucus, as well as support from Quebec and other francophone regions of the country; most in the party felt that it was now the turn of a French Canadian to lead it; the chief organizer of the convention, Gordon Fogo, appeared to be taking orders directly from the prime minister's staff; no Nova Scotian MP had mentioned Macdonald's name or even asked him if he were interested; and finally, 'the Upper Canadian papers' again portrayed Macdonald as the leader of the anti-Ottawa faction for his role in protesting the BTC decision, though the organization of the Seven Premiers had been a group effort.[95]

In May the question of Macdonald's candidacy again came up, but it was raised by Howe, a solid St Laurent supporter. In Halifax to collect an honorary degree from Dalhousie University, Howe encouraged Macdonald to run, saying 'it would be a good thing to have a number of candidates.' Macdonald declined and seemed rather hurt that Howe would suggest he run when he expected him to lose: 'butchered to make a Roman holiday.'[96]

In July the press finally mentioned Macdonald as a serious candidate. A reporter asked Halifax MP Gordon Isnor whom he would be supporting at the convention; Isnor replied that he would wait until he saw what Macdonald would do. The story then ran that Isnor was lining up delegates from the East to support Macdonald.[97] A few days later, an article by Macdonald on liberalism appeared in the *Winnipeg Free Press*. In this piece, Macdonald called for a platform of general principles rather than positions on many issues, arguing that principles could better guide the party through difficult decisions. His discussion of liberal ideology praised individual freedoms above possible security, and he warned that state planning, necessary as it might have been in war, was impractical and dangerous in peace.[98] Supporters quickly pressed Macdonald to run.[99]

As the convention neared, St Laurent's position seemed to falter, thanks to the strong showing by Duplessis in the Quebec provincial election and to Gardiner's aggressive campaign to recruit delegates. Moreover, the anticipation that St Laurent would win in a walk had caused most Canadians – including Liberal delegates – to be bored by the convention. Kirk Cameron argued that delegates could be swayed by someone with 'colour and substance,' presumably Macdonald. 'I have a conviction that what the people of this country look for, long for, hope for is a leader with the soul of a poet and the hard common sense of a mathematician.'[100] Such words may have stoked Macdonald's ambition, but an upset such as he had won in 1930 would require an extraordinary combination of events.

Leadership conventions, unfortunately, leave little in the way of paper trails. Negotiations and canvassing are carried on face-to-face on the convention floor or in back rooms, unrecorded except as rumours in newspapers or faintly recalled in memoirs. The 1948 National Liberal Convention is typical; there is a record of speeches from the podium, the text of the resolutions, and a few secondary accounts that relate how smoothly the convention moved to anoint Louis St Laurent as leader.[101] Missing from most of these accounts is a discussion of the 'draft Macdonald' campaign and its quiet smothering. Even King's diary, usually a rich source for political history, is unhelpful on this point; King seemed to spend the entire weekend marvelling at the culmination of his career as the chosen instrument of Divine Order.[102]

Macdonald went to Ottawa undecided about whether to allow his name to be put forward as a candidate, though he rather leaned away from the possibility. He arrived early to get a sense of the situation and decided that St Laurent's momentum was irresistible. On the first night of the convention, Macdonald told Nova Scotia's seventy-eight delegates that he would not be a candidate.[103] The second day of the convention, however, had a restless tone, one more conducive to a dark horse. Delegates seemed frustrated to find that the convention was being so carefully managed by organizers. Young Liberals, who hoped to introduce significant changes to the party's platform, felt they were being silenced.[104] On Friday afternoon, a young group of Liberals, noisily proclaiming, 'We're for [Paul] Martin,' interrupted King's farewell speech, much to the embarrassment of the ambitious young minister of national health and welfare.[105]

After King spoke, Macdonald rose to move a resolution in favour of national unity. In his address Macdonald warned the party that it did not have a 'divine right to govern,' that it must abide by the principles of democracy and responsible government, and that it had to shake off the 'war psychology' of government by order-in-council.

The people of this country desire to be governed by their elected representatives, whom they know and whom they can call to account at stated intervals. They do not wish to be governed by other people, no matter how able or how well-intentioned they may be. They do not wish to be governed by people whom they don't know and who are not responsible to the great masses of people in this country.

Journalists called Macdonald's speech 'brilliant' and said it 'made a deep impression' on delegates; it also scared the organizers of St Laurent's campaign.[106]

To Macdonald's refusal to offer his name as a candidate, Prince Edward Island's premier Walter Jones reportedly said, 'Never mind, we'll draft you anyway.'[107] That seemed to be the mood of many delegates from the Maritimes on Saturday, the last day of the convention. A plan emerged from somewhere that McNair and Jones would nominate Macdonald, and Macdonald would refuse to stand; each would take the opportunity to voice the many Maritime and provincial grievances before a national audience. The Young Liberal delegate Dalton Camp ran into Robert Winters, MP for Lunenburg-Queens and soon to be Ilsley's replacement as the Nova Scotia minister in the cabinet. 'Isn't it great,' Camp enthused, 'McNair is nominating Angus L. and we're going to put our Maritime resolutions on the floor.' 'In a pig's ass,' Winters said, as he went off to try to squelch the scheme.[108] If the three premiers had settled on such a proposal, they soon dropped it. Macdonald did not run, and St Laurent won on the first ballot, taking almost 70 per cent of the votes.[109] St Laurent became leader of the Liberal party, though Mackenzie King held onto the title of prime minister until November, once he had safely beaten Sir Robert Walpole's endurance record.

Macdonald did not need much convincing to stay out of the race.[110] His decision rested partly on party loyalty and partly on an assessment of his chances in the *next* leadership race. Macdonald and his close friends surmised that most French Canadian delegates believed it was 'Quebec's turn' at the leadership, and the party elite was trying to establish a tradition of alternating between French and English Canadian leaders. If Macdonald had challenged St Laurent, he would have antagonized Quebec, the bulwark of the Liberal party for fifty years. Even a protest candidacy would have created rifts within the party, making it very difficult for Macdonald to serve as leader later.[111]

This was the heart of Macdonald's decision not to run: he made a poor protest candidate simply because he had such potential as a legitimate candidate in the future. St Laurent was sixty-six, while Macdonald was not yet fifty-eight. The Liberal government had seemed in rapid decline in recent months, with various signs of ineptitude and arrogance. The CCF remained a factor, and the Progressive Conservatives were about to choose the able and popular George Drew as their leader. The next election would not be an easy one, no matter who led the Liberals. Furthermore, if Macdonald had run and won in 1948, he would have been saddled with Mackenzie King's political organization, unable to tailor it to his own tastes in the two years remaining in the life of the government. Far better to catch the party on the way back up than on the way down; this scenario had worked wonderfully for Macdonald in 1930, and the premiership of Nova Scotia would provide a very comfortable base from which to await the next leadership convention.

It does not appear that Macdonald opted to stand aside as part of a quid pro quo with St Laurent and his supporters in cabinet. Though Ottawa did soon move on the question of a royal commission on transportation, Macdonald did not win any other major points. The federal government persisted in using fixed, per capita subsidies when the tax rental agreements were renewed in 1952 and 1957. Scheduled, annual federal-provincial conferences were not on the horizon. There was no constitutional reform in the works, and the 1950s witnessed a continuation of the pattern of economic policies and public projects – such as the St Lawrence Seaway and the TransCanada Pipeline – that benefited primarily Central Canada.

Macdonald did not see Louis St Laurent as the saviour of liberalism in Canada, but he could hardly be as bad as Mackenzie King, who seemed willing to sacrifice all for expediency and for his legacy. Macdonald's temper flashed less often in the St Laurent era, though the federal government continued to trod on areas of provincial jurisdiction. Macdonald may have grown weary after almost two decades in public life, battles with his ulcer, and quixotic errands to resurrect Rowell-Sirois liberalism.

5 Limits of the Liberal State

Angus Macdonald maintained his political dominance in Nova Scotia until his death in 1954. The strong ministers of the pre-war cabinets had departed, and on the whole the new ministers were weaker and unable to challenge him on policy, even had they wanted to do so. Macdonald generally left each to run his own department, but on key issues the premier usually convinced his colleagues of the wisdom of his views.[1] Government policy, therefore, remained consistent with Macdonald's philosophy of the role of the liberal state.

Macdonald cautiously combined the frustrations of the disadvantaged with the rhetoric of individual liberty and mobility. Nova Scotians suffered from the centrist policies of the federal government, but they were a hardy, enduring lot, too proud to accept direct government assistance. The state, he argued, should provide them with the tools to achieve economic and cultural self-improvement, but not actively interfere with economic forces. His administration after the Second World War accordingly played an active-but-indirect role in the Nova Scotian economy to preserve the structures of private enterprise and to quell agitation for a truly interventionist state. Macdonald committed the province's resources to developing a modern infrastructure – including roads, educational services, energy distribution, and cold-storage facilities – to promoting the province and its products, and to lobbying Ottawa for constitutional change and more favourable transportation policies. Meanwhile, the province resisted public ownership of industry and avoided direct financial assistance to businesses. Macdonald sought to create an environment conducive to economic development but declined to sponsor that development directly.

In the decade following the Second World War, revenues of the government of Nova Scotia increased by more than 240 per cent. Even though expenditures more than matched this remarkable growth – rising more than 270 per cent – the provincial government did have discretionary control over considerable amounts of money, something it had not enjoyed in the 1930s. Macdonald's postwar administration balanced the budget seven out of nine years, producing a cumulative surplus of more than $21 million. Nova Scotia's economy also grew. Between 1946 and 1954 the Gross Provincial Product (GPP) rose by almost 66 per cent. The province's economic performance did not, however, keep pace with the national economy, as the Gross National Product (GNP) fully doubled in the same period. Nova Scotia's share of GNP fell from 3.5 per cent in 1945 to 2.8 per cent in 1954. The economic marginalization of the province, a process begun in the late nineteenth century, continued in spite of the government's growing returns.[2]

Nova Scotian industries, including coal mining, agriculture, and the fishery, faced painful adjustments. Dwindling or vanishing markets, external competition, and sharp increases in shipping costs crippled profits and discouraged new investment. Those investors that remained tended to focus on the mechanization of existing production methods rather than new development and looked to increased efficiencies and reduced labour costs to secure future profits. In each of the province's resource industries investment and revenue increased significantly between 1945 and 1954; at the same time, employment in these industries dropped sharply.[3] The provincial government, meanwhile, remained an indirect participant in the economy, trusting that a modern infrastructure and market forces would spur development and employment.

Macdonald's government changed considerably in the period, with the departure of old colleagues through death, patronage appointments, or defeat. Attorney-General Josiah MacQuarrie took a seat on the bench in September 1947. Minister of Health Frank Davis died in September 1948. The affable Acadian representative in government, J. Willie Comeau, found a seat in the Senate in late 1948. Macdonald's college roommate and minister of labour, Lauchie Currie, was elevated to the bench in November 1949. The Speaker of the House, Gordon Romkey, lost in the 1953 election, twenty-five years after he had first won a seat. Macdonald found himself surrounded by young, sometimes arrogant ministers, few of whom he considered friends.[4]

In the 1930s, Macdonald had known many, if not most, of the public employees in Halifax. By the 1950s, government business was handled impersonally by a professional civil service, now 4000-strong. Macdonald was familiar with large-scale bureaucracy from his time in Ottawa, but at times did things 'the old way.' Henry Hicks, his future successor, recalled the premier holding up a cabinet meeting to edit the language of a bill, which Hicks believed could have been done by an assistant.[5]

On the federal scene the transition from Mackenzie King to Louis St Laurent did not proceed as smoothly as Liberals would have liked. Though St Laurent had won the leadership convention in early August, King remained as prime minister until November 1948, partly to make one last trip to Europe as Canada's leader, but mainly to establish a Commonwealth record as prime minister. Meanwhile, the Progressive Conservatives chose George Drew as their leader. Momentum lay with the Tories, and J.W. Pickersgill recalls that many believed 'the defeat of the Liberal government was almost certain in the next election.'[6]

The St Laurent–Drew contest previewed with a key by-election, held on 13 December 1948 in J.L. Ilsley's former seat of Digby-Annapolis-Kings. Ilsley, a member of Parliament for twenty-two years, resigned at the end of the 1948 session. Though he was just fifty-four, stress had taken a toll on his physical and mental health; he moved to Montreal to assist the ailing J.L. Ralston with his law practice.[7] Ilsley had won the Digby-Annapolis-Kings riding easily in the three elections since its creation in 1935. C.D. Howe, Gordon Fogo, and several other leading Liberals assumed that the riding would stay with the government, but voters used the occasion to express their discontent with the state of the federation.[8]

Perhaps no industry in Nova Scotia suffered as badly in the two world wars as the Annapolis Valley apple industry, which had previously enjoyed a profitable market in Britain. When the British market collapsed, Ottawa responded not by assisting in marketing, as it frequently had done with Western wheat, but by grudgingly subsidizing the contraction of the industry in Nova Scotia. Growers received compensation based on the number of trees they uprooted, and a once-thriving industry became relegated to a tiny share of the domestic market. Some voters grumbled as well about new federal income tax forms, which appeared overly complicated. In 1948 Annapolis Valley farmers and their neighbours were in no mood to support Liberals in Ottawa.[9]

To retain Digby-Annapolis-Kings and stimulate western Nova Scotia's economy, the federal government reopened HMCS Cornwallis as a naval training base. Defence minister Brooke Claxton made the announcement on 2 December, less than a fortnight before the by-election.[10] Although Ottawa planned to increase defence spending in general and expand the RCN in particular, the Cornwallis base – consisting of now-rotting temporary buildings big enough to house 10,000 naval recruits – was clearly a political plum. It joined another large military base in the riding, as the Royal Canadian Air Force maintained its installation at Greenwood.

All three parties took the by-election seriously, and each national leader made an appearance in the riding during the campaign. The Liberals nominated J.D. McKenzie, minister of highways under A.S. MacMillan. George Nowlan, a well-known lawyer and political organizer, ran for the Conservatives. The CCF put forward its provincial secretary, industrialist Lloyd Shaw. Nowlan ran an anti-government campaign, asking people in the riding to register their 'protest vote' with him. The frustrations of the apple growers trumped the sop of military spending: though the two western counties went Liberal, Nowlan carried a 2000-vote majority in his home county of Kings. Voters in the riding recognized that they were not sharing in the post-war boom, and King feared that his protégé St Laurent had lost the 'first real contest' with Drew.[11]

Macdonald called a provincial election for 9 June 1949, confident of winning another majority. A federal election followed the provincial by less than three weeks. Members of Nova Scotia's federal caucus initially asked Macdonald to delay Nova Scotia's vote; they assumed that the Progressive Conservatives would make some gains in the province and worried that these would hurt the federal party's chances. Macdonald argued that the provincial party was stronger than the federal and that the latter could ride his coattails. He felt he was doing it a great service by having the provincial election first: 'I am most eager to help St Laurent in any way.'[12]

Nova Scotia's government continued to post budget surpluses, and Macdonald's personal appeal remained almost irresistible, as indicated by the Liberals' prosaic campaign slogan, 'All's Well With Angus L.' Opposition to the party remained weak, with the CCF confined to urban, industrial Cape Breton, and the Conservatives starting from scratch with no seats and a raw new leader. Thirty-five-year-old Robert Stanfield came from one of Nova Scotia's leading industrial and Conservative families and moved almost unexpectedly into politics. He had been 'unenthusiastic about the practice of law' and had enough personal wealth that he could serve as leader and chief organizer for the Tories.[13] Yet in 1949, the party's organization was still a work in progress.

Macdonald was satisfied with the Liberal performance – the party dropped from twenty-eight of thirty seats to twenty-seven of thirty-seven and won 51 per cent of the vote – though he thought more ridings could have been won with better organizational work.[14] The Conservatives under Stanfield made impressive gains. Not only did they return to the House with eight seats, they also increased their share of the popular vote by 6 per cent, largely at the expense of the CCF.[15]

By the spring of 1949, Macdonald was quite impressed with St Laurent as the Liberal leader. 'St Laurent,' Macdonald wrote, has gotten 'much nearer to the people than King ever did. He [is] frank and straightforward instead of being obscure and devious.' Thus, the premier worked much harder on the 1949 federal campaign than he had in 1945. In addition to stumping within Nova Scotia, Macdonald also made his now regular trip to Eastern Ontario to speak in Kingston and the surrounding ridings. The election went smoothly for the Liberals, and Macdonald gave most of the credit to the party's new leader. 'He left the impression everywhere of a man of ability and character, a safe man.' George Drew, by contrast, came off as a petty squabbler.[16]

Macdonald was personally embarrassed when Joseph P. Connolly, an old friend, and Dan Lewis Macdonald, his brother, both stood for the Progressive Conservatives. During the war Connolly had been the RCN captain in charge of the stage and screen production Meet the Navy; politically he was neither active nor astute. His former law partner, J. McGregor Stewart, convinced him to run.[17] Dan Lewis's motives for offering were less clear, though at the time he said: '[T]he Mackenzie King–St Laurent government ha[s] departed from the true principles of Liberalism.'[18] Both Connolly and Dan Lewis were defeated soundly.

In the provincial campaign Stanfield had made three central criticisms of the Macdonald government: it engaged in nefarious dealings with liquor companies and their agents, it did not fund municipalities adequately, and it had no industrial policy.[19] The first charge was more or less true, as the Liberal party raised much of its funds from elements of the liquor trade. On the second score, the administration had devised a scheme to more equitably fund municipal governments, but it lacked the political will to implement it unilaterally. Stanfield was incorrect when he said that Macdonald had no industrial policy; indeed, it was in the province's economy that the premier gave freest rein to his liberalism.

Conservatives charged that 'secret liquor agents' operated in the province. These agents allegedly worked for breweries and distilleries to secure contracts from the government-run Nova Scotia Liquor Commission (NSLC) in exchange for contributions to the Liberal party. Macdonald claimed that the NSLC dealt directly with the companies, and that liquor agents did not exist. Technically Macdonald was correct, but in reality most companies doing business with the NSLC seem to have employed 'representatives' who were close to or often the same people as Liberal party bagmen. For example, Joe Reardon was president of the Halifax County Liberal Association and an 'employee' of Melchers Distilleries of Montreal.[20] Macdonald's former executive assistant, John J. Connolly, emerged as one of the most important fund-raisers for Nova Scotia Liberals outside the province. He also represented Noah Turno, director of Jordan Wines and Danforth Distilleries. Typically, companies were expected to kick back 2 per cent of their sales in the province to the party. Connolly pressed for more NSLC business for his client, pointing out that Turno gladly contributed whereas a certain competitor 'did not help to the extent of 2 per cent.' Connolly also 'put the touch' on the Bronfman interests for the Nova Scotia Liberals.[21]

Party coffers were fed as well by considerable sums raised through the Provincial Bottle Exchange. The Exchange, established shortly after the 1933 election, had a virtual monopoly on the empty beer bottle market in the province, and most of its profits went directly to the Liberal party of Nova Scotia. This arrangement very nearly exploded in the government's face on the eve of the 1953 election when the Department of National Revenue threatened to begin proceedings against W.B. Moriarty, president of the Exchange, for failing to pay about $95,000 in corporate taxes in the late 1940s. Moriarty, a city alderman and party organizer, used his connections within the federal Liberal party to avoid a scandal. Halifax MP John Dickey and Nova Scotia cabinet representative Robert Winters met with Minister of National Revenue James MacKinnon to set up a deal: the company would pay the taxes owed plus a 25 per cent fine, and National Revenue would not pursue charges.[22] The tax problems of the Bottle Exchange never became public.

For his part, Macdonald avoided personal dealings on the subject of liquor, recognizing the political pitfalls of even above-board relationships. In 1947 the discreet Geoffrey Stevens, minister without portfolio, took charge of the NSLC from the attorney-general's office. Macdonald rarely corresponded with either Stevens or Commissioner A.S. Mahon and left almost all liquor matters to them. Occasionally, he warned local patronage committees that the government could tolerate no improprieties on the part of NSLC workers, most of whom were patronage appointees.[23]

Stanfield was correct in saying that many of Nova Scotia's municipalities were in dire straits; they had not fully recovered from the losses to their revenue bases in the 1920s and 1930s and continued to struggle in the post-war period. The province had provided some financial assistance, including grants and guaranteed loans, but the basis of resource allocation was insufficient for modern municipal needs. Recognizing the shifting balances of government powers and resources, Macdonald attempted to address the problems of provincial-municipal affairs by commissioning Donald C. Rowat of Dalhousie's Institute of Public Affairs to study the situation and suggest ways to make municipal government more relevant and sustainable. He also arranged a conference between the province and the Union of Nova Scotia Municipalities. Murray Beck writes that Macdonald

> hoped to follow the course he had been recommending for the solution of federal-provincial financial problems ... The conference would first examine the distribution of authority between the province and the municipal governments with a view to determining what services each level could provide more effectively. Only then would it be appropriate to consider the allocation of financial resources.

To Macdonald's disappointment, the January 1948 conference produced only calls from the Union of Municipalities for more money.[24]

Rowat's report, delivered in early 1949, reflected several of the themes of the Rowell-Sirois report on dominion–provincial relations and paralleled Macdonald's thinking that 'local government [should serve] as an agency of democratic education and participation.'[25] The premier reasoned that municipal government could be the model of participatory democracy in Canada, but only if it were relevant to its citizens. To rejuvenate the third level of the state, Rowat proposed that municipalities be 'made directly responsible for administering a significant proportion of all the governmental services supplied within [their] borders.' This approach necessarily required expansion of the financial and administrative resources of Nova Scotia's municipalities.

Rowat found that municipal tax bases and administrations had been allowed to atrophy somewhat since the 1920s. The growth of the other two levels of government exacerbated the problem:

> In the last few years in particular it appears that, because of the rapid expansion of Dominion and provincial expenditures upon social services,

municipalities have not lived up to their responsibility for raising taxes to expand this field; they have hung back, simply because the provincial government was expanding its own services.

He pointed out that Nova Scotia's provincial government taxes were 19 per cent above the Canadian average, while municipal taxes were 31 per cent below the national average. Rowat argued that property-tax bases needed to be developed and rationalized. Yet he also recognized the disparities among the province's counties and towns and, while he favoured shifting some sources of revenues to municipalities to strengthen their autonomy, he warned that different levels of resources would negatively affect the delivery of services. Thus, Rowat proposed an 'equalization' scheme, administered by the province and based on 'revenue-raising ability' and 'expenditure requirements.' Municipalities with weak revenue bases and large populations would qualify for extra consideration.

Rowat also believed that Nova Scotia's municipalities – established long before modern communications systems – were too small to provide a good bureaucratic infrastructure for service delivery. He suggested a second tier of local government, supra-municipal units of at least 30,000 people, organized along 'natural geographic and economic' lines, to administer 'public health, hospitals, poor relief, County Homes, and possibly education' as well as regional planning. Rowat estimated that Nova Scotia's eighteen counties could be divided into ten large units; he did not suggest that the counties be dissolved nor did he specifically describe these units in his report. Entry to the regional units would be voluntary for municipalities, but would be a prerequisite to obtaining further provincial grants. In turn, these units would be able to support skilled bureaucrats and provide invaluable training to novice politicians.

Although the Rowat report represented Macdonald's ideal for provincial–municipal relations, Beck argues that it 'proved of little direct use to the provincial government, for in recommending a two-tier system of local government, it proposed a remedy which, however sound in theory, appeared to be altogether impracticable.'[26] The province continued to host large, annual meetings with the municipalities; it worked closely with them on projects for new schools and hospitals; it pushed municipalities to draw more from their tax bases, and it eliminated several taxes that municipalities paid to the province – including the highway tax and a rural poll tax – but it shied away from implementing fundamental changes to municipal structures.[27] This is understandable when one considers that municipal government already provided something more than a 'training ground' for provincial politics. Mayors, aldermen, county wardens, and county councillors were often the local distributors of patronage, and a county councillor upset with the provincial government could conceivably change the election result in a riding, either through personal influence or by rewarding the wrong people with jobs on the highways. With little municipal backing for Rowat's plans, Macdonald chose to let sleeping dogs lie.

Stanfield's contention that the province lacked an industrial policy missed the ideological nature of the province's approach. Following Macdonald's liberal principles the government worked 'to create conditions under which citizens should work out their own salvation,' but – with a few exceptions – avoided playing a direct role in the economy. James Bickerton writes: '[T]here were no notable provincial [development] initiatives at that time. Constricted finances were no doubt a major factor, but so was Macdonald's economic orthodoxy.'[28] The government willingly invested resources only in infrastructure, education, and research. In 1949 it established the Nova Scotia Research Foundation (NSRF) to aid the development of industry. Macdonald also promised $100 million over five years on a public works program to develop the province's intellectual and physical infrastructure, giving individual Nova Scotians the tools to improve their economy.[29] The program included rural high schools, cold storage plants for the fishery, the continuation of the highway paving and tourism programs, and bridges across the Halifax Harbour and the Strait of Canso.

Macdonald established the NSRF in 1946 with a million-dollar endowment and hired two professors to direct it.[30] Harold Innis had suggested a research council to guide government and industry in his complimentary report to the Jones commission in 1934.[31] The royal commission on post-war development and rehabilitation, directed by R. MacGregor Dawson, repeated the call for an advisory board on research and development to aid Nova Scotia's economy.[32] Innis, Dawson, and Macdonald reasoned that only the government could afford to fund long-term research into problems facing the province's primary industries. The NSRF also became quite active in trying to attract new industry to Nova Scotia and to secure new contracts for existing industries.[33]

The government flirted with direct aid to industry in 1948, creating a $1 million business loans program, administered by Harold Connolly's Department of Tourism and Industry.[34] Nova Scotia assisted in the establishment of the Bendix appliance factory in Amherst and the Cossar television and radar factory in Halifax through direct government loans.[35] Most of the loan applications the government received, however, came from small motel and hotel operators; all too frequently, the loans were not recovered, and the government moved to bureaucratize the program in 1950.[36]

Macdonald disagreed with some of Dawson's proposals for the post-war development of Nova Scotia, but adopted many of his ideas when provincial resources allowed. The Dawson report viewed 'encouragement of industry' as crucial to the reconstruction period, but did not spell out clearly what forms that encouragement should take.[37] Given that the province collected no income tax and only a small corporation tax, manipulation of taxation rates was unlikely to attract new industry. Large loans or grants to industry were beyond the resources of the province – even with one or two huge post-war surpluses – and outside Macdonald's liberal ideology. Million-dollar loans to private firms might result in more employment, but he believed that the state should avoid taking such risks with public funds. The risks of failure ought not to be discounted. Shortly after Macdonald's death, the Liberal government was embarrassed by the bankruptcy of Mercury Fisheries, which had been given an unsecured loan of $367,000 to develop a herring fishery off Cape Breton's west coast.[38]

The CCF called for public ownership of the province's steel, power generation, and coal industries. Predictably, the Liberals rejected such ideas, though political pressures in Macdonald's home county kept the government-owned Inverness Mine operating for twenty years. The miners had taken over operations in 1925 when the company failed. They received assistance from the Rhodes-Harrington government, but in 1934 Macdonald's administration took control of the mine outright. The province had no long-term plan for the mine, other than selling it, and did not invest significantly to improve its efficiency. The mine never posted a surplus and by the time it closed in 1951 it had lost $3,664,000 of public money.[39]

The post-war Macdonald governments made substantial changes to the province's intellectual infrastructure. No grants were yet made to universities to aid undergraduate programs, but assistance to Dalhousie's schools of law and medicine was increased.[40] More important, the province extended to thousands of students the opportunity of secondary education by providing capital loans to municipalities and launching a program to build rural high schools. The latter were intended both to provide Nova Scotians with the skills required in a modern economy and to slow rural out-migration. The province also stepped in to bail out the floundering teachers' pension scheme and to subsidize increases in teachers' wages throughout the province.

All of these moves sharply increased provincial spending on education. In 1939 the province contributed about $1.3 million towards the cost of education, covering less than 30 per cent of the overall cost; by 1950, it spent $7.6 million, about a fifth of the provincial budget, and covered 55.7 per cent of the cost. Representing such a significant portion of public spending, education obviously warranted ministerial control through a bureaucratized administration. Nova Scotia had long relied on a superintendent of education – always a Protestant – and emphasized local control of schools, attempting to avoid the divisive battles over religion that existed in other provinces. In 1949 Macdonald created a Ministry of Education under Henry Hicks, hoping to avoid political capriciousness and sectarianism.[41]

Macdonald's Liberal government attempted to stimulate the province's economy indirectly through the modernization of its physical infrastructure, as when it built a cold storage plant to bolster the fishery around the depressed area of Louisbourg. Macdonald took a more aggressive stance on the fishery after the war, following a report written by Stewart Bates, assistant deputy minister of fisheries, for the Dawson commission. Bates saw modernization as the solution to problems in the fishery, and in the mid-1940s modernization meant quick-frozen, filleted fish, marketed to the urban middle class of North America. This required a comprehensive program of modernization of all aspects of the fishery, from an increase in the number of trawlers and cold storage plants to refrigerated rail cars and freezers in retail stores. Only by abandoning 'traditional' production practices could fishers participate in a modern, industrialized economy.[42]

Bates recommended carefully spaced fish-processing plants and cold storage facilities along Nova Scotia's coast. In 1946 Macdonald announced plans for a joint project at Louisbourg to complement privately owned plants at Yarmouth, Lunenburg, and Halifax. The province would build and operate a cold storage plant at a cost of $300,000; the Dominion would construct a large wharf for $210,000, and two American companies would put up $250,000 each to establish processing plants to be supplied by the companies' trawlers.[43] Ottawa dragged its feet over the wharf, however, delaying construction until 1948.[44] Meanwhile domestic opposition from South Shore fishers and other fishing interests mounted; National Seafoods' president Ralph Bell argued that the logic of the market should dictate whether such development should occur at Louisbourg.[45] Conditions in the post-war fishery improved slightly, but not as significantly as planners had expected.[46]

Other infrastructure projects begun before the war were resumed, including extending electrical power to rural sections of the province, developing tourism areas such as the Cape Breton Highlands National Park, and expanding the network of paved roads in the province. While these endeavours provided a distinct political benefit by directly employing workers for a time, Macdonald saw the long-term results as the true return on investment. He believed that efficient transportation systems would retain and attract industry. In the post-war period, two large projects drew most of his attention: the Halifax-Dartmouth bridge and the Canso Causeway.

The idea of bridging the Halifax harbour was not new, though two nineteenth-century spans had collapsed.[47] Mackenzie King's government had commissioned a design and cost estimate for a bridge or tunnel connecting the cities of Halifax and Dartmouth in 1929. King's defeat and the Great Depression squelched those plans. Soon after war's end, however, local politicians resurrected the scheme, forming the Halifax-Dartmouth Bridge Association in 1947. Macdonald hired Dr Philip Pratley of Montreal, who had conducted the 1929–30 survey, to draw up new plans and present an updated estimate. In September 1948, Pratley submitted a scheme for a bridge priced at $4,468,400, later revised to $6.2 million.[48]

A project even nearer to Macdonald's heart was a permanent link between Cape Breton and mainland Nova Scotia across the Strait of Canso. This long-standing dream gained momentum in 1947, as an economic slump in Cape Breton coincided with the need to renovate the ferry system at Mulgrave. Macdonald initially favoured tunnels for both Halifax and Canso, reasoning that they would require less steel and concrete – materials in great shortage after the war – and would provide more local employment, especially of surplus labour from Cape Breton's coal mines. Cost estimates and geological concerns soon eliminated the tunnel option.[49]

Macdonald led a delegation from industrial Cape Breton and the Canso Strait area to Ottawa to meet with Howe, Ilsley, and Minister of Transportation Lionel Chevrier in July 1947. Macdonald pointed out that the cost of new ferries and yearly operation of the service ran to about $500,000; this, he argued, could be better spent on a mortgage for a causeway or bridge. D.W. McLachlan, Ottawa's senior engineer, estimated that a causeway with a lock would cost $35 million, and a bridge $54 million. Macdonald noted that this was considerably higher than the estimate McLachlan made to a parliamentary committee in 1943. Then, McLachlan had priced a causeway and lock at $12 million and a bridge at $20 million. Macdonald said that even allowing for inflation, McLachlan's new estimate showed that he either had not studied the proposal or was inexplicably hostile to it. Some members of Nova Scotia's delegation had grown hostile to McLachlan and eagerly awaited his pending retirement.[50]

Both the Halifax and Canso projects faced significant obstacles, and Macdonald played a central role in keeping them on course. In Halifax, the only practical site for the bridge cut across H.M.C. Dockyard Halifax and probably required a pier within the naval base. Defence minister Brooke Claxton objected that a bridge overlooking the dockyard would present a security problem. Macdonald had Halifax MP Gordon Isnor work on Claxton. After more than a year of Nova Scotia's lobbying, Defence dropped its objections to the North Street site and the project moved ahead.[51] For the Canso crossing, Ottawa and the railways accepted McLachlan's high estimate and prepared to refurbish the ferry facilities. Chevrier wrote that the idea of a causeway had been abandoned; however, as a favour to Macdonald he would recommend an independent study to cabinet. The federal government set up a three-member panel to look into the matter, splitting the cost with the province; Nova Scotia nominated Dr Pratley as its representative.[52]

The panel rescued the fixed crossing scheme as viable, though at first it favoured a Pratley-designed bridge for $13.5 million before settling on a lock-and-causeway. Engineers in both Ottawa and Nova Scotia questioned Pratley's design, arguing that the strength of the Strait's currents and the pressure of ice packs would topple the piers. His pride wounded and professional reputation at stake, Pratley threatened to withdraw from both the Halifax and Canso projects, but Macdonald soothed his battered ego and kept him working on the Halifax-Dartmouth bridge.[53] Just as remarkably, Macdonald prevented the demise of the Canso bridge plan from defeating the whole idea of a crossing. The railway companies went back to discussing the ferry option, and Canadian National Railways president Donald Gordon went so far as to say publicly that he was opposed to either a bridge or a causeway. Macdonald won over Ottawa, which finally settled on a relatively inexpensive causeway with a lock to allow for shipping and ice flow.[54] The

Halifax-Dartmouth Bridge and the Canso Causeway came to symbolize Macdonald's infrastructure liberalism.

Soon after St Laurent's convention victory, Macdonald resumed organizing the provinces outside Central Canada and pressed the 'acting Prime Minister' to secure a commission of inquiry into the matter of transportation. The dominion cabinet agreed to meet with the Seven Premiers once more on 27 and 28 September 1948. The premiers had rather more success than before, and Ottawa agreed that the Board of Transport Commissioners had erred in its ruling by failing to differentiate between the railway revenues of Canadian Pacific and those of its other operations when calculating liabilities. Order-in-council 4678, passed 14 October, directed the board to make this distinction but said nothing about a royal commission.[55] Macdonald thanked St Laurent for finally accepting the provinces' point, but repeated the Seven Premiers' contention that only a royal commission could properly investigate the crisis in transportation costs. St Laurent finally agreed and asked Macdonald to suggest names of potential commissioners.[56]

Macdonald cabled the other premiers for their ideas and soon fashioned a list of potential commissioners, including several international experts, but the federal government preferred to go with three Canadians.[57] Justice W.F.A. Turgeon was named chair. Saskatchewan's attorney-general before moving to the bench, he had sat on numerous royal commissions and later served as Canada's ambassador to Argentina, Chile, Mexico, Belgium, and Ireland. No grand ideas were expected of Turgeon; rather, he was seen as a peace-maker who was adept at calming tensions.[58] Any vision on transportation issues would come from the two professors appointed to the commission, H.A. Innis and H.F. Angus. University of Toronto political economist Harold Innis, perhaps Canada's most acclaimed academic, had written his doctoral dissertation on the Canadian Pacific Railway and had experience on provincial royal commissions.[59] Henry Angus, an economist from the University of British Columbia, specialized in matters of trade and had served on the much-vaunted Rowell-Sirois Commission on Dominion-Provincial Relations.

The terms of reference instructed the commission to

review and report upon the effect, if any, of economic, geographic or other disadvantages under which certain sections of Canada find themselves in relation to the various transportation services therein, and recommend what measures should be initiated in order that the national transportation policy may best serve the general economic well-being of all Canada.

Ottawa also ordered an examination of the railways' accounting methods and the extent of their cooperation under the Railway Act and the Canadian National–Canadian Pacific Act of 1933.[60] Significantly, the terms made no mention of the impact of tariffs, which Macdonald considered a correlative to transportation in the Canadian economy. Industries in Nova Scotia required affordable access to the Central Canadian market mainly because the tariff structure closed off other potential markets or did not provide sufficient protection, as in the case of coal. An inquiry into transportation policy, therefore, had to take heed of the national policy to be comprehensive.[61]

The case that Nova Scotia put to the Royal Commission on Transportation was ably researched and prepared by the Transportation Commission of the Maritime Board of Trade (MBT). The MBT – proportionally funded by Nova Scotia, New Brunswick, and Prince Edward Island – had been formed amid the Maritime Rights movement of the 1920s and resurrected in 1933 in an unprecedented example of interprovincial cooperation.[62] Rand Matheson, an expert on railway operations, headed the MBT's Transportation Commission, which represented the three provinces before the BTC. It also compiled information on the Maritime economy and the effects of transportation policy, kept the premiers apprised of developments in transportation, and occasionally negotiated rates with the railways on behalf of shippers in the region.

Nova Scotia hosted the Turgeon commission from 12 to 14 July 1949. Matheson had intended to present one brief on behalf of the three provinces, but Macdonald argued that as the royal commission resulted directly from the pressure brought to bear by the Seven Premiers, each province should make a presentation.[63] Macdonald welcomed the commission by recalling the work of the Duncan Commission on Maritime Claims (1926–7) and the Duff Commission on Transportation (1931), though he noted that their recommendations remained ignored or imperfectly implemented. He then approvingly cited Alberta premier Ernest Manning's testimony on transportation policy, arguing that the commission 'should not necessarily accept conditions as they are, but should be designed to ensure an essential equality of conditions for economic enterprises in so far as man-made conditions are concerned.'[64]

After his fifteen-minute address, Macdonald left the rest of the province's presentation to Matheson and Frank Smith. They laid out a detailed argument favouring a reinvigorated Maritime Freight Rates Act, the continuation of coal subventions, and the adjustment of April–November port rates in the Maritimes to make them competitive with Montreal's. They expressly opposed horizontal rate increases and, significantly, advocated giving broader powers to the Board of Transport Commissioners. The new board, in their view, would be able to consider economic policies and conditions in its rulings and would be in a position to compel cooperation between railway companies to lower costs. Predictably, Nova Scotia and the MBT did not support Prince Edward Island's call for national ownership of all railways.[65]

The report of the Turgeon Commission on Transportation, tabled on 9 February 1951, was a disappointment to Macdonald. The commissioners had laboured for two years, enduring almost endless travel and detailed testimony. Harold Innis, for one, found the experience completely draining. From Regina he wrote his wife: 'I am afraid I am getting more and more disgusted and that my character is slowly deteriorating through not having enough courage to resign. I go on saying that things will improve and find them getting worse. But I doubt whether I can stand it very much longer.' He found the work totally unfulfilling and, in July 1950, fell seriously ill as the report was being written.[66] In the end, Innis found it necessary to submit a separate 'Memorandum on Transportation,' and Henry Angus signed the report only after attaching a list of his 'Reservations and Observations.'[67]

The report represented compromises on most of the central issues and had no substantial recommendations. The commissioners rejected full public ownership of the railways and failed to define 'a reasonable rate of return' for the railway companies. They damned horizontal rate increases and praised the equalization of rates, but offered no mechanisms to deal with either, leaving matters to the board. The central theme in the report involved equalization: consistency in rates charged throughout Canada, based on mileage and tonnage. According to the commissioners, 'the broad general principle of equalization throughout the country is now accepted ... The time has come for the abolition of regional differences.' Yet the report acknowledged the value and purpose of both the Crow's Nest Pass rates and the Maritime Freight Rates Act and recommended that these be exempt from equalization legislation.[68]

In his memorandum, Innis wrote that competitive rates in Central Canada created an imbalance that threatened Confederation. His work in political economy attuned him to the dangers of liberal economics

within the Canadian federation, but he could not bring himself to recommend policies that would contravene liberalism.[69] He supported the
Maritime Freight Rates Act, but held that no one policy – not even
equalization, long requested by Western Canadians – could restrain the
centralizing economic forces of the last two decades.

> No scheme of equalization can be devised which will overcome the effects
> of competition in the St Lawrence region as reflected particularly in com-
> petitive rates. An obsession with equalization will obscure the handicaps
> of the Maritimes and of Western Canada and perpetuate their paralyzing
> effects. A reorganization of the regulatory bodies concerned with trans-
> portation will facilitate collection of vital statistical facts and offset the
> most serious effects ... In this way more precise methods can be devised to
> meet the problems of transportation in Canada.[70]

Innis clearly saw the Turgeon commission as a first step in a long process of careful study.

By the end of 1951, Ottawa had prepared legislation to give shape to
the commission's recommendation of rate equalization. Rand Matheson
appeared before the Commons committee dealing with the bill and was
overjoyed when he secured a subsection exempting territory covered
under the Maritime Freight Rates Act.[71] Rather than redressing Maritime grievances, the Turgeon commission proved a bullet to be dodged.
In March 1953 the BTC awarded the railways yet another rise in freight
rates, representing a total increase in rates of 98 per cent in six years.[72]

After the commission completed its work, Innis corresponded with
Frank Covert, the commission's legal counsel. Innis was disturbed by
the comments of one observer that the commission's 'prime object [had
been] to establish real political peace and to leave the vital problems of
transportation to the B.T.C.' Covert apparently accepted this assessment and replied that

> the Report really did establish political peace by delay, by a few admoni-
> tions to the Board, by the recommending of equalization (in a bastard sort
> of way), by the retaining of the Crow's Nest Pass rates, and by preserving
> the Maritime Freight Rates Act, and by giving the Government an oppor-
> tunity to fix up the C.N.R.'s capitalization.[73]

The peace was temporary; within a decade another commission was
convened on transportation.[74]

Taking a bolder step than any Mackenzie King had dared venture, Louis St Laurent invited the premiers to Ottawa in January 1950 to discuss the British North America Act and a possible amending formula. C.G. 'Chubby' Power offered Macdonald the use of his office on Parliament Hill. Power attached some conditions: first that Macdonald 'bow his haughty head in acknowledgement of the superiority, mental, intellectual and judicial, of his superiors in Ottawa.' Second, Power warned: 'I won't have you plotting with Duplessis within its confines. This is an honest man's room, and no dark conspiracy is to be hatched therein.'[75] Power's joking aside, this conference was marked by cooperation unseen in twenty years.

When the delegates gathered on 10 January 1950, Ottawa presented no concrete proposal for an amending formula, thus avoiding giving belligerent premiers something to criticize. The federal delegates sat mum as Saskatchewan's T.C. Douglas took one pole and Quebec's Maurice Duplessis the other. Douglas urged the federal government to play a larger role in constructing social welfare programs, in labour legislation, and in the marketing of natural resources. Duplessis, as expected, flatly opposed giving up one iota of provincial prerogative, though he did so without bombast. A long-overdue, constructive discussion of constitutional issues appeared to be at hand.[76]

While other premiers spoke in generalities – either hesitant or unprepared to offer clear suggestions – Macdonald arrived prepared with a specific proposal for constitutional talks. He resurrected the scheme of separate amending formulae for different sections of the constitution, first raised in 1935. Under the 'Macdonald Plan' the federal and provincial attorneys-general would form a continuing committee to identify categories of the constitution and to propose an amending formula for each.[77] Nova Scotia's attorney-general Malcolm Patterson presented a draft resolution, setting up four categories into which constitutional powers could be placed: federal powers, provincial powers, shared powers, and entrenched, fundamental rights.[78] This compartmentalization became the basis for future talks.

The prime minister did not wholly abandon unilateralism. St Laurent agreed with Macdonald that the constitution could be compartmentalized, but he argued that Ottawa could alter any provision of the BNA Act that dealt with federal responsibility; provincial consultation, much less consent, was unnecessary. He even held that Parliament could amend the constitution in matters of shared power, provided provincial powers later agreed to the changes.[79]

Privately, Macdonald explained his hesitation about accepting St Laurent's method in response to an article in the *Financial Post* by Bora Laskin on constitutional change. Laskin suggested that Parliament could unilaterally alter the structures of the federal government, as the provincial legislatures could for their own governments. Macdonald disagreed, arguing that it mattered not at all to Ontario when Nova Scotia abolished its Legislative Council in 1928, for example, but that it would matter to all provinces if Parliament changed the composition of the Senate. That body had been consciously constructed to represent provincial and regional interests within Parliament, in recognition of the fact that provinces have an interest in the actions of the federal government. Macdonald did not favour an amending formula so stringent as to prevent all constitutional change, but he did believe that on issues of national importance – such as the admission of Newfoundland to Confederation or the abolition of appeals to the Privy Council – Ottawa had a moral, if not constitutional, obligation to consult the provinces.[80]

Macdonald pursued other methods of amending the constitution as well. In 1947 his government passed a law stipulating that the provincial and federal governments could delegate powers to each other. Nova Scotia's attorney-general Josiah MacQuarrie immediately referred the bill to the Supreme Court of Nova Scotia. This 'amending shortcut' would allow the transfer of jurisdiction in labour law from the province to Ottawa, opening the door to a federal labour code. In return, Ottawa would delegate to the province the power to collect revenue through indirect taxation – a sales tax. Nova Scotia's Court rejected the idea, and the Supreme Court of Canada unanimously ruled the bill *ultra vires* the Nova Scotia Legislature in early October. It ruled that delegation of powers violated the constitution, although later, in *PEI Potato Marketing Board v. H.B. Willis Inc.* (1952), the court ruled that Parliament could delegate powers not to a provincial legislature, but to an administrative body created by that legislature.[81]

In August 1950 the attorneys-general met and apportioned 96 of the 147 sections of the BNA Act into six categories. They divided powers into provincial, federal, or shared categories and indicated whether the powers were to be entrenched or mutable. The six categories each had an amending formula, ranging from a simple act of Parliament to the unanimous agreement of Ottawa and the provinces.[82] Much work remained to be done, but things appeared to be moving forward by the time of the federal-provincial conference of late September in Quebec City. This conference opened against the backdrop of two emerging crises: a strike by the nation's railway workers and the developing conflict in Korea.[83] Douglas and Duplessis again took up opposing positions, and – lacking direction or pressure from the federal delegates – this meeting also ended pleasantly but without accomplishment.

Macdonald did not know it at the time, but comprehensive constitutional talks had been spiked for his lifetime. The provinces met with the federal government again in December, but the focus of the talks was the next round of tax rental agreements; Ottawa used the Korean War as justification for not seeking a more permanent solution on constitutional change. External affairs minister Lester Pearson, defence minister Brooke Claxton, and finance minister Douglas Abbott each painted a bleak picture of the international situation and spoke of the need for greater defence spending. According to Pickersgill, this tactic succeeded in making the premiers more compliant.[84] The federal government offered to boost the guaranteed minimum revenues for the provinces by 50 per cent of the 1945 offer. Macdonald cabled his provincial colleagues from Ottawa, asking their opinion. 'All agree that we must concur in Federal proposals largely because of political considerations,' came the response. 'People here not too happy over manner in which proposals were advanced but feel that we cannot afford to disagree.' Nova Scotia signed the deal along with all the other provinces except Quebec.[85]

In addition to the tax rental agreement, Ottawa also put the Old Age Pension (OAP) and a provincial sales tax on the table, though it refused to discuss a national health scheme.[86] The federal government offered to cover the cost of universal pensions for those over seventy and half the cost for a means-tested pension for those aged sixty-five to seventy. All provinces, including Quebec, agreed to the constitutional amendment necessary to grant Ottawa shared jurisdiction over pensions. Yet Macdonald worried that lowering the pensionable age was another Ottawa-led step that would cost the province money. He expected that the means test would not survive long against public opinion and that the province would soon be called upon to pay pensions to everyone over sixty-five.[87]

After the war, revenues from liquor and the federal-provincial tax rental agreement had provided some astonishing surpluses, but – as Macdonald warned with every budget speech – demand for more social spending and infrastructure drove up public expenditures much faster than revenues grew. In the fiscal year 1946–7 the province had recorded a surplus of more than $9,507,000; in 1947–8 the surplus dropped to $4,875,000, and in 1948–9 it was just $113,000.[88] By the 1950s the surpluses had dried up. Initial estimates for the 1949–51 budget

anticipated a deficit of $5,369,000 and sent Macdonald searching franti-
cally for spending cuts and new taxes.[89] Macdonald advised all ministers to spare no effort locating savings as they prepared their
departmental estimates. Things had improved by the time Macdonald
presented his budget speech in April 1950, but he was still forced to
predict the first deficit in ten years: $1,835,000 on revenues of
$47,655,000. Macdonald told the Assembly that this one deficit did not
concern him, but the trend of the last few years troubled him greatly.
How far was government to go?[90]

In 1950 the province considered a 'turnover tax' on retail sales – British Columbia, Saskatchewan, Quebec, and New Brunswick already had
such taxes – but it chose instead to reduce expenditures and expand
some existing taxes. Calculations for 1951–2, however, indicated that a
sales tax might be essential to Nova Scotia's financial stability. Including a provincial sales tax of 3 per cent that could generate about $2 mil-
lion in revenue, the estimates showed a deficit of $850,000 on revenues
of more than $40,500,000.[91]

Early in 1951 Stuart Garson, now the federal minister of justice, circulated two proposed amendments to the constitution: 95.2, allowing
Ottawa the power to legislate in the matter of pensions, and 92.2, allowing provinces to collect a sales tax.[92] Macdonald solicited the advice of
C.J. Burchell, a former law partner of Ralston's and frequent counsel to
the province. Burchell observed that provinces that had introduced
'turnover' taxes had required lengthy descriptions of what was and
was not taxable; Burchell doubted whether the BNA Act was the place
for such detail. He agreed with Macdonald that services ought to be
taxed along with goods, but warned that this could strengthen the hand
of central provinces even further, as Ontario and Quebec could tax
transactions of the stock exchanges in their provinces, drawing more
wealth from the outlying regions. Finally, Burchell noted that since the
Privy Council had ruled that provinces could collect sales taxes as
direct taxes under section 92, an amendment might not be necessary.[93]

Macdonald heard from others opposed to the amendment. Margaret
Hyndman, a lawyer representing the Canadian Retail Federation,
argued that requiring the agreement of all the provinces and the
Dominion for the sales tax amendment would prove a damaging precedent. Hyndman warned this would mean that

the constitutional development of Canada must be attuned to the most
conservative, and perhaps the most selfish, of the Provinces, any one of

whom could block Constitutional changes. Surely it would be better for the Provinces now to face up to the problem of working out an equitable and fair method for amending our Constitution.[94]

Hyndman's clients obviously opposed the tax for non-constitutional reasons, but it is telling that she relied on this argument when addressing Macdonald.

The premier denied that this would set a precedent for future amendments and noted that Ottawa and the provinces were 'in the midst of an attempt at devising a general method of amending the constitution.' He agreed with Hyndman that more comprehensive constitutional change in the allocation of taxation was needed:

> I have been advocating this for some seventeen or eighteen years with, however, little or no support from Governments at Ottawa. In my judgment the parts of the BNA Act conferring tax jurisdiction on the Dominion and the provinces were grossly unfair to the provinces ... Virtually what the BNA Act did in 1867 was to give the Dominion the power to completely cripple the taxing ability of the provinces. This need not have been done and was not done in the United States. The proposal to allow the provinces to impose a turn over tax was the first sign that I had seen that the Federal authorities were beginning to see the unfairness of the relative positions.[95]

Macdonald did not relish imposing a sales tax, but he was delighted to see Ottawa finally do something to increase the taxation capacity of the provinces.

That delight ended with Douglas Abbott's budget speech on 10 April 1951. Abbott announced an increase from 8 per cent to 10 per cent in the federal government's sales tax, applied at the manufacturer's level.[96] Macdonald immediately protested. Had Nova Scotia known at the conference in December that Ottawa would raise its sales tax, the province would not have been interested in a provincial sales tax. 'Difficult as it may be to do,' the premier wrote, 'we may simply have to say that we cannot impose a sales tax in view of the increase in the Dominion rate, and that it will therefore become necessary for us to cut some services.' Abbott expressed surprise at Macdonald's claim. He could see no impediment to Nova Scotia's adopting a sales tax, whether or not Ottawa increased its tax rates. Macdonald fumed that dominion revenues always took precedence, even though these revenues were needed solely because Ottawa 'thrusts itself into fields that are traditionally Provincial ... The Provinces, with their already vast, inescapable and ever increasing burdens ... are somehow expected to get along ... while their meagre taxing rights which were granted them at Confederation are being constantly whittled away.'[97]

Macdonald's ire showed again in a dispute over the OAP. A conference of dominion and provincial health ministers had been held on 23 and 24 May 1951 to discuss details of the new plan. The conference addressed an income ceiling for the means test – the maximum income a person aged sixty-five to sixty-nine could earn and still be eligible for the OAP – and Harold Connolly said Nova Scotia favoured keeping it at $600. Most of the provinces, save Saskatchewan, seemed to accept this proposal, though Ontario and Quebec indicated that they would not oppose raising the ceiling.[98] When health minister Paul Martin introduced legislation for the means-tested OAP to Parliament, he announced a rise in the income ceiling to $720.[99] Macdonald fired off telegrams to Martin, St Laurent, and Robert Winters, protesting that unilateral action by Ottawa again was costing the Province of Nova Scotia money. Martin replied that, although the majority of provinces favoured keeping the ceiling at $600, he sensed 'the disposition of most provinces was to provide some modest upward adjustment.' Martin maintained that Nova Scotia need not match the $720 ceiling, but Macdonald correctly pointed out that this would be politically impossible. If provincial opinions were to be ignored by the federal government on matters of shared jurisdiction, Macdonald asked rhetorically, why bother with a conference at all?[100]

Provincial autonomy remained a foundation of Macdonald's liberalism in the St Laurent era. Until the constitution defined jurisdictions and taxation powers in exclusive terms, Macdonald believed, dominion policies would continue to undermine the independence of provincial governments, and voters would not know which government to hold accountable. Macdonald may have enjoyed warmer relations with St Laurent, but the new prime minister appeared just as willing to accept federal unilateralism as had his predecessor.

On 22 July 1950 Mackenzie King passed away at Kingsmere. In the weeks and months after King's death, Macdonald and his friends quietly and cynically observed the rituals of mourning and homage that went on in Ottawa. Leonard Brockington, formerly a bitter critic of the late prime minister, took to the airways in fulsome praise in a series of radio broadcasts. Macdonald never criticized King publicly, but he kept a watchful eye on the activities of the biographers, anticipating that they would 'depict Mackenzie King as a noble, disinterested and high-minded spirit ... Knowing King as we did, we realize that the diaries and memoirs would be written always with an eye to posterity, and only one side of the story would be given.'[101] Macdonald and his friends understood how much consideration King had given to his legacy throughout his life and observed that he took steps to 'perpetuate his memory' in his will. Referring to King's bequest for university scholarships, Macdonald noted: 'All due offerings have been made to the muse of history.'[102]

Macdonald, Crerar, Alex Johnston, Chubby Power, and Kirk Cameron made a hobby of scrutinizing King biographies. Shortly after King's death, R. MacGregor Dawson began work on an official biography, Bruce Hutchison prepared a journalistic one, and Bernard Ostry and H.S. Ferns collaborated on an 'exposé' account.[103] In 1949 H. Reginald Hardy had published a 'King-approved' biography of the former prime minister, allowing his subject final approval of the manuscript in exchange for information.[104] Hardy's comments on the conscription crisis, in particular, provoked Macdonald to respond publicly. In late December 1949 Macdonald issued a press release defending J.L. Ralston and, by extension, attacking King; dozens of letters of praise and thanks poured in to the premier's office.[105] At the prodding of *Maclean's* editor W.A. Irwin, Macdonald considered writing his own account of the conscription issue, but after making some chapter outlines, he set the project aside, presumably for his retirement.[106]

Bruce Hutchison enjoyed a friendship with Crerar and Macdonald, but his *Incredible Canadian* unsettled them. They concluded that Hutchison had spoken at length with King about key parts of the book and agreed with King's self-image. Macdonald wrote to John Connolly that he found it 'difficult to accept [Hutchison's] estimate that King as a public figure was greater than Macdonald or Laurier.'[107]

John Stevenson, who had written his own short attack on the former prime minister, gleefully reported on the progress of Ferns and Ostry and directed the pair towards Macdonald, though he died before meeting them. Ferns, formerly on King's staff, had 'acquired an acute distaste' for the prime minister. Stevenson found Ostry a 'brilliant young man of tireless industry and he says that the more he delves into W. L. M. K.'s career, the more astonished he is that he escaped exposure so long.' Macdonald suggested that they talk to Kirk Cameron about King's years with the Rockefeller Foundation.[108] Cameron, an inveterate King-hater, dismissed any hint of greatness about King. 'He was a political, mental, and maybe a physical "Hermaphrodite." Look at the evidence. He never conceived anything. He never created anything ... He never sponsored any cause or reform. He never organized anything in his life.'[109] Macdonald took comfort in such assessments of his former leader.

Late in his fourth administration, Macdonald found new pleasure in his job. Three sessions of the legislature had passed without his being able to report a surplus, and he could barely contain his pride when he presented the fiscal year 1952–3 budget calling for a surplus of $525,000.[110] This news completely revived Macdonald. The seven years after the war had been as stressful for him as the seven years of depression preceding it, and he was now in his sixties, not his forties. Signs that he should pass on his mantle were all around him: Ilsley and Currie had gone to the Nova Scotia Supreme Court in 1949; Macdonald lost his dear friends and confidants J.L. Ralston, in 1948, and Alex Johnston, in 1951; Harold Innis was dying of cancer; and in September 1952 J.B. McNair's government was upset by New Brunswick's Progressive Conservatives, led by Hugh John Flemming.[111] Yet Macdonald showed new life in the 1952 session. He opened with a moving eulogy of the late King George and a poetic tribute to the new queen, drawing from the Archbishop of Canterbury's speech in the fifth act of *Henry VIII*.[112] Macdonald presided at the opening of construction on the Halifax-Dartmouth Bridge on 1 March and, with transport minister Chevrier, on the Canso Causeway on 16 September 1952. Infrastructure programs in the province progressed, and the government was able to increase spending on its highway program and on education.[113]

Nova Scotia's tourism industry, very much a pet project for the premier, flourished under a spreading veneer of 'tartanism.' Macdonald had drawn from his father an abiding pride in his Highland heritage.[114] His efforts to shape Nova Scotia into a veritable 'New Scotland' for the tourists' gaze were inspired partly by a desire to cash in on public demand for nostalgia and 'otherness' and partly by his own romantic conviction that the best of Scots culture could be found in the province.[115] Historical tourism need not be Celtic. In the Annapolis Valley and on the province's western shore, for example, 'traditional' Acadian culture took precedence based, in large part, on Henry Wadsworth Longfellow's poem *Evangeline*. Macdonald once referred to Longfellow as 'the best writer of tourist literature we ever had.'[116]

Things Scottish did take personal preference for Macdonald, who saw in the romanticized tradition elements of his liberalism, with its emphasis on self-reliance, local authority, and education. He rejected some of the more radical and expensive schemes of tartanism – such as planting heather along the province's highways or importing Highland cattle to roam the Cape Breton Highlands National Park[117] – but he put a piper at the Nova Scotia–New Brunswick border, hired a 'Gaelic advisor' for the Department of Education, and sent the province's archivist on a mission to Edinburgh Castle in search of the spot where Nova Scotia's baronets had received their knighthoods in the 1620s.[118]

Macdonald's interest in tourism combined his romantic, anti-modern self-identity and his liberal ideas about the role of the state. The government of Nova Scotia could publish advertisements and brochures, set up booths at trade shows, and even make short films about the province as 'a place out of time' without directly entering the private economic sphere. The pre-industrial themes of this invented tradition were ones Macdonald warmed to: the principled-but-lost cause of Culloden, the loyalty of Flora Macdonald, and the democratic dignity of Robert Burns's poetry. Though he did not take direct charge of the tourism program, Macdonald's values shaped the presentation of his province through his influence, suggestions, and speeches.

Macdonald had regained fighting form for the provincial and federal elections of 1953. As early as June 1952, he had signalled that he would contest a fifth election, when he urged his riding association to begin organizational preparation; in November the premier told the Halifax City and County associations to get ready and not be troubled by McNair's recent loss in New Brunswick.[119]

Macdonald looked for portents in the municipal elections in October 1952. He had members of caucus report on their local elections, attempting to spot trends or trouble. Each report focused on local issues to explain gains by Progressive Conservative candidates: personal jealousies and bruised egos, poor habits of finance and drink among certain Liberal organizers, and especially Tory shenanigans, including threats and shady deals. Some mentioned the boost provided to the Tories by Hugh John Flemming's victory in New Brunswick, but none suggested that provincial government policies were to blame. Save for the quantity of patronage each had to dispense, members of the Liberal caucus seemed greatly contented with Macdonald's leadership and the government's performance.[120]

Two key sections of the province's economy were struggling in early 1953: the fishery and the coal industry. Fishers faced declining prices, caused in part by increasing competition from Newfoundland and Scandinavia.[121] The concentration of control that existed in the fishery almost certainly exacerbated the fishers' problems, though the two leading spokespersons for the fish companies quickly denied responsibility to Macdonald. Ralph Bell and O.F. Mackenzie blamed Ottawa's investment in the Newfoundland fishery and foreign over-fishing for the decline in prices. Mackenzie granted that there might be some who would take advantage of the situation to lower prices unfairly, but faithfully asserted that in 'any industry in a free competitive economy will be found enough men aware of their social and moral responsibility to set the pace for the less scrupulous.'[122]

In the coal fields, the United Mine Workers (UMW) union again was negotiating with the Dominion Steel and Coal Corporation (DOSCO) and its affiliated companies. Negotiations failed, as the UMW asked for wage increases and DOSCO demanded greater productivity at the same rates. When the existing contract expired on 31 January 1953, the Macdonald government appointed a conciliation board to investigate and report. The board's report supported DOSCO's position, but Minister of Labour and Mines A.H. MacKinnon sat on the report until after the election. Though a strike was avoided, tensions ran high in industrial Cape Breton.[123]

In the spring session of the legislature the government predicted another surplus, but the Opposition scored some points.[124] Using the venue of the Public Accounts Committee (PAC) of the Legislature, Stanfield's Conservatives asked pointed and embarrassing questions of the government. When W.H. Pipe, chair of the PAC, quashed discussion by ruling that the questions of liquor agents and the collapse of a securities company were beyond its jurisdiction, Conservatives knew they had hit soft spots. On at least two matters that did reach the PAC – theft of materials from the Inverness mine and irregularities in the pay records of one highway foreman – the Progressive Conservative members succeeded in linking the government with corruption.

Although the slings and arrows rained a little heavier than in 1949, the 1953 campaign stirred little interest. When the Liberals announced they were running on their record, the Conservatives worked to make them defend it. The Tories' slogan was 'Twenty's Plenty,' and they ran daily advertisements, with copy written by Dalton Camp, attacking the government for dealing with liquor agents, introducing pensions for cabinet ministers, and failing to stimulate industrial growth.[125]

Tory attacks on the Liberal record hinted at a government grown hard in the arteries and forced the Grits onto the defensive, unfamiliar ground for Macdonald. He defended some small loans made under the Industrial Loan Board and denied once more the existence of liquor agents. 'There may be liquor agents in the province,' he lamely explained at a rally. 'However, if I were on oath, I could not say that there were. We do not recognize liquor agencies. We pay them no commission and they have no effect on the price of liquor in this province.'[126] Just days before the vote, Camp learned that Health Minister Harold Connolly had been given shares in Wine Securities Limited, a company that did considerable business with the NSLC. Camp put the revelation into a Stanfield speech, but the challenger felt uneasy making the accusation and reportedly blew the delivery. The media and the public essentially ignored the charge.[127]

The election produced another clear Liberal victory, though the Progressive Conservatives made substantial gains, taking five seats from the government. The Liberals held twenty-two seats in the Legislature, the Conservatives thirteen, and the CCF two. The Tories' share of the popular vote rose 4 per cent, most of which came at the expense of the CCF.[128]

The Liberal losses generally occurred in areas where the government failed to ameliorate local economic problems. On the province's South Shore, in the heart of the fishery, highways minister Merrill Rawding and the Speaker of the House, Gordon Romkey, were soundly beaten; the minister of industry, W.T. Dauphinee, narrowly kept his seat. In the Annapolis Valley, where apple growers had not yet recovered from the decimation of their industry, government whip D.D. Sutton was ousted. In the Sydney–Glace Bay area, the CCF kept their two seats in spite of a vigorous Liberal campaign.

Though the government benches had been lightly thinned, Macdonald took a great deal of personal satisfaction from the results. He saw no evidence that voters were unduly upset with the Liberals' record; he believed the losses were based almost entirely on 'local campaigns' and, in many cases, could have been avoided given stronger candidates and better organization. 'After twenty straight years of rather overwhelming victories,' he wrote Tom Crerar, 'it is hard to keep the workers on the bit.'[129] Macdonald saw to it that many of the defeated Liberal MLAs and several long-time party workers soon received patronage appointments to tide them over. Speculation was rife that Macdonald would soon accept a well-earned sinecure.[130]

In the autumn of 1953, Macdonald made a final pilgrimage to the Old

Country to preside over the Jubilee Gaelic Mod at Oban, Scotland. He and Agnes sailed for the United Kingdom on 17 September and spent the first week of October travelling in Ireland before going to Scotland, where Angus made a number of speeches and went everywhere in his Clanranald kilt. After the Mod, he unveiled a plaque marking Nova Scotian soil within the walls of Edinburgh Castle.[131] Before sailing for Halifax the Macdonalds spent a few days in London, where Angus fell ill. He told Crerar: 'As long as I was in Scotland and wearing a kilt, I was in good health, but on getting to London I made the great mistake of donning the common garb of the city and immediately got a cold!'[132] As he stepped off the ship in Halifax on 6 November, he told reporters that he would retire 'sometime between today and my 91st birthday,' but he immediately turned his attention to the work of the government and the upcoming session.[133]

In January 1954 Macdonald announced a cabinet shuffle, forced by the departure of two ministers. Alex MacKinnon left the Ministry of Labour and Mines for the bench; A.B. DeWolfe, faced with diabetes and deteriorating health, gave up the provincial secretary's job. No new ministers were added, but younger ministers picked up new portfolios. After the election Macdonald had taken on the sensitive Department of Highways and Public Works, but he now finally handed the post of provincial treasurer to R.M. Fielding.[134] Other than this one move, he did not lighten his workload, even flying to Edmonton to make the Toast to the Immortal Memory on Burns Night, 25 January 1954.[135] He continued to oversee work on the bridge and causeway, pulling strings with C.D. Howe to ensure that the steel contract for the latter went to DOSCO over the Steel Company of Canada, its Hamilton rival.[136]

Macdonald had never fully shaken the cold he caught in Britain, and his workload began to take its toll on him. His haggard appearance in the Legislature reportedly became a 'source of silent concern' for members on both sides of the Speaker and led several of his friends to push for his swift retirement.[137] From Ottawa, Tom Crerar and Chubby Power each wrote to 'invite' him to accept a Senate seat; they were sure St Laurent would offer one if asked. They argued that Macdonald would add prestige to the Upper House and that his abilities would help them to make the Senate a useful body once more.[138] The idea of joining some of his closest friends – Crerar, Power, John Connolly, Norman Lambert, Wishart Robertson, and others – must have been tempting for Macdonald. He preferred Halifax to Ottawa, however, and had no faith in the Senate. Macdonald told Power it would take more than a 'half a dozen good appointments [to] restore the Senate to favour in the eyes of the Canadian people,' even if he and Power were among those appointed. He could not 'see any way of making the Senate effective except by having a certain number of elected Senators. I do not agree with the idea that Provincial Parliaments should name a certain number to the Senate. That mixes up the two spheres of jurisdiction.'[139] He remained concerned with constitutional questions, even in the matter of his retirement.

The most plausible rumour about Macdonald's career after politics had him teaching at a university.[140] His sister Mairi, Sister St Veronica, taught history at St Francis Xavier University and complained to her brother that the university did nothing for Gaelic or Scottish studies, hinting that there might be a role for him in Antigonish. 'They pay no more attention to St. Andrew's Day than to any other day in the week, but St. Patrick's rates a banquet and other forms of celebration.'[141] Macdonald, however, probably preferred to teach at Dalhousie and remain in Halifax.

All this was put aside until he had piloted his government through at least one more session of the Legislature. He continued work at his regular pace until Sunday, 11 April 1954. That evening, he suffered a 'mild heart attack' and was admitted to the Victoria General hospital.[142] Even from his hospital bed, he continued working; on Monday afternoon, he prepared the estimates for his department and that evening he discussed politics with Senator Charles Hawkins.[143] Some time early in the morning of Tuesday, 13 April 1954, Macdonald died in his sleep, four months shy of his sixty-forth birthday.

The pageantry of mourning fit the man. It combined a romantic vision of a passing Scottish chieftain with estimations of Macdonald's place in his province's political history. The Legislature sat on the day of his death, with Macdonald's chair draped in Clanranald tartan and his desk decorated with a sprig of heather.[144] His body lay in state for three days in Province House, and more than 100,000 people filed past to pay their respects. The comparisons offered were not to George Murray or even William Fielding, but to Nova Scotia's most celebrated politician, Joseph Howe. Conservatives Robert Stanfield and H.P. MacKeen served as pallbearers, along with CCF leader Michael MacDonald, and Liberal Stan Rafuse. Honorary pallbearers included C.D. Howe, J.L. Ilsley, C.G. Power, Douglas Abbott, Brooke Claxton, Robert Winters, and Macdonald's cabinet. Significantly, Macdonald was buried in a Catholic cemetery just outside the capital, rather than in either of his two Cape Breton homes, Dunvegan or Port Hood; his achievements as premier had done much to raise a provincial identity above local ones.

Macdonald left his government in a sound financial position, with another surplus for 1954–5. The Halifax-Dartmouth Bridge and the Canso Causeway would soon be completed, and the official opening of each over the next sixteen months was a gushing tribute to the late premier.[145] Yet much remained unfinished. Macdonald, in spite of years of effort, had not succeeded in securing constitutional revision and renewal. The auspicious beginnings of 1950 were unexploited, and there the issue lay for decades. The Maritime Freight Rates Act had been reaffirmed, but freight rates continued to rise, squeezing industries in the region to the point of breaking. Things had improved, but national economic policies did not yet adequately address regional disparities.

The matter of a successor also remained undecided. It is unlikely that Macdonald would have attempted to anoint an heir, but had he lived he certainly could have prevented the damaging and divisive struggle that occurred. The cabinet chose Harold Connolly, now the senior minister, to lead until a convention could be held in the fall. Connolly may have pledged that he would not seek the leadership at the convention, but would serve only as the interim chief.[146] By the time of the convention on 9 September 1954, Connolly had had a change of heart and threw his hat in the ring. The other cabinet contenders were Hicks, Fielding, Malcolm Patterson, and agriculture minister A.W. Mackenzie.[147]

At the convention, Connolly came very close to saying that he was Macdonald's 'legitimate heir,' suggesting it was the late premier's deathbed request that the Irish Catholic MLA from Halifax North succeed him. Richard and Eileen Donahoe, close friends of the Macdonalds, recalled that Connolly's claim shocked Agnes and that she privately rebuked him for it later.[148] The contest took on the feeling of Connolly against everyone else. Connolly led on the first three ballots, but his support did not grow, and Hicks prevailed on the fifth. Many Catholic Liberals in the province cried bigotry, and Hicks failed to win all of them back during the next two years. For his part, Connolly resigned rather than serve under Hicks and went to the Senate the following July.[149] The Stanfield Conservatives defeated the remnants of Macdonald's Liberal machine on 30 October 1956.[150]

Conclusion

The opening ceremonies of the Canso Causeway attracted some 35,000 people in August 1955. Premier Henry Hicks chaired the event and welcomed federal dignitaries C.D. Howe, minister of trade and Commerce, and Donald Gordon, president of Canadian National Railways. He then introduced Father Stanley Macdonald to offer a Gaelic welcome.

> When I was asked to say a few words in Gaelic, they told me they would allow me one minute. Then they got generous and their hearts expanded and they gave me two minutes. Of course, we must make allowances for them. As you know the city of Ottawa is quite young and cities are like human beings – in their youth they can be quite devoid of manners and they often lack common sense and understanding. It is not so long since Ottawa was but a camp in the depths of the untamed forest. It seems that something of the camp atmosphere still prevails, and quite a noticeable stench of spruce still lingers about them.

Hicks, Howe, and Gordon followed the lead of Gaelic-speaking people in the crowd, smiling, laughing, and applauding Father Stanley when it seemed appropriate. The priest's harmless jest hinted at bitterness, a resentment of the power that Ottawa at times wielded so capriciously. The honoured guests did not comprehend Father Stanley's gibes any more than they seemed to understand his brother's defence of provincial autonomy.[1]

The causeway's opening was laden with 'Highland' imagery in addition to Father Stanley's Gaelic address. Crowds watched Howe cut a tartan ribbon with a claymore, officially opening the link. A hundred bagpipers paraded across playing 'The Road to the Isles' in fulfilment of

Angus L. Macdonald's vision. Tourists so inclined could travel the highway past folk legend Giant MacAskill's home to the Highlands, or at
least to a national park of that name. The causeway fit as seamlessly into
the province's tourism scheme as it had into Macdonald's liberalism.[2]

Macdonald developed his liberalism between the wars, adding a set
of political and intellectual principles to a familial partisanship. He
embraced the ideals of individual freedom and equality that he saw in
liberal democracy, but the economic disaster that befell Nova Scotia
between 1921 and 1939 convinced him of the need for state intervention. He and the politicians and intellectuals with whom he shared
friendships – including J.L. Ralston, J.L. Ilsley, Norman Rogers, J.W.
Dafoe, Harold Innis, C.G. Power, T.A. Crerar, and J.A. Corry – did not
trust the state to take a direct role in the economy. They did, however,
accept its power to stimulate growth indirectly and to provide emergency assistance, triggered automatically, in the form of direct payments to citizens in need.

Macdonald's 'infrastructure liberalism' sought to promote economic
development indirectly, through the creation of a climate for economic
development. Macdonald viewed the causeway as a relief-work
project, an efficient transportation link for the island's industries, and a
tourist attraction in itself, and expected it to ease the economic decline
of Cape Breton and the eastern mainland of Nova Scotia.[3] Several royal
commissions pointed to the instability of the local steel industry and
warned that the coal industry would constrict dramatically in the 1950s
with the spread of diesel trains and oil furnaces. These commissions
advised the province to promote supplemental industries such as tourism.[4] The causeway and the Halifax-Dartmouth Bridge – named for the
late premier at its opening – were the culmination of Macdonald's
'paved road' campaigns of the mid-1930s.

Macdonald believed that the state should, within its means, provide
the infrastructure necessary for individual self-realization or 'blossom-
ing.'[5] Although this included material improvement, Macdonald placed
greater emphasis on the moral and intellectual improvement of individuals. His first political battle concerned the creation of a large, secular
university that could offer a first-rate education to Nova Scotians. After
the Second World War, his government invested heavily in research and
a provincially funded rural high school system. Macdonald's celebration of 'tartanism' can also be traced to his concern for moral and intellectual development. He pointed to the poetry of Robert Burns and the
romance of Highland life as models of cultural development and self-

reliance. Though he recognized the value of tartanism for the tourism industry, Macdonald also believed that it could help Nova Scotians towards self-realization.

Macdonald's rejection of substantial state intervention almost surely contributed to Nova Scotia's relative decline after 1945. Yet even had he succeeded in securing reduced freight rates and greater provincial control of certain tax fields, Macdonald's limited approach could not have reversed Nova Scotia's economic slide. Regional development – a deliberate effort by the federal and provincial governments to address regional disparity through state intervention – would have to await changes of government in Nova Scotia and Ottawa.[6] Macdonald's stature, perhaps, could have hastened the acceptance of state intervention had he thrown his political weight behind the idea. Instead, he succeeded in quelling calls for public ownership of coal mines and utilities and greater public investment in private industry, even as he won three majority governments in the post-war period. Margaret Conrad argues that the region's decline led much of the public to support state planning with generous federal assistance, well ahead of the political leadership.[7] Macdonald's political domination of the province, reflected in the image of an unbeatable 'Angus L.,' prevented an effective lobby for federal or provincial intervention.

The power of Macdonald's image also may have prevented him from developing better communication skills. In his home province, he did not need to court the press, and even Conservative newspapers trod carefully when criticizing the premier after 1937. Nationally, however, he failed to 'connect' despite close personal relationships with some of Canada's leading journalists, including Grant Dexter, Bruce Hutchison, J.W. Dafoe, Rupert Davies, Leslie Roberts and Grattan O'Leary. Macdonald could not convince most Canadians that the post-war tax rental agreements embodied a dangerous shift in the federal balance and marked a sharp detour from the path laid out in the Rowell-Sirois report. The national media did not even put forward his name as a potential candidate to succeed Mackenzie King until the eve of the 1948 leadership conference, far too late to affect the outcome.

Macdonald's unwillingness or inability to cultivate good relations with a broader section of Ottawa's press gallery was one of the central factors in his political failure in federal politics. He took a seat in King's cabinet in 1940 as one of the most respected Liberal politicians in the country, widely expected to contend for the prime minister's chair some day. Within two years, however, observers noted their disappointment

with his performance, sensing that he had squandered an opportunity.[8]
Macdonald's administration of the Department of National Defence for
Naval Affairs was not flawless, but it compared favourably to that of
other wartime departments. He did not, however, rise to his reputation
in parliamentary debate nor did he garner laudatory public attention as
did Howe or Ilsley, for example. His complete personal break with
Mackenzie King contributed to Macdonald's gloom in Ottawa, but the
prime minister could safely reject the opinions of a minister who had
such little influence by 1943.

Macdonald enjoyed some success in Ottawa, most notably in the
1944 conscription crisis. He and T.A. Crerar managed to bring almost
the entire government to the very difficult decision to enforce conscription for overseas service. Though most historians have credited King
with victory in this crisis, a careful analysis of events reveals that Macdonald triumphed in securing reinforcements for Canada's infantry
without bringing down the government. He may have been tempted to
destroy King, but he realized that to do so would split the Liberal party
for decades. Macdonald and Crerar applied just enough pressure at just
the right time to change the government's direction.

Macdonald's principled stand in the conscription crisis contributed
to his political success in Nova Scotia. He returned in 1945 as a hero, all
the more popular for having received no political reward from King.
The Liberal party rode his coattails to a near-sweep in the 1945 provincial election, somewhat masking the strong showing by the Co-operative Commonwealth Federation (CCF) in the election. Though one in
seven Nova Scotian voters supported the CCF and indicated their
approval of state planning, that remained improbable with Macdonald
so solidly entrenched in power.

The infrastructure and tourism policies of the Macdonald government contributed to the provincial economy's growth. Under Macdonald, the province modernized its roads and schools without large
deficits, though the significant expansion of the public debt would
prove a problem in the future, as interest rates exceeded 3 per cent. The
province's paved roads and tourism campaign attracted almost 500,000
visitors and generated as much revenue – about $44 million annually by
the time of Macdonald's death – as the fishery.[9] The economic activity
spawned indirectly by the government must have pleased the premier.

Macdonald's most important success was also his greatest disappointment. Over the course of the 1930s, he worked with other liberal
intellectuals and politicians to modernize the British North America

Act. Through study groups and a series of royal commissions, Macdonald and the 'new liberals' gradually arrived at a plan to reallocate powers and resources to meet the needs of an industrialized, federal nation. Their aspirations to rationalize taxation, distribute the nation's wealth more equitably, and strengthen provincial autonomy were embraced by the Rowell-Sirois report. The report echoed Nova Scotia's submission point-by-point, and Macdonald eagerly anticipated reshaping Confederation in line with its recommendations.

The abortive Dominion-Provincial Conference of 1941 disappointed Macdonald, to be sure, but he could see no reason why discussion might not resume immediately following the war. By 1945, however, Rowell-Sirois's strongest supporters were dead, out of the government, or exhausted by the war effort. Ilsley, for example, despaired of getting provincial agreement to any deal that did not bankrupt the federal treasury; he apparently gave no thought to a reconsideration of the royal commission's report.[10] For his part, Mackenzie King wanted only to avoid difficulties and unpleasantness. Ottawa, therefore, abandoned serious discussion of constitutional reform in favour of ad hoc changes by means of cabinet decisions, intergovernmental agreements, and accepted practice.[11]

Macdonald, now from stubbornness as much as principle, continued to defend Rowell-Sirois late into the 1940s, even when it was obviously a dead letter. His arguments for provincial autonomy were like Father Stanley's Gaelic: unintelligible to Ottawa ears. Liberalism had moved on, absorbing a measure of state economic planning to enervate the CCF's appeal for substantial socialist programs. The efficiency of the new fiscal federalism was assumed, even if it proved no more effective than Macdonald's indirect intervention at redressing regional disparity.[12]

Macdonald's liberalism told him that provinces must remain autonomous in local matters if Canada's federal system were to survive. He rejected the political convenience of shared costs and overlapping jurisdictions; powers and resources should remain exclusive wherever possible to bolster responsible government, in Macdonald's mind. That the party of Mowat, Fielding, and Laurier was presiding over the destruction of provincial autonomy especially incensed Macdonald. His occasional public outbursts about the blind tyranny of Liberal Ottawa led some to conclude that he was really a Tory at heart.

Macdonald died, as most do, with work undone. Several of his proposals were adopted in the years following his death. In 1956 the government of Louis St Laurent introduced a scheme for equalization to enable all provinces to provide an average level of services to their citizens. Annual federal-provincial conferences eventually gained acceptance, and in 1957 the Atlantic premiers managed to draw expressions of solidarity from the federal Liberals and Conservatives.[13] The dawning of regional development owed much to Macdonald's post-war battles with Ottawa.

The province became relevant to Nova Scotians under Angus L. Macdonald as it never had been before. It appeared physically in almost every community in the form of a road or a school; citizens increasingly came into contact with the province's bureaucracy, whether through Old Age Pensions, small loans to fishers and businesses, or tourism programs. Macdonald even developed a language for 'Nova Scotianess': tartanism. This expression of a romantic, organic – and predominantly Scottish – past may have been affected largely for tourists, but it proved an enduring myth in the province's culture.

On a more rational level, Macdonald developed a rather vague regional 'awareness' into an articulate provincialism. Regional identity in Nova Scotia usually emerged in a populist rhetoric of anger and frustration, as in W.S. Fielding's repeal campaign in the 1880s or the Maritime Rights movement of the 1920s.[14] Macdonald's provincialism often expressed frustration, but fundamentally it was rooted in classical federalism: constitutionally distinct powers and resources for Ottawa and the provinces. This view of Canadian federalism has been often ignored and disparaged since the Second World War.[15] The result, much as Macdonald predicted, has been a greater centralization of economic and political power.

Notes

Introduction

1 See, for example, Robert Bothwell, Ian Drummond, and John English, *Canada since 1945: Power, Politics and Provincialism* (Toronto: University of Toronto Press, 1989), 75 and 79, and James Bickerton, *Nova Scotia, Ottawa, and the Politics, of Regional Development* (Toronto: University of Toronto Press, 1990), 117–18 and 129.

   The only extended examination of Macdonald is John Hawkins's hagiographic *The Life and Times of Angus L.* (Windsor, NS: Lancelot Press, 1969), though J. Murray Beck chronicles the public events of Macdonald's career as premier of Nova Scotia in *Politics of Nova Scotia*, Volume 2, *Murray–Buchanan, 1896–1988* (Tantallon, NS: Four East Publications, 1988), 153–86 and 205–37.

2 A.R.M. Lower and Donald Creighton, for example, consciously sought to strengthen the national conscience through their work, though from very different political perspectives. Carl Berger, *The Writing of Canadian History: Aspects of English-Canadian Historical Writing since 1900* (Toronto: University of Toronto Press, 1976), 112–36 and 228–9.

3 Ibid., 260–2.

4 Ian McKay, 'A Note on "Region" in Writing the History of Atlantic Canada,' *Acadiensis* 29.2 (Spring 2000): 90–1 and 93; see also McKay, 'After Canada: On Amnesia and the Apocalypse in the Contemporary Crisis,' *Acadiensis* 28.1 (Autumn 1998): 76–97.

5 See, for example, Robert J. Brym and R. James Sacouman, eds., *Underdevelopment and Social Movements in Atlantic Canada* (Toronto: New Hogtown Press, 1979).

6 For correctives to 'national narratives' see, for example, Nolan Reilly, 'The

General Strike in Amherst, Nova Scotia, 1919,' *Acadiensis* 9.2 (Spring 1980): 56–77, and E.R. Forbes, 'The Ideas of Carol Bacchi and the Suffragists of Halifax,' in *Challenging the Regional Stereotype: Essays on the 20th Century Maritimes* (Fredericton: Acadiensis Press, 1989), 90–9.

7 David Bercuson, ed., *Canada and the Burden of Unity* (Toronto: Gage, 1980), 6.

8 John English, 'The Second Time Around: Political Scientists Writing History,' *Canadian Historical Review* 67.4 (1986): 7.

9 See, for example, Bothwell et al., *Canada since 1945*. 74–5, and Margaret Prang, *N.W. Rowell: Ontario Nationalist* (Toronto: University of Toronto Press, 1975), 493.

10 On the contributions and shortfalls of political science's discussion of the development of Canada's federal system, see Barry Ferguson and Robert Wardhaugh, '"Impossible Conditions of Inequality": John Dafoe, The Rowell-Sirois Commission, and the Interpretation of Canadian Federalism,' *Canadian Historical Review* 84.4 (December 2003): 552–3.

11 See especially Donald V. Smiley, 'The Rowell-Sirois Report, Provincial Autonomy, and Postwar Canadian Federalism,' *Canadian Journal of Economics and Political Science* 28.1 (February 1962): 54–69.

12 Paul Romney, *Getting It Wrong: How Canadians Forgot Their Past and Imperilled Confederation* (Toronto: University of Toronto Press, 1999); see also Romney, 'Provincial Equality, Special Status and the Compact Theory of Canadian Confederation,' *Canadian Journal of Political Science* 32.1 (March 1999): 21–39.

13 Ian McKay, 'The Liberal Order Framework: A Prospectus for a Reconnaissance of Canadian History,' *Canadian Historical Review* 81.4 (December 2000): 623.

14 Ibid., 623–4, and Gad Horowitz, 'Conservatism, Liberalism and Socialism in Canada: An Interpretation,' in Janet Ajzenstat and Peter J. Smith, eds., *Canada's Origins: Liberal, Tory, or Republican?* (Ottawa: Carleton University Press, 1995), 35–7.

15 Fernande Roy, *Progrès, Harmonie, Liberté: Le libéralisme des milieux d'affaires francophones à Montréal au tournant du siècle* (Montreal: Boréal, 1988), 45.

16 McKay, 'Liberal Order,' 640. See also Rainer Knopff, 'The Triumph of Liberalism in Canada: Laurier on Representation and Party Government,' *Journal of Canadian Studies* 26.2 (Summer 1991): 72.

17 Barry Ferguson, *Remaking Liberalism: The Intellectual Legacy of Adam Shortt, O.D. Skelton, W.C. Clark, and W.A. Mackintosh, 1890–1925* (Montreal and Kingston: McGill-Queen's University Press, 1993), xiii–xv.

18 C.B. Macpherson, *The Political Theory of Possessive Individualism: Hobbes to Locke* (Toronto: Oxford University Press, 1962), 2–3.

19 Ferguson, *Remaking Liberalism*, xii-xiii and 7. See also Marlene Shore, *The Science of Social Redemption: McGill, the Chicago School, and the Origins of Social Research in Canada* (Toronto: University of Toronto Press, 1987) and Doug Owram, *The Government Generation: Canadian Intellectuals and the State, 1900–1945* (Toronto: University of Toronto Press, 1986).

20 On differences between the major parties in a later period, see Ian Stewart, *Roasting Chestnuts: The Mythology of Maritime Political Culture* (Vancouver: UBC Press, 1994).

21 Leo XIII, *Encyclical Letter on Condition of the Working Classes (Rerum Novarum)* (1891, Washington: Apostolic Delegation, 1942). On the encyclical's impact on the diocese of Antigonish, see Jim Lotz and Michael R. Welton, *Father Jimmy: The Life and Times of Father Jimmy Tompkins* (Wreck Cove, NS: Breton Books, 1997), 19–20.

22 James D. Cameron, *For the People: A History of St. Francis Xavier University* (Montreal and Kingston: McGill-Queen's University Press, 1996), 151–4.

23 A.L. Macdonald, 'Liabilities of Possessors of Premises,' SJD thesis, Harvard Law School, 1929. On legal realism, see William Twining, *Karl Llewellyn and the Realist Movement* (London: Weidenfeld and Nicolson, 1973), 7–8, and Allen Mills, 'Of Charters and Justice: The Social Thought of F. R. Scott, 1930–1985,' *Journal of Canadian Studies* 32.1 (1997): 46.

24 See J.A. Corry, *Difficulties of Divided Jurisdiction* (Ottawa: Patenaude, 1939), prepared for the Royal Commission on Dominion-Provincial Relations.

25 See Smiley, 'Rowell-Sirois,' 67.

26 For studies of the commission, see Smiley, 'Rowell-Sirois'; David W. Fransen, '"Unscrewing the Unscrutable": The Rowell-Sirois Commission, the Ottawa Bureaucracy and Public Finance Reform, 1935–1941,' PhD dissertation, University of Toronto, 1984; Owram, *Government Generation*, 221–53, and Ferguson and Wardhaugh, '"Impossible Conditions of Inequality."' Journalist J.B. McGeachy gave this name to the commissioners; see 'Confederation Clinic, 1867–1937,' *Winnipeg Free Press*, 4 February 1938.

27 See, for example, Macdonald to Alexander Johnston, 7 February 1939, Angus L. Macdonald Papers, Nova Scotia Archives and Records Management, MG 2, vol. 1504, file 405.

28 Arthur C. Parks, *The Economy of the Atlantic Provinces, 1940–1957* (Halifax and Fredericton: Atlantic Provinces Economic Council, 1959), 1–2.

1. Dunvegan to Halifax

1 On the notion of 'sub-region' see Carmen Miller, 'The Restoration of Greater Nova Scotia,' in David Jay Bercuson, ed., *Canada and the Burden of Unity* (Toronto: Macmillan, 1977), 45 and passim.

2 On this process in Quebec / Lower Canada see Jean-Marie Fecteau, *Un nouvel ordre des choses: La pauvreté, le crime, l'État au Québec, de la fin du XVIIIe
   siècle à 1840* (Outremont, QC: VLB Éditeur, 1989), and Allan Greer, *Peasant,
   Lord, and Merchant: Rural Society in Three Quebec Parishes, 1740–1840* (Toronto: University of Toronto Press, 1985).

3 Georges Arsenault, 'Stanislaus Perry,' *Dictionary of Canadian Biography:* Volume 12, *1891–1900* (Toronto: University of Toronto Press, 1990), 836–8.

4 J.M. Bumsted, *The People's Clearance: Highland Emigration to British North
   America* (Edinburgh: Edinburgh University Press, 1982), 27–53, and
   Stephen J. Hornsby, *Nineteenth-Century Cape Breton: A Historical Geography*
   (Montreal and Kingston: McGill-Queen's University Press, 1992), 33–45.

5 See 'Copies of Land Grants and Genealogical Information,' Angus L. Macdonald Papers, Nova Scotia Archives and Records Management (NSARM),
   MG2 (hereafter ALM Papers), vol. 1506, file 428.

6 See, for example, Macdonald, 'Speech at Windsor, Nova Scotia,' 13 September 1951, ALM Papers, vol. 966, file 40-6.

7 See 'Copies of Land Grants.'

8 See *1881 Census,* Nova Scotia District 4, Inverness County, Subdistrict J,
   Broad Cove Marsh, pp. 23–4, and *1891 Census*, Nova Scotia District 36, Subdistrict A, Broad Cove Marsh, pp. 7–8.

9 See John Hawkins interview with Donald 'Dan' Lewis Macdonald,
   25 August 1967, Hawkins Fonds, AR 9066, NSARM; Hawkins, *The Life and
   Times of Angus L.* (Windsor, NS: Lancelot Press, 1969), 13–14, and 'Mrs.
   Lewis Macdonald,' *Franciscan Review* 39.4 (April 1943): 135–6.

10 *1881, 1891,* and *1901 Census.*

11 Hawkins interview with Dan Lewis Macdonald, and Angus L. Macdonald
   to Flora Jane Gentry, 14 December 1934, ALM Papers, vol. 1535, file 1368.
   See also Alan R. MacNeil, 'Cultural Stereotypes and Highland Farming in
   Eastern Nova Scotia, 1827–1861,' *Histoire sociale / Social History* 19.37 (May
   1986): 39–56.

12 Hawkins interview with Agnes Macdonald, 16 August 1967, Hawkins
   Fonds, AR 9063, NSARM; see also J.L. MacDougall, *History of Inverness
   County, Nova Scotia* (1922, Belleville, ON: Mika Publishing, 1972), 116–17.

13 See Hawkins, *Life and Times*, 13–14, and *Belcher's Farmers' Almanac, 1888*
   (Halifax: McAlpine Publishing, 1888). William B. Hamilton, *Place Names of
   Atlantic Canada* (Toronto: University of Toronto Press, 1996), 319–20.

14 On the repetitiveness of names in Cape Breton communities, see William
   Davey and Richard MacKinnon, 'Nicknaming Patterns and Traditions
   among Cape Breton Coal Miners,' *Acadiensis* 30.2 (Spring 2001): 79–80.

15 See 'Mrs. Lewis Macdonald,' 136, and *1901 Census.*

16 Hawkins interviews with Agnes Macdonald and Dan Lewis Macdonald.

17 Hawkins interview with Dan Lewis Macdonald.

18 Kenneth M. McLaughlin, 'Race, Religion and Politics: The Election of 1896 in Canada,' PhD thesis, University of Toronto, 1974, 159–60.

19 See J. Murray Beck, *Politics of Nova Scotia*, Volume 1, *Nicholson–Fielding, 1710–1896* (Tantallon, NS: Four East Publications, 1985), 157–80, and P.B. Waite, *The Man from Halifax: Sir John Thompson, Prime Minister* (Toronto: University of Toronto Press, 1985), 69–70.

20 *1901 Census*, Nova Scotia District 35R, Port Hood, p. 2.

21 *Halifax Chronicle*, 3 October 1901.

22 *Belcher's Farmers' Almanac, 1904–1906*.

23 See J. Murray Beck, *The Evolution of Municipal Government in Nova Scotia, 1749–1973* (Halifax: n.p., 1973), 29.

24 Hawkins interview with Agnes Macdonald.

25 Allister W.D. MacBean, *The Inverness and Richmond Railway* (Halifax: Tennant Publishing, 1987), 5–13.

26 See MacDougall, *History of Inverness County*, 96–8 and 117–19, and *Belcher's Farmers' Almanac, 1904–1906*.

27 See Hawkins, *Life and Times*, 25–7, and Macdonald to Ralph P. Bell, 20 April 1950, ALM Papers, vol. 955(II), file 31-2.

28 For the history of St FX, see James D. Cameron, *For the People: A History of St. Francis Xavier University* (Montreal and Kingston: McGill-Queen's University Press, 1996); on the diocese of Arichat/Antigonish, see Rev. Angus Anthony Johnston, *A History of the Catholic Church in Eastern Nova Scotia*, Volume 2, *1827–1880* (Antigonish, NS: St. Francis Xavier University Press, 1971).

29 Cameron, *For the People*, 52–5, 70–4, and 407 n. 36.

30 Ibid., 75–6.

31 Ibid., 84–6 and 107.

32 See George Boyle, *Father Tompkins of Nova Scotia* (New York: P.J. Kennedy and Sons, 1953), and Jim Lotz and Michael R. Welton, *Father Jimmy: The Life and Times of Father Jimmy Tompkins* (Wreck Cove, NS: Breton Books, 1997). Poor health prevented Tompkins from completing his studies.

33 Cameron, *For the People*, 111–13 and 151–54. Cameron does not identify the new faculty members.

34 See *Xaverian* 19.1 (November 1914): 11, in ALM Papers, vol. 1531, file 1321.

35 Cameron, *For the People*, 102–5.

36 Hawkins, *Life and Times*, 29–30 and 37.

37 Hawkins interview with Dan Lewis Macdonald. See also Cameron, *For the People*, 155–6, for the 'militarization' of the St FX campus.

38 Cameron, *For the People*, 115–17, 151, and 457–8 n. 88. On Father Coady see
    Alexander F. Laidlaw, ed., *The Man from Margaree: Writings and Speeches of
    M.M. Coady* (Toronto: McClelland and Stewart, 1971), and Michael R. Wel-
    ton, *Little Mosie from the Margaree: A Biography of Moses Michael Coady* (Tor-
    onto: Thompson Educational Publishing, 2001).
39 Boyle, *Father Tompkins*, 47–8. For the former model, see Roger Fieldhouse,
    The Workers' Educational Association: Aims and Achievements, 1903–1977 (Syr-
    acuse, NY: Syracuse University Press, 1977); for the latter, see O'Dwyer's
    pamphlet 'A University for Catholics in Relation to the Material Interests of
    Ireland' (Dublin: Catholic Truth Society, 1900), cited in Boyle, *Father Tomp-
    kins*, 48.
40 Ian McKay and Suzanne Morton, 'The Maritimes: Expanding the Circle of
    Resistance,' in Craig Heron, ed., *The Workers' Revolt in Canada, 1917–1925*
    (Toronto: University of Toronto Press, 1998), 43–4. Antigonish County was
    perhaps hardest hit by rural depopulation, losing more than 40% of its
    population in the first two decades of the twentieth century. See Paul
    Brown, '"Come East, Young Man!" The Politics of Rural Depopulation in
    Nova Scotia, 1900–1921,' *Journal of the Royal Nova Scotia Historical Society* 1
    (1998): 49.
41 Lotz and Welton, *Father Jimmy*, 25–27.
42 Ibid., 27–9. The leading scholar of the Antigonish Movement describes it as
    a 'middle way' between the forces of capitalism and socialism. R. James
    Sacouman, 'Underdevelopment and the Structural Origins of Antigonish
    Movement Co-operatives in Eastern Nova Scotia,' *Acadiensis* 7.1 (Autumn
    1977): 68, and Sacouman, 'The Social Origins of Antigonish Co-operative
    Associations in Eastern Nova Scotia,' PhD thesis, University of Toronto,
    1976.
43 See, for example, Tompkins to Macdonald, 11 August 1922, ALM Papers,
    vol. 1532, file 1348.
44 Tompkins wanted to offer education to working-class adults to improve
    their standard of living and to broaden their horizons. His first 'People's
    School' ran at St FX from January to March, 1921 and drew 51 students.
    Lotz and Welton, *Father Jimmy*, 44–9.
45 G.W.L. Nicholson, *The Canadian Expeditionary Force, 1914–1919: Official His-
    tory of the Canadian Army in the First World War* (Ottawa: Queen's Printer,
    1962), 224–7.
46 Macdonald's service file is located in RG 150, Box 6702, file 23, Library and
    Archives Canada (LAC).
47 Angus L. Macdonald, 'The 185th Battalion (Cape Breton Highlanders),' in
    M.S. Hunt, ed., *Nova Scotia's Part in the Great War* (Halifax: Nova Scotia Vet-
    eran Publishing Co., 1920), 122–9.

48 See Macdonald to Sister St Veronica, 1916, ALM Papers, vol. 1506, file 424; Macdonald to Veronica Perry Macdonald, December 1916, ibid.

49 Colin's file is located in RG 150, vol. 6742, box 9, LAC.

50 See Macdonald, 'The 185th,' 123 and 126, and Macdonald to Donald M.R. Vince, 21 November 1949, ALM Papers, vol. 955(II), file 31-1.

51 See Nicholson, *Canadian Expeditionary Force*, 223–4.

52 For details of the 25th Battalion's activities from May to November 1918, see 'War Diaries of the 25th Battalion, 1918,' RG 9, III D3, Vol. 4933, LAC.

53 See ALM Papers, vol. 1506, file 424.

54 Macdonald to Sister St Veronica, n.d. (1917?), ibid.

55 Macdonald to Sister St Veronica, 1 September 1918, ibid.

56 Macdonald to Sister St Veronica, 5 September 1918, ibid. On 'deification' of the dead as a coping strategy, see Jonathan Vance, *Death So Noble: Memory, Meaning, and the First World War* (Vancouver: UBC Press, 1997). Vance takes his title from John Milton's 'Samson Agonistes,' a work that Macdonald probably knew.

57 Macdonald, 'Casualty Form,' RG 150, vol. 6702, Box 23, LAC.

58 'War Diaries of the 25th,' 7 November 1918, and Nicholson, *Canadian Expeditionary Force*, 479.

59 Macdonald to Veronica Perry Macdonald, 15 November 1918 and 12 December 1918, ALM Papers, vol. 1506, file 424.

60 Macdonald, 'Medical History Sheet,' RG150, Vol. 6702, Box 23, LAC.

61 Sister St Veronica to Agnes Macdonald, n.d. (1954?), ALM Papers, vol. 1506, file 424.

62 Ibid., vol. 1535, file 1376.

63 Macdonald to Ralph Bell, 20 April 1950, ALM Papers, Vol. 955(II), File 31-2.

64 See *Belcher's Farmers' Almanac, 1920.*

65 Hawkins interviews with R.A. Fielding, 22 August 1967, Hawkins Fonds, AR 9065, and with G.M. Logan, 21 August 1967, Hawkins Fonds, AR 9064, NSARM.

66 See John Willis, *A History of Dalhousie Law School* (Toronto: University of Toronto Press, 1979), 78.

67 See Macdonald to D.A. Cameron, 17 May 1928, ALM Papers, vol. 1533, file 1351.

68 Ernest R. Forbes, 'Never the Twain Did Meet: Prairie-Maritime Relations, 1910–27,' *Canadian Historical Review* 59.1 (1978): 25–7; J. Murray Beck, *Politics of Nova Scotia*, Volume 2, *Murray–Buchanan, 1896–1988* (Tantallon, NS: Four East Publications, 1988), 422, and A.A. MacKenzie, 'The Rise and Fall of the Farmer-Labour Party in Nova Scotia,' MA thesis, Dalhousie University, 1969.

69 J. Archy Macdonald to Angus L. Macdonald, 18 October 1921, and A.A.

Kennedy to J. Archy Macdonald, 8 October 1921, ALM Papers, vol. 1530, file 1301. See also Macdonald to Cameron, 17 May 1928.

70 Beck, *Politics of Nova Scotia*, 2:428.

71 David Frank, *J.B. McLachlan: A Biography* (Toronto: James Lorimer, 1999).

72 On the relationship see Hawkins interview with Agnes Macdonald and interview with Eileen and Richard Donahoe, 16 July 1999. For examples of her poetry, see Agnes Foley Macdonald, *Once and Again* (Port Royal, NS: Abenaki Press, 1950); 'The Native Speaks,' *Dalhousie Review* 29.1 (April 1949): 50; and 'A Christmas Carol,' *Atlantic Advocate* 51.4 (December 1960): 83.

73 Waite, *Lives of Dalhousie*, 1:203–4.

74 William S. Learned and Kenneth C.M. Sills, *Education in the Maritime Provinces of Canada* (New York: Carnegie Foundation for the Advancement of Teaching, 1922).

75 Cameron, *For the People*, 179–81, and Waite, *Lives of Dalhousie*, 1:258–81.

76 See 'For the People,' *Casket*, 20 and 27 April 1922.

77 Father J. Boyle to Macdonald, 30 December 1922, ALM Papers, vol. 1532, file 1348.

78 Cameron, *For the People*, 182–3.

79 Ibid., 183–4.

80 Ibid., 185–7.

81 *Casket*, 26 October 1922.

82 Tompkins to Macdonald, 11 August 1922, ALM Papers, vol. 1532, file 1348.

83 Tompkins to Macdonald, 20, 26(?), and 27 October, ibid.

84 *Casket*, 30 November 1922.

85 See Cameron, *For the People*, 190–1; Boyle, *Father Tompkins*, 108–11; and Lotz and Welton, *Father Jimmy*, 54–5.

86 Tompkins to Macdonald, 23 November, 21 December 1922, and 5 February 1923, ALM Papers, vol. 1532, files 1348 and 1348(A). Following his March on Rome in October 1922, Benito Mussolini impressed many Canadians, Catholic and Protestant alike, with his apparent vitality and anti-Communism.

87 The report may be found in the appendix of MacDougall's *History of Inverness County*, 642–83.

88 *Casket*, 7 December 1922.

89 *Casket*, 14 December 1922, 11 and 18 January, 1, 15, and 22 February, and 1 and 8 March 1923; the *Sydney Post*, 22, 29, and 30 December 1922, 5, 6, 10, 13, and 16 January, 5, 6, 8, 14, 16, 20, 21, 22, 27, and 28 February 1923.

90 *The Casket*, 18 January 1923. Phalen quoted from Veblen's *The Higher Learning in America: A Memorandum on the Conduct of Universities by Business Men* (New York: B.W. Huebsch, 1918).

91 ALM Papers, vol. 1532, file 1384(A).

92 *Sydney Post*, 14 February 1923.

93 Ibid., 29 December 1922 and 8 and 22 February 1923.

94 Cameron, *For the People*, 185–6 and 191–3.

95 *Halifax Chronicle*, 17 February 1923; Waite, Lives of Dalhousie, 1:271–2, and Acadia Board of Governors Minutes, 31 May 1922 and 16 February 1923, Acadia University Archives.

96 See Waite, *Lives of Dalhousie*, 1:271–81, and Learned to Tompkins, 22 June 1923, ALM Papers, vol. 1532, file 1348(A). Kings had been unable to fund the reconstruction of its main buildings in Windsor, destroyed by fire in 1920.

97 Macdonald to Florence Clark, 3 January 1927, ALM Papers, vol. 1533, file 1351, and Macdonald to Carleton Stanley, 22 February 1937, ALM Papers, vol. 1536, file 1399.

98 Campbell to Macdonald, 30 December 1922; see also P.J. Webb to Macdonald, 12 January 1923, and Rev. J.J. MacKinnon to Macdonald, 15 January 1923, ALM Papers, vol. 1532, files 1348 and 1348(A).

99 Tompkins to Macdonald, 21 February and 9 March 1923, ALM Papers, vol. 1532, file 1348(A).

100 Macdonald to Tompkins, 23 January 1923, ibid.

101 On the Weldon tradition, named for the founding dean, R.C. Weldon, see Hawkins interview with Horace Read, 12 December 1967, Hawkins Fonds, AR 9068, and Willis, *Dalhousie Law School*, appendix II, 255–8.

102 'Scrapbook,' kept by Sister St Veronica, 1933–4, ALM Papers, vol. 1533, file 1350.

103 William Twining, *Karl Llewellyn and the Realist Movement* (London: Weidenfeld and Nicolson, 1973), 7–8 and 41–55.

104 Hawkins interview with Read.

105 See Beck, *Politics of Nova Scotia*, 2:91–4. On the economic downturn, see Forbes, *Maritime Rights*, 54–72; on the radicalization of labour in Nova Scotia in the period, see Frank, *McLachlan*, 233–392, and McKay and Morton, 'The Maritimes,' in Heron, ed., *The Workers' Revolt*, 48–51.

106 E.R. Forbes, 'The Rise and Fall of the Conservative Party in the Provincial Politics of Nova Scotia, 1922–1933,' MA thesis, Dalhousie University, 1967, 8, and Forbes, *Maritime Rights*, 130–9.

107 Forbes, *Maritime Rights*, 25–7, 80–1, and 87.

108 Brown, '"Come East,"' 47–78.

109 Beck, *Politics of Nova Scotia*, 2:11–14 and 377–9; Forbes, 'Rise and Fall,' 26–36 and 60–5; A. Jeffrey Wright, 'The Hapless Politician: E.H. Armstrong of Nova Scotia,' *Nova Scotia Historical Quarterly* 6 (September 1976): 259–79;

David Frank, 'The Cape Breton Coal Industry and the Rise and Fall of the British Empire Steel Corporation,' *Acadiensis* 7.1 (1977): 23; L. Anders Sandberg, 'Forest Policy in Nova Scotia: The Big Lease, Cape Breton Island, 1899–1960,' *Acadiensis* 18.2 (Spring 1990): 105–15; and Escott Reid interview with G. Fred Pearson, 14 October 1931, Reid Papers, MG 31, E46, vol. 1, LAC.

110 See Forbes, 'Rise and Fall,' 42–53; Frank, *McLachlan*, 327–33 and 355–92; Frank, 'Cape Breton Coal Industry,' 225–8; and Hawkins interview with H.B. Jefferson, 24 April 1969, Hawkins Fonds, AR 9070, NSARM.

111 Macdonald, 'Continuous Record of the Liberal Government,' 1925, ALM Papers, vol. 1531, file 1325.

112 Forbes, 'Rise and Fall,' 3, 54–7, and 60–5; Beck, *Politics of Nova Scotia*, 2:138 and 422; and Hawkins interview with Fielding.

113 Beck, *Politics of Nova Scotia*, 2:428.

114 See Frank, *McLachlan*, 312–15 and 379–80; McKay and Morton, 'Expanding the Circle of Resistance,' 50–1; and Macdonald, 'Notes of Conciliation Board,' 18 May 1927, ALM Papers, vol. 1533, file 1349.

115 See 'Presentation of Malcolm J. MacLean and Alex L. McIsaac,' 18 May 1927; Macdonald, 'Notes on Conciliation Board'; H.H. Ward, Deputy Minister of Labour, to Macdonald, 12 May 1927, ALM Papers, vol. 1530, file 1301; and *Halifax Chronicle*, 19 May 1927.

116 'Minutes of the Board of Commissioners,' 18 and 19 May 1927, and Macdonald to Malcolm MacLean, 31 May 1927, ALM Papers, vol. 1533, file 1349.

117 *Halifax Chronicle*, 27 May 1927.

118 On Nova Scotia see Reid's interviews, conducted in October 1931, with Dr Arthur Kendal, Liberal MP for Cape Breton East, 1904–11; William Chisholm, Liberal leader, 1925–30; Don Sinclair, president of the Nova Scotia Liberal Association; Carleton Stanley, president of Dalhousie University; G. Fred Pearson, chair of Dalhousie's board of governors and key Liberal organizer; and Angus L. Macdonald, Liberal leader after 1930. Reid summarized his conclusions in an unpublished paper, 'Party Organization in Nova Scotia,' written in 1932 or 1933. See Escott Reid Papers, MG 31, E46, vols. 1 and 23, LAC.

119 Reid interview with Don Sinclair, 13 October 1931.

120 Reid interviews with Sinclair, William Chisholm, 12 October, and G. Fred Pearson, 14 October 1931.

121 For evidence of Macdonald's involvement in organization, see Macdonald to B. W. Russell, 25 May 1925; Ralston to Macdonald, 7 April and 30 August 1927; Macdonald to Ralston, 14 February 1927 and 5 April 1928;

Florence Clark to Macdonald, 24 March 1928; and Macdonald to Clark, 5 April 1928, ALM Papers, vol. 1533, file 1351.

122 See 'James Layton Ralston,' in J.K. Johnson, ed., *The Canadian Directory of Parliament, 1867–1967* (Ottawa: Public Archives, 1968).

123 'Edward Mortimer Macdonald,' in *Directory of Parliament*. For the wisdom of Ralston's selection, see Forbes, *Maritime Rights*, 171.

124 Macdonald to Currie, 5 February 1926, ALM Papers, vol. 1533, file 1351.

125 Sandberg, 'The Big Lease,' 116–18, and Cahill, *The Thousandth Man*, 95–101.

126 Halifax's newspapers were openly partisan until the late 1930s and 1940s. The Conservatives controlled the *Herald* and the *Mail*, while the Liberal operated the *Chronicle* and the *Star*. See Margaret Conrad, 'The Art of Regional Protest: The Political Cartoons of Donald McRitchie, 1904–1937,' *Acadiensis* 21.1 (Autumn 1991): 12–14.

127 Potter to Macdonald, 1 April 1927, ALM Papers, vol. 1533, file 1351.

128 See, for example, Hawkins interview with Fielding.

129 See Roy McNutt to Macdonald, 22 August 1928, ALM Papers, vol. 1531, file 1318.

130 Beck, *Politics of Nova Scotia, Volume Two*, 120 and 126–7; Forbes, 'Rise and Fall,' 80–2, 91, and 103; and Forbes, *Maritime Rights*, 158–72.

131 Beck, *Politics of Nova Scotia*, 2:128–9; and Forbes, 'Rise and Fall,' 103–7 and 109–10.

132 Beck, *Politics of Nova Scotia*, 2:127.

133 Forbes, 'Rise and Fall,' 112. For a discussion of the OAP bill and its passage, see Blair Neatby, *William Lyon Mackenzie King, 1924–1932: The Lonely Heights* (Toronto: University of Toronto Press, 1963), 110–11 and 125–6.

134 Beck, *Politics of Nova Scotia*, 2:422.

135 Allen Mills, 'Of Charters and Justice: The Social Thought of F.R. Scott, 1930–1985,' *Journal of Canadian Studies* 32.1 (1997): 46. On Pound's legal realism, see Twining, *Llewellyn and the Realist Movement*, 70–2. On the role of the legal realists in the progressive movement in the United States, see Barbara H. Fried, *The Progressive Assault on Laissez Faire: Robert Hale and the First Law and Economics Movement* (Cambridge, MA: Harvard University Press, 1998).

136 Charles Gavsie to Macdonald, 30 January 1929, ALM Papers, vol. 1530, file 1301.

137 A.L. Macdonald, 'Liabilities of Possessors of Premises,' 39–40, 64–5, and 116–21.

138 Horace Read to Macdonald, 27 January, 12 February, and 18 March 1929; Vincent Macdonald to Angus Macdonald, 6 March 1929, and Smith to Macdonald, 22 February 1929, ALM Papers, vol. 1531, file 1319. See also Willis, *Dalhousie Law School*, 90, 96–7, and 100–1.

139 Smith to Macdonald, 11 and 22 February and 19 April 1929, ALM Papers, vol. 1531, file 1319.

140 Smith to Macdonald, 12 and 19 April and 9 May 1929, and Read to Macdonald, 2 May 1929, ibid.

141 Interview with Richard and Eileen Donahoe, 16 July 1999.

142 Beck, *Politics of Nova Scotia:* 2:133, *Halifax Herald,* 3 September 1929, and Forbes, 'Rise and Fall,' 128–9.

143 See Hawkins interviews with Horace Read and Ronald Fielding.

144 See 'Robert Emmet Finn,' in *Directory of Parliament.*

145 Ralston to Macdonald, 7 December 1929, ALM Papers, vol. 1533, file 1351.

146 Beck, *Politics of Nova Scotia,* 2:134–5. The final majority was 5128.

147 Hawkins interview with Fielding.

148 See Ilsley to Macdonald, 1 May 1930, ALM Papers, vol. 1533, file 1352.

149 See Ralston to Macdonald, 6 May 1930, ibid. Macdonald described the political events of 1930 in a diary entry several years later: 'Diary,' 25 January 1937, ALM Papers, vol. 1503, file 387.

150 Ralston to Macdonald, 21 May 1930, ALM Papers, vol. 1533, file 1352; Macdonald, 'Diary,' 25 January 1937; Hawkins interview with Fielding; *Halifax Chronicle,* 12 June 1930; and entries for 'Alexander William Chisholm,' 'Moses Elijah McGarry,' and 'Donald MacLennan' in *Directory of Parliament.*

151 Macdonald, 'Diary,' 25 January 1937.

152 See Macdonald to Gordon Harrington, Minister of Mines, 7 July 1930, ALM Papers, vol. 1531, file 1310, and I. D. Macdougall, 'Letter to Voters,' *Halifax Herald,* 26 July 1930. On Nova Scotia's inability to afford the OAP plan, which called for the province to pay half the costs, see E.R. Forbes, 'Cutting the Pie into Smaller Pieces: Matching Grants and Relief in the Maritime Provinces during the 1930s,' *Acadiensis* 17.1 (Autumn 1987): 39.

153 Macdonald, 'Letter to the Electors of Inverness,' July 1930, ALM Papers, vol. 1531, file 1326.

154 Heenan to Macdonald, 21 July 1930, ibid.

155 See Macdonald to Rev. Dr. J. M. Shaw, 26 June 1930, and Shaw to Macdonald, 4 July 1930, ALM Papers, vol. 1533, file 1349.

156 Macdonald, 'Diary,' 25 January 1937.

157 See Hawkins interviews with Agnes Macdonald and Dan Lewis Macdonald.

158 Macdougall's total was 4909 to Macdonald's 4720. *Halifax Chronicle,* 29 July 1930.

159 Hawkins interviews with Fielding and Horace Read.

160 Beck, *Politics of Nova Scotia,* 2:138.

161 Macdonald, 'Diary,' 25 January 1937.

162 *Halifax Chronicle*, 2 October 1930.
163 See Macdonald, 'Diary,' 25 January 1937, and *Halifax Chronicle*, 2 October 1930.
164 See Beck, *Politics of Nova Scotia*, 2:100–1.
165 On Duff's connections with rum-runners, see D. Frank Matheson to Macdonald, 6 May 1933, ALM Papers, vol. 1531, File 1305.
166 For MacMillan's career to 1930 see Forbes, 'Rise and Fall,' 108–9, and Beck, *Politics of Nova Scotia*, 2:85, 105, 113, and 138–9. On MacMillan's hesitance to stand, see Hawkins interview with Fielding.
167 Ilsley to Macdonald, 12 September 1930, ALM Papers, vol. 1533, file 1352.
168 Beck, *Politics of Nova Scotia*, 2:139.
169 Hawkins interview with Fielding.
170 Macdonald, 'Diary,' 25 January 1937.
171 *Halifax Chronicle*, 2 October 1930.
172 A.S. MacMillan, Private papers, Document 12, quoted in Beck, *Politics of Nova Scotia*, 2:138–9.
173 Hawkins interview with Fielding, and *Halifax Chronicle*, 2 October 1930.
174 Macdonald, 'Diary,' 25 January 1937. See also *Halifax Chronicle* and *Halifax Herald*, 2 October 1930.
175 Macdonald, 'Diary,' 25 January 1937.
176 *Halifax Chronicle*, 2 October 1930.
177 Macdonald, 'Diary,' 25 January 1937, and *Halifax Herald*, 2 October 1930.
178 *Ottawa Journal*, 27 July 1940.
179 Macdonald won 314 votes, Kinley 110, and Duff 64. *Halifax Chronicle*, 2 October 1930, and Macdonald, 'Diary,' 25 January 1937.
180 Hawkins interview with Logan.
181 Hawkins interviews with Fielding and Gordon B. Isnor, 15 August 1967, Hawkins Fonds, AR 9062, NSARM.

2. The Macdonald Decade

1 See, for example, Paul Martin to Macdonald, October 1930, Angus L. Macdonald Papers, Nova Scotia Archives and Records Management (NSARM) MG 2 (hereafter ALM Papers), vol. 1531, file 1311, J.L. Ralston to King, 19 November 1930, and King to Macdonald, 21 November 1930, W.L. Mackenzie King Papers, MG 26, J1, vol. 180, pp. 153,528 and 150,603–4, Library and Archives Canada (LAC).
2 Interview with Eileen and Richard Donahoe, 16 July 1999.
3 Macdonald to E.M. Macdonald, 9 March 1936, ALM Papers, vol. 1536, file 1389.

4 J. Murray Beck, *Politics of Nova Scotia*, Volume 2, *Murray–Buchanan, 1896–1988* (Tantallon, NS: Four East Publications, 1988), 140–2.

5 For intimate accounts of Macdonald's personality, see the series of interviews conducted by John Hawkins; for example, interviews with Fielding; with Gordon B. Isnor, 15 August 1967, AR 9062; with Agnes Macdonald, 16 August 1967, AR 9063; with Dr Guy Murray Logan, 21 August 1967, AR 9064; with Henry Hicks, 29 November 1967, AR 9067; with Horace Read, 12 December 1967, AR 9067; and with J.A. Walker, 1967(?), AR 9074, Hawkins Fonds, NSARM. See also Thomas Raddall to Kenneth Mackenzie, 23 April 1954, Thomas Raddall Papers, MS-2-202 S-506, Dalhousie University Archives.

6 Hawkins interview with Hicks.

7 Ilsley to Macdonald, 2 October 1930, ALM Papers, vol. 1531, file 1311.

8 Macdonald to L.D. Currie, 5 February 1926, ALM Papers, vol. 1533, file 1351.

9 Macdonald, 'Speech to the inaugural meeting of the 20th Century Club of New Glasgow,' 9 July 1931, ALM Papers, vol. 1531, file 1328, and A.L. Macdonald, 'Liabilities of Possessors of Premises,' SJD thesis, Harvard Law School, 1929.

10 Macdonald, 'Speech to the Progressive Club of Halifax,' no date, but before 1933, ALM Papers, vol. 1531, file 1328.

11 On King's liberalism, see H. Blair Neatby, *William Lyon Mackenzie King, 1924–1932: The Lonely Heights* (Toronto: University of Toronto, 1963), 207, 245, 307–11, and 344, and Neatby, *William Lyon Mackenzie King, 1932–1939: The Prism of Unity* (Toronto: University of Toronto Press, 1976), 12 and 36–8.

12 Macdonald to King, 9 March 1933, King Papers, MG 26, J1, vol. 197, reel C-3673, p. 167,384, LAC.

13 King's speech is in House of Commons, *Debates*, 27 February 1933, pp. 2492–9; see also, Neatby, *Prism of Unity*, 36–8.

14 Beck, *Politics of Nova Scotia*, 2:142, and *The Canadian Annual Review, 1930–1931* (Toronto: Canadian Review Company, 1931), 187.

15 See, for example, the *Chronicle* story of 16 February 1932: 'Liberal Party Will View Nova Scotia's Problems Scientifically, Says Provincial Liberal Leader.'

16 James Bickerton, *Nova Scotia, Ottawa, and the Politics of Regional Development* (Toronto: University of Toronto Press, 1990), 85. For a definition of populism, see Peter Worsley, 'The Concept of Populism,' in Ghita Ionescu and Ernest Gellner, eds., *Populism, Its Meaning and National Characteristics* (London: Weidenfeld and Nicolson, 1969).

17 Hawkins interview with Dan Lewis Macdonald, 25 August 1967, Hawkins Fonds, AR 9066, NSARM. See also, Beck, *Politics of Nova Scotia*, 2:235–6.

18 See 'Minutes of First Meeting of Group,' 13 January 1931, ALM Papers, vol. 1532, file 1330.

19 Macdonald to Bennie Young, Jr, 3 April 1933, ALM Papers, vol. 1531, file 1305. See also Macdonald to Bob Hawkins, 30 December 1930, ALM Papers, vol. 1531, file 1311.

20 'First Meeting,' 13 January 1931, and 'Meeting,' 26 January 1931, ALM Papers, vol. 1532, file 1330.

21 'Speech to the Progressive Club of Halifax.'

22 E.R. Forbes, 'Cutting the Pie into Smaller Pieces: Matching Grants and Relief in the Maritime Provinces during the 1930s,' *Acadiensis* 17.1 (Autumn 1987): 36–7.

23 Beck, *Politics of Nova Scotia*, 2:141–5, and *Chronicle*, 10 December 1931, 3 March 1932, 31 January and 19 April 1933. For accusations of partisan hiring practices, see Melvin MacPhie to Macdonald, 3 April 1933, ALM Papers, vol. 1531, file 1305.

24 Beck, *Politics of Nova Scotia*, 2:133 and 135–6, and *Canadian Annual Review, 1930–1931*, 195.

25 See Barry Cahill, *The Thousandth Man: A Biography of James McGregor Stewart* (Toronto: University of Toronto Press, 2000), 108–9.

26 See Forbes, 'Rise and Fall,' 112–14, and 'Cutting the Pie,' 39–40.

27 On the commission, the wage cut, and the failed coal order, see *Chronicle*, 20 February, 14 and 15 March and 27 April 1932; *Halifax Herald*, 29 April 1932; *Canadian Annual Review, 1932*, 191; Forbes, 'Rise and Fall,' 154–7; and Michael Earle, 'The Coalminers and Their "Red" Union: The Amalgamated Mine Workers of Nova Scotia, 1932–1936,' *Labour / Le Travail* 22 (Fall 1988): 117–18.

28 Beck, *Politics of Nova Scotia*, 2:136; L. Anders Sandberg, 'Forest Policy in Nova Scotia: The Big Lease, Cape Breton Island, 1899–1960,' *Acadiensis* 18.2 (Spring 1990): 117–18; and L. Anders Sandberg and Bill Parenteau, 'From Weapons to Symbols of Privilege: Political Cartoons and the Rise and Fall of the Pulpwood Embargo Debate in Nova Scotia, 1923–1933,' *Acadiensis* 26.2 (Spring 1997): 48.

29 Beck, *Politics of Nova Scotia*, 2:142–3.

30 *Chronicle*, 14 April 1931.

31 Robert Gass to Macdonald, 17 February 1932; see also H.B. Crosscup to Macdonald, 26 February 1932, ALM Papers, vol. 1530, file 1304.

32 E.M. Macdonald to Macdonald, 18 March 1932 and 9 April 1932, ALM Papers, vol. 1532, file 1331. Beck disputes the partisanship of the bill, noting that six of the thirteen seats eliminated had been won in 1928 by Conservatives. Beck, *Politics of Nova Scotia*, 2:132 and 144.

33 *Chronicle*, 18 May 1933.

34 Beck, *Politics of Nova Scotia*, 2:146, and *Canadian Annual Review, 1933*, 207.

35 Macdonald, 'Diary,' 20 June 1933, ALM Papers, NSARM, vol. 1503, file 387.

36 See *Herald*, 22 July 1933, and *Chronicle*, 2 August 1933.

37 Ian Stewart, *Roasting Chestnuts: The Mythology of Maritime Political Culture* (Vancouver: UBC Press, 1994), 73–88. Stewart quotes Nova Scotia Premier John Buchanan as saying in 1984: 'I don't believe that elections should be fought on issues.'

38 On the franchise affair see Beck, *Politics of Nova Scotia*, 2:147–51; Cahill, *Thousandth Man*, 110, 113, and 224 n. 46; and Margaret Conrad, *George Nowlan: Maritime Conservative in National Politics* (Toronto: University of Toronto Press, 1986), 52–4.

39 Macdonald to Harrington and Doull, 18 July 1933, and Harrington to Macdonald, 19 July 1933, ALM Papers, vol. 1534, file 1357.

40 See Cahill, *Thousandth Man*, 224 n. 46, and *Chronicle*, 20 July 1933.

41 See *Chronicle*, 25 July 1933, and Nova Scotia, *Journals of the House of Assembly, 1934*, part III, appendix 32 (Halifax: King's Printer, 1934), 64–92.

42 *Chronicle*, 31 July 1933.

43 Macdonald, 'Diary,' 30 July 1933.

44 *Chronicle*, 25 and 26 July 1933.

45 Macdonald, 'Speech to the Reform Club of Montreal,' 17 March 1934, ALM Papers, vol. 1531, file 1328.

46 *Chronicle*, 27, 28, and 29 July 1933, and Macdonald et al. to Harrington, 28 July 1933, ALM Papers, vol. 1534, file 1357. Robert Chambers's cartoon from 29 July 1933 depicted many of the alleged stalling tactics employed by registrars.

47 Harrington, 'Speech at the Capitol Theatre,' 2 August 1933. About 27,000 votes were cast in the City of Halifax in the 1933 election.

48 Beck, *Politics of Nova Scotia*, 2:148.

49 See 'To all members of the Loyal Orange Association, County of Colchester,' and 'To the Orangemen of Nova Scotia,' pamphlets in the ALM Papers, vol. 1532, file 1333 and vol. 1534, file 1358.

50 See Conrad, *George Nowlan*, 54–5, and Forbes, 'Rise and Fall,' 195.

51 For the results of the election, see *Herald* and *Chronicle*, 23 August 1933, and Beck, *Politics of Nova Scotia*, appendix C, 2:423.

52 W.C. Dunlop to Macdonald, 11 April 1933, ALM Papers, vol. 1531, file 1305.

53 See, for example, Chambers's cartoons in the *Chronicle* for 18 and 27 April and 3 and 16 August 1933. For a discussion of Chambers's artistic techniques, see Margaret Conrad, 'The Battle of the Cartoonists: The Cartoon Art of Donald McRitchie and Robert Chambers in Halifax Newspapers,

1933–1937,' in Gwendolyn Davies, ed., *Myth and Milieu: Atlantic Literature and Culture, 1918–1939* (Fredericton: Acadiensis Press, 1993), 22–4.

54 Forbes, 'Rise and Fall,' 145. On the introduction of the RCMP into Nova Scotia, see Greg Marquis, 'The History of Policing in the Maritime Provinces: Themes and Prospects,' *Urban History Review* 19.1–2 (1990): 84–99.

55 See Hawkins interviews with R.M. Fielding, G.B. Isnor, and Gordon Purdy, and *Herald*, 28 July 1933.

56 McKenzie to Macdonald, 25 August 1933, ALM Papers, vol. 1534, file 1361. See also Hawkins interviews with Fielding and Isnor, and Beck, *Politics of Nova Scotia*, 2:83 and 95.

57 Margaret Conrad, 'Apple Blossom Time in the Annapolis Valley, 1880– 1957,' *Acadiensis* 9.2 (Spring 1980): 24.

58 Fr Stanley Macdonald to Macdonald, 28 August 1933, ALM Papers, vol. 1534, file 1364.

59 Smiley to Macdonald, 3 September 1933, ALM Papers, vol. 1534, file 1361. This file also contains the letters written in support of Smiley.

60 Interview with J. Murray Beck, 21 August 1998.

61 Fr Stanley to Angus Macdonald, 10 September 1933 and Angus to Fr Stanley, 13 September 1933, ALM Papers, vol. 1534, file 1364.

62 John Crowe to H.B. Havey, MD, 15 August 1933, ALM Papers, vol. 1534, file 1357.

63 For some of the lists kept on Halifax South workers and senior provincial positions, see ALM Papers, vol. 1534, files 1362 and 1363.

64 'List of Applicants Circulated for Rating,' n.d., ALM Papers, vol. 1534, file 1362.

65 See Macdonald to Rev. Ronald Macdonald, 23 April and 2 May 1924, ALM Papers, vol. 1530, file 1301.

66 Fr Stanley Macdonald to Macdonald, 2 March 1936, and Macdonald to Fr Stanley Macdonald, 3 March 1936, ALM Papers, vol. 1535, file 1385.

67 G. Fred Pearson, 'Memorandum,' 27 August 1933, ALM Papers, vol. 1534, file 1358.

68 Dawson prepared a 23-page report on the civil service for the Jones inquiry. *Report of the Royal Commission Provincial Economic Inquiry, Appendices* (Halifax: King's Printers, 1934), 48–9.

69 On this development in Canadian politics, see John English, *The Decline of Politics: The Conservatives and the Party System, 1901–1920* (Toronto: University of Toronto Press, 1977) and Reginald Whitaker, 'Between Patronage and Bureaucracy: Democratic Politics in Transition,' *Journal of Canadian Studies* 22.2 (Summer 1987): 55–71.

70 Rod McColl to Michael Dwyer, 16 February 1934, ALM Papers, vol. 1534,

file 1365; 'Unemployment Relief – Approximate Figures in Round Numbers,' 19 September 1933, and 'Direct Relief,' late 1933(?), ALM Papers, vol. 1534, file 1366. See also James Struthers, *No Fault of Their Own: Unemployment and the Canadian Welfare State, 1914–1941* (Toronto: University of Toronto Press, 1983), 47–70.

71 Interview with Angus L. Macdonald, Jr, 10 December 1998; Hawkins interviews with Agnes Macdonald and Fielding.

72 Angus Lloyd MacLean, M.D., to Macdonald, 8 December 1933, ALM Papers, vol. 1535, file 1369.

73 See, for example, W.A. Macdonald to Angus Macdonald, 27 December 1933 and 12 February 1934, ALM Papers, vol. 1534, file 1364.

74 Struthers, *No Fault of Their Own*, 71.

75 'Unemployment Relief – Approximate Figures,' 19 September 1933.

76 Macdonald to Gordon, 23 September 1933; Gordon to Macdonald, 19 October 1933; Macdonald to Gordon, 25 October 1933; and Gordon to Macdonald, 15 December 1933, ALM Papers, vol. 1534, file 1365.

77 'Speech from the Throne,' 1 March 1934, ALM Papers, vol. 1534, file 1363.

78 Sessional speech, 1934, ALM Papers, vol. 1534, file 1366.

79 A.E. Safarian, *The Canadian Economy in the Great Depression* (1959; Toronto: McClelland and Stewart, 1970), 141–6.

80 Veronica Macdonald to Angus Macdonald, 15 April 1934, ALM Papers, vol. 1534, file 1364.

81 Emelyn MacKenzie to Macdonald, 7 January 1934, ALM Papers, vol. 1535, file 1369.

82 Forbes, 'Cutting the Pie,' 40.

83 See Macdonald to Norman Rogers, 23 October 1933, Norman McLeod Rogers Papers, collection 2125, box 1, Queen's University Archives (QUA).

84 Macdonald to Rogers, 6 October 1933, ibid.

85 See John R. Rowell, 'An Intellectual in Politics: Norman Rogers as an Intellectual and Minister of Labour, 1929–1939,' MA thesis, Queen's University, 1979.

86 See Macdonald to Robertson, 14 October 1933, and Macdonald to Layton, 13 January 1934, ALM Papers, vol. 1531, file 1308; Macdonald to MacFadyean, 20 February 1934, and Macdonald to Layton, 28 February 1934, ALM Papers, vol. 1531, file 1309.

87 Macdonald to G. Fred Pearson, 30 July 1934.

88 On Johnston's career, see 'Alexander Johnston,' in J.K. Johnson, ed., *The Canadian Dictionary of Parliament, 1867–1967* (Ottawa: Public Archives, 1968). For Macdonald's invitation, see Johnston, 'Diaries, 1933–1939,' entries for 9, 21, and 29 July 1934, Alexander Johnston Papers, MG 30, E70, reel M-64, LAC.

89 Macdonald to Turgeon, 23 April 1934, and Macdonald to Rogers, 17 May 1934, ALM Papers, vol. 1531, file 1309.

90 For Innis's research trips to the Maritimes, see Harold Adams Innis Papers, B1972-003, series 4, box 006, files 8–13 and 19, University of Toronto Archives.

91 *Provincial Economic Inquiry*, 3–4.

92 Ibid., 131–230, and *Appendices*, 18–40, 43–65, and 121–33. On requests for Rogers' brief, see, for example, Sidney Smith to Macdonald, 17 September 1934, ALM Papers, vol. 1535, file 1370, and Rogers to Innis, 10 December 1934, Rogers Papers, box 1, QUA.

93 *Provincial Economic Inquiry*, 79–86.

94 Ibid., 69–70 and 86–7.

95 Ibid., 71–7.

96 Ibid., 87–8, 184–6 and *Appendices*, 51–2 and 58–60. See also Bickerton, *Politics of Regional Development*, 83–84.

97 *Provincial Economic Inquiry*, 88–90 and 96.

98 Ibid., 90–2, and H. Scott Gordon, 'The Trawler Question in the United Kingdom and Canada,' *Dalhousie Review* 31.2 (Summer 1951): 117–27.

99 Macdonald to J.L. Ilsley, 17 May 1938, ALM Papers, vol. 1504, file 397.

100 *Montreal Gazette*, 8 December 1934, and *Halifax Chronicle*, 10 December 1934.

101 See Rogers to J.H. Jones, 12 December 1934, Rogers Papers, box 1, QUA.

102 *Montreal Gazette*, 10 December 1934.

103 Johnston, 'Diaries,' entries for 8, 15, and 27 December 1934.

104 See March, *Red Line*, 394, 396, and 398, for circulation rates of both papers. In 1934, for example, the *Herald* sold an average of 28,000 papers daily, while the *Chronicle* managed just under 13,000.

105 See *Herald*, 11 August 1934, and March, *Red Line*, 278 n. 18.

106 Beck, *Politics of Nova Scotia*, 2:154.

107 *Canadian Annual Review, 1934*, 235.

108 Ibid., 237; and table T147–194, 'Motor Vehicle Registrations, by Province, 1903 to 1975,' in Leacy, ed., *Historical Statistics of Canada*.

109 See 'Gasoline Bill, 1934,' ALM Papers, vol. 1535, file 1373; *Canadian Annual Review, 1935–1936*, 435–6; and Nova Scotia, 'Highway Report,' *Journals of the House of Assembly, 1935*, appendix 10 (Halifax: King's Printer, 1935).

110 See Struthers, *No Fault of Their Own*, 109–11 and 116–18; Christopher Armstrong, *The Politics of Federalism: Ontario's Relations with the Federal Government, 1867–1942* (Toronto: University of Toronto Press, 1981), 152–4; and *Chronicle*, 31 July, 1 August 1934.

111 See *Report of the Royal Commission on Financial Arrangements between the Dominion and the Maritime Provinces* (Ottawa: King's Printer, 1935); Forbes, *Maritime Rights*, 161, 176–7; and *Chronicle*, 2 August 1934.

112 *Canadian Annual Review, 1937–1938*, 252 and 267.
113 *Report of the Royal Commission on Dominion-Provincial Relations: Book I* (Ottawa: King's Printer, 1940), 222–3.
114 Forbes, *Maritime Rights*, 188–9.
115 On tourism in the Macdonald era, see Ian McKay, 'Tartanism Triumphant: The Construction of Scottishness in Nova Scotia, 1933–1954,' *Acadiensis* 21.2 (Spring 1992): 5–47. McKay writes that Macdonald placed his faith in a '19th-century "nightwatchman state."' Ibid., 21. Yet Macdonald's government displayed an affinity for the 'new liberalism' of the interwar years with its active promotion of the province's tourism industry.
116 Ibid., 16–17.
117 The Jones and Rowell-Sirois Commissions shared this opinion. See *Provincial Economic Inquiry*, 97–8, and *Dominion-Provincial Relations, Book I*, 223.
118 'A Toast to Canada,' in *Speeches of Angus L. Macdonald* (Toronto: Longmans, Green and Co., 1960), 18–27.
119 Ian McKay, *The Quest of the Folk: Antimodernism and Cultural Selection in Twentieth-Century Nova Scotia* (Montreal and Kingston: McGill-Queen's University Press, 1994), 37–8 and passim.
120 See, for example, Bird, *This Is Nova Scotia* (Toronto: Ryerson, 1950); Adams, *Glimpses of Nova Scotia* (Halifax: Bureau of Information, c. 1932); Raddall, *Tambour and Other Stories* (Toronto: McClelland and Stewart, 1945); MacNeil, *The Highland Heart in Nova Scotia* (New York: S.J.R. Saunders, 1958); and Day, *Rockbound* (1940; Toronto: University of Toronto Press, 1989; repr. 1998).
121 *Halifax Herald*, 25 July 1934; *Canadian Annual Review, 1935–1936*, 424–5; and Alan MacEachern, *Natural Selections: National Parks in Atlantic Canada, 1935–1970* (Montreal and Kingston: McGill-Queen's University Press, 2001), 68–70.
122 McKay, 'Tartanism Triumphant,' 8–9.
123 Neatby, *Prism of Unity*, 38.
124 *Canadian Annual Review, 1934*, 229 and 237; *Provincial Economic Inquiry*, 88–90; and Beck, *Politics of Nova Scotia*, 2:160.
125 See Rogers to Macdonald, 5 November 1935, ALM Papers, vol. 1534, file 1379; Macdonald to Alex Johnston, 27 August 1935, ALM Papers, vol. 1535, file 1377; Michael Dewan to Macdonald, 10 September 1935, ALM Papers, vol. 1535, file 1376; John T. Saywell, *'Just Call Me Mitch': The Life of Mitchell F. Hepburn* (Toronto: University of Toronto Press, 1991), 234; and Neatby, *Prism of Unity*, 116–17.
126 W.L. Mackenzie King, *Mackenzie King Diaries, 1932–1949* (Toronto: University of Toronto Press, 1980), entry for 4 September 1935.

127 Liberals won in British Columbia in November 1933, Saskatchewan and Ontario in June 1934, and New Brunswick and Prince Edward Island in June 1935.

128 King, *Diaries*, 17 October 1935. See also Neatby, *Prism of Unity*, 130, and Lita-Rose Betcherman, *Ernest Lapointe: Mackenzie King's Great Quebec Lieutenant* (Toronto: University of Toronto Press, 2002), 199–201.

129 Macdonald to W.A. Macdonald, 18 October 1935, ALM Papers, vol. 1535, file 1385.

130 Chisholm to Macdonald, 3 and 14 March 1936, and Macdonald to Chisholm, 18 March 1936, ALM Papers, vol. 1536, file 1386; and Ilsley to Macdonald, 2 March 1936, and Macdonald to Ilsley, 18 September 1936, ALM Papers, vol. 1536, file 1388.

131 Ilsley to MacDonald, 18 January 1936; Macdonald to Isley, 27 January 1936; Ilsley to Macdonald, 2 March 1936; Macdonald to James L. Regan, 3 March 1936; and Macdonald to Ilsley, 9 March 1936, ALM Papers, vol. 1536, file 1388. Some members of Macdonald's cabinet feared that the positon of 'organizer' would provide Regan with too many temptations to drink. The job was given to former Liberal MLA Wishart Robertson, and Regan was placed on a $500 yearly retainer to look out for the province's interests in matters or trade.

132 See *Dominion-Provincial Conference, 1935: Record of Proceedings* (Ottawa: King's Printer, 1936); Neatby, *Prism of Unity*, 148–52; Armstrong, *Politics of Federalism*, 199–206; and Saywell, *'Just Call Me Mitch,'* 247–53.

133 Armstrong, *Politics of Federalism*, 199–201, and Saywell, *'Just Call Me Mitch,'* 237–40 and 248–9.

134 *Dominion-Provincial Conference, 1935*, 51.

135 Armstrong, *Politics of Federalism*, 205–6.

136 *Dominion-Provincial Conference, 1935*, 37–8. On New Brunswick's suspicions of constitutional amendment, see E.R. Forbes, 'The 1930s: Depression and Retrenchment,' in E.R. Forbes and D.A. Muise, eds., *The Atlantic Provinces in Confederation* (Toronto: University of Toronto Press, 1993), 301–3.

137 Armstrong, *Politics of Federalism*, 206.

138 See A.P. Paterson, *The True Story of Confederation* (Saint John: Saint John Board of Trade, 1926), and Kenneth H. LeBlanc, 'A.P. Paterson and New Brunswick's Response to Constitutional Change, 1935–1939,' MA thesis, University of New Brunswick, 1989, 31 and passim.

139 *Dominion-Provincial Conference, 1935*, 52; Armstrong, *Politics of Federalism*, 202; and Neatby, *Prism of Unity*, 150–1.

140 See Leo Dolan to Macdonald, 23 December 1935, ALM Papers, vol. 1535, file 1376.

141 Macdonald to Alex Johnston, 23 December 1935, ALM Papers, vol. 1535, file 1377; *Financial Post*, 21 December 1935.

142 Macdonald to W.A. Macdonald, 18 October 1935, ALM Papers, vol. 1535, file 1385.

143 *Canadian Annual Review, 1935–1936*, 425, 429, and 434, and *Chronicle*, 3 March 1936. See also Safarian, *Canadian Economy*, 137–60.

144 *Chronicle*, 14 to 23 April 1936.

145 *Chronicle*, 2 May 1936, and Alex Johnston to Macdonald, 1 May 1936, ALM Papers, vol. 1536, file 1388; the speech may be found in *Speeches of Angus L. Macdonald*, 28–34.

146 See Macdonald to Johnston, 16 May 1936, ALM Papers, vol. 1536, file 1388.

147 Macdonald to Fraser, 16 September 1935, ALM Papers, vol. 1535, file 1376, and C.F. Jubien to Macdonald, 5 November, 1935, ALM Papers, vol. 1535. file 1377.

148 Fr Stanley Macdonald to Angus Macdonald, 14 May 1946, ALM Papers, vol. 922, file 31-44.

149 Aileen Veronica was eleven, Angus Lewis Jr ten, and Coline Foley five.

150 Interview with Angus L. Macdonald Jr and Hawkins interview with Agnes Macdonald.

151 Macdonald to Flora Jane Macdonald Gentry, 14 December 1934, ALM Papers, vol. 1535, file 1368.

152 Chisholm to Angus Macdonald, 3 March 1936, ALM Papers, vol. 1536, file 1386. See also Helen Donovan to Angus Macdonald, 15 August and 18 October 1939, ALM Papers, vol. 1504, file 404.

153 Angus Macdonald to W.A. Macdonald, 20 February 1936, ALM Papers, vol. 1535, file 1385.

154 Fr Stanley Macdonald to Angus Macdonald, 2 March 1926, and Macdonald to Father Stanley, 3 March 1936, ALM Papers, vol. 1535, file 1385.

155 D.J. MacDonald to W.F. Carroll, 18 March 1938, St Francis Xavier Archives (SFXA), President MacDonald Papers, RG 5, vol. 10, #525, and Dr Moses Coady to Fr Lewis MacLellan, 21 April 1951, SFXA, Coady Papers, RG 30–2, vol. 1, #2904.

156 See Angus Macdonald to Alex Johnston, 17 February 1937; Johnston to Macdonald, 2 March 1937; and Macdonald to Johnston, 9 March 1937, ALM Papers, vol. 1536, file 1397.

157 See Father Stanley to Macdonald, 21 May 1937, ALM Papers, vol. 1536, file 1398; and Father Stanley to Macdonald, 16 August 1937, 25 May 1938, and 3 November 1939, ALM Papers, vol. 1506, file 422.

158 For the 1937 session, see Beck, *Politics of Nova Scotia*, 2:167–70, and the *Canadian Annual Review, 1937–1938*, 256–8.

159 *Chronicle*, 9 March 1937.
160 *Canadian Annual Review, 1935–1936*, 425 and 429, and *1937–1938*, 256–7, and Beck, *Politics of Nova Scotia*, 2:169.
161 See Hawkins interview with H.B. Jefferson, 24 April 1969, Hawkins' Fonds, AR 9070, NSARM; *Chronicle*, 10 April 1937; and *Canadian Annual Review, 1937–1938*, 258.
162 See, for example, Craig Heron, *The Canadian Labour Movement: A Short History* (Toronto: James Lorimer and Co., 1989), 71–2; David Frank, *J.B. McLachlan: A Biography* (Toronto: James Lorimer and Co., 1999), 503–8; and Earle, 'Coalminers and Their "Red" Union,' 130–2.
163 On the Oshawa strike, see Irving M. Abella, 'Oshawa, 1937,' in Abella, ed., *On Strike: Six Key Labour Struggles in Canada, 1919–1949* (Toronto: James Lewis and Samuel, 1974), 93–128, and Saywell, 'Just Call Me Mitch,' 303–32.
164 Judy Fudge and Eric Tucker, *Labour before the Law: The Regulation of Workers' Collective Action in Canada, 1900–1948* (Toronto: Oxford University Press, 2001), 217–18.
165 For an account of this meeting see David Frank and Donald MacGillivray, eds., *George MacEachern, An Autobiography: The Story of a Cape Breton Labour Radical* (Sydney: University College of Cape Breton Press, 1987), 75–7.
166 Under a yellow dog contract, an employee had to agree not to join a union while working for the employer.
167 *Chronicle*, 14, 17, 19, and 23 April 1937. On the SWOC, see Irving Abella, *Nationalism, Communism, and Canadian Labour: The CIO, the Communist Party, and the Canadian Congress of Labour, 1935–1956* (Toronto: University of Toronto Press, 1973), 54–65, and Ron Crawley, 'What Kind of Unionism: Struggles among Sydney Steel Workers in the SWOC Years, 1936–1942,' *Labour / Le Travail* 39 (Spring 1997): 99–123.
168 For an account of the trip, see Macdonald, 'Diaries,' 23 April to 11 May 1937.
169 *Chronicle*, 21 May 1937.
170 *Herald*, 22 May to 29 June. Of the 35 Chambers cartoons that appeared in the *Herald* during the campaign, 29 were printed on the front page.
171 See, for example, *Chronicle*, 22–29 May 1937.
172 *Chronicle*, 8 June 1937.
173 *Chronicle*, 15 June 1937.
174 See *Herald* and *Chronicle*, 30 June 1937; Beck, *Politics of Nova Scotia*, 2:171 and 423; and Conrad, *Nowlan*, 64–5.
175 See, for example, Emelyn MacKenzie to Macdonald, 7 November 1934, and Macdonald to MacKenzie, 20 February 1934, ALM Papers, vol. 1535,

file 1369, and Joseph Bernard to Macdonald, 31 December 1934, ALM Papers, vol. 1535, file 1375.

176 *Canadian Annual Review, 1937–1938*, 252.

177 Neatby, *Prism of Unity*, 186–7 and 195–201. On the Rowell-Sirois Commission, see Struthers, *No Fault of Their Own*, 175–84; David W. Fransen, '"Unscrewing the Unscrutable": The Rowell-Sirois Commission, the Ottawa Bureaucracy and Public Finance Reform, 1935–1941,' PhD thesis, University of Toronto, 1984; and Barry Ferguson and Robert Wardhaugh, '"Impossible Conditions of Inequality": John Dafoe, the Rowell-Sirois Commission, and the Interpretation of Canadian Federalism,' *Canadian Historical Review* 84.4 (December 2003): 551–83.

178 Rogers, 'The Constitutional *Impasse*,' *Queen's Quarterly* 46.4 (Winter 1934): 475–86.

179 See, for example, Macdonald to Alex Johnston, 10 January 1938, ALM Papers, NSARM, vol. 1504, file 398; Macdonald to Prof. Robert M. Haig, Columbia University, 9 February 1938, ALM Papers, vol. 1504, file 397; and Macdonald to Sister Veronica (Mary Macdonald), 12 February 1940, ALM Papers, vol. 1506, file 414. Macdonald wrote the introduction to the brief, as well as the section on finances. The attorney-general's department drafted the section on constitutional amendments.

180 For an account of the Halifax hearings, see J.B. McGeachy's column – 'Confederation Clinic, 1867–1937' – in the *Winnipeg Free Press*, 4 to 9 February 1938.

181 *Nova Scotia Submission*, 14, 15, 21, and 46.

182 Ibid., 6, 15–16, 52, 61–7, and 129.

183 See ibid., 24–6 and 67–78, and Australia, *Report of the Royal Commission on the Constitution* (Canberra: Commonwealth Government Printer, 1929).

184 *Nova Scotia Submission*, 15 and 40–1.

185 See, for example, Saywell, *'Just Call Me Mitch,'* 377–82.

186 See 'Value of fish landed, by province, 1911 to 1975,' and 'Number of persons engaged in primary fishing operations, by province, 1878 to 1975,' tables N1–11 and N38–48, in Leacy, ed., *Historical Statistics of Canada*.

187 See Macdonald to Johnston, 10 January 1938, and Johnston to Macdonald, 14 January 1938, ALM Papers, vol. 1504, file 398.

188 *Nova Scotia Submission*, 139.

189 Margaret Prang, *N.W. Rowell: Ontario Nationalist* (Toronto: University of Toronto Press, 1975), 493.

190 Fransen, '"Unscrewing the Unscrutable,"' 164–6.

191 *Report of the Royal Commission on Dominion-Provincial Relations, Book 2* (Ottawa: King's Printer, 1940), 31–2, 55, 69–73, 118–20, and 155–6.

192 Ibid., 83–4 and 125–7. On the commission's delays and the arduous task of preparing the report, see Fransen, '"Unscrewing the Unscrutable,"' 286–361, and Ferguson and Wardhough, '"Impossible Conditions of Inequality,"' 572–4.

193 *Canadian Annual Review, 1937–1938*, 262, and Beck, *Politics of Nova Scotia*, 2:175 and 178.

194 Macdonald to Don Fraser, editor of the *Eastern Chronicle*, 16 July 1938, ALM Papers, vol. 1504, file 397. See also Beck, *Politics of Nova Scotia*, 2:173–6.

195 See Fraser to Macdonald, 15 July 1938, ALM Papers, vol. 1504, file 397, and Macdonald to O'Leary, 16 September 1938, ALM Papers, vol. 1504, file 400.

196 See Macdonald to J.L. Ilsley, 21 March 1938, and Ilsley to Macdonald, 1 April 1938, ALM Papers, vol. 1504, file 397; Macdonald to Johnston, 28 June 1938, ALM Papers, vol. 1504, file 398; *Canadian Annual Review, 1937–1938*, 259; and 'Index of prices received by fishermen, 1913 to 1974,' tables 114–17, in Leacy, ed., *Historical Statistics of Canada*.

197 *Herald*, 12, 20, 22, and 24 August and 2 and 5 September 1938; *Globe and Mail*, 22 August 1938, and *Ottawa Citizen*, 25 August 1938. See also 'Rideau Banks' – aka Norman MacLeod – 'Maritimes Are Restive,' *Saturday Night* 53.42 (20 August 1938): 5.

198 *Herald*, 27 August and 2 September 1938.

199 Macdonald to Johnston, 10 September 1938, ALM Papers, vol. 1504, file 398, and Macdonald to Don Fraser, 12 September 1938, ALM Papers, vol. 1504, file 397.

200 Rose to Macdonald, 13 September 1938, ALM Papers, vol. 1504, file 400.

201 Macdonald to Johnston, 7 February 1939, ALM Papers, vol. 1504, file 405.

202 House of Commons, *Debates*, 23 and 30 January 1939, 214–15 and 458–9.

203 *Chronicle*, 4 February 1939, and MacMillan to Macdonald, 12 February 1939, ALM Papers, vol. 1504, file 406.

204 George Gordon to Macdonald, 17 May 1938, ALM Papers, vol. 1504, file 397.

205 Joseph P. McIsaac to Macdonald, 21 June 1938, ALM Papers, vol. 1504, file 399.

206 Crerar to Macdonald, 18 July 1938, ALM Papers, vol. 1504, file 396; Macdonald to Johnston, 10 September 1938, and Johnston to Macdonald, 14 September 1938, ALM Papers, vol. 1504, file 398.

207 On the tour, see Neatby, *Prism of Unity*, 310–14, and Macdonald 'Diaries,' 15 June 1939.

208 See, for example, Joseph Bernard to Macdonald, 21 June 1939, and Dorothy Crerar to Macdonald, 24 November 1939, ALM Papers, vol. 1504, file 404.

209 Quoted in Macdonald to W.C. Rean, 26 August 1939, ALM Papers, vol. 1505, file 407. Asquith was praising Sir Donald MacLean, a Liberal cabinet minister.
210 Robert Bothwell and William Kilbourn, *C.D. Howe: A Biography* (Toronto: McClelland and Stewart, 1979), 104–13. For Macdonald's account of the trip, see his 'Diaries,' 11–24 August 1939.
211 Compare the coverage in the *Free Press* on 12 and 17 August 1939.
212 See Macdonald, 'Diaries,' 21–4 August 1939.

3. Macdonald versus King

 1 Macdonald, 'Memorandum for Sir Howard D'Egville,' 30 September 1939, and D'Egville to Macdonald, 1 September 1939, Angus L. Macdonald Papers (hereafter ALM Papers), Nova Scotia Archives and Records Management (NSARM), MG 2, vol. 1504, file 404. D'Egville asked Macdonald for a summary of Canadian perceptions of the international situation to circulate among members of the British government. See also Macdonald to Alex Johnston, 8 September 1939, and Johnston to Macdonald, 17 September 1939, ALM Papers, vol. 1504, file 405.
 2 *Toronto Globe and Mail*, 19 January 1940. Hepburn's very public feud with King is well chronicled in John T. Saywell, *'Just Call Me Mitch': The Life of Mitchell F. Hepburn* (Toronto: University of Toronto Press, 1991).
 3 Macdonald to Johnston, 25 January 1940, ALM Papers, vol. 1505, file 412.
 4 See J.L. Granatstein, *Canada's War: The Politics of the Mackenzie King Government, 1939–1945* (Toronto: University of Toronto Press, 1975), 77–8.
 5 Macdonald to Johnston, 26 January, 5 and 22 February 1940, ALM Papers, vol. 1505, file 412. See also King to Macdonald, 15 February 1940, King Papers, MG 26, vol. 290, reel C4570, p. 245534, Library and Archives Canada (LAC).
 6 Granatstein, *Canada's War*, 91.
 7 Ibid., 84, and House of Commons, *Debates*, 21 and 28 May 1940.
 8 F.W. Gibson and Barbara Robertson, eds., *Ottawa at War: The Grant Dexter Memoranda, 1939–1945* (Winnipeg: Manitoba Record Society, 1994), 66 and 70, Grant Dexter memos to J.W. Dafoe, 31 May and 7 June 1940. This collection of reports and memos written by Dexter to his editors at the *Winnipeg Free Press*, Dafoe and George V. Ferguson, provides valuable and perceptive insights into the political world of Ottawa throughout the war. Dexter enjoyed intimate contact with many bureaucrats and ministers in the federal government – including King, Macdonald, and T.A. Crerar – and his memos invariably display his perspicacity.

9 W.L. Mackenzie King, *Mackenzie King Diaries, 1932–1949* (Toronto: University of Toronto Press, 1980), entries for 30 March, 27 May, and 10 June 1940. On King's distaste of coalition governments, see R. MacGregor Dawson, *William Lyon Mackenzie King: A Political Biography, 1874–1923* (Toronto: University of Toronto Press, 1958), 258–314.

10 King, *Diaries*, 27 June 1940.

11 Ibid., 6, 27, and 28 June 1940, and Macdonald, 'Diaries,' 28 June 1940, ALM Papers, vol. 1503, file 388.

12 J.H. Fisher, 'Premier Plans to Bring "Heir" to His Cabinet,' *Toronto Evening Telegram*, 8 June 1940.

13 John Hawkins interview with Gordon Purdy, 1967(?), Hawkins fonds, AR 9073, NSARM.

14 King, *Diaries*, 5 and 22 July 1940; Macdonald, 'Diaries,' 3 July 1940.

15 Macdonald, 'Diaries,' 17 July 1940.

16 King, *Diaries*, 12 July 1940, Macdonald, 'Diaries,' 12 July 1940, and Macdonald to A.J. Baxter, 1 August 1940, ALM Papers, vol. 1516, file 690.

17 See Rupert Davies, editor of the *Kingston Whig-Standard*, to King, 10 July 1940, King Papers, MG 26, J1, vol. 286, reel C4586, p. 242299, LAC; W.C. Crozier, president of Kingston Conservative Association, 8 August 1940, King Papers, vol. 286, reel C4586, p. 242178, and W.M. Nickle, KC, to King, 12 August 1940, King Papers, vol. 293, reel C4572, p. 248097. See also *Kingston Whig-Standard*, 8 August 1940.

18 Macdonald, 'Diaries,' 17 July 1940; King, *Diaries*, 15 July 1940, and Macdonald to A.S. MacMillan, 5 August 1940, ALM Papers, vol. 1518, file 757.

19 King, *Diaries*, 5 September 1940.

20 Ibid., 1 and 23 October, 4 December 1940, 12 March and 6 February 1941.

21 King, *Diaries*, 27 June 1940.

22 See Marc Milner, *Canada's Navy: The First Century* (Toronto: University of Toronto Press, 1999), 104; Melner, *North Atlantic Run: The Royal Canadian Navy and the Battle for the Convoys* (Toronto: University of Toronto Press, 1985), 14–20; Joseph Schull, *The Far Distant Ships: An Official Account of Canadian Naval Operations in the Second World War* (Ottawa: King's Printer, 1950), 1, 74, 425–6; and Dan van der Vat, *The Atlantic Campaign: World War II's Great Struggle at Sea* (New York: Harper and Row, 1988), 135. Macdonald established the Women's Royal Canadian Naval Service (Wrens) on 31 July 1942.

23 Quoted in S. Matthew Davis, 'The "St. Laurent" Decision: Genesis of a Canadian Fleet,' in W.A.B. Douglas, ed., *The RCN in Transition, 1910–1985* (Vancouver: UBC Press, 1988), 189.

24 Milner, *North Atlantic Run*, 7, and W.A.B. Douglas, 'Conflict and Innovation

in the Royal Canadian Navy, 1939–1945,' in Gerald Jordan, ed., *Naval Warfare in the 20th Century: Essays in Honor of Arthur Marder* (New York: Crane Russak, 1977), 210–32.

25 See, for example, Milner, *North Atlantic Run*, and *The U-Boat Hunters: The Royal Canadian Navy and the Offensive against Germany's Submarines* (Toronto: University of Toronto Press, 1994); Commander Tony German, *The Sea Is at Our Gates: The History of the Canadian Navy* (Toronto: McClelland and Stewart, 1990); and David Zimmerman, *The Great Naval Battle of Ottawa* (Toronto: University of Toronto Press, 1989).

26 John Hawkins interview with Read, 12 December 1967, John Hawkins Fonds, AR 9068, NSARM.

27 Gibson and Robertson, eds., *Ottawa at War*, 200; Dexter memo to Dafoe, 10 October 1941.

28 C.G. Power, Memorandum on War Cabinet, 17 November 1942, ALM Papers, vol. 1500, file 277.

29 Macdonald to Power, 24 March 1943, ibid.

30 On Naval Services' administration, see Gilbert Tucker, *The Naval Service of Canada*, Volume 2, *Activities on Shore during the Second World War* (Ottawa: King's Printer, 1952), 418–35.

31 See ALM Papers, vol. 1513, file 589. Connolly earned his MA and PhD at Notre Dame and his LLB at McGill; see Charles Murphy to Connolly, 13 January 1931, John J. Connolly Papers, MG 32, C71, vol. 2, file 1, LAC.

32 Macdonald to Nelles, 3 April 1944, quoted in Douglas, 'Conflict and Innovation,' 226. See also James Eayrs, *In Defence of Canada*, Volume 3, *Peacemaking and Deterrence* (Toronto: University of Toronto Press, 1972) 82–3, and Milner, *North Atlantic Run*, 155. American naval officers had a difficult time distinguishing between the British and Canadian navies.

33 See John Connolly to Richard Jackson, Ottawa Press Gallery, 24 October 1944, Connolly Papers, MG 32, C71, vol. 3, file 1, LAC, and the *Ottawa Journal*, 31 October 1944.

34 See Eayrs, *Peacemaking and Deterrence*, 130–1, and L.C. Audette, 'The Lower Deck and the Mainguy Report of 1949,' in James A. Boutilier, ed., *The RCN in Retrospect, 1910–1968* (Vancouver: UBC Press, 1982), 247. Eayrs argues that the language policy was simply a nod to RN customs.

35 Hawkins interview with Read; and Tucker, *Naval Service*, 2:434–5.

36 Appreciation dated 6 October 1940, cited in 'Development of Canadian Naval Policy,' 9 December 1943, Connolly Papers, MG 32, C71, vol. 4, file 11, LAC.

37 'Development of Canadian Naval Policy,' 9 December 1943; and Milner, *North Atlantic Run*, 88 and 153.

38 See 'Ilsley Likeliest Successor to Prime Minister King,' *Ottawa Journal*, 24 October 1942, and *Globe and Mail*, 8 October 1941. The *Ottawa Journal*, on 13 February 1941, reported Macdonald's reaction to a security breach without mentioning any specific incident.

39 Austin Cross, 'Career Sketches,' *Canadian Business* 15.8 (Aug. 1942): 36–43; see also Cross, *The People's Mouths* (Toronto: Macmillan, 1943), 94 and 96.

40 McArdle to Macdonald, 25 August 1942, Macdonald to McArdle, 9 September 1942, and Macdonald to McArdle, 13 October 1942, ALM Papers, vol. 1516, file 685.

41 Grant Dexter, 'First Lord,' *Maclean's* 52.6 (15 March 1942): 40.

42 See also Hawkins interview with Purdy.

43 See Granatstein, *Canada's War*, 114–58 and 175–87; and Gibson and Robertson, eds., *Ottawa at War*, 201–11, 430–1, and 428, Dexter memos to Ferguson, 9 and 10 October 1941, 9 September 1943, and 22 September 1944.

44 Granatstein, *Canada's War*, 162–3.

45 'Plenary Session, 14 January,' in *Dominion-Provincial Conference, 1941* (Ottawa: King's Printer, 1941) 11–12. See also J.E. Rea, *T.A. Crerar: A Political Life* (Montreal and Kingston: McGill-Queen's University Press, 1997), 204–5.

46 Macdonald to King, 14 January 1941, quoted in Saywell, '*Mitch*,' 461, and 'Plenary Session, 15 January,' *Conference*, 84–7.

47 Granatstein, *Canada's War*, 172

48 Christopher Armstrong, 'Ceremonial Politics: Federal-Provincial Meetings before the Second World War,' in R. Kenneth Carty and W. Peter Ward, eds., *National Politics and Community in Canada* (Vancouver: UBC Press, 1986), 139.

49 This system was formalized in the Dominion-Provincial Tax Agreement Act, 1942; see Granatstein, *Canada's War*, 173–4.

50 Macdonald to Dexter, 1 November 1945, ALM Papers, vol. 900, file 28-3A; and Rea, *Crerar*, 202–5.

51 House of Commons, *Debates*, 18 June 1940, 854. On the fears of Quebec Liberals, see Lita-Rose Betcherman, *Ernest Lapointe: Mackenzie King's Great Quebec Lieutenant* (Toronto: University of Toronto Press, 2002), 312–19.

52 King, *Diaries*, 18 December 1941.

53 Gibson and Robertson, eds., *Ottawa at War*, 185, letter from Ferguson to Dexter, 12 July 1941.

54 Macdonald, 'Diaries,' 11 December 1941.

55 See King, *Diaries*, 23 April and 9 May 1941, and Gibson and Robertson, eds., *Ottawa at War*, 167 and 174–8, Dexter memos, 7 May and 12 June 1941.

56 See C.P. Stacey, *Arms, Men and Governments: The War Policies of Canada, 1939–1945* (Ottawa: Queen's Printers, 1970), 43–5.

57 Macdonald, 'Diaries,' 10 June 1941.
58 King, *Diaries*, 10 June 1941.
59 Granatstein, *Canada's War*, 207–8.
60 King, *Diaries*, 23 September 1941. Lapointe died on 26 November 1941 of pancreatic cancer; Betcherman, *Lapointe*, 340–5.
61 For accounts of Macdonald's poor health, see Tweedsmuir to King, 14 June 1937, King Papers, MG 26, J1, vol. 243, reel C3730, pp. 209309–12, LAC; Cross, *The People's Mouths*, 96; Gibson and Robertson, eds., *Ottawa at War*, 452, Dexter memo to Ferguson, 23 December 1943; 'The Navy Minister's Position,' *Ottawa Journal*, 4 November 1944; and Hawkins interview with Agnes Foley Macdonald, 16 August 1967, Hawkins Fonds, AR 9063.
62 See J.L. Granatstein, *The Politics of Survival: The Conservative Party of Canada, 1939–1945* (Toronto: University of Toronto Press, 1967), 82–112, and Granatstein, *Canada's War*, 204–6.
63 See Michael D. Stevenson, *Canada's Greatest Wartime Muddle: National Selective Service and the Mobilization of Human Resources during World War II* (Montreal and Kingston: McGill-Queen's University Press, 2001), 4–5; Gibson and Robertson, eds., *Ottawa at War*, 222–4 and 227, Dexter memo to Dafoe, 18 and 20 November 1941; Macdonald, 'Diaries,' 1 and 2 December 1941; and Granatstein, *Canada's War*, 209–11.
64 Gibson and Robertson, eds., *Ottawa at War*, 231, Dexter memo to Dafoe, 8 December 1941.
65 Ibid., 256, Dexter memo to Ferguson, 12 January 1942.
66 See King, *Diaries*, 9 and 10 December, and Macdonald, 'Diaries,' 9 and 11 December 1941.
67 See King, *Diaries*, 11 and 16 December 1941.
68 Gibson and Robertson, eds., *Ottawa at War*, 296, Dexter memo to Ferguson, 13 March 1942; emphasis in original.
69 See, for example, King, *Diaries*, 4 December 1941.
70 J.L. Granatstein and J.M. Hitsman, *Broken Promises: A History of Conscription in Canada* (Toronto: Oxford University Press, 1977), 68.
71 Dafoe to Crerar, 12 January 1942, Dafoe Papers, MG 30, D45, reel M-80, LAC, and Macdonald, 'Diaries,' 18 December 1941. The Quebec ministers in King's cabinet had promised their province that a Liberal government would never conscript soldiers for overseas combat; see Betcherman, *Lapointe*, 279–83.
72 See Macdonald, 'Diaries,' 27 and 28 December 1941, and King, *Diaries*, 28 December 1941.
73 See King, *Diaries*, 5 January 1942.

74 Gibson and Robertson, eds., *Ottawa at War*, 254–5 and 296–7, Dexter memos to Ferguson, 6 January and 13 March 1942.
75 See King, *Diaries*, 6 January 1942.
76 Granatstein and Hitsman, *Broken Promises*, 177; see also Macdonald, 'Diaries,' 28 January 1942, ALM Papers, vol. 1503, file 390.
77 Quoted in Granatstein, *Canada's War*, 219; author's translation.
78 Macdonald, 'Diaries,' 31 January 1942.
79 Gibson and Robertson, eds., *Ottawa at War*, 237, Dexter memo to Dafoe, 22 December 1941, and Granatstein, *Canada's War*, 221.
80 Granatstein and Hitsman, *Broken Promises*, 163–72.
81 Macdonald, 'Diaries,' 28 April 1942.
82 Gibson and Robertson, eds., *Ottawa at War*, 315–18, Dexter memo to Ferguson, 7 May 1942.
83 King, *Diaries*, 5 May 1942.
84 Gibson and Robertson, eds., *Ottawa at War*, 318 and 323, Dexter memos to Ferguson, 7 and 13 May 1942.
85 Quoted in Dexter memo, 13 May 1942.
86 King, *Diaries*, 7 May 1942.
87 Quoted in Granatstein, *Canada's War*, 231.
88 Macdonald, 'Diaries,' 27 May 1942.
89 Macdonald to King, 28 May 1942, King Papers, MG 26, J1, vol. 327, reel C6808, pp. 279092–3, LAC.
90 Macdonald, 'Diaries,' 4 June 1942.
91 King, *Diaries*, 8 June 1942.
92 House of Commons, *Debates*, 10 June 1942, 3236.
93 Gibson and Robertson, eds., *Ottawa at War*, 326, Dexter memo to Ferguson, 15 June 1942.
94 King, *Diaries*, 12 June 1942, and Macdonald, 'Diaries,' 12 June 1942. Dafoe agreed with Macdonald's logic; see 'Memorandum of conversation with J.W. Dafoe,' 29 May 1942, ALM Papers, vol. 1503, file 390.
95 Gibson and Robertson, eds., *Ottawa at War*, 327, Dafoe memo to Ferguson, 17 June 1942.
96 Gibson and Robertson, eds., *Ottawa at War*, 330–1, Dexter memo to Ferguson, 4 July 1942.
97 See Macdonald, 'Diaries,' 7 July 1942, and 'Ralston Memo, 1942,' ALM Papers, vol. 1503, file 379. For Ralston's letter of resignation, see Ralston to King, J.L. Ralston Papers, MG 27, III, B11, vol. 85, LAC.
98 Macdonald, 'Diaries,' 8 July 1942. Crerar told King of Macdonald's position and his efforts to keep Ralston from resigning; see King, *Diaries*, 9 July 1942.

99 See King to Ralston, 11 July, and Ralston to King, 13 July 1942, Ralston Papers, MG27, III, B11, vol. 85.

100 See especially Gibson and Robertson, eds., *Ottawa at War*, 317–18, 321–3, 326–30, 333, and 345, Dexter memos to Ferguson, 7, 11, and 13 May, 15, 17, and 25 June, and 4, 9, and 19 July 1942.

101 Marc Milner, 'Inshore ASW: The Canadian Experience in Home Waters,' in Douglas, ed., *The RCN in Transition*, 146, and Milner, *Canada's Navy*, 104.

102 See Milner, 'Canadian Experience,' 147–52, and Michael L. Hadley, 'Inshore ASW in the Second World War: The U-Boat Experience,' in Douglas, ed., *The RCN in Transition*, 140–1.

103 See Zimmerman, *Great Naval Battle*, 90–1; E.R. Forbes, 'Consolidating Disparity: The Maritimes and the Industrialization of Canada during the Second World War,' *Acadiensis* 15.2 (Spring 1986): 25–7; and Tucker, *Naval Service*, 2:391–5.

104 Tucker, *Naval Service*, 2:391–2; Marc Milner, 'The Royal Canadian Navy and 1943: A Year Best Forgotten?' in Paul Dickson, ed., *1943: The Beginning of the End* (Ottawa: Canadian Committee for the History of the Second World War, 1995), 124–5; and Michael L. Hadley, *U-Boats Against Canada: German Submarines in Canadian Waters* (Montreal and Kingston: McGill-Queen's University Press, 1985), 38–40.

105 House of Commons, *Debates*, 13 July 1942, 4124–6.

106 King, *Diaries*, 28 October 1942.

107 The best account of this period is Milner, *North Atlantic Run*, 185–241.

108 Zimmerman, *Great Naval Battle*, 32–3; Milner, *North Atlantic Run*, 77–8 and 123–4; and Milner, *Canada's Navy*, 162–3.

109 The USN had just one escort group in the theatre during this time. Milner, *North Atlantic Run*, 129 and 190.

110 Attlee to King, 17 December 1942, King Papers, MG 26 J1, vol. 350, reel C7043, pp. 287012–13, LAC.

111 Milner, '1943,' 125.

112 Milner, *North Atlantic Run*, 193–4, 198–200, and 219.

113 See Macdonald, 'Diaries,' 23 December 1942.

114 Zimmerman, *Great Naval Battle*, 104.

115 Milner, *U-Boat Hunters*, 51.

116 See Nelles to Macdonald, 27 November 1943, ALM Papers, vol. 1500, file 276.

117 Milner, *North Atlantic Run*, 212, 220–2, 225–41, and 277–8, and Milner, 'Royal Canadian Navy Participation in the Battle of the Atlantic Crisis of 1943,' in Boutilier, ed., *The RCN in Retrospect*, 171–2.

118 Milner, 'Royal Canadian Navy Participation,' 171–2.

119 Milner, '1943,' 126, and Milner, *North Atlantic Run*, 222, 240, 242, and 277–8.

120 See Macdonald, 'Diaries,' 26 May 1943, ALM Papers, vol. 1503, file 391.

121 Onésime Gagnon of the Union Nationale led the attack. See Hadley, *U-Boats*, 23.

122 *Globe and Mail*, 16 and 18 March 1943.

123 Tucker, *Naval Service*, 2:393–4.

124 The Canadian zone covered the Atlantic west of 47°W and north of 40°N. See W.G.D. Lund, 'The Royal Canadian Navy's Quest for Autonomy in the Northwest Atlantic, 1941–43,' in Boutilier, ed., *The RCN in Retrospect*, 152–3.

125 See Milner, *North Atlantic Run*, 239, and Milner, 'Royal Canadian Navy Participation,' 172–4.

126 See Milner, *North Atlantic Run*, 245–51.

127 Ibid., 252–3, and Stacey, *Arms, Men and Governments*, 315–16. Adams's report can be found in the Percy Walker Nelles Fonds (hereafter Nelles Papers), Directorate of History and Heritage (DHist), folder B, file 10.

128 Richard Oliver Mayne, 'A Covert Naval Investigation: Overseas Officers, John J. Connolly, and the Equipment Crisis of 1943,' *Northern Mariner* 10.1 (January 2000): 39. For the political slide, see Granatstein, *Canada's War*, 264–5.

129 Milner, '1943,' 127, and Gibson and Robertson, eds., *Ottawa at War*, 422–4, Dexter memo to Ferguson, 1 September 1943.

130 Macdonald to Nelles, 21 August 1943, RG 24, vol. 3995, NSS 1057-1-27, LAC, quoted in Milner, *North Atlantic Run*, 255.

131 Milner, *North Atlantic Run*, 255–56.

132 Connolly's trip is described in full detail in his diary; see John J. Connolly, 'Diary, June to December 1943' and 'Diary, Trip to the U.K., October 1943,' Connolly Papers, MG 32, C71, vol. 2, files 6 and 7, LAC.

133 Stacey, *Arms, Men and Governments*, 318, and Milner, *North Atlantic Run*, 258.

134 'I am not entirely in favour here. That, of course, is one of the penalties which must be paid and I am prepared to accept it, as I was before I assume the responsibility for the statements which I made. I hope none of them were exaggerated because I tried particularly to avoid exaggeration.' Connolly to Commander R. A. Pennington, London, 7 December 1943, Connolly Papers, MG 32, C71, vol. 2, file 18, LAC.

135 Macdonald to Nelles, 23(?) November 1943, ALM Papers, vol. 1500, file 276.

136 Nelles to Macdonald, 4 December 1943, ibid.

137 Macdonald to Nelles, 10 December 1943, ibid.

138 Nelles's duties were neither clear nor unique. He helped with liaison work, but his role overlapped with those of the Senior Canadian Naval Officer in London. Nelles returned to Ottawa in April and May to pester Macdonald about his terms of reference, but the minister wished only to be rid of him. See Macdonald, 'Notes on Naval Matters,' 5 May 1944, ALM Papers, vol. 1501, file 305, and Nelles Papers, folder C, files 3, 4, 6, 14, 25, 38, 39 and 40.

139 Stacey, *Arms, Men and Governments*, 316–17; Zimmerman, *Great Naval Battle*, 139–40; German, *Our Gates*, 147; Richard Oliver Mayne, 'A Political Execution: Expediency and the Firing of Vice Admiral Percy W. Nelles, 1943–1944,' *American Review of Canadian Studies* 29.4 (Winter 1999): 557–92; and Milner, *U-Boat Hunters*, 52, *North Atlantic Run*, 259 and 264–6, and '1943,' 133.

140 King, *Diaries*, 7 January 1944. On the government's optimism about the U-boat threat, see Gibson and Robertson, eds., *Ottawa at War*, 429, Dexter memos to Ferguson, 9 September and 21 October 1943.

141 See Granatstein, *Canada's War*, 264–5.

142 Gibson and Robertson, eds., *Ottawa at War*, 431–2 and 440, Dexter memo to Ferguson, 9 September 1943, and Dafoe memo to Dexter, 15 September 1943. Macdonald used Dexter as a go-between to Dafoe.

143 King, *Diaries*, 24 March 1943.

144 Gibson and Robertson, eds., *Ottawa at War*, 441–2, Dexter memo to Ferguson, 17 September 1943.

145 See *Report on Social Security for Canada* (Ottawa: King's Printer, 1943); Granatstein, *Canada's War*, 254–62; and Brigitte Kitchen, 'The Marsh Report Revisited,' *Journal of Canadian Studies* 21.2 (1986): 38–48.

146 Gibson and Robertson, eds., *Ottawa at War*, 405, Dexter memo to Ferguson, 23 March 1943. Mackenzie's department had also been developing a plan for health insurance.

147 King, *Diaries*, 9 June 1943, and Granatstein, *Canada's War*, 262 and 269.

148 Gibson and Robertson, eds., *Ottawa at War*, 445–7, Dexter memo to Ferguson, 1 November 1943.

149 Granatstein, *Canada's War*, 281. Granatstein argues that Pickersgill changed King's mind.

150 King, *Diaries*, 4 December 1943, and Granatstein, *Canada's War*, 274.

151 Macdonald, 'Memorandum on Reconstruction,' 12 January 1944, King Papers, MG 26, J1, vol. 364, reel C7053, pp. 315881–6.

152 Macdonald to King, 22 January 1944, ibid. pp. 315889–90. On Clark's presentation, see Macdonald, 'Diaries,' 22 January 1944, ALM Papers, vol. 1503, file 392.

153 King, *Diaries*, 22 January 1944.

154 See House of Commons, *Debates*, 27 January 1945, 1–3, and Granatstein, *Canada's War*, 275.

155 Power to Hutchison, 26 March 1952, C.G. Power Papers, no. 2150, box 6, series I-C, Queen's University Archives (hereafter QUA); Bruce Hutchison, *The Incredible Canadian – A Candid Portrait of Mackenzie King: His Work, His Times, and His Nation* (Toronto: Longmans, Green and Co., 1952).

156 See King, *Diaries*, 15 June 1944, and Macdonald, 'Diaries,' 15 and 20 June 1944. Grant Dexter passed this comment along to Macdonald.

157 Macdonald, 'Diaries,' 15, 21, and 22 June 1944.

158 See, e.g., King, *Diaries*, 14 January and 15 September 1943.

159 King, *Diaries*, 10 November 1943.

160 King, *Diaries*, 29 March, 5 and 13 April 1943.

161 Macdonald, 'Diaries,' 31 August and 8 September 1943, and Macdonald to Leslie Roberts, 3 December 1946, ALM Papers, vol. 290, file 31-2.

162 Macdonald, 'Diaries,' 5 January 1944.

163 King, *Diaries*, 12 January 1944.

164 King, *Diaries*, 31 August 1944.

165 Macdonald, 'Diaries,' 6, 13, 20, and 22 September 1944.

166 Macdonald, 'Diaries,' 5 and 11 October 1944, and King, *Diaries*, 11 October 1944.

167 Connolly, 'Diary, September 1944 – April 1945,' entry 13 October 1944, Connolly Papers, MG 32, C71, vol. 2, file 8, LAC.

168 See, for example, Hutchison, *Incredible Canadian*, 340–98; R. MacGregor Dawson, *The Conscription Crisis of 1944* (Toronto: University of Toronto Press, 1961); Maurice Pope, *Soldiers and Politicians: The Memoirs of Lt.-Gen. Maurice A. Pope, C.B., M.C.* (Toronto: University of Toronto Press, 1962), 247–61; C.G. Power, *A Party Politician: The Memoirs of Chubby Power*, ed. Norman Ward (Toronto: Macmillan of Canada, 1966), 150–78; J.L. Granatstein, *Conscription in the Second World War: A Study in Political Management* (Toronto: McGraw-Hill Ryerson, 1969); Stacey, *Arms, Men, and Governments*, 424–81; Granatstein, *Canada's War*, 333–81; Granatstein and Hitsman, *Broken Promises*, 185–244; and T. Stephen Henderson, 'Angus L. Macdonald and the Conscription Crisis of 1944,' *Acadiensis* 27.1 (Autumn 1997): 85–104.

169 King, *Diaries*, 3 August 1944.

170 Stacey, *Arms, Men, and Governments*, 432 and 437–8, and Macdonald, 'Diaries,' 19 October 1944.

171 Quoted in Stacey, *Arms, Men, and Governments*, 437–8.

172 See Drew to King, 30 September 1944, King Papers, MG 26, J1, vol. 359, reel C7050, LAC, and *Montreal Gazette*, 19 September 1944.

173 King, *Diaries*, 18 and 19 October 1944, and Macdonald, 'Diaries,' 19 October 1944.

174 Macdonald, 'Diaries,' 24 October 1944.

175 King, *Diaries*, 18 October 1944.

176 J.E. Rea, 'A View from the Lectern,' *Journal of the Canadian Historical Association*, new series, 2 (1991): 15.

177 King, *Diaries*, 25 and 26 October 1944, and Macdonald, 'Diaries,' 26 October 1944.

178 Power, *Party Politician*, 154–5.

179 Macdonald, 'Diaries,' 27 October 1944.

180 King, *Diaries*, 20 and 25 October 1944, and Power to Dexter, 10 December 1944, Power Papers, QUA, 2150, box 12, series I-E.

181 Macdonald, untitled memorandum of the events of 1 November 1944, prepared 2 or 3 November 1944, ALM Papers, vol. 1503, file 385. See also King, *Diaries*, 31 October 1944.

182 Conversation reported in Reginald H. Roy, *For Most Conspicuous Bravery: A Biography of Major-General George V. Pearkes, V.C., Through Two World Wars* (Vancouver: UBC Press, 1977), 220–2.

183 See Macdonald, untitled memo, 2 or 3 November 1944, and John Swettenham, *McNaughton*, Volume 3, *1944–1946* (Toronto: Ryerson Press, 1969), 45–6.

184 King, *Diaries*, 18 and 31 October 1944; on the Ralston-McNaughton affair, see J.L. Granatstein, *The Generals: The Canadian Army's Senior Commanders in the Second World War* (Toronto: Stoddard,1993), 61–80.

185 See House of Commons, *Debates*, 27 November 1944, 6603; King, *Diaries*, 17 March 1942; and Gibson and Robertson, eds., *Ottawa at War*, 303–4, Dexter memo to Dafoe, 19 March 1942.

186 King, *Diaries*, 19, 20, and 31 October 1944.

187 Macdonald, 'Diaries,' 31 October 1944.

188 King, *Diaries*, 24 and 30 October and 1 November 1944.

189 King, *Diaries*, 1 November 1944. For other accounts of the events on 1 November, see Macdonald, untitled memo, 2 or 3 November; J.L. Ilsley, 'Memorandum of events leading up to the resignation of Colonel Ralston, ... prepared some weeks after Nov. 1st,' ALM Papers, vol. 1503, no. 385; Crerar, 'Notes for the record on the recent crisis in the Government over reinforcements,' 26 December 1944, T.A. Crerar Papers, collection 2117, box 119, QUA; and Power, 'Notes of discussions on the conscription crisis,' November 1944, Power Papers, no. 2150, box 12.

190 Gibson and Robertson, eds., *Ottawa at War*, 489, Dexter memo to Ferguson, 6 November 1944.

191 Rumours of Macdonald's departure were in the air; see Gibson and Robertson, eds., *Ottawa at War*, 483, Dexter memo to Ferguson, 25 September 1944; King, *Diaries*, 29 September 1944 *Ottawa Journal*, 25 October 1944, and Rod MacSween to Macdonald, 26 October 1944, ALM Papers, vol. 1518, no. 764.

192 J.J. Connolly to Macdonald, 2 November 1944, ALM Papers, vol. 1500, no. 291. See also 'Home Defence Army Will Again Be Debated?' *Halifax Herald*, 30 October 1944, and 'Cabinet Crisis in 8th Day,' *Winnipeg Free Press*, 1 November 1944.

193 Dawson, *Conscription Crisis*, 51.

194 Granatstein, *Conscription in the Second World War*, 59.

195 Stacey, *Arms, Men and Governments*, 458.

196 See Macdonald, untitled memo (n. 181 above); Ilsley, 'Memorandum'; and Crerar, 'Notes for the record.'

197 Macdonald, 'Diaries,' 1 November 1944.

198 Macdonald to MacMillan, 7 November 1944, ALM Papers, vol. 1503, file 385.

199 Rea, 'View from the Lectern,' 15; Macdonald, 'Diaries,' 1 November 1944; and King, *Diaries*, 19 October 1944.

200 Granatstein, *Canada's War*, 338.

201 Stacey, *Arms, Men and Governments*, 439–40. Stuart's telegram to the Chief of the General Staff was dated 26 August 1944.

202 King, *Diaries*, 19 October 1944. At the meeting of 3 August 1944, King and his cabinet reluctantly agreed to reinforce the 5th Canadian Armoured Division with a second infantry brigade, based on assurances from Stuart that this would not aggravate the reinforcement situation.

203 Sifton to Ralston, 1 March 1944, Ralston Papers, MG 27, III, B11, vol. 57, LAC.

204 King, *Diaries*, 31 October 1944. McNaughton placed Stuart on leave pending retirement. Minutes of the War Committee, 9 November 1944, RG 2, vol. 16, LAC.

205 Gibson and Robertson, eds., *Ottawa at War*, 431, Dexter memo to Ferguson, 9 September 1943.

206 Stacey, *Arms, Men and Governments*, 468–9, 476–7, and Roy, *For Most Conspicuous Bravery*, 225–36.

207 Pope, *Soldiers and Politicians*, 248–51; Power, *Party Politician*, 154; and Minutes of the War Committee, 24 October 1944.

208 Minutes of the War Committee, 19 October 1944.

209 King, *Diaries*, 21 October 1944.

210 Granatstein and Hitsman, *Broken Promises*, 190–2.

211 Howe missed the 1 November cabinet meeting and did not commit to conscription until 22 November. See King, *Diaries*, 1 November 1944, and Crerar, 'Notes for the record.'

212 King, *Diaries*, 1 November 1944.

213 Macdonald, 'Diaries,' 1 November 1944.

214 Connolly to Macdonald, 2 November 1944, ALM Papers, vol. 1500, file 291; see also Bernard Charles LeBlanc, 'A Reluctant Recruit: Angus L. Macdonald and Conscription, 1940–1945,' MA thesis, Queen's University, 1987, 77–8.

215 Rupert Davies to Macdonald, 6 February 1945, ALM Papers, vol. 1518, file 764.

216 J.A. Corry to Macdonald, 17 November 1944, ALM Papers, vol. 1500, file 291.

217 Macdonald to MacMillan, 7 November 1944, and MacMillan to Macdonald, 20 November 1944, ALM Papers, vol. 1503, file 385.

218 Macdonald to Frank Davis, 5 November 1944, and Davis to Macdonald, 14 November 1944, ibid.

219 Macdonald, 'Diaries,' 3 November 1944.

220 See Macdonald, 'Diaries,' 5 November 1944, for his conversations in Montreal.

221 King to Macdonald, 15 November 1944, King Papers, MG 26, J1, vol. 364, reel C7053, LAC.

222 King, *Diaries*, 9 November 1944.

223 *Public Opinion Quarterly* 8 (Winter 1944–5): 591, quoted in Granatstein and Hitsman, *Broken Promises*, 222–3.

224 Connolly, 'Diary, September 1944–April 1945,' 10 and 14 November 1944.

225 Macdonald, 'Diaries,' 10 November 1944, emphasis in original. Macdonald also spoke to at least three backbenchers about the possibility of forming an independent Liberal group; see his 'Diaries,' 12, 14, and 15 November 1944.

226 Macdonald to Ralston, 18 November 1944, ALM Papers, vol. 1503, file 385. At the bottom of the letter, Macdonald wrote, 'This had better be destroyed once read.'

227 Macdonald, 'Diaries,' 20 November 1944, and King, *Diaries*, 20 November 1944.

228 Macdonald, 'Diaries,' 21 November 1944.

229 Macdonald, 'Diaries,' 22 November 1944, and Crerar, 'Notes for the record.'

230 Power to Macdonald, 15 November 1952, ALM Papers, vol. 1503, file 382.

231 Granatstein, *Canada's War*, 372–3.

232 See King, *Diaries*, 18, 19, 20, 25, and 30 October 1944.

233 See King, *Diaries*, 19, 20, 25, 26, 30, and 31 October, and 1 November 1944.

234 Macdonald to MacMillan, 7 November 1944, and Macdonald to Edward Young, 22 November 1944, ALM Papers, vol. 1500, file 291.

235 Power to Hutchison, 20 June 1951, Power Papers, Collection 2150, box 6, series I-C, QUA.

236 King, *Diaries*, 3 October 1941.

237 Macdonald, 'Diaries,' 2 to 5 January 1945, ALM Papers, vol. 1503, file 393.

238 See Macdonald, 'Diaries,' 12 January to 2 February 1945; Connolly, 'Diary of 2nd Trip Overseas, 1945,' Connolly Papers, MG 32, C71, vol. 2, file 11, LAC; and Vincent Massey, *What's Past Is Prologue: The Memoirs of the Right Honourable Vincent Massey* (Toronto: Macmillan, 1963).

239 King, *Diaries*, 22 December 1944 and 2 January 1945.

240 Compare King, *Diaries*, 9 January 1945, and Gibson and Robertson, eds., *Ottawa at War*, 494, Dexter memo to Ferguson, 9–10 January 1945.

241 Rea, *Crerar*, and *Globe and Mail*, 19 April 1945.

242 See Connolly, 'Diary, 2nd Trip Overseas,' 26 January 1945.

243 Macdonald, 'Diaries,' 9 February 1945.

244 Macdonald to King, 18 April 1945, King Papers, MG 26, J1, vol. 386, reel C9876, 345981–2, LAC.

245 King, *Diaries*, 11 April 1945.

246 Connolly to Macdonald, 22 April 1945, Connolly Papers, MG 32, C71, vol. 4, file 15, LAC.

4. The Provinces' Champion

1 On the VE day riots, see Stephen Kimber, *Sailors, Slackers and Blind Pigs: Halifax At War* (Toronto: Anchor, 2003); R.H. Caldwell, 'The VE Day Riots in Halifax, 7–8 May 1945,' *Northern Mariner* 10.1 (2000): 3–20; Stanley R. Redman, *Open Gangway: An Account of the Halifax Riots, 1945* (Hantsport, NS: Lancelot Press, 1981); and James M. Cameron, *Murray: The Martyred Admiral* (Hantsport, NS: Lancelot Press, 1981), 102–291.

2 P.B. Waite, *The Lives of Dalhousie University: Volume Two, 1925–1980: The Old College Transformed* (Montreal and Kingston: McGill-Queen's University Press, 1998), 129–40.

3 Ray Smith to Dr Dinty Moore, 26 March 1945, Angus L. Macdonald Papers, Nova Scotia Archives and Records Management (NSARM), MG 2 (hereafter ALM Papers), vol. 1501, file 307.

4 W.L.M. King, *Mackenzie King Diaries, 1932–1945* (Toronto: University of Toronto, 1980), 29 September 1944.

5 Frederick W. Gibson and Barbara Robertson, eds., *Ottawa at War: The Grant Dexter Memoranda, 1939–1945* (Winnipeg: Manitoba Records Society, 1994), 501, Grant Dexter memo to George V. Ferguson, 14 June 1945.

6 Macdonald to MacMillan, 19 April 1945, ALM Papers, vol. 1518, file 764.

7 For reports of MacMillan's less-than-deft abilities, see Davis to Macdonald, 26 October 1944, and L.D. 'Lauchie' Currie, Minister of Labour, to Macdonald, 8 September 1940, ALM Papers, vol. 1513, file 596.

8 Macdonald to MacMillan, 19 February 1945, MacMillan to Macdonald, 24 February 1945, Macdonald to MacMillan, 19 April 1945, MacMillan to Macdonald, 21 May 1945, Macdonald to MacMillan, 26 May 1945, Macdonald to MacMillan, 23 June 1945, and Macdonald to MacMillan, 26 May 1945, ALM Papers, vol. 1518, file 764. See also Davis to Macdonald, 26 October 1944, and Macdonald to Davis, 8 November 1944, ibid., vol. 1503, file 385.

9 J. Murray Beck, *The Politics of Nova Scotia*, Volume 2, *Murray–Buchanan, 1896–1988* (Tantallon, NS: Four East, 1988), 193.

10 See Macdonald, 'Speech on Dominion-Provincial Relations in the Legislative Assembly,' 8 May 1947, ALM Papers, vol. 920, file 31-3.

11 Janine Brodie, *The Political Economy of Canadian Regionalism* (Toronto: Harcourt Brace Jovanovich, 1990), 29 and 155–6.

12 J.A. Corry, *My Life and Work: A Happy Partnership* (Kingston: Queen's University Press, 1981), 111–12. On Corry's work for Rowell-Sirois, see his *Difficulties of Divided Jurisdiction: A Study Prepared for the Royal Commission on Dominion-Provincial Relations* (Ottawa: King's Printer, 1939).

13 Gibson and Robertson, eds., *Ottawa at War*, 496–500, Dexter memo to Ferguson, 1 March 1945. For the careers of Skelton and Mackintosh, see J.L. Granatstein, *The Ottawa Men: The Civil Service Mandarins, 1935–1957* (Toronto: Oxford University Press, 1982), and Barry Ferguson, *Remaking Liberalism: The Intellectual Legacy of Adam Shortt, O.D. Skelton, W.C. Clark, and W.A. Mackintosh, 1890–1925* (Montreal and Kingston: McGill-Queen's University Press, 1993).

14 *Dominion-Provincial Conference (1945): Dominion and Provincial Submissions and Plenary Conference Discussions* (Ottawa: King's Printer, 1946), 5, 21–2, and 124–8.

15 Johnston to Macdonald, 11 August 1945, ALM Papers, vol. 904, file 28. Nova Scotian governments of the period had typically had seven or eight cabinet ministers. Catholics constituted roughly 30% of the population of Nova Scotia, and premiers typically had no more than three Catholics in their cabinets. Macdonald was sensitive on this point, fearful that he would

be seen as favouring Catholics. Nevertheless, after the 1945 election Macdonald's cabinet had three Protestants and four Catholics; Currie went to the Supreme Court of Nova Scotia in 1949.

16 See Macdonald, 'Diary,' 29 to 31 August 1945, ALM Papers, vol. 1503, file 393.

17 Macdonald, 'Diaries,' 31 August 1945.

18 *Halifax Chronicle*, 10 September 1945, quoted in Beck, *Politics of Nova Scotia*, 2:205.

19 See 'Liberals Meet,' *Halifax Herald*, 4 October 1945.

20 Macdonald, 'Speeches,' 25 September, 2 October and 20 October 1945, ALM Papers, vol. 903, file 28 (A1).

21 Interview with Dalton Camp, 20 December 1999, and Camp, *Gentlemen, Players and Politicians* (Toronto: McClelland and Stewart, 1970), 111. For the results of the election, see Beck, *Politics of Nova Scotia*, 2:424. The Liberals drew 52.7% of the popular vote, the Conservatives took 33.5%, and the CCF won 13.6%, its best showing until 1978.

22 'Preliminary Statement of Province of Nova Scotia,' 28 November 1945, in *Dominion-Provincial Conference (1945)*, 215–18.

23 'Reply by Dominion Government to Questions Raised in the Preliminary Statement of Province of Nova Scotia,' 5 December 1945, in *Dominion-Provincial Conference (1945)*, 219.

24 For a discussion of historians' misinterpretation of Rowell-Sirois, see Barry Ferguson and Robert Wardhaugh, '"Impossible Conditions of Inequality": John Dafoe, the Rowell-Sirois Commission, and the Interpretation of Canadian Federalism,' *Canadian Historical Review* 84.4 (December 2003): 555–6.

25 Robert Bothwell, Ian Drummond, and John English, *Canada: 1900–1945* (Toronto: University of Toronto Press, 1987), 276, and Bothwell et al., *Canada since 1945: Power, Politics, and Provincialism* (Toronto: University of Toronto Press, 1981), 73.

26 Macdonald to John Connolly, 8 November 1946, ALM Papers, vol. 901, file 28(A2).

27 Macdonald to Corry and Macdonald to Innis, 16 January 1946, ALM Papers, vol. 898, file 19½(D).

28 Corry to Macdonald, 17 January 1946, ibid.

29 Innis to Macdonald, 17 January 1946, H.A. Innis Papers, B1972–0003, box 005, file 18, University of Toronto Archives. See also Brodie, *Political Economy of Canadian Regionalism*, 155–6.

30 'Submissions by the Government of Nova Scotia to the Dominion-Provincial Conference, 1945–1946,' 26 January 1946, *Dominion-Provincial Conference (1945)*, 315–17.

31 Macdonald, 'Address on Dominion–Provincial Relations,' 8 February 1946, ALM Papers, vol. 898, file 19½(D).

32 'Replies by the Dominion Government to the Questions Put by the Provincial Premiers, January 1946,' 25 April 1946, *Dominion-Provincial Conference (1945)*, 333–8.

33 'Dominion-Provincial Conference,' 29 April 1946, *Dominion-Provincial Conference (1945)*, 416–19.

34 King, *Diaries*, 26 April 1946.

35 'Dominion-Provincial Conference,' 29 April 1946, *Dominion-Provincial Conference (1945)*, 510–11.

36 See Macdonald to Douglas Abbott, 26 March 1947, ALM Papers, vol. 913, file 14.

37 'Dominion-Provincial Conference,' 29 April 1946, *Dominion-Provincial Conference (1945)*, 603–4.

38 House of Commons, *Debates*, 27 June 1946, 2906–14.

39 Beck, *Politics of Nova Scotia*, 209.

40 See Macdonald to Alex Johnston, 18 January 1946, ALM Papers, vol. 903, file 28(A2), and Macdonald to W.A. Macdonald, 25 February 1947, ALM Papers, vol. 920, file 31-2.

41 For an account of the meeting in Montreal, see Macdonald, 'Diaries,' 17 November 1946, ALM Papers, vol. 1503, file 394, and 'Notes for 4 November 1946' and 'Notes for 18 November 1946,' ALM Papers, vol. 898, file 19½(D).

42 King, *Diaries*, 16 January 1947.

43 See Macdonald, 'Notes for 26 and 30 November 1946,' ALM Papers, vol. 898, file 19½(D).

44 McNair to King, 17 December 1946, J.B. McNair Papers, RS414, C6, file A2, Public Archives of New Brunswick; see also Macdonald, 'Notes for 17 December 1946,' ALM Papers, vol. 898, file 19½(D).

45 John J. Connolly to Macdonald, 26 March 1947, ALM Papers, vol. 918, file 31-1(B).

46 Macdonald to Connolly, 9 April 1947, ibid.

47 Crerar to Macdonald, 21 December 1946, ibid. See also J.E. Rea, *T.A. Crerar: A Political Life* (Montreal and Kingston: McGill-Queen's University Press, 1997), 223–4, for Crerar's support of Rowell-Sirois and the autonomy of provinces.

48 Macdonald to Crerar, 13 January 1947, ALM Papers, vol. 918, file 31-1(B).

49 Douglas Abbott replaced Ilsley as minister of finance late in 1946. Power to Macdonald, 27 January 1947, ALM Papers, vol. 920, file 31-2.

50 Douglas Abbott to Macdonald, 21 April 1947, ALM Papers, vol. 911, file 11.

51 Macdonald, 'Dominion–Provincial Relations,' 8 May 1947, ALM Papers, vol. 920, file 31-3.

52 James Bickerton, *Nova Scotia, Ottawa, and the Politics of Regional Development* (Toronto: University of Toronto Press, 1990), 124.

53 Macdonald, 'Budget Speech,' 2 April 1947, ALM Papers, vol. 914, file 15-8; 'Financial Statements, 1947,' ALM Papers, vol. 913, file 15; and Macdonald, 'Radio Address,' 10 May 1948, ALM Papers, vol. 934, file 31-2(A).

54 Macdonald, 'Dominion–Provincial Relations,' 8 May 1947.

55 Macdonald to Ralph M. Kelley, 29 August 1947, ALM Papers, vol. 919, file 31-1(C).

56 See, for example, Macdonald's speech 'Federalism in Canada,' delivered to the Canadian Club of Toronto, 1 December 1947, ALM Papers, vol. 920, file 31-1(A).

57 See Taylor Hollander, 'Making Reform Happen: The Passage of Canada's Collective-Bargaining Policy, 1943–1944,' *Journal of Policy History* 13.3 (2001): 299–328, and Judy Fudge and Eric Tucker, *Labour before the Law: The Regulation of Workers' Collective Action in Canada, 1900–1948*, (Toronto: Oxford University Press, 2001), 261–5 and 273–6.

58 Fudge and Tucker, *Labour before the Law*, 276–91 and 294, and Paul MacEwan, *Miners and Steelworkers: Labour in Cape Breton* (Toronto: Hakkert, 1976), 259–65.

59 Currie to Macdonald, 4 November 1941, ALM Papers, vol. 1516, file 688.

60 Mitchell to Currie, 11 February 1947, ALM Papers, vol. 923, file 34-4.

61 Dr R.D. Howland, Deputy Minister of Labour, to Currie, 24 March 1947; Thomas Kennedy, Secretary-Treasurer, UMW, Washington, D.C., to Macdonald 2 and 6 May 1947, ibid. See also Fudge and Tucker, *Labour before the Law*, 291–2, and MacEwan, *Miners and Steelworkers*, 265–74.

62 For the creation of National Sea Products Limited, see L. Gene Barrett, 'Development and Underdevelopment, and the Rise of Trade Unionism in the Fishing Industry of Nova Scotia, 1900–1950,' MA thesis, Dalhousie University, 1976, 129–34; Barry Cahill, *The Thousandth Man: A Biography of James McGregor Stewart* (Toronto: University of Toronto Press, 2000), 87–8; and Stephen Kimber, *Net Profits: The Story of National Sea* (Halifax: Nimbus, 1989). Bell, a friend of Macdonald's, served as director-general of aircraft production during the war.

63 For a discussion of the Lunenburg 64 system, as well as the 1947 strike, see E. Jean Nisbet, '"Free Enterprise at Its Best": The State, National Sea, and the Defeat of the Nova Scotia Fishermen, 1946–1947,' in Michael Earle, ed., *Workers and the State in Twentieth Century Nova Scotia* (Fredericton: Acadiensis Press, 1989), 171–90.

64 Nisbet, '"Free Enterprise,"' 176–81, and Fudge and Tucker, *Labour before the Law,* 297.

65 See, for example, advertisements in the *Halifax Chronicle,* 11, 19, and 27 January, and 26 February 1947, and Nisbet, '"Free Enterprise,"' 182–5.

66 Bell to Macdonald, 22 January 1947, ALM Papers, vol. 914, file 16-3.

67 *Time,* 13 January 1947: 14. This article was clipped and forwarded to Macdonald by Bell; see Bell to Macdonald, 22 January 1947, ALM Papers, vol. 914, file 16-3.

68 Nisbet, '"Free Enterprise,"' 184–6, and ALM Papers, vol. 914, file 16-3.

69 MacKenzie to Macdonald, 15 February 1947, ibid.

70 See *Halifax Herald,* 15 February 1947, and Nisbet, '"Free Enterprise,"' 185.

71 See Nisbet, '"Free Enterprise,"' 187–8; for Sullivan's defection, see John Stanton, *The Life and Death of a Union: The Canadian Seaman's Union, 1936–1949* (Toronto: Steel Rail Education Publishing, 1978), 97–9; William Kaplan, *Everything That Floats: Sullivan, Banks, and the CSU* (Toronto: University of Toronto Press, 1987), 49–50; and Jim Green, *Against the Tide: The Story of the Canadian Seaman's Union* (Toronto: Progress Books, 1986), 151–61.

72 Nisbet, '"Free Enterprise,"' 189–90.

73 Ibid., 189.

74 I am relying here on a definition of industrial legality offered by David Frank: 'an accommodation between labour and capital, as each of these partners in industrial society accepts common rules under which they are prepared to compete for advantage.' David Frank, *J.B. McLachlan: A Biography* (Toronto: James Lorimer, 1999), 179–80.

75 Macdonald, 'Speech,' 26 March 1947, ALM Papers, vol. 914, file 15-8.

76 Crerar to Macdonald, 27 January 1948, ALM Papers, vol. 933, file 27-3. See also Macdonald to Johnston, 18 January 1946; Johnston to Macdonald, 19 February 1946, Crerar to Macdonald, 19 February 1946, and Macdonald to Crerar, 28 February 1946, ALM Papers, vol. 903, file 28(A2).

77 See C.J. Burchell, 'Memorandum on BTC Decision,' 17(?) April 1948, ALM Papers, vol. 935, file 32.

78 Burchell, 'Memorandum.' Burchell pointed out that freight accounted for just 48% of CP's revenue in 1947.

79 See E.R. Forbes, 'Misguided Symmetry: The Destruction of Regional Transportation Policy for the Maritimes,' in *Challenging the Regional Stereotype: Essays on the 20th Century Maritimes* (Fredericton: Acadiensis, 1989), 129–30.

80 'Rough Draft of Argument Presented by Seven Premiers,' in ALM Papers, vol. 935, file 32.

81 By Order-in-Council P.C. 1487, 7 April 1948.

82 King to Macdonald, 1 July 1948, ALM Papers, vol. 935, file 32.

83 'Brief of Provincial Premiers, Submitted to the Federal Cabinet,' 20 July 1948, ALM Papers, vol. 935, file 32(A).

84 C.J. Burchell to Macdonald, 30 July 1948, ALM Papers, vol. 935, file 32.

85 See, for example, E.C. Manning to Macdonald, 3 August 1948, Macdonald to Manning, 12 August 1948, Macdonald to McNair, 24 August 1948, and Macdonald to Jones, 24 August 1948, ALM Papers, vol. 935, file 32–2.

86 See Macdonald to Manning, 12 August 1948, Rand Matheson to Macdonald, 18 September 1948, Manning to Macdonald, 25 September 1948; Macdonald, 'Press Statement,' 15 October 1948; Macdonald to St Laurent, 22 October 1948, and St Laurent to Macdonald, 27 October 1948, ibid.

87 Macdonald to T.A. Crerar, 24 January 1948, ALM Papers, vol. 933, file 27-3.

88 See ibid.

89 See Crerar to Macdonald, 27 January 1948, ibid.

90 Johnston to Macdonald, 11 February 1948, ibid.

91 Power to Macdonald, 5 February 1948, ibid. Sir Richard Acland, 'Morality and British Politics: Two Views,' *Listener*, 14 January 1948. For Crerar's and Leslie Roberts's views on the need for ideological renewal, see Crerar to Macdonald, 14 February 1948, and Roberts to Macdonald, 7 February 1948, ALM Papers, vol. 933, file 27-3.

92 Macdonald to Crerar, 19 February 1948, ibid.

93 Macdonald to Johnston, 29 March 1948, ibid.

94 See Connolly to Macdonald, 1 and 13 March 1948, ibid.

95 See Macdonald to Connolly, 12 April 1948, and Macdonald to Johnston, 12 April 1948, ibid.

96 Macdonald to Johnston, 17 May 1948, ibid.

97 See *Ottawa Journal*, 6 July 1948; and Macdonald to Connolly, 12 July 1948, and Connolly to Macdonald, 14 July 1948, ibid.

98 Macdonald, 'Task Confronting Liberalism,' *Winnipeg Free Press*, 9 July 1948.

99 See, for example, F.X. Ferguson to Macdonald, 14 July 1948, Donald A. MacDonald to Macdonald, 19 July 1948, Col. Wilfrid Bovey to Macdonald, 21 July 1948, and A.J. Mason to Macdonald, 24 July 1948, ALM Papers, vol. 933, file 27–3.

100 Cameron to Macdonald, 31 July 1948; see also Crerar to Macdonald, 24 July 1948, and Macdonald to Crerar, 29 July 1948, ibid.

101 Liberal Party of Canada, *Report of the Proceedings of the National Liberal Convention Called by the National Liberal Federation of Canada at the Request of W.L. Mackenzie King* (Ottawa: National Liberal Federation of Canada, 1948); Dale Thomson, *Louis St. Laurent: Canadian* (Toronto: Macmillan, 1967); J.W. Pickersgill, *My Years with Louis St. Laurent: A Political Memoir* (Toronto: University of Toronto Press, 1975); Paul Martin, *A Very Political*

Life (Ottawa: Deneau, 1983), and C.G. Power, *A Party Politician: The Memoirs of Chubby Power*, ed. Norman Ward (Toronto: Macmillan, 1966).

102 See King, *Diaries*, 5–7 August 1948.

103 See 'Race Narrowed Down to Three at Convention,' *Halifax Herald*, 6 August 1948; 'Macdonald Says He's Not a Candidate for Leadership,' *Ottawa Journal*, 6 August 1948; and 'St Laurent Win Now Seems Sure,' *Globe and Mail*, 6 August 1948.

104 See Tufts, 'Race Narrowed'; *Ottawa Journal*, 6 August 1948; J.B. McGeachy, 'Liberals in Convention,' *Globe and Mail*, 7 August 1948; 'Recognize Us, or Another Party Will,' *Montreal Star*, 7 August 1948; and Camp, *Gentlemen*, 2–5.

105 See 'Macdonald, Martin Still in Race with Big Three,' *Halifax Herald*, 7 August 1948; 'Liberal Convention Continues,' *Ottawa Journal*, 7 August 1948; and 'Five Possible Candidates for Leadership as Voting Hour Nears,' *Globe and Mail*, 7 August 1948.

106 Backstage at Ottawa, 'Harsh Words at Liberal Love Feast,' *Maclean's* 61.18 (15 September 1948): 15; 'Leadership Race in Stride,' *Ottawa Journal*, 7 August 1948; 'N. S. Premier Demands Return to Liberalism, Provincial Autonomy,' *Globe and Mail*, 7 August 1948; 'Macdonald Warns Liberal Party Has No Divine Right to Govern,' *Ottawa Journal*, 7 August 1948, and 'Macdonald, Martin Still in Race,' *Halifax Herald*.

107 'Macdonald Says He's Not a Candidate,' *Ottawa Journal*.

108 Camp, *Gentlemen*, 6.

109 St Laurent won 848 votes, Gardiner 323, and Power 56. *Halifax Herald*, 9 August 1948.

110 Power later wrote that Agnes had urged her husband to run, a point that she contradicted later. See Power, *A Party Politician*, 396–7, and John Hawkins's interview with Agnes Macdonald, 16 August 1967, John Hawkins Fonds, AR 9063, NSARM.

111 For Macdonald's reasons for not offering, see, for example, Macdonald to Johnston, 29 March 1948, Johnston to Macdonald, 5 April 1948, Macdonald to Crerar, 6 July 1948, Earl Urquhart to Macdonald, 17 August 1948, and Macdonald to Jennie Fraser, 23 August 1948, ALM Papers, vol. 933, file 27–3; and Macdonald to Fr Stanley Macdonald, 24 June 1948, ALM Papers, vol. 934, file 31-1(E).

5. Limits of the Liberal State

1 See John Hawkins interview with Henry Hicks, 29 November 1967, Hawkins Fonds, AR 9067, Nova Scotia Archives and Records Management (NSARM).

2 Arthur C. Parks, *The Economy of the Atlantic Provinces, 1940–1957* (Halifax and Fredericton: Atlantic Provinces Economic Council, 1959), i and 1–2. Parks acknowledges that his GPP calculations are imperfect, as it is difficult to track profits, wages, and dividends that cross provincial borders. On the economic marginalization of the region, see T.W. Acheson, 'The National Policy and the Industrialization of the Maritimes, 1880–1910,' *Acadiensis* 1.2 (Spring 1972): 3–28.

3 Parks, *Economy of the Atlantic Provinces*, 37–8.

4 John Hawkins interview with Agnes Macdonald, 16 August 1967, Hawkins Fonds, AR 9063.

5 Hawkins interview with Hicks.

6 J.W. Pickersgill, *My Years with Louis St. Laurent: A Political Memoir* (Toronto: University of Toronto Press, 1975), 49–50; Macdonald to Crerar, 6 July 1948, and Crerar to Macdonald, 24 July 1948, Angus L. Macdonald Papers, NSARM, MG 2 (hereafter ALM Papers), vol. 933, file 27-3.

7 Alex Johnston to Macdonald, 5 April 1948, ALM Papers, vol. 933, file 27-3.

8 T.A. Crerar to Macdonald, 22 December 1948, ALM Papers, vol. 945, file 31.

9 Margaret Conrad, 'Apple Blossom Time in the Annapolis Valley, 1880–1957,' *Acadiensis* 9.2 (Spring 1980): 30–5.

10 See 'Deep Brook Naval Base Will Reopen as Training Centre,' *Halifax Herald*, 3 December 1948, and 'Cornwallis Naval Base, Largest in Empire, to Reopen,' *Digby Courier*, 9 December 1949.

11 W.L. Mackenzie King, *Mackenzie King Diaries, 1932–1949* (Toronto: University of Toronto Press, 1980), 13 December 1948. The final election results were: Nowlan 14,192, McKenzie 12,490, and Shaw 1968. *Digby Courier*, 16 December 1948.

12 Macdonald to Johnston, 13 April 1949, ALM Papers, NSARM, vol. 945, file 31-2.

13 Stanfield awaits an academic biographer, but Geoffrey Stevens's *Stanfield* (Toronto: McClelland and Stewart, 1973) is quite readable if strongly partisan. For Stanfield's early career as leader of the Opposition, see Margaret Conrad, *George Nowlan: Maritime Conservative in National Politics* (Toronto: University of Toronto Press, 1986), 91, 95–6.

14 Macdonald to Johnston, 4 July 1949, ALM Papers, vol. 944, file 27-12. The riding of Hants West, always extremely close, remained in dispute for some months. On election night it went Conservative by four votes. A recount produced a tie, and Liberal G.B. Cole prevailed over Conservative G.H. Wilson by virtue of the Returning Officer's vote. Each side presented evidence of voting irregularity, and the courts ordered a new election. The by-election, held on 27 November 1950, resulted in a narrow win for the Tories. See ibid. vol. 953, file 27-10(A).

15 The Tories' share of the vote rose from 33.5% in 1945 to 39.2%; the CCF's dropped from 13.6% to 9.6%, but it retained its two seats in industrial Cape Breton.

16 Macdonald to Johnston, 4 July 1949, ALM Papers, vol. 944, file 27-12; Macdonald to Harry Hamilton, 14 June 1949, and Macdonald to John J. Connolly, 17 June 1949, ALM Papers, vol. 944, file 27-11.

17 See Barry Cahill, *The Thousandth Man: A Biography of James McGregor Stewart* (Toronto: University of Toronto Press, 2000), 112, and Alex Johnston to Macdonald, 31 May 1949, ALM Papers, vol. 944, file 27-11.

18 *Halifax Chronicle-Herald*, 16 May 1949.

19 See Stevens, *Stanfield*, 88–9; Macdonald, 'Speech in Kentville,' 25 April 1949, ALM Papers, NSARM, vol. 944, file 27–9; *Globe and Mail*, 6 June 1949; and J. Murray Beck, *Politics of Nova Scotia, Volume 2, Murray–Buchanan, 1896–1988* (Tantallon, NS: Four East Publications, 1988), 214.

20 Joe Reardon to Macdonald, 23 March 1949, ALM Papers, vol. 944, file 27-2.

21 John J. Connolly to Macdonald, 7 May 1949, ALM Papers, vol. 945, file 31.

22 E.J. Cragg to John Dickey, 20 March 1953, copy to Macdonald, ALM Papers, vol. 978, file 31-2.

23 See, for example, Macdonald to Colin MacKenzie 8(?) April 1946, ALM Papers, vol. 903, file 28.

24 J. Murray Beck, *The Evolution of Municipal Government in Nova Scotia, 1749–1973: A Study Prepared for the Nova Scotia Royal Commission on Education, Public Services and Provincial-Municipal Relations* (Halifax: n.p., 1973), 35, and *Halifax Herald*, 24 January 1948. See also Peter Johnson, 'Relations between the Government of Nova Scotia and the Union of Nova Scotia Municipalities, 1906–1966,' MA thesis, Dalhousie University, 1968.

25 D. C. Rowat, 'Basic Proposals for the Reorganization of Provincial-Municipal Relations,' 28 February 1949 ALM Papers, vol. 943, file 22-3 (hereafter the Rowat report).

26 Beck, *Evolution of Municipal Government*, 35.

27 Ibid. and Macdonald to James McLenaghen, Attorney-General for Manitoba, 13 March 1950, ALM Papers, vol. 952, file 22-3.

28 James Bickerton, *Nova Scotia, Ottawa and the Politics of Regional Development* (Toronto: University of Toronto Press, 1990), 129.

29 Beck, *Politics of Nova Scotia*, 2:217, and *Globe and Mail*, 6 June 1949.

30 Macdonald, 'Research Council Speech,' 4 September 1946, ALM Papers, vol. 893, file 12, and vol. 911, file 12. Dr H.D. Smith, an engineer from the University of British Columbia, was named chair, and Dr Robert Howland, an economist serving as deputy minister of labour, was vice-chair.

31 *Report of the Royal Commission Provincial Economic Inquiry* (Halifax: King's Printer, 1934), 88–90 and 198–201.

32 *Report of the Royal Commission on Provincial Development and Rehabilitation*, Volume One (Halifax: King's Printer, 1944), 77–8.

33 See, for example, ALM Papers, vol. 939, file 12, for the activities of the NSRF in 1949.

34 *Halifax Herald*, 25 March 1948.

35 Macdonald, 'Radio Address,' 10 May 1948, ALM Papers, vol. 934, file 32-2(A).

36 ALM Papers, vol. 932, Files 21–3 and 21–4, and vol. 942, files 21-3 and 21-4.

37 Macdonald to Dawson, 26 March 1946, ALM Papers, vol. 898, file 19½(C); see also *Report on Development and Rehabilitation*, 72–3.

38 Beck, *Politics of Nova Scotia*, 2:243 and 246–7.

39 Macdonald, 'Address,' 12 June 1951, ALM Papers, vol. 963, file 26.

40 See, for example, Alex Kerr to Macdonald, 31 March 1946, ALM Papers, vol. 901, file 28A(05).

41 See ALM Papers, vol. 911, file 13-2, and vol. 958, file 13-2.

42 *Report on Development and Rehabilitation*, 62–5. For a perceptive discussion of the industrialization of the Atlantic fishery, see Miriam Wright, *A Fishery for Modern Times: The State and the Industrialization of the Newfoundland Fishery, 1934–1968* (Toronto: Oxford University Press, 2001).

43 See *Halifax Herald*, 22 August 1946, and ALM Papers, vol. 932, file 21-2.

44 Macdonald to C.D. Howe, 26 June 1948, and Howe to Macdonald, 18 July 1948, ALM Papers, vol. 932, file 21-2.

45 Ralph Bell to Macdonald, 28 August and 25 September 1946, Bell to Dr D.L. Cooper, 20 August 1947, Gordon Romkey to Macdonald, 9 October 1948, and Macdonald to Romkey, 13 October 1948, ALM Papers, vol. 932, file 21-2.

46 On expectations for the fishery, see *Report of Provincial Economic Inquiry*, 90–4, and *Report on Development and Rehabilitation*, 61–2.

47 See Thomas H. Raddall, *Halifax: Warden of the North* (New York: Doubleday, 1965), 224.

48 Arthur C. Petipas to Macdonald, 29 September 1947, Macdonald to Philip Pratley, 22 December 1947, Pratley to Macdonald, 23 December 1947, and Pratley to Macdonald, 24 September 1948 and 19 November 1948, ALM Papers, vol. 936, file 35.

49 See Macdonald to C.A. Fowler, 28 November 1947, ALM Papers, vol. 936, file 35.

50 Macdonald, 'Notes of Meeting,' 16 July 1947, W.S. Wilson to Macdonald, 21 July 1947, and Macdonald to Wilson, 23 July 1947, ALM Papers, vol. 981, file 2, and Macdonald to Chevrier, 12 January 1948, ALM Papers, vol. 981, file 3. For a history of the Canso Causeway, see Meaghan Beaton, 'The Canso Causeway: Regionalism, Reconstruction, Representations and Results,' MA thesis, Saint Mary's University, 2001.

51 See Macdonald to Grant, 2 February 1948, Pratley to Macdonald, 8 March 1948, Pratley to Grant, 8 March 1948, Claxton to Macdonald, 10 June 1948, Macdonald to Grant, 18 October 1948, Macdonald to Isnor, 2 November 1948, and Isnor to Macdonald, 5 November 1948, ALM Papers, vol. 936, file 35, and Isnor to Macdonald, 3 May 1949, ALM Papers, vol. 947, file 35-3.

52 Chevrier to Macdonald, 8 January 1948, and Macdonald to Chevrier, 30 January 1948, ALM Papers, vol. 981, file 3. Arthur Surveyor chaired the panel, and D.S. Ellis acted as the third member.

53 See *Halifax Chronicle-Herald*, 15 March 1949; Macdonald to Pratley, 9 August 1950, Pratley to Macdonald, 11 August 1950, Chevrier to Macdonald, 8 September 1950, R.W. McColough, Executive Assistant, Ministry of Highways, to Merrill Rawding, Minister of Highways, 11 September 1950, Macdonald to Pratley, 22 September 1950, and Macdonald to Pratley, 15 December 1950, ALM Papers, vol. 982, file 2.

54 See Macdonald, 'Notes of a Conversation with Dr. Pratley,' 19 February 1951, Macdonald to Chevrier, 16 August 1951, and Macdonald to Alex Johnston, 20 August 1951, ALM Papers, vol. 982, file 3. See the *Sydney Post-Record*, 15 June 1951, for Gordon's statement.

55 Macdonald to St Laurent, 21 August 1948, ALM Papers, vol. 935, file 32-2; A.D.P. Heeney, Secretary of the Cabinet, to Macdonald, 16 September 1948, Heeney to Macdonald, 13 October 1948, containing PC 4678, and Macdonald, 'Statement to the Press,' 15 October 1948, ALM Papers, vol. 935, file 32-2(2).

56 Macdonald to St Laurent, 22 October 1948, and St Laurent to Macdonald, 27 October 1948, ALM Papers, vol. 935, file 32-2(2).

57 See Macdonald to St Laurent, 22 October, St Laurent to Macdonald, 27 October, Walter Jones to Macdonald, 29 October, Manning to Macdonald, 5 November, J.B. McNair to Macdonald, 5 November, and T.C. Douglas to Macdonald, 26 November 1948, ALM Papers, vol. 935, file 32-2(2). The names offered ranged from the venerable Andrew Duncan to justices Ivan Rand and Thane Campbell, to economists such as Ralph Dewey of the University of Ohio and G.E. Britnell of the University of Saskatchewan.

58 See Royal Commission on Transportation (hereafter Turgeon commission), *Hearings*, vol. 2, Winnipeg, 1 June 1949. Frank Covert, counsel to the commission, later wrote to Harold Innis: 'Judge Turgeon was a liberal in politics and had been appointed again and again by the Government to head Royal Commissions and to settle questions in a manner which would ease pressure on the Government.' Covert to Innis, 25 July 1952, H.A. Innis Papers, University of Toronto Archives, B1972-003, box 005, file 16.

59 See Innis, *A History of the Canadian Pacific Railway* (1923; Toronto: University of Toronto Press, 1971). Innis sat on Nova Scotia's 1934 Royal Commission of Provincial Economic Inquiry and Manitoba's 1946 Royal Commission on Adult Education.

60 *Report of the Royal Commission on Transportation, 1951* (Ottawa: King's Printer, 1951), 5–6.

61 See, for example, 'Rough Draft of Argument Presented by Seven Premiers,' 26 April 1948, ALM Papers, vol. 935, file 32.

62 See 'Proceedings of the Conference of Maritime Premiers, Amherst, Nova Scotia,' 7 November 1933, J.B. McNair Papers, RS 414 (hereafter McNair Papers), folder C4, file C, Public Archives of New Brunswick (PANB).

63 See Macdonald to D.R. Turnbull, 19 April 1949, ALM Papers, vol. 946, file 32-2, and C.J. Burchell to Macdonald, 23 April 1949, ALM Papers, vol. 946, file 32-1.

64 Turgeon commission, *Hearings*, vol. 11, 1930 [Manning], vol. 18, 3276–7 [Macdonald].

65 Transportation Commission of the Maritime Board of Trade, 'Submission to the Royal Commission on Transportation,' vol. I (July 1949). On Prince Edward Island's proposal to nationalize railways, see Turgeon commission, *Hearings*, vol. 127, 22858–68; see also T. Stephen Henderson, 'A Defensive Alliance: The Maritime Provinces and the Turgeon Commission on Transportation, 1948–1951,' *Acadiensis* 35.2 (Spring 2006): 1–18.

66 Harold Innis to Mary Innis, June(?) 1949, Innis Papers, box 005, file 13, and Donald Creighton, *Harold Adams Innis: Portrait of a Scholar* (Toronto: University of Toronto Press, 1957), 135–40.

67 *Report on Transportation*, 282–307.

68 Ibid., 69–70, 87, 125–57, 228–52, and 276. See also Rand Matheson, 'Memorandum on Some Aspects of the Report of the Royal Commission on Transportation in Relation to the Maritimes,' 16 April 1951, ALM Papers, vol. 965, file 32-1.

69 See T. Stephen Henderson, "Harold Innis and Canadian Federalism," paper presented at the 2005 Congress at the University of Western Ontario.

70 *Report on Transportation*, 307.

71 See Matheson to Macdonald, 12 December 1951, and Matheson, 'Memo RE Maritimes' Provisions of the National Freight Rate Policy,' 18 June 1952, Atlantic Provinces Transportation Commission Papers, MC 204, MS12, F1, PANB.

72 *Chronicle-Herald*, 10 March 1953.

73 Covert to Innis, 25 July 1952. William T. Jackman had given Innis a critique of the commission's work. Jackman was the author of *Economic Principles of Transportation* (Toronto: University of Toronto Press, 1935).

74 This commission was headed by M.A. MacPherson; see *Royal Commission on Transportation, Report*, 2 vols. (Ottawa: Queen's Printer, 1961).

75 Power to Macdonald, 10 December 1949, ALM Papers, vol. 945, file 31.

76 For the January 1950 conference, see *Proceedings of the Constitutional Conference of Federal and Provincial Governments, January 10–12, 1950* (Ottawa: King's Printer, 1950); Thomson, *St. Laurent*, 280–2; and Pickersgill, *My Years with St. Laurent*, 118–19.

77 See *Proceedings, January*, 17–21, 51–4, and 65, and *Globe and Mail*, 13 January 1950. Former American ambassador to Canada Norman Armour praised the committee idea as the 'Macdonald Plan'; see Armour to Macdonald, 3 March 1950, ALM Papers, vol. 955, file 31-1.

78 'Draft Resolution Submitted by the Attorney-General of Nova Scotia to the Committee of Attorneys-General,' 12 January 1950, *Proceedings, January*, 113.

79 St Laurent, 'Opening Address,' 10 January 1950, ALM Papers, vol. 952, file 22-5; Thomson, *St. Laurent*, 280; and Pickersgill, *My Years with Louis St. Laurent*, 111–17.

80 Macdonald to W.F. Carroll, 24 February 1950, ALM Papers, vol. 953, file 31. On the Senate's intended role as representative of the provinces, see Frederick Vaughn, *The Canadian Federalist Experiment: From Defiant Monarchy to Reluctant Republic* (Montreal and Kingston: McGill-Queen's University Press, 2003), 113. Laskin's article appeared in *Financial Post*, 11 February 1950.

81 See *Halifax Chronicle-Herald*, 26 May 1950; *Globe and Mail*, 4 October 1950; and Peter Russell, ed., *Leading Constitutional Decisions: Cases on the British North America Act*, rev. ed. (Toronto: McClelland and Stewart, 1973), 264–77.

82 See appendix IV, *Proceedings of the Constitutional Conference of Federal and Provincial Governments, Quebec, September 25–28, 1950* (Ottawa: King's Printer, 1950), 86–130, and Thomson, *St. Laurent*, 299–300.

83 See Macdonald to Johnston, 22 August 1950, and Pickersgill, *My Years with St. Laurent*, 120–1.

84 See *Proceedings, September*, 9–18; Thomson, *St. Laurent*, 301–2; and Pickersgill, *My Years with St. Laurent*, 134–9.

85 Harold Connolly to Macdonald, 6 December 1950, ALM Papers, vol., 952, file 22-5.

86 'Statement to the Press by the Right Honourable Louis-S. St-Laurent at the Conclusion of the Conference,' appendix VI, *Proceedings, September*, 137.

87 Macdonald to Robert Winters, 16 December 1950, ALM Papers, vol. 953, file 31.

88 See 'Nova Scotia Prospectus, 1953,' prepared for a debenture issue in New York, ALM Papers, vol. 974, file 15-3. After the 1948–9 fiscal year, Nova Scotia made its fiscal year compatible with Ottawa's by moving the end date from 30 November to 31 March, resulting in a 16-month budget for 1949–51.

89 Macdonald to H. E. Potter, 28 February 1950, vol. 953, file 26-2.

90 Macdonald, 'Budget Speech,' 17 April 1950, ALM Papers, vol. 953, file 26-2.

91 Macdonald, 'Estimates, 1951,' ALM Papers, vol. 959, file 15.

92 Garson to Macdonald, 2 January 1951, ALM Papers, vol. 961, file 15-5(A).

93 Burchell to Macdonald, 6 February 1951, ibid.

94 Hyndman to Macdonald, 6 April 1951, ibid.

95 Macdonald to Hyndman, 17 April 1951, ibid.

96 See *Debates of the House of Commons*, 10 April 1951, 1812–13.

97 Macdonald to Abbott, 28 April and 11 June 1951, ALM Papers, vol. 961, file 15-5(A), and Abbott to Macdonald, 8 May 1951, ALM Papers, vol. 961, file 18-4(A).

98 Macdonald to Martin, 29 June 1951, and Martin to Macdonald, 24 September 1951, ALM Papers, vol. 961, file 18-4(A).

99 *Debates of the House of Commons*, 23 June 1951, 4579–81.

100 Macdonald to St Laurent, Martin, and Winters, 26 June 1951, ALM Papers, vol. 958, file 14; Martin to Macdonald, 24 September 1951, and Macdonald to Martin, 29 June 1951, ALM Papers, vol. 961, file 18-4(A).

101 Macdonald to Crerar, 15 January 1951, ALM Papers, vol. 964, file 31-2.

102 Johnston to Macdonald, 14 August 1950, and Macdonald to Johnston, 22 August 1950, ALM Papers, vol. 955, file 31-1.

103 Dawson died in 1958, managing to complete only one volume on King: *William Lyon Mackenzie King: A Political Biography, 1874–1923* (Toronto: University of Toronto Press, 1958); Blair Neatby carried on the work for two more volumes. Hutchison produced *The Incredible Canadian: A Candid Portrait of Mackenzie King, His Works, His Times and His Nation* (Toronto: Longmans, Green, 1952). Ferns and Ostry published *The Age of Mackenzie King: The Rise of the Leader* (London: Heinemann, 1955), which was released in Canada under the title *Mackenzie King and the First World War* (Toronto: University of Toronto Press, 1955).

104 H.R. Hardy, *Mackenzie King of Canada* (London: Oxford University Press, 1949). Grant Dexter assured Alex Johnston that King had vetted the manuscript; see Johnston to Macdonald, 27 November 1949, and Macdonald to Johnston, 2 December 1949, ALM Papers, vol. 1503, file 379.

105 See ALM Papers, vol. 1503, file 379. The press release began as a rebuttal to

a rather positive review of Hardy's book; see B.K. Sandwell, 'Mr. King: Politician vs. Human Being,' *Saturday Night*, 22 November 1949, 13.

106 Irwin to Macdonald, 6 December 1949, ALM Papers, vol. 1503, file 379. Notes for three chapters exist in the file.

107 Macdonald to Connolly, 13 December 1952, ALM Papers, vol. 1503, file 382.

108 Stevenson to Macdonald, 18 February 1954, and Macdonald to Stevenson, 20 February 1954, ALM Papers, vol. 980, file 50. See also John A. Stevenson, 'The Career of Mackenzie King,' *Political Quarterly* 21.4 (October 1950): 395–410.

109 Cameron to Crerar, 10 December 1952, ALM Papers, vol. 1503, file 382.

110 Macdonald, 'Budget Address,' 7 March 1952, ALM Papers, vol. 969, file 15-8.

111 See Dalton Camp, *Gentlemen, Players and Politicians* (Toronto: McClelland and Stewart, 1970), 68–94.

112 Macdonald, 'Speech,' 19 February 1952, ALM Papers, vol. 971, file 26-1.

113 See ALM Papers, vol. 970, file 19-8; Beaton, 'Canso Causeway,' 81; and Macdonald, 'Budget Address,' 7 March 1952.

114 See Hawkins interview with Dan Lewis Macdonald.

115 The best discussion of Macdonald's efforts to 'tartanize' Nova Scotia is Ian McKay, 'Tartanism Triumphant: The Construction of Scottishness in Nova Scotia, 1933–1954,' *Acadiensis* 21.2 (Spring 1992): 5–27. See also MacKay, *Quest for the Folk: Antimodernism and Cultural Selection in Twentieth-Century Nova Scotia* (Montreal and Kingston: McGill-Queen's University Press, 1994), and Beaton, 'Canso Causeway,' 83–110.

116 Macdonald to Col. H.R. Alley, 12 August 1948, ALM Papers, vol. 934, file 31-1(A). On Acadian themes in tourism promotion, see Barbara LeBlanc, 'Evangeline as Identity Myth,' *Canadian Folklore Canadien* 15.2 (1993): 139–53, and Jay White, '"A Vista of Infinite Development": Surveying Nova Scotia's Early Tourism Industry,' *Journal of the Royal Nova Scotia Historical Society* 6 (2003): 144–69.

117 See Macdonald to T.J. Courtney, 19 September 1949, Courtney to Macdonald, 11 March 1950, and Macdonald to Courtney, 11 March 1950, ALM Papers, vol. 956, file 40-5; and I.H. Macdonald, Canadian Daily Newspaper Association, to Macdonald, 18 August 1952, ALM Papers, vol. 972, file 40-1.

118 See MacKay, 'Tartanism Triumphant,' 5–6, 21–4, and 29–30; Macdonald to Harold G. Sutherland, 17 April 1952, ALM Papers, vol. 972, file 40-2; and Macdonald to D.C. Harvey, Provincial Archivist, 6 May 1952, ALM Papers, vol. 972, file 40-1.

119 Macdonald, 'Political Speeches,' 20 June and 6 November 1952, ALM Papers, vol. 971, file 31-4.

120 See, for example, Gordon Romkey to Macdonald, 30 October 1952, Earl Urquhart to Macdonald, 31 October 1952, and Donald J. Fraser to Macdonald, 3 November 1952, ALM Papers, vol. 972, file 36-1.

121 *Chronicle-Herald*, 24 January 1953.

122 Mackenzie to Macdonald, 2 May 1953, ALM Papers, vol. 974, file 16-1, and Bell to Macdonald, 28 January 1953, ALM Papers, vol. 978, file 31-2.

123 See Freeman Jenkins to Macdonald, 23 May 1953, and Macdonald to Jenkins, 25 May 1953, ALM Papers, vol. 976, file 23-5, and Paul MacEwan, *Miners and Steelworkers: Labour in Cape Breton* (Toronto: Hakkert, 1976), 285–7.

124 Macdonald, 'Budget Speech,' 13 February 1953, ALM Papers, vol. 976, file 26.

125 See, for example, the *Chronicle-Herald*, 4, 9, 14, 22, and 24 May 1953.

126 Ibid., 14 and 21 May 1953.

127 Interview with Camp, 20 December 1999; Camp, *Gentlemen, Players and Politicians*, 127–9; and *Chronicle-Herald*, 22 May 1953.

128 For election results, see *Chronicle-Herald*, 27 May 1953. The percentage changes, 1949–53, were: Liberals, 51–49.4%; Conservatives, 39.2–43.5%; and CCF, 9.6–6.6%. This time the riding of Hants East remained in dispute for some months. The first count showed Conservative Ernest Ettinger had won by one vote over Liberal Alfred Reid. A recount put Reid ahead by one, but there were allegations of typical Hants County voting irregularities. Ettinger won the by-election, held in November, by 13 votes. See ALM Papers, vol. 977, file 27-10.

129 Macdonald to Crerar, 10 June 1953; see also Macdonald to Grant Dexter, 29 May 1953, Macdonald to Douglas Campbell, premier of Manitoba, 29 May 1953, Macdonald to Norman Lambert, 9 June 1953, and Macdonald to Senator John A. McDonald, 9 June 1953, ALM Papers, vol. 977, file 27-12(A).

130 On government appointments after the election, see ALM Papers, vol. 976, file 24-2, and *Chronicle-Herald*, 1 September 1953. St Laurent also appointed Macdonald's former assistant John Connolly to the Senate in June 1953; Connolly to Macdonald, 12 June 1953, ALM Papers, vol. 978, file 31-1.

131 See James Stuart, Secretary of State for Scotland, to Macdonald, 3 June 1953, ALM Papers, vol. 978, file 30(A).

132 Macdonald to Crerar, 12 December 1953, ALM Papers, vol. 978, file 31-1.

133 *Chronicle-Herald*, 7 November 1953.

134 'Press Release,' 19 January 1954, ALM Papers, vol. 980, file 48. Macdonald

noted that it was almost impossible for a rural MLA to serve as minister of highways without drawing accusations of favouritism and corruption. Macdonald to Senator John A. McDonald, 6 August 1953, ALM Papers, vol. 975, file 19-2.

135 See ALM Papers, vol. 1507, file 447.

136 See Macdonald to Howe, 12 February 1954, and Howe to Macdonald, 16 February 1954, ALM Papers, vol. 980, file 50.

137 *Halifax Mail-Star*, 13 April 1954.

138 Power to Macdonald, 10 March 1954, ALM Papers, vol. 980, file 50, and Crerar to Macdonald, 11 March 1954, ALM Papers, vol. 980, file 49.

139 See Macdonald to Power, 25 March 1954, ALM Papers, vol. 980, file 50.

140 This was reported in the *Halifax Mail-Star* on the day of Macdonald's death. His widow also indicated that he hoped to return to teaching. Hawkins interview with Agnes Macdonald, 16 August 1967.

141 Sister St Veronica to Macdonald, 3 December 1953, ALM Papers, vol. 980, file 49.

142 *Mail-Star*, 13 April 1954.

143 Interview with Charles Hawkins' son George, 13 July 1999. Macdonald reportedly told Hawkins's that he worried for his cabinet, as only Connolly qualified for a pension.

144 *Chronicle-Herald*, 14 April 1954.

145 See Beaton, 'Canso Causeway,' 83–91, and 'Opening of the Angus L. Macdonald Bridge,' 2 April 1955, CHNS Radio Fonds, AR1953, NSARM.

146 Interview with George Hawkins, 13 July 1999; interview with Richard and Eileen Donahoe, 16 July 1999. Camp and Beck argue that Connolly never gave this commitment, but concede that most of cabinet assumed he would not run for the leadership. Camp, *Gentlemen, Players and Politicians*, 149–50, and Beck, *Politics of Nova Scotia*, 2:239–40.

147 Beck, *Politics of Nova Scotia*, 2:240.

148 Interview with Richard and Eileen Donahoe, 16 July 1999.

149 Beck, *Politics of Nova Scotia*, 2:240, and Camp, *Gentlemen, Players and Politicians*, 152–3.

150 Beck *Politics of Nova Scotia*, 2:425.

Conclusion

1 A copy of Father Stanley's speech in translation was provided by Sister Margaret MacDonnell, CND. See also interview with Richard and Eileen Donahoe, 16 July 1999. On the opening ceremonies of the Canso Causeway, see *Halifax Chronicle-Herald* and *Globe and Mail*, 15 August 1955; L.J.

Doucet, *The Road to the Isle: 'The World's Deepest Causeway'* (Fredericton: University of New Brunswick Press, 1955); and Meaghan Beaton, 'The Canso Causeway: Regionalism, Reconstruction, Representations and Results,' MA thesis, St Mary's University, 2001.

2 Doucet, *Road to the Isle*. Macdonald had mentioned the idea of the pipers at the ground-breaking ceremony; see *Chronicle-Herald*, 17 September 1952. On the Cape Breton Highlands National Park and its 'Scottish' character, see Alan MacEachern, *Natural Selections: National Parks in Atlantic Canada, 1935–1970* (Montreal and Kingston: McGill-Queen's University Press, 2001), 47–72.

3 Ian McKay, 'History and the Tourist Gaze: The Politics of Commemoration in Nova Scotia, 1935–1964,' *Acadiensis* 22.2 (Spring 1993): 131–2. On the region's economic difficulties, see Arthur C. Parks, *The Economy of the Atlantic Provinces, 1940–1957* (Halifax: Atlantic Provinces Economic Council, 1959), 6, 12–14, 28, and 36–8.

4 See, for example, *Report of the Royal Commission Provincial Economic Inquiry* (Halifax: King's Printer, 1934); *Report of the Royal Commission on Dominion-Provincial Relations: Book I* (Ottawa: King's Printer, 1940); *Report of the Royal Commission on Provincial Development and Rehabilitation* (Halifax: King's Printer, 1944); and *Report of the Royal Commission on Coal* (Ottawa: King's Printer, 1946).

5 C.B. MacPherson, *The Political Theory of Possessive Individualism: Hobbes to Locke* (Toronto: Oxford University Press, 1962), 2–3.

6 Margaret Conrad, 'The "Atlantic Revolution" of the 1950s,' in Berkeley Fleming, ed., *Beyond Anger and Longing: Community and Development in Atlantic Canada* (Fredericton: Acadiensis, 1988), 55–6.

7 Conrad, '"Atlantic Revolution,"' 60–1.

8 See, for example, Austin F. Cross, *The People's Mouths* (Toronto: Macmillan, 1943), 94 and 96.

9 Nova Scotia, *Department of Trade and Industry Annual Report, 1955* (Halifax: Queen's Printer, 1955), 17–18, and Parks, *Economy of the Atlantic Provinces*, 38.

10 W. Gibson and Barbara Robertson, eds., *Ottawa at War: The Grant Dexter Memoranda, 1939–1945* (Winnipeg: Manitoba Records Society, 1994), 496–500, Dexter memorandum to George V. Ferguson, 1 March 1945.

11 Donald V. Smiley, 'The Rowell-Sirois Report, Provincial Autonomy, and Postwar Canadian Federalism,' *Canadian Journal of Economics and Political Science* 28.1 (February 1962): 59.

12 Janine Brodie, *The Political Economy of Canadian Regionalism* (Toronto: Harcourt Brace Jovanovich, 1990), 155–6.

13 Margaret Conrad, 'The 1950s: The Decade of Development,' in E.R. Forbes and D.A. Muise, eds., *The Atlantic Provinces in Confederation* (Toronto: University of Toronto Press, 1993), 407 and 410.

14 See Colin Howell, 'W. S. Fielding and the Repeal Elections of 1886 and 1887 in Nova Scotia,' *Acadiensis* 8.2 (Spring 1979): 28–46, and E.R. Forbes, *The Maritime Rights Movement, 1919–1927: A Study in Canadian Regionalism* (Montreal and Kingston: McGill-Queen's University Press, 1979).

15 See Paul Romney, *Getting It Wrong: How Canadians Forgot Their Past and Imperilled Confederation* (Toronto: University of Toronto Press, 1999).

Bibliography

Manuscript Sources

Nova Scotia Archives and Records Management
CHNS Radio Fonds
John Hawkins Fonds
Angus L. Macdonald Papers

Library and Archives Canada
Canadian Expeditionary Force Collection
Canadian Writers' Foundation Papers
John J. Connolly Papers
C.D. Howe Papers
Alexander Johnston Papers
W.L. Mackenzie King Papers
J.L. Ralston Papers
Escott Reid Papers
Louis-Stephen St Laurent Papers
War Committee of Cabinet Minutes

Provincial Archives of New Brunswick
Atlantic Provinces Transportation Commission Fonds
Hugh John Flemming Papers
J.B. McNair Papers

Directorate of History and Heritage
Percy Walker Nelles Fonds

Acadia University Archives
Board of Governors Minutes

Dalhousie University Archives
Thomas Raddall Papers
Carleton Stanley Papers

Queen's University Archives
T.A. Crerar Papers
Grant Dexter Papers
C.G. Power Papers
Norman McL. Rogers Papers

St Francis Xavier University Archives
M.M. Coady Papers
President D.J. Macdonald Papers
President Nicholson Papers

University of Toronto Archives
Harold Adams Innis Papers

Newspapers and Periodicals

Acadian Recorder
Antigonish Casket
Belcher's Farmers' Almanac
Canadian Annual Review
Canadian Forum
Digby Courier
Financial Post
Franciscan Review
Halifax Chronicle
Halifax Chronicle-Herald
Halifax Gazette
Halifax Herald
Halifax Mail-Star
Kingston Whig-Standard
Listener
Maclean's
Montreal Gazette

Montreal Star
Ottawa Citizen
Ottawa Journal
Saturday Night
Sydney Post
Sydney Post-Record
Time
Toronto Evening Telegram
Toronto Globe and Mail
Winnipeg Free Press
Xaverian

Government Publications

Australia. *Report of the Royal Commission on the Constitution*. Canberra: Commonwealth Government Printer, 1929.
Census of Canada, 1871,1881, 1891.
Dominion-Provincial Conference, 1935. Ottawa: King's Printer, 1936.
Dominion-Provincial Conference, 1941. Ottawa: King's Printer, 1941.
Dominion-Provincial Conference, 1945. Ottawa: King's Printer, 1946.
House of Commons, *Debates*.
Maritime Board of Trade. *Submission to the Royal Commission on Transportation*. 2 vols. 1949.
Nova Scotia. *Journals of the House of Assembly,* 1925–54.
– *Department of Trade and Industry Annual Report, 1955*. Halifax: Queen's Printer, 1955.
Proceedings of the Constitutional Conference of Federal and Provincial Governments, January 10–12, 1950. Ottawa: King's Printer, 1950.
Proceedings of the Constitutional Conference of Federal and Provincial Governments, Quebec, September 25–28, 1950. Ottawa: King's Printer, 1950.
Report of the Royal Commission on Coal. Ottawa: King's Printer, 1946.
Report of the Royal Commission on Dominion-Provincial Relations. Books I and II. Ottawa: King's Printer, 1940.
Report of the Royal Commission on Financial Arrangements between the Dominion and the Maritime Provinces. Ottawa: King's Printer, 1935.
Report of the Royal Commission on Maritime Claims. Ottawa: King's Printer, 1927.
Report of the Royal Commission on Provincial Development and Rehabilitation. Halifax: King's Printer, 1944.
Report of the Royal Commission Provincial Economic Inquiry. Halifax: King's Printers, 1934.

Report of the Royal Commission on Transportation. Ottawa: King's Printer, 1951.
Report on Social Security for Canada. Ottawa: King's Printer, 1943.
Submission of the Government of the Province of Nova Scotia to the Royal Commission on Dominion-Provincial Relations, February 1938. Halifax: King's Printer, 1938.

Secondary Sources

Abella, Irving M. *Nationalism, Communism, and Canadian Labour: The CIO, the Communist Party, and the Canadian Congress of Labour, 1935–1956*. Toronto: University of Toronto Press, 1973.
– ed. *On Strike: Six Key Labour Struggles in Canada, 1919–1949*. Toronto: James Lewis and Samuel, 1974.
Acheson, T.W. 'The National Policy and the Industrialization of the Maritimes, 1880–1910.' *Acadiensis* 1.2 (Spring 1972): 3–28.
Adachi, Ken. *The Enemy That Never Was: A History of the Japanese Canadians*. Toronto: McClelland and Stewart, 1976.
Adams, George Matthew. *Glimpses of Nova Scotia*. Halifax: Bureau of Information, c. 1932.
Ajzenstat, Janet, and Peter J. Smith, eds. *Canada's Origins: Liberal, Tory, or Republican?* Ottawa: Carleton University Press, 1995.
Allan, Richard. *The Social Passion: Religion and Social Reform in Canada, 1914–1928*. Toronto: University of Toronto Press, 1971.
Armstrong, Christopher. *The Politics of Federalism: Ontario's Relations with the Federal Government, 1867–1942*. Toronto: University of Toronto Press, 1981.
Arsenault, Georges. 'Stanislaus Perry.' *Dictionary of Canadian Biography: Volume XII, 1891–1900*. Toronto: University of Toronto Press, 1990.
Barrett, L. Gene. 'Development and Underdevelopment, and the Rise of Trade Unionism in the Fishing Industry of Nova Scotia, 1900–1950.' MA thesis. Dalhousie University, 1976.
Beaton, Meaghan. 'The Canso Causeway: Regionalism, Reconstruction, Representations and Results.' MA thesis. Saint Mary's University, 2001.
Beck, J. Murray. *The Evolution of Municipal Government in Nova Scotia, 1749–1973: A Study Prepared for the Nova Scotia Royal Commission on Education, Public Services and Provincial–Municipal Relations*. Halifax: n.p., 1973.
– *The Government of Nova Scotia*. Toronto: University of Toronto Press, 1957.
– *Politics of Nova Scotia*. Volume 1. *Nicholson–Fielding, 1710–1896*. Tantallon, NS: Four East Publications, 1985.
– *Politics of Nova Scotia*. Volume 2. *Murray–Buchanan, 1896–1988*. Tantallon, NS: Four East Publications, 1988.

– ed., *Joseph Howe: Voice of Nova Scotia*. Toronto: McClelland and Stewart, 1964.

Bent, David L. 'Going Forward: Agricultural Modernity in Nova Scotia, 1933–1956.' MA thesis. University of New Brunswick, 2004.

Bercuson, David Jay, ed. *Canada and the Burden of Unity*. Toronto: Macmillan, 1977; Gage, 1980.

Berger, Carl. *The Writing of Canadian History: Aspects of English-Canadian Historical Writing since 1900*. Toronto: University of Toronto Press, 1976.

Betcherman, Lita-Rose. *Ernest Lapointe: Mackenzie King's Great Quebec Lieutenant*. Toronto: University of Toronto Press, 2002.

Bickerton, James. *Nova Scotia, Ottawa, and the Politics of Regional Development*. Toronto: University of Toronto Press, 1990.

Bird, Will R. *This Is Nova Scotia*. Toronto: Ryerson, 1950.

Black, Conrad. *Duplessis*. Toronto: McClelland and Stewart, 1977.

Bothwell, Robert, Ian Drummond, and John English. *Canada: 1900–1945*. Toronto: University of Toronto Press, 1987.

– *Canada since 1945: Power, Politics, and Provincialism*. Toronto: University of Toronto Press, 1989.

Bothwell, Robert, and William Kilbourn. *C.D. Howe: A Biography*. Toronto: McClelland and Stewart, 1979.

Boutilier, James A., ed. *The RCN in Retrospect, 1910–1968*. Vancouver: UBC Press, 1982.

Bowman, Charles A. *Ottawa Editor: The Memoirs of Charles A. Bowman*. Sidney, BC: Gray's, 1966.

Boyle, George. *Father Tompkins of Nova Scotia*. New York: P.J. Kennedy and Sons, 1953.

Brodie, Janine. *The Political Economy of Canadian Regionalism*. Toronto: Harcourt Brace Jovanovich, 1990.

Brown, Paul. '"Come East, Young Man!": The Politics of Rural Depopulation in Nova Scotia, 1900–1925.' *Journal of the Royal Nova Scotia Historical Society* 1 (1998): 47–78.

Brown, Robert Craig, and Ramsay Cook. *Canada 1896–1921: A Nation Transformed*. Toronto: McClelland and Stewart, 1974.

Bryce, Viscount. *Modern Democracies*. London: Macmillan, 1921.

Brym, Robert J., and R. James Sacouman, eds. *Underdevelopment and Social Movements in Atlantic Canada*. Toronto: New Hogtown Press, 1979.

Buckner, P.A., David Frank, and Gail Campbell, eds. *Atlantic Canada after Confederation: The Acadiensis Reader*. Volume 2. 3rd ed. Fredericton: Acadiensis Press, 1999.

Bumstead, J.M. *The People's Clearance: Highland Emigration to British North America*. Edinburgh: Edinburgh University Press, 1982.

Cahill, Barry. *The Thousandth Man: A Biography of James McGregor Stewart*. Toronto: University of Toronto Press, 2000.

Caldwell, R.H. 'The VE Day Riots in Halifax, 7–8 May 1945.' *Northern Mariner* 10.1 (2000): 3–20.

Cameron, James D. *For the People: A History of St. Francis Xavier University.* Montreal and Kingston: McGill-Queen's University Press, 1996.

Cameron, James M. *Murray: The Martyred Admiral*. Hantsport, NS: Lancelot Press, 1981.

Camp, Dalton. *Gentlemen, Players and Politicians*. Toronto: McClelland and Stewart, 1970.

Campbell, G.G. *The History of Nova Scotia*. Toronto: Ryerson, 1948.

Careless, Anthony. *Initiative and Response: The Adaptation of Canadian Federalism to Regional Economic Development*. Montreal and Kingston: McGill-Queen's University Press, 1977.

Careless, J.M.S. '"Limited Identities" in Canada.' *Canadian Historical Review* 50 (March 1969): 1–10.

Carty, R. Kenneth, and W. Peter Ward, eds. *National Politics and Community in Canada*. Vancouver: UBC Press, 1986.

Catholics of the Diocese of Antigonish, Nova Scotia, and the War, 1914–1919, With Nominal Enlistment Rolls by Parish. Antigonish: St Francis Xavier University, 1920.

Conrad, Margaret. 'Apple Blossom Time in the Annapolis Valley, 1880–1957.' *Acadiensis* 9.2 (Spring 1980): 14–39.

– 'The Art of Regional Protest: The Political Cartoons of Donald McRitchie, 1904–1937.' *Acadiensis* 21.1 (Autumn 1991): 5–29.

– *George Nowlan: Maritime Conservative in National Politics*. Toronto: University of Toronto Press, 1986.

Cook, Ramsay. 'Canadian Centennial Celebrations.' *International Journal* 31 (Autumn 1967): 663.

– 'The Golden Age of Canadian Historical Writing.' *Historical Reflections* 14 (Summer 1977): 148.

– *The Regenerators: Social Criticism in Late Victorian English Canada*. Toronto: University of Toronto Press, 1985.

Corry, J.A. *Difficulties of Divided Jurisdiction: A Study Prepared for the Royal Commission on Dominion-Provincial Relations*. Ottawa: King's Printer, 1939.

– *My Life and Work: A Happy Partnership*. Kingston: Queen's University Press, 1981.

Craven, Paul. *'An Impartial Umpire': Industrial Relations and the Canadian State, 1900–1911*. Toronto: University of Toronto Press, 1980.

Crawley, Ron. 'What Kind of Unionism: Struggles among Sydney Steel Workers in the SWOC Years, 1936–1942.' *Labour / Le Travail* 39 (Spring 1997): 99–123.

Creighton, Donald. *Harold Adams Innis: Portrait of a Scholar*. Toronto: University of Toronto Press, 1957.

Cross, Austin. 'Career Sketches.' *Canadian Business* 15.8 (August 1942): 36–43.
– *The People's Mouths*. Toronto: Macmillan, 1943.

Cruikshank, Ken. *Close Ties: Railways, Government and the Board of Railway Commissioners, 1851–1933*. Montreal and Kingston: McGill-Queen's University Press, 1991.

Davey, William, and Richard MacKinnon. 'Nicknaming Patterns and Traditions among Cape Breton Coal Miners.' *Acadiensis* 30.2 (Spring 2001): 71–83.

Davies, Gwendolyn, ed. *Myth and Milieu: Atlantic Literature and Culture, 1918–1939*. Fredericton: Acadiensis Press, 1993.

Dawson, R. MacGregor. *The Conscription Crisis of 1944*. Toronto: University of Toronto Press, 1961.
– *William Lyon Mackenzie King: A Political Biography, 1874–1923*. Toronto: University of Toronto Press, 1958.

Day, Frank Parker. *Rockbound*. 1940; Toronto: University of Toronto Press, 1989; reprinted 1998.

Dickson, Paul, ed. *1943: The Beginning of the End*. Ottawa: Canadian Committee for the History of the Second World War, 1995.

Doucet, L.J. *The Road to the Isle: 'The World's Deepest Causeway.'* Fredericton: University of New Brunswick Press, 1955.

Douglas, W.A.B., ed. *The RCN in Transition, 1910–1985*. Vancouver: UBC Press, 1988.

Earle, Michael. 'The Coalminers and Their "Red" Union: The Amalgamated Mine Workers of Nova Scotia, 1932–1936.' *Labour / Le Travail* 22 (Fall 1988): 99–137.

Earle, Michael, ed. *Workers and the State in Twentieth Century Nova Scotia*. Fredericton: Acadiensis Press, 1989.

Eayrs, James. *In Defence of Canada*. Volume. 3. *Peacemaking and Deterrence*. Toronto: University of Toronto Press, 1972.

English, John. *The Decline of Politics: The Conservatives and the Party System, 1901–1920*. Toronto: University of Toronto Press, 1977.
– 'The Second Time Around: Political Scientists Writing History,' *Canadian Historical Review* 67.4 (1986): 1–16.

Fecteau, Jean-Marie. *Un nouvel ordre des choses: La pauvreté, le crime, l'État au Québec, de la fin du XVIIIe siècle à 1840*. Outremont, QC: VLB Éditeur, 1989.

Ferguson, Barry. *Remaking Liberalism: The Intellectual Legacy of Adam Shortt, O.D.*

Skelton, W.C. Clark, and W.A. Mackintosh, 1890–1925. Montreal and Kingston: McGill-Queen's University Press, 1993.

Ferguson, Barry, and Robert Wardhaugh. '"Impossible Conditions of Inequality": John Dafoe, the Rowell-Sirois Commission, and the Interpretation of Canadian Federalism.' *Canadian Historical Review* 84.4 (December 2003): 551–83.

Ferns, H.S., and Bernard Ostry. *Mackenzie King and the First World War.* Toronto: University of Toronto Press, 1955

Fieldhouse, Roger. *The Workers' Educational Association: Aims and Achievements, 1903–1977.* Syracuse, NY: Syracuse University Press, 1977.

Fleming, Berkeley. *Beyond Anger and Longing: Community and Development in Atlantic Canada.* Fredericton: Acadiensis, 1988.

Fontana, Benedetto. *Hegemony and Power: On the Relation between Gramsci and Machiavelli.* Minneapolis: University of Minnesota Press, 1993.

Forbes, E.R. *Challenging the Regional Stereotype: Essays on the 20th Century Maritimes.* Fredericton: Acadiensis Press, 1989.

– 'Consolidating Disparity: The Maritimes and the Industrialization of Canada during the Second World War.' *Acadiensis* 15.2 (Spring 1986): 3–27.

– 'Cutting the Pie into Smaller Pieces: Matching Grants and Relief in the Maritime Provinces during the 1930s.' *Acadiensis* 17.1 (Autumn 1987): 34–55.

– 'In Search of a Post-Confederation Maritime Historiography, 1900–1967.' *Acadiensis* 8.1 (Autumn 1978): 7–19.

– *The Maritime Rights Movement, 1919–1927: A Study in Canadian Regionalism.* Montreal and Kingston: McGill-Queen's University Press, 1979.

– 'Never the Twain Did Meet: Prairie-Maritime Relations, 1910–27.' *Canadian Historical Review* 59.1 (1978): 18–37.

– 'The Rise and Fall of the Conservative Party in the Provincial Politics of Nova Scotia, 1922–1933.' MA thesis. Dalhousie University, 1967.

Forbes, E.R., and D.A. Muise, eds. *The Atlantic Provinces in Confederation.* Toronto: University of Toronto Press, 1993.

Frank, David. 'The Cape Breton Coal Industry and the Rise and Fall of the British Empire Steel Corporation.' *Acadiensis* 7.1 (1977): 3–34.

– *J.B. McLachlan: A Biography.* Toronto: James Lorimer, 1999.

Frank, David, and Donald MacGillivray, eds. *George MacEachern, An Autobiography: The Story of a Cape Breton Labour Radical.* Sydney: University College of Cape Breton Press, 1987.

Fransen, David W. '"Unscrewing the Unscrutable": The Rowell-Sirois Commission, the Ottawa Bureaucracy and Public Finance Reform, 1935–1941.' PhD dissertation. University of Toronto, 1984.

Fried, Barbara H. *The Progressive Assault on Laissez Faire: Robert Hale and the First*

Law and Economics Movement. Cambridge, MA: Harvard University Press, 1998.

Fudge, Judy, and Eric Tucker. *Labour before the Law: The Regulation of Workers' Collective Action in Canada, 1900–1948*. Toronto: Oxford University Press, 2001.

Gagnon, Alain G., ed. *Intellectuals in Liberal Democracies: Political Influence and Social Involvement*. New York: Praeger, 1987.

German, Commander Tony. *The Sea Is at Our Gates: The History of the Canadian Navy*. Toronto: McClelland and Stewart, 1990.

Gibson, F.W., and Barbara Robertson, eds. *Ottawa at War: The Grant Dexter Memoranda, 1939–1945*. Winnipeg: Manitoba Record Society, 1994.

Gilbert, Martin. *Winston S. Churchill: Finest Hour, 1939–1941*. Vol. 6. London: Heineman, 1983.

Girard, Philip, and Jim Phillips, eds. *Essays in the History of Canadian Law*. Volume 3. *Nova Scotia*. Toronto: University of Toronto Press, 1987.

Girouard, Mark. *The Return to Camelot: Chivalry and the English Gentleman*. New Haven: Yale University Press, 1981.

Gordon, H. Scott. 'The Trawler Question in the United Kingdom and Canada, *Dalhousie Review* 31.2 (Summer 1951): 117–27.

Gramsci, Antonio. *Selections from the Prison Notebooks*. Ed. and trans. Quentin Hoare and Geoffrey Nowell Smith. New York: International Publishers, 1971.

Granatstein, J.L., *Canada's War: The Politics of the Mackenzie King Government, 1939–1945*. Toronto: University of Toronto Press, 1975.

– *Conscription in the Second World War: A Study in Political Management*. Toronto: McGraw-Hill Ryerson, 1969.

– *The Generals: The Canadian Army's Senior Commanders in the Second World War*. Toronto: Stoddart, 1993.

– *How Britain's Weakness Forced Canada into the Arms of the United States*. Toronto: University of Toronto Press, 1989.

– *The Ottawa Men: The Civil Service Mandarins, 1935–1957*. Toronto: Oxford University Press, 1982.

– *The Politics of Survival: The Conservative Party of Canada, 1939–1945*. Toronto: University of Toronto Press, 1967.

Granatstein, J.L., and J.M. Hitsman. *Broken Promises: A History of Conscription in Canada*. Toronto: Oxford University Press, 1977.

Green, Jim. *Against the Tide: The Story of the Canadian Seaman's Union*. Toronto: Progress Books, 1986.

Greenfield, Nathan M. *The Battle of the St. Lawrence: The Second World War in Canada*. Toronto: HarperCollins, 2004.

Greer, Allan. *Peasant, Lord, and Merchant: Rural Society in Three Quebec Parishes, 1740–1840*. Toronto: University of Toronto Press, 1985.

Grierson, Frank. *William Lyon Mackenzie King: A Memoir*. Ottawa, 1952.

Hadley, Michael L. *U-boats Against Canada: German Submarines in Canadian Waters*. Montreal and Kingston: McGill-Queen's University Press, 1985.

Hamilton, William B. *Place Names of Atlantic Canada*. Toronto: University of Toronto Press, 1996.

Harris, Richard. 'Flattered but Not Imitated: Co-operative Self-Help and the Nova Scotia Housing Commission, 1936–1973.' *Acadiensis* 31.1 (Autumn 2001): 103–28.

Hawkins, John. *The Life and Times of Angus L*. Windsor, NS: Lancelot Press, 1969.

Henderson, T. Stephen. 'Angus L. Macdonald and the Conscription Crisis of 1944.' *Acadiensis* 27.1 (Autumn 1997): 85–104.

– 'A Defensive Alliance: The Maritime Provinces and the Turgeon Commission on Transportation, 1948–1951.' *Acadiensis* 35.2 (Spring 2006): 1–18.

Heron, Craig. *The Canadian Labour Movement: A Short History*. Toronto: James Lorimer and Company, 1989.

– ed. *The Workers' Revolt in Canada, 1917–1925*. Toronto: University of Toronto Press, 1998.

Hobsbawm, Eric, and Terence Ranger, eds. *The Invention of Tradition*. New York: Cambridge University Press, 1983.

Hofstadter, Richard. *Anti-Intellectualism in American Life*. New York: Alfred A. Knopf, 1963.

Hollander, Taylor. 'Making Reform Happen: The Passage of Canada's Collective-Bargaining Policy, 1943–1944.' *Journal of Policy History* 13.3 (2001): 299–328.

Hornsby, Stephen J. *Nineteenth-Century Cape Breton: A Historical Geography*. Montreal and Kingston: McGill-Queen's University Press, 1992.

Howell, Colin. 'W. S. Fielding and the Repeal Elections of 1886 and 1887 in Nova Scotia.' *Acadiensis* 8.2 (Spring 1979): 28–46.

Hunt, M.S., ed. *Nova Scotia's Part in the Great War*. Halifax: Nova Scotia Veteran Publishing Company, 1920.

Hutchison, Bruce. *The Incredible Canadian – A Candid Portrait of Mackenzie King: His Work, His Times, and His Nation*. Toronto: Longmans, Green and Com., 1952.

Ionescu, Ghita, and Ernest Gellner, eds. *Populism, Its Meaning and National Characteristics*. London: Weidenfeld and Nicolson, 1969.

Johnson, J.K., ed. *The Canadian Directory of Parliament, 1867–1967*. Ottawa: Public Archives, 1968.

Johnson, Peter. 'Relations between the Government of Nova Scotia and the Union of Nova Scotia Municipalities, 1906–1966.' MA thesis. Dalhousie University, 1968.

Johnston, Rev. Angus Anthony. *A History of the Catholic Church in Eastern Nova Scotia. Volume 2., 1827–1880.* Antigonish, NS: St Francis Xavier University Press, 1971.

Jordan, Gerald, ed. *Naval Warfare in the 20th Century: Essays in Honor of Arthur Marder.* New York: Crane Russak, 1977.

Kaplan, William. *Everything That Floats: Sullivan, Banks, and the CSU.* Toronto: University of Toronto Press, 1987.

Katz, Michael B. *In the Shadow of the Poorhouse: A Social History of Welfare in America.* New York: Basic Books, 1986.

Kimber, Stephen. *Net Profits: The Story of National Sea.* Halifax: Nimbus, 1989.

– *Sailors, Slackers and Blind Pigs: Halifax at War.* Toronto: Anchor, 2003.

King, W.L. Mackenzie. *Mackenzie King Diaries, 1896–1932.* Toronto: University of Toronto Press, 1973. Microfilm.

– *Mackenzie King Diaries, 1932–1949.* Toronto: University of Toronto, 1980. Microfilm.

Kitchen, Brigitte. 'The Marsh Report Revisited.' *Journal of Canadian Studies* 21.2 (1986): 38–48.

Knopff, Rainer. 'The Triumph of Liberalism in Canada: Laurier on Representation and Party Government.' *Journal of Canadian Studies* 26.2 (Summer 1991): 72–86.

Laidlaw, Alexander F., ed. *The Man from Margaree: Writings and Speeches of M. M. Coady.* Toronto: McClelland and Stewart, 1971.

Leacy, F.H., ed. *Historical Statistics of Canada.* Ottawa: Statistics Canada, 1983.

Learned, William S., and Kenneth C.M. Sills. *Education in the Maritime Provinces of Canada.* New York: Carnegie Foundation for the Advancement of Teaching, 1922.

LeBlanc, Barbara. 'Evangeline as Identity Myth.' *Canadian Folklore* 15.2 (1993): 139–53.

LeBlanc, Bernard Charles. 'A Reluctant Recruit: Angus L. Macdonald and Conscription, 1940–1945.' MA thesis. Queen's University, 1987.

LeBlanc, Kenneth H. 'A.P. Paterson and New Brunswick's Response to Constitutional Change, 1935–1939.' MA thesis, University of New Brunswick, 1989.

Leo XIII. *Encyclical Letter on Condition of the Working Classes (Rerum Novarum).* 1891. Washington: Apostolic Delegation, 1942.

Liberal Party of Canada. *Report of the Proceedings of the National Liberal Convention Called by the National Liberal Federation of Canada at the Request of W.L. Mackenzie King.* Ottawa: National Liberal Federation of Canada, 1948.

Lotz, Jim, and Michael R. Welton. *Father Jimmy: The Life and Times of Father Jimmy Tompkins*. Wreck Cove, NS: Breton Books, 1997.

MacBean, Allister W.D. *The Inverness and Richmond Railway*. Halifax: Tennant Publishing, 1987.

Macdonald, Agnes Foley. 'A Christmas Carol.' *Atlantic Advocate* 51.4 (December 1960): 83.

– 'The Native Speaks.' *Dalhousie Review* 29.1 (April 1949): 50.

– *Once and Again*. Port Royal, NS: Abenaki Press, 1950.

Macdonald, Angus L. 'Liabilities of Possessors of Premise.' SJD thesis. Harvard Law School, 1929.

– *Speeches of Angus L. Macdonald*. Ed. T.A. Crerar. Toronto: Longmans, Green and Company, 1960.

MacDougall, J.L. *History of Inverness County, Nova Scotia*. 1922. Belleville, Ontario: Mika Publishing, 1972.

MacEachern, Alan. *Natural Selections: National Parks in Atlantic Canada, 1935–1970*. Montreal and Kingston: McGill-Queen's University Press, 2001.

MacEwan, Paul. *Miners and Steelworkers: Labour in Cape Breton*. Toronto: Hakkert, 1976.

MacKenzie, A.A. 'The Rise and Fall of the Farmer-Labour Party in Nova Scotia.' MA thesis. Dalhousie University, 1969.

MacNeil, Alan R. 'Cultural Stereotypes and Highland Farming in Eastern Nova Scotia, 1827–1861.' *Histoire sociale / Social History* 19.37 (May 1986): 39–56.

MacNeil, Neil. *The Highland Heart in Nova Scotia*. New York: S.J.R. Saunders, 1958.

Macpherson, C.B. *The Political Theory of Possessive Individualism: Hobbes to Locke*. Toronto: Oxford University Press, 1962.

Mangan, J.A. *The Games Ethic and Imperialism: Aspects of the Diffusion of an Ideal*. New York: Viking, 1986.

March, William. *Red Line: The* Chronicle-Herald *and the* Mail-Star, *1875–1954*. Halifax: Chebucto Agencies, 1986.

Marquis, Greg. 'The History of Policing in the Maritime Provinces: Themes and Prospects.' *Urban History Review* 19.1–2 (1990): 84–99.

Martin, Paul. *A Very Political Life*. Ottawa: Deneau, 1983.

Massey, Vincent. *What's Past Is Prologue: The Memoirs of the Right Honourable Vincent Massey*. Toronto: Macmillan, 1963.

Mayne, Richard Oliver. 'A Covert Naval Investigation: Overseas Officers, John J. Connolly, and the Equipment Crisis of 1943.' *Northern Mariner* 10.1 (January 2000): 37–52.

– 'A Political Execution: Expediency and the Firing of Vice Admiral Percy W.

Nelles, 1943–1944.' *American Review of Canadian Studies* 29.4 (Winter 1999): 557–92.

McGee, R. Harley. *Getting in Right: Regional Development in Canada*. Montreal and Kingston: McGill-Queen's University Press, 1992.

McKay, Ian. 'After Canada: On Amnesia and the Apocalypse in the Contemporary Crisis.' *Acadiensis* 28.1 (Autumn 1998): 76–97.

– 'History and the Tourist Gaze: The Politics of Commemoration in Nova Scotia, 1935–1964.' *Acadiensis* 22.2 (Spring 1993): 102–38.

– 'The Liberal Order Framework: A Prospectus for a Reconnaissance of Canadian History.' *Canadian Historical Review* 81.4 (December 2000): 617–45.

– 'A Note on "Region" in Writing the History of Atlantic Canada.' *Acadiensis* 29.2 (Spring 2000): 89–101.

– *The Quest of the Folk: Antimodernism and Cultural Selection in Twentieth-Century Nova Scotia*. Montreal and Kingston: McGill-Queen's University Press, 1994.

– 'Tartanism Triumphant: The Construction of Scottishness in Nova Scotia, 1933–1954.' *Acadiensis* 21.2 (Spring 1992): 5–47.

McKillop, A.B. *A Disciplined Intelligence: Critical Inquiry and Canadian Thought in the Victorian Era*. Montreal and Kingston: McGill-Queen's University Press, 1979.

McLaughlin, Kenneth M. 'Race, Religion and Politics: The Election of 1896 in Canada.' PhD dissertation, University of Toronto, 1974.

Mills, Allen. 'Of Charters and Justice: The Social Thought of F.R. Scott, 1930–1985.' *Journal of Canadian Studies* 32.1 (1997): 44–62.

Milner, Marc. *Canada's Navy: The First Century*. Toronto: University of Toronto, 1999.

– *North Atlantic Run: The Royal Canadian Navy and the Battle for the Convoys*. Toronto: University of Toronto Press, 1985.

– *The U-Boat Hunters: The Royal Canadian Navy and the Offensive against Germany's Submarines*. Toronto: University of Toronto Press, 1994.

Neatby, Blair. *William Lyon Mackenzie King, 1924–1932: The Lonely Heights*. Toronto: University of Toronto Press, 1963.

– *William Lyon Mackenzie King, 1932–1939: The Prism of Unity*. Toronto: University of Toronto Press, 1976.

Nicholson, G.W.L. *The Canadian Expeditionary Force, 1914–1919: Official History of the Canadian Army in the First World War*. Ottawa: Queen's Printer, 1962.

Nolan, Brian. *King's War: Mackenzie King and the Politics of War, 1939–1945*. Toronto: Random House, 1988.

Owram, Doug. *The Government Generation: Canadian Intellectuals and the State, 1900–1945*. Toronto: University of Toronto Press, 1986.

Parks, Arthur C. *The Economy of the Atlantic Provinces, 1940–1957*. Halifax and Fredericton: Atlantic Provinces Economic Council, 1959.

Paterson, A.P. *The True Story of Confederation*. Saint John: Saint John Board of Trade, 1926.

Perlin, George C. *The Tory Syndrome: Leadership Politics in the Progressive Conservative Party*. Montreal and Kingston: McGill-Queen's University Press, 1980.

Pickersgill, J.W. *My Years with Louis St. Laurent: A Political Memoir*. Toronto: University of Toronto Press, 1975.

Pickersgill, J.W., and D.F. Forster. *The Mackenzie King Record: Volume 2, 1944–1945*. Toronto: University of Toronto Press, 1968.

Pope, Maurice. *Soldiers and Politicians: The Memoirs of Lt.-Gen. Maurice A. Pope, C.B., M.C.* Toronto: University of Toronto Press, 1962.

Power, C.G. *A Party Politician: The Memoirs of Chubby Power*. Ed. Norman Ward. Toronto: Macmillan, 1966.

Prang, Margaret. *N.W. Rowell: Ontario Nationalist*. Toronto: University of Toronto Press, 1975.

– *Halifax: Warden of the North*. New York: Doubleday, 1965.

Raddall, Thomas H. *Tambour and Other Stories*. Toronto: McClelland and Stewart, 1945.

Rasmussen, Ken. 'The Administrative Liberalism of R. MacGregor Dawson.' *Canadian Public Administration* 33.1 (Spring 1990): 37–51.

Rea, J.E. 'The Mackenzie King Controversy: "Clay from Feet to Forehead."' *Beaver* 73.2 (April–May 1993): 27–34.

– *T.A. Crerar: A Political Life*. Montreal and Kingston: McGill-Queen's University Press, 1997.

– 'A View from the Lectern.' *Journal of the Canadian Historical Association*, new series, 2 (1991): 3–16.

Redman, Stanley R. *Open Gangway: An Account of the Halifax Riots, 1945*. Hantsport, NS: Lancelot Press, 1981.

Reilly, Nolan. 'The General Strike in Amherst, Nova Scotia, 1919.' *Acadiensis* 9.2 (Spring 1980): 56–77.

Rogers, Norman. 'The Constitutional *Impasse*.' *Queen's Quarterly* 46.4 (Winter 1934): 475–86

Romney, Paul. *Getting It Wrong: How Canadians Forgot Their Past and Imperilled Confederation*. Toronto: University of Toronto Press, 1999.

– 'Provincial Equality, Special Status and the Compact Theory of Canadian Confederation.' *Canadian Journal of Political Science* 32.1 (March 1999): 21–39.

Rowell, John R. 'An Intellectual in Politics: Norman Rogers as an Intellectual and Minister of Labour, 1929–1939.' MA thesis, Queen's University, 1979.

Roy, Fernande. *Progrès, Harmonie, Liberté: Le libéralisme des milieux d'affaires fran-cophones à Montréal au tournant du siècle*. Montreal: Boréal, 1988.

Roy, Reginald H. *For Most Conspicuous Bravery: A Biography of Major-General George V. Pearkes, V.C., through Two World Wars*. Vancouver: UBC Press, 1977.

Russell, Peter H., ed. *Leading Constitutional Decisions: Cases on the British North America Act*. Rev. ed. Toronto: McClelland and Stewart, 1973.

Sacouman, R. James. 'The Social Origins of Antigonish Co-operative Associa-tions in Eastern Nova Scotia.' PhD dissertation, University of Toronto, 1976.

– 'Underdevelopment and the Structural Origins of Antigonish Movement Co-operatives in Eastern Nova Scotia.' *Acadiensis* 7.1 (Autumn 1977): 66–85.

Safarian, A.E. *The Canadian Economy in the Great Depression*. 1959. Toronto: McClelland and Stewart, 1970.

Sandberg, L. Anders, 'Forest Policy in Nova Scotia: The Big Lease, Cape Breton Island, 1899–1960.' *Acadiensis* 18.2 (Spring 1990): 105–28.

Sandberg, L. Anders and Bill Parenteau. 'From Weapons to Symbols of Privi-lege: Political Cartoons and the Rise and Fall of the Pulpwood Embargo Debate in Nova Scotia, 1923–1933.' *Acadiensis* 26.2 (Spring 1997): 31–58.

Saywell, John T. *'Just Call Me Mitch': The Life of Mitchell F. Hepburn*. Toronto: University of Toronto Press, 1991.

– *The Lawmakers: Judicial Power and the Shaping of Canadian Federalism*. Toronto: University of Toronto Press, 2002.

Schull, Joseph. *The Far Distant Ships: An Official Account of Canadian Naval Oper-ations in the Second World War*. Ottawa: King's Printer, 1950.

Shore, Marlene. *The Science of Social Redemption: McGill, the Chicago School, and the Origins of Social Research in Canada*. Toronto: University of Toronto Press, 1987.

Smiley, Donald V. 'The Rowell-Sirois Report, Provincial Autonomy, and Post-war Canadian Federalism.' *Canadian Journal of Economics and Political Science* 28.1 (February 1962): 54–69.

Smith, H.A. *Federalism in North America: A Comparative Study of Institutions in the United States and Canada*. Boston: Chipman, 1923.

Stacey, C.P. *Arms, Men and Governments: The War Policies of Canada, 1939–1945*. Ottawa: Queen's Printers, 1970.

Stanton, John. *The Life and Death of a Union: The Canadian Seaman's Union, 1936–1949*. Toronto: Steel Rail Education Publishing, 1978.

Stevens, Geoffrey. *Stanfield*. Toronto: McClelland and Stewart, 1973.

Stevenson, John A. 'The Career of Mackenzie King.' *Political Quarterly* 21.4 (October 1950): 395–410.

Stevenson, Michael D. *Canada's Greatest Wartime Muddle: National Selective Ser-*

vice and the Mobilization of Human Resources during World War II. Montreal and Kingston: McGill-Queen's University Press, 2001.

Stewart, Ian. Roasting Chestnuts: The Mythology of Maritime Political Culture. Vancouver: UBC Press, 1994.

Stokesbury, James L. A Short History of World War II. New York: William and Morrow, 1980.

Struthers, James. No Fault of Their Own: Unemployment and the Canadian Welfare State, 1914–1941. Toronto: University of Toronto Press, 1983.

Swettenham, John. McNaughton. Volume 3. 1944–1946. Toronto: Ryerson Press, 1969.

Thompson, Dale. Louis St. Laurent: Canadian. Toronto: Macmillan, 1967.

Tucker, Gilbert N. The Naval Service of Canada. 2 vols. Ottawa: King's Printer, 1952.

Twining, William. Karl Llewellyn and the Realist Movement. London: Weidenfeld and Nicolson, 1973.

Vance, Jonathan. Death So Noble: Memory, Meaning, and the First World War. Vancouver: UBC Press, 1997.

Vat, Dan van der. The Atlantic Campaign: World War II's Great Struggle at Sea. New York: Harper and Row, 1988.

Vaughan, Frederick. The Canadian Federalist Experiment: From Defiant Monarchy to Reluctant Republic. Montreal and Kingston: McGill-Queen's University Press, 2003.

Veblen, Thorstein. The Higher Learning in America: A Memorandum on the Conduct of Universities by Business Men. New York, 1918.

Waite, P.B. The Lives of Dalhousie University. 2 vols. Montreal and Kingston: McGill-Queen's University Press, 1994, 1998.

– The Man from Halifax: Sir John Thompson, Prime Minister. Toronto: University of Toronto Press, 1985.

Ward, Norman, and David Smith. Jimmy Gardiner: Relentless Liberal. Toronto: University of Toronto Press, 1990.

Welton, Michael R. Little Mosie from the Margaree: A Biography of Moses Michael Coady. Toronto: Thompson Educational Publishing, 2001.

Whitaker, Reginald. 'Between Patronage and Bureaucracy: Democratic Politics in Transition.' Journal of Canadian Studies 22.2 (Summer 1987): 55–71.

– The Government Party: Organizing and Financing the Liberal Party of Canada, 1930–58. Toronto: University of Toronto Press, 1977.

White, Jay. '"A Vista of Infinite Development": Surveying Nova Scotia's Early Tourism Industry.' Journal of the Royal Nova Scotia Historical Society 6 (2003): 144–69.

Willis, John. A History of Dalhousie Law School. Toronto: University of Toronto Press, 1979.

Wright, A. Jeffrey. 'The Hapless Politician: E.H. Armstrong of Nova Scotia.' *Nova Scotia Historical Quarterly* 6 (September 1976): 259–79.

Wright, Miriam. *A Fishery for Modern Times: The State and the Industrialization of the Newfoundland Fishery, 1934–1968*. Toronto: Oxford University Press, 2001.

Zimmerman, David. *The Great Naval Battle of Ottawa*. Toronto: University of Toronto Press, 1989.

Index